The Amphibians and Reptiles of New York State

D1560019

"... in the ancient days of creation, the world was all water and the only living creatures dwelt upon the back of a huge tortoise, floating on the deep. These creatures held council to find a way of obtaining mud from the bottom of the ocean—mud from which an "earth" could be made, large enough for them all. The muskrat dove to try his luck, but he became exhausted and failed. The beaver tried, but he, too, failed. Then the crayfish made an attempt, and he was successful. From the mud the earth was built upon the back of the tortoise. The animals and people of the world dwell upon the island formed on the dome of his carapace and, among them, the small turtles still crawl about on the earth."

The Haudenosaunee (Six Nations) creation myth, as recorded by Speck (1943)
(Image: © 2005, David N. Edwards).

The Amphibians and Reptiles of New York State
Identification, Natural History, and Conservation

JAMES P. GIBBS
State University of New York College of Environmental Science
and Forestry, Syracuse

ALVIN R. BREISCH
New York State Department of Environmental Conservation, Albany

PETER K. DUCEY
State University of New York at Cortland

GLENN JOHNSON
State University of New York at Potsdam

JOHN L. BEHLER
Wildlife Conservation Society, Bronx

RICHARD C. BOTHNER
St. Bonaventure University, Olean

OXFORD
UNIVERSITY PRESS

2007

OXFORD
UNIVERSITY PRESS

Oxford University Press, Inc., publishes works that further
Oxford University's objective of excellence
in research, scholarship, and education.

Oxford   New York
Auckland   Cape Town   Dar es Salaam   Hong Kong   Karachi
Kuala Lumpur   Madrid   Melbourne   Mexico City   Nairobi
New Delhi   Shanghai   Taipei   Toronto

With offices in
Argentina   Austria   Brazil   Chile   Czech Republic   France   Greece
Guatemala   Hungary   Italy   Japan   Poland   Portugal   Singapore
South Korea   Switzerland   Thailand   Turkey   Ukraine   Vietnam

Published by Oxford University Press, Inc.
198 Madison Avenue, New York, New York 10016

www.oup.com

This project was developed with subsidy support from the New York State
Biodiversity Research Institute.

Library of Congress Cataloging-in-Publication Data The amphibians
and reptiles of New York State : identification, natural history, and conservation /
James P. Gibbs . . . [et al.].
   p. cm.
Includes bibliographical references and index.
ISBN 978-0-19-530430-5
ISBN 978-0-19-530444-2 (pbk.)
1. Amphibians-New York (State).   2. Reptiles-New York (State).   I.   Gibbs, James P.
QL653.N7A47 2007
597.909747—dc22   2006005024

9 8 7 6 5 4 3 2
Printed in the United States of America
on acid-free paper

To the efts, Hamish and Shay

IN MEMORIAM

JOHN LUTHER BEHLER
June 1943–January 2006

Distinguished herpetologist, committed conservationist,
colleague, and friend

*John Behler in a field near his home in Westchester County with one of
his favorite species, the spotted turtle. (Wildlife Conservation Society)*

Acknowledgments

Many individuals contributed to this book. The distributional data were generated by the New York Department of Environmental Conservation's Amphibian and Reptile Atlas Project, which was recently completed with the help of thousands of volunteers from across New York State who contributed tens of thousands of observations. The Atlas project was funded by many sources, including the New York State Biodiversity Research Institute, Sabin Conservation Fund, Harvey and Bernice Weinstein, Society for the Study of Amphibians and Reptiles, Institute for Ecosystem Studies, State University of New York at Cortland, Mohonk Preserve Hudson River Estuary Action Plan Project, New York Cooperative Fish and Wildlife Research Unit at Cornell University, The Wildlife Society, New York Natural Heritage Program, Upstate Herpetological Association, New York Turtle and Tortoise Society, US Fish and Wildlife Service Federal Aid to Endangered Species (Section 6), Return a Gift to Wildlife Tax Checkoff, and US Fish and Wildlife Service Partnerships for Wildlife. The range maps presented are based on data structures developed by John W. Ozard and the considerable technical expertise of Matthew F. Buff and Pablo I. Ramirez de Arellano who converted the Atlas data into map form.

Some of the species accounts were initiated by James Arrigoni, Todd Castoe, Simon Long, and David Steen. Thane Joyal helped compile the folklore chapter, much material of which the New York Folklore Society generously permitted us to reprint herein. The Philadelphia Zoo permitted reprinting of the frontispiece material. Tammy Kubinec proofed the Literature Cited section, and Collin Shepherd provided much assistance with literature reviews and data gathering. Nick Conrad and David VanLuven provided Natural Heritage Program species ranks, which were revised and updated by Paul Novak and Jesse Jaycox. Ellen Pehek kindly shared with us her records of the New York City herpetofauna. In researching the text, we depended heavily on the libraries (and librarians) of the State University of New York's College of Environmental Science and Forestry, Syracuse University, Cornell University, and the American Museum of Natural History. Allen Salzberg and Russell Burke also were extremely helpful in providing leads on information. Nancy Karraker's infectious enthusiasm for the subject matter helped move the book forward. Four anonymous reviewers along with Richard L. Wyman reviewed the manuscript and offered many, useful suggestions that improved it greatly.

We are humbled by the generosity of the 33 photographers who contributed *gratis* the images showcased in the plates and figures of this book. Their work evinces an intense curiosity and fondness for amphibians and reptiles that we are privileged to exhibit here. In order of number of images contributed, they are Sean T. Giery, B. M. Glorioso, Michael Graziano, Nancy E. Karraker, Twan Leenders, Charles Eichelberger, David N. Edwards, Victor S. Lamoureux, Ariana Breisch, James Harding, Aaron C. Jacobsen, Frank T. Burbrink, Jack Hecht, Kenneth Barnett, Russell Burke, Suzanne L. Collins, Aaron R. Greene, Allan J. Lindberg, David A. Steen, Jason Gibson, Jeremy Feinberg, Jerry Czech, Joel Strong, John C. Maerz, John Schmid, Kenneth Roblee, Matthew F. Buff, Michael Unold, Randy Stechert, Ross MacColloch, Wayne Jones, Jeffrey Humphries, Matthew Kull, M. Watson, Kirstin Breisch, and William Capitano. Jacqualine Grant kindly contributed the sea turtle illustrations. Others who helped secure images for use herein were Barbara Mathe of the American Museum of Natural History, Priya Nanjappa of the US Geological Survey Northeast Amphibian Research and Monitoring Initiative, the staff of the Wildlife Conservation Society, the New York State Department of Transportation, and Glenn Graves of the *Walton Reporter*.

We are most grateful to Peter Prescott, Life Sciences Senior Editor at Oxford University Press, for patiently guiding this book through an extended publishing process and for steadfastly encouraging us to produce the best book possible. Production Editors Rosanne Hallowell and Paul Hobson and Copy Editor Martha Cushman also made many valuable suggestions. Last, a generous educational grant of the New York State Biodiversity Research Institute to Oxford University Press enabled more extensive use of color images in the volume and reduced its final purchase price.

A Note about Royalties

All royalties from this book are deposited at the State University of New York's College of Environmental Science and Forestry and put toward research and advocacy efforts for amphibian and reptile conservation.

Contents

Species Accounts (Chapters 4-7)

The Amphibians and Reptiles of New York State

1

Introduction

New York State hosts a magnificent suite of some 69 native species of amphibians and reptiles. These include such wonders as stinkpots, hellbenders, queen snakes, softshells, tiger salamanders, red efts, mink frogs, and spadefoots. This said, a general guide to the state's salamanders, frogs, turtles, lizards, and snakes has long been lacking. The primary reason has been a scarcity of detailed information about the distributions of New York's herpetofauna (i.e., the amphibian and reptile species living in an area, from the Latin "herpes" or "creeping things").

Fortunately, the New York State Department of Environmental Conservation recently completed its ambitious "Amphibian and Reptile Atlas Project." The so-called "Herp Atlas" ("herp" is a shortened version of herpetofauna) was a 10-year survey designed to document the geographic distribution of New York State's amphibians and reptiles. The survey began in 1990 and continued through 1999. During this period some 59,000 reports were submitted by more than 1,800 volunteers. The "Herp Atlas" also collected more than 28,000, pre-1990 records from various sources, including museums, field notes, graduate theses, agency reports, and published literature. The "Herp Atlas" has spawned a series of popular articles on New York's herpetofauna (Bothner and Breisch 2001, Breisch and Behler 2002, Breisch and Gibbs 2002, Breisch and Ducey 2003a and 2003b, Stegeman and Breisch 2005, Breisch and Bothner 2006, Breisch and Jaycox 2006), which updated an earlier series by Reilly (1955, 1957, and 1958) and Wright (1955). The "Herp Atlas" has provided a foundation to create this first general guide to the amphibians and reptiles of New York State.

This book is intended as a modest contribution in a long series of publications in herpetology that has originated in New York. Many early, prominent herpetologists began their careers in the state, including James DeKay, author of *Zoology of New York* in 1842, which presented the first scientific treatment of the state's herpetofauna. An earlier work by James Macauley (1829) listed 25 species of amphibians and reptiles for the state, but his descriptions were too imprecise to determine which species he recognized. Raymond Ditmars, curator of Herpetology at the Bronx Zoo in the early 1900s, made the study of reptiles and amphibians a popular pastime worldwide, especially with his *Reptiles of the World*. Sherman C. Bishop, while at the University of Rochester, conducted the first systematic studies of salamanders of the United States; his 1941 *Salamanders of New York* and 1943 *Handbook of Salamanders* remain "classics" of the herpetology literature. Cornell University's Albert Hazen Wright and his wife Anna produced the 1947 *Handbook of Frogs and Toads of the United States and Canada* and the 1957 *Handbook of Snakes of the United States and Canada*. As a result of the efforts of these and other herpetologists, New York is the type locality (location of first individual ever described) for at least 18 taxa of amphibians and reptiles (see Chapter 2). A more complete listing of historical publications on New York's herpetofauna can be found in Moriarty and Bauer (2000).

The work of some of these herpetologists is germane to this day. For example, John Treadwell Nichols of the American Museum of Natural History marked numerous eastern box turtles on his Long Island estate in the early 1900s (figure 1.1). Some of Nichols' turtles are still alive and well and teaching us much about the longevity of turtles in the wild (see Chapter 6: Eastern box turtle: Other Intriguing Facts).

New York's significance in herpetology is not simply historical; several scholarly institutions retain an important focus on herpetology. Herpetologists at Cornell University in Ithaca focus primarily on questions in behavior, ecology, and evolution, and those at the American Museum of Natural History in New York City focus on classifying the world's herpetofauna (Myers 2000). This long tradition of herpetological research is increasingly being directed at questions concerning conservation of New York's herpetofauna (see Chapter 11, Conservation

Figure 1.1. One of J.T. Nichols' marked eastern box turtles photographed after being marked 35 years previously. Turtles initially marked by Nichols have been recently found alive at more than 100 years of age (see figure 6.17b). Suffolk Co., New York. (Neg./Trans. no. 101050, American Museum of Natural History Library.)

Case Studies). Two major organizations that are internationally active in reptile and amphibian conservation are based in New York. The Wildlife Conservation Society at the Bronx Zoo breeds a number of species in captivity that would otherwise face extinction in the wild. It also provides spectacular exhibits to the public of amphibians and reptiles from around the world (figure 1.2). Last but certainly not

Figure 1.2. A reticulated python named Samantha at the Bronx Zoo in New York City. She was obtained in 1973 from hide hunters who had caught her at a cave entrance near a remote village 50 miles from Samarinda, Borneo. Pigs were her favorite food—she ate one a month while in captivity in the Bronx and grew to more than 26 ft. (7.9 m) and 275 lb. (125 kg) before she died on November 22, 2002. Coauthor John L. Behler is on the far left. (Do DeMello © Wildlife Conservation Society.)

least, the New York Turtle and Tortoise Society has long played a critical role in advocating for turtle conservation around the world.

Despite the impressive herpetological activity in New York State, conspicuous has been the lack of a guide available with which to venture out into the field and identify the state's amphibians and reptiles. Residents of both New York State and adjacent regions have long desired an accessible, informative, and up-to-date treatment of the state's herpetofauna. We developed this book primarily to address this need. We were also looking for an outlet to express our long-standing fascination with these creatures and our collective concern for their well-being. More specifically, New York's extraordinary herpetofauna is being steadily displaced by the state's human inhabitants. Several species in New York are on the brink of extirpation, and population extirpations are widespread. Moreover, New York State's amphibians and reptiles, despite their beauty and venerability, are regarded by many with loathing, disdain, or, at best, indifference. This is unfortunate, given that these creatures play an important role in ecosystems as both predators and prey, some are valuable indicators of environmental quality for all organisms (including humans), and others still are model organisms for medical research.

This book is based on our many collective decades of teaching about and conducting research on New York State's herpetofauna, as well as working to conserve it. During our careers, each of us has developed a tremendous interest and fondness for these creatures, which we hope to share. The book has three primary themes: identification, natural history, and conservation. In detailed species accounts are key characteristics and geographical ranges to permit the confident identification of every reptile or amphibian native to New York State (as well as a few introduced species). In addition, the species accounts also contain short discussions of the natural history and habitat associations of each species (as well as, surprisingly often, mention of what biologists do not yet know about them). Supplementary sections offer an overview of the biology and habitats of the animals.

Most of the descriptions of the animals themselves as well as the habitats that they occupy are based on our personal experience. We have also drawn occasionally from other sources as needed. For species descriptions of salamanders we examined Bishop (1941), Pfingsten and Downs (1989), and Petranka (1998); for frogs and toads, Dickerson (1969) and Wright and Wright (1949); for turtles, Ernst et al. (1994) and Carr (1952); for snakes, Wright and Wright (1957), Ernst and Barbour (1989), and Ernst and Ernst (2003); and for lizards, Smith (1995). Habitat descriptions are based largely on our own observations and augmented by reports in the technical literature that are cited in each species' account.

Mapping where species do and do not occur is problematic for any group of organisms. The distribution maps presented herein are our best approximation of the current distributions of amphibians and reptiles in New York based on the extensive records compiled by the New York State "Herp Atlas" project between 1990 and 2005. Shaded areas on a given species' map are areas with clusters of "Herp Atlas" records. Isolated dots are seemingly legitimate records too remote from any others to map them as part of an obvious aggregation of records (a small number of significant but isolated records from before 1990 are included to augment the 1990–2005 Atlas records). The remaining blank areas have no known records. This said, the blank areas may or may not truly reflect the absence of a particular species. Despite the enormous number of records compiled by the "Herp Atlas," New York State covers a huge swath of territory. Much of it is quite rural (most of central, western, and northern New York) or even downright remote (e.g., Adirondack Mountain region). In other words, a great deal of searching for "herps" in the state has occurred, and much remains to done. Therefore, the blank spots on the distribution maps should be considered a strong hypothesis about a particular species' absence. In addition, these blank spots should be considered worthy targets for further searching. Collection of additional distributional information using the Atlas format is continuing and you are encouraged to contribute records (see "Herp Atlas" Report Card).

The theme of conservation appears throughout the book. A set of habitat conservation guidelines for land managers, landowners, and concerned citizens is presented, as are case studies of specific conservation efforts in New York State. Elsewhere a section on how to study and enjoy amphibians and reptiles along with a sampling of the "unnatural history" of these creatures, including New Yorkers' curious perspectives on "herps" as recorded in the state's folklore, is presented. Collectively, the book is intended to provide a comprehensive look at the diversity, distribution, and natural history of New York's magnificent herpetofauna as well as approaches, opportunities, and reasons for conserving it.

Take this book out into the field, perhaps with a child, parent, friend, or even a politician. Use it to learn more about New York's amphibians and reptiles and involve yourself in their conservation. As a result, perhaps your grandchildren will also have the opportunity to gaze upon New York's stinkpots, hellbenders, spadefoots, tiger salamanders, and more, with wonder and delight.

2

Herpetofauna of New York

Here we present the species of amphibians and reptiles known to occur in New York State. We also provide an overview of the biology
of these fascinating organisms by examining their similarities and
contrasting their differences. Later in the book, at the beginning of
each collection of species accounts, we provide overviews of each of
the major groups of amphibians and reptiles of New York State, that
is, the salamanders (see Chapter 4), frogs and toads (see Chapter 5),
turtles (see Chapter 6), and lizards and snakes (see Chapter 7).

Amphibians and Reptiles of New York State

Just how many species of amphibians and reptiles are native to New
York State? The answer is generally accepted as 69: 18 salamanders
and 14 frogs and toads (table 2.1) and 17 turtles, 3 lizards, and 17
snakes (table 2.2). Quite notably, the state is the type locality for some
18 taxa, including 5 salamanders, 5 frogs, 4 snakes, and 4 turtles (table
2.3). In addition, there are three particularly widespread, introduced
species. Accounts for all these species are provided later in the book,
with one exception: the hawksbill seaturtle, whose occurrence in
New York State is based on just a single record from Long Island
Sound in 1938.

After perusing tables 2.1 and 2.2, those of you who may have
learned your salamanders by reading Bishop (1941) may wonder: what
happened to the purple salamander? (It's now the spring salamander).
Or you may note that Bishop's *Triturus* was changed to *Diemictylus*
and is now *Notophthalmus*. Or if you have been a student of older

Table 2.1.
Amphibians of New York State and Their Status[a]

Scientific Name	Common Name	New York Natural Heritage Program State Rank[b]	NatureServe Global Rank[c]	New York State Listing[d]	Federal Listing
Caudata	Salamanders				
CRYPTOBRANCHIDAE	GIANT SALAMANDERS				
Cryptobranchus alleganiensis	Hellbender	S2	G3G4	Special Concern	
PROTEIDAE	WATERDOGS				
Necturus maculosus	Mudpuppy [Common Mudpuppy]	S4	G5		
AMBYSTOMATIDAE	MOLE SALAMANDERS				
Ambystoma jeffersonianum	Jefferson Salamander	S4	G4	Special Concern	
Ambystoma laterale	Blue-spotted Salamander	S4	G5	Special Concern	
Ambystoma maculatum	Spotted Salamander	S5	G5		
Ambystoma opacum	Marbled Salamander	S3	G5	Special Concern	

Ambystoma tigrinum	Tiger Salamander [Eastern Tiger Salamander]	S1S2	G5	Endangered
SALAMANDRIDAE	TRUE SALAMANDERS			
Notophthalmus viridescens	Eastern Newt	S5	G5	
PLETHODONTIDAE	LUNGLESS SALAMANDERS			
Desmognathus fuscus	Northern Dusky Salamander	S5	G5	
Desmognathus ochrophaeus	Allegheny Mountain Dusky Salamander [Allegheny Dusky Salamander]	S5	G5	
Eurycea bislineata	Northern Two-lined Salamander	S5	G5	
Eurycea longicauda	Long-tailed Salamander [Longtail Salamander]	S2S3	G5	Special Concern
Gyrinophilus porphyriticus	Spring Salamander [Northern Spring Salamander]	S5	G5	
Hemidactylium scutatum	Four-toed Salamander	S5	G5	
Plethodon cinereus	Eastern Red-backed Salamander [Northern Redback Salamander]	S5	G5	

Table 2.1. (continued)

Scientific Name	Common Name	New York Natural Heritage Program State Rank[b]	NatureServe Global Rank[c]	New York State Listing[d]	Federal Listing
Plethodon glutinosus	Northern Slimy Salamander	S5	G5		
Plethodon wehrlei	Wehrle's Salamander	S3	G4		
Pseudotriton ruber	Red Salamander	S3S4	G5		
Anurans	Frogs				
PELOBATIDAE	SPADEFOOT TOADS				
Scaphiopus holbrookii	Eastern Spadefoot	S2S3	G5	Special Concern	
BUFONIDAE	TRUE TOADS				
Bufo americanus	American Toad	S5	G5		
Bufo fowleri	Fowler's Toad	S4	G5		
HYLIDAE	TREEFROGS				
Acris crepitans	Northern Cricket Frog	S1	G5	Endangered	
Hyla versicolor	Gray Treefrog	S5	G5		

Pseudacris triseriata	Western Chorus Frog	S4	G5	
Pseudacris crucifer	Spring Peeper	S5	G5	
RANIDAE	TRUE FROGS			
Rana catesbeiana	Bullfrog	S5	G5	
Rana clamitans	Green Frog	S5	G5	
Rana palustris	Pickerel Frog	S5	G5	
Rana pipiens	Northern Leopard Frog	S5	G5	
Rana septentrionalis	Mink Frog	S5	G5	
Rana sylvatica	Wood Frog	S5	G5	
Rana sphenocephala	Southern Leopard Frog	S1S2	G5	Special Concern

[a]Names follow Crother et al. (2000/2001, 2003) and Collins and Taggart (2005, in brackets, where different).

[b]New York Natural Heritage State Ranks (as of February 2006) are: S1–typically 5 or fewer occurrences or some factor of its biology making it especially vulnerable in New York State; S2–typically 6–20 occurrences or factors demonstrably making it very vulnerable; S3–typically 21–100 occurrences; S4–apparently secure; S5–demonstrably secure in New York State.

[c]NatureServe Global Ranks are: G1–critically imperiled globally because of extreme rarity (5 or fewer occurrences) or especially vulnerable to extinction because of some factor of its biology; G2–imperiled globally because of rarity (6–20 occurrences) or very vulnerable to extinction throughout its range because of other factors; G3–either rare and local throughout its range (21–100 occurrences), or found locally (even abundantly at some of its locations) in a restricted range (e.g., a physiographic region), or vulnerable to extinction throughout its range because of other factors; G4–apparently secure globally, although it may be quite rare in parts of its range, especially at the periphery; G5–demonstrably secure globally, although it may be quite rare.

[d]In 2006 all native amphibians and reptiles in New York State were classified as "game" providing NYS DEC the authority to regulate their harvest, which in practice is currently restricted to frogs of the genus *Rana*, snapping turtle, and diamond-backed terrapin (see Chapter 9).

Table 2.2.

Reptiles of New York State and Their Status[a]

Scientific Name	Common Name	New York Natural Heritage State Rank	NatureServe Global Rank	New York State Listing	Federal Listing
Testudines	Turtles				
Chelydridae	Snapping Turtles				
Chelydra serpentina	Snapping Turtle [Common Snapping Turtle]	S5	G5		
Kinosternidae	Mud and Musk Turtles				
Kinosternon subrubrum	Eastern Mud Turtle	S1	G5	Endangered	
Sternotherus odoratum	Stinkpot [Common Musk Turtle]	S5	G5		
Emydidae	Pond Turtles				
Chrysemys picta	Painted Turtle	S5	G5		
Clemmys guttata	Spotted Turtle	S3	G5	Special Concern	

Glyptemys insculpta	Wood Turtle	S3	G4	Special Concern	
Glyptemys muhlenbergii	Bog Turtle	S2	G3	Endangered	Threatened
Emydoidea blandingii	Blanding's Turtle	S2S3	G4	Threatened	
Graptemys geographica	Northern Map Turtle [Common Map Turtle]	S3	G5		
Malaclemys terrapin	Diamond-backed Terrapin [Diamondback Terrapin]	S3	G4		
Pseudemys rubriventris	Northern Red-Bellied Cooter [Eastern Redbelly Turtle]	Introduced	G5	Unprotected	
Terrapene carolina	Eastern Box Turtle	S3	G5	Special Concern	
Trachemys scripta	Pond Slider [Slider]	Introduced	G5	Unprotected	
Cheloniidae	Seaturtles				
Caretta caretta	Loggerhead	S1	G3	Threatened	Threatened
Chelonia mydas	Green Seaturtle [Green Turtle]	S1	G3	Threatened	Threatened

Table 2.2. (continued)

Scientific Name	Common Name	New York Natural Heritage State Rank	NatureServe Global Rank	New York State Listing	Federal Listing
Eretmochelys imbricata	Hawksbill Seaturtle [Hawksbill]	SN	G3	Endangered	Endangered
Lepidochelys kempii	Kemp's Ridley Seaturtle [Atlantic Ridley]	S1	G1	Endangered	Endangered
Dermochelyidae	Leatherback Seaturtles				
Dermochelys coriacea	Leatherback Seaturtle [Leatherback]	S1N	G2	Endangered	Endangered
Trionychidae	Softshell Turtles				
Apalone spinifera	Spiny Softshell	S2S3	G5	Special Concern	
Squamata	Lizards/Snakes				
Sauria	Lizards				
Phrynosomatidae	Sceloporine Lizards				
Sceloporus undulatus	Eastern Fence Lizard	S1	G5	Threatened	

Lacertidae	Wall Lizards		
Podarcis sicula	Italian Wall Lizard	Introduced	G5
Scincidae	Skinks		
Eumeces anthracinus	Coal Skink	S2S3	G5
Eumeces fasciatus	Common Five-lined Skink [Five-lined Skink]	S3	G5
Squamata	Snakes		
Colubridae	Colubrids		
Carphophis amoenus	Eastern Wormsnake [Eastern Worm Snake]	S2	G5	Special Concern
Coluber constrictor	Eastern Racer	S4	G5
Diadophis punctatus	Ring-necked Snake [Ringneck Snake]	S5	G5
Elaphe alleghaniensis	Eastern Ratsnake [Eastern Rat Snake]	S4	G5

Table 2.2. (continued)

Scientific Name	Common Name	New York Natural Heritage State Rank	NatureServe Global Rank	New York State Listing	Federal Listing
Heterodon platirhinos	Eastern Hog-nosed Snake [Eastern Hognose Snake]	S3	G5	Special Concern	
Lampropeltis triangulum	Milksnake [Milk Snake]	S5	G5		
Liochlorophis vernalis	Smooth Greensnake [Smooth Green Snake]	S4	G5		
Nerodia sipedon	Northern Watersnake [Northern Water Snake]	S5	G5		
Regina septemvittata	Queen Snake	S1	G5	Endangered	
Storeria dekayi	Dekay's Brownsnake [Brown Snake]	S5	G5		
Storeria occipitomaculata	Red-bellied Snake [Redbelly Snake]	S5	G5		

Thamnophis brachystoma	Short-headed Gartersnake [Shorthead Garter Snake]	S3	G4		
Thamnophis sauritus	Eastern Ribbonsnake [Eastern Ribbon Snake]	S4	G5		
Thamnophis sirtalis	Common Gartersnake [Common Garter Snake]	S5	G5		
Viperidae	Pitvipers				
Agkistrodon contortrix	Copperhead	S3	G5		
Crotalus horridus	Timber Rattlesnake	S3	G4	Threatened	
Sistrurus catenatus	Massasauga	S1	G3G4	Endangered	Candidate

[a]Names follow Crother et al. (2000/2001, 2003) and Collins and Taggart (2005, in brackets, where different). Status designations are as given in Table 2.1.

Table 2.3.

Places in New York Where Specimens Used to Fix a Name to a New Type of Amphibians and Reptiles Were Found

Common Name	Species	Type Locality	Notes	Source
Salamanders				
Marbled Salamander	*Ambystoma opacum*	New York	Originally reported by Gravenhorst 1807, collector unknown	Anderson (1967)
Northern Dusky Salamander	*Desmognathus fuscus*	Northern parts of New York State	Originally reported by Rafinesque 1820	McCoy (1982)
Eastern Newt	*Notophthalmus viridescens*	Lake George, Lake Champlain, and the springs and brooks of the neighborhood	Originally reported by Rafinesque 1820, collector unknown	Mecham (1967)
Eastern Red-backed Salamander	*Plethodon cinereus*	Hudson Highlands of New York	Originally reported by Rafinesque 1818	Smith (1963)
Frogs and Toads				
Northern Cricket Frog	*Acris crepitans*	Vicinity of Queens, New York	Originally reported in DeKay 1842	Smith et al. (1995)
Gray Treefrog	*Hyla versicolor*	Restricted to the vicinity of New York City	As reported in Schmidt 1953	Schmidt (1953), McCoy (1982)

Green Frog	*Rana clamitans*	Lake Champlain and Lake George	Subspecies *melanota*, originally reported by Rafinesque 1820	Stewart (1983)
Northern leopard frog	*Rana pipiens*	Fall Creek, Etna, Tompkins County	As reported in Pace 1974	Pace (1974), McCoy (1982)
Mink Frog	*Rana septentrionalis*	Sackett's Harbor, Jefferson County	Originally reported by Baird 1854	Hedeen (1977)
Wood Frog	*Rana sylvatica.*	Vicinity of New York City	Originally reported by LeConte 1825	Martof (1970)
Turtles				
Snapping Turtle	*Chelydra serpentina*	Vicinity of New York City	Originally reported by Linnaeus	Gibbons et al. (1988)
Painted Turtle	*Chrysemys picta*	Vicinity of New York City	Originally reported by Schneider 1783	Ernst (1971)

Table 2.3. (continued)

Common Name	Species	Type Locality	Notes	Source
Wood Turtle	*Glyptemys insculpta*	Vicinity of New York City	As reported in Schmidt 1953	Schmidt (1953), McCoy (1982)
Diamond-backed Terrapin	*Malaclemys terrapin*	Coastal waters of Long Island	Originally reported by Schoepff 1793	Ernst (1982)
Snakes				
Timber Rattlesnake	*Crotalus horridus*	Vicinity of New York City	Originally reported by Linnaeus 1758	Collins and Knight (1980)
Milksnake	*Lampropeltis triangulum*	Vicinity of New York City	Originally reported by Lacepede 1788	Williams (1994)
Northern Watersnake	*Nerodia sipedon*	Vicinity of New York City	As reported in Schmidt 1953	Schmidt (1953), McCoy (1982)
Common Gartersnake	*Thamnophis sauritus*	Michigan Hollow, near Ithaca, Tompkins County	Subspecies *septentrionalis* Collected by J.A. Bartley in 1959	Fossman (1970)

field guides, you will find Muhlenberg's turtle is now the bog turtle and the entire genus *Natrix* is missing, replaced by two "new" genera: *Nerodia* and *Regina*. A renewed interest in amphibians and reptiles over the past two decades, coupled with novel insights derived from genetic analyses, has resulted in changes to accepted common and scientific names of many species, a process that will doubtlessly continue.

Three remaining groups of amphibians and reptiles that live on Earth but are not native to New York State may be found under unusual circumstances in the state. The caecilians (sometimes known as "rubber eels") are a group of limbless, worm-like amphibians found across the tropical parts of the world but confined to zoos and pet shops in New York. Another group that is not native to the state is the crocodilians, familiar to most as occasional denizens of New York City's sewer system (see box: "Are there really alligators in New York City sewers?"). A final group not known to New York under any circumstance is sphenodon (or tuatara), an obscure and endangered, lizard-like reptile that only occurs in New Zealand.

Are There Really Alligators in New York City Sewers?

Alligators are prominent in the folklore of New York City. While swarms of flushed pets do not lurk and breed in the Gotham's sewers, such tales are not baseless. Reports of alligators in the city have indeed been recorded since the 1930s. In June of 1932, two small boys collected a dead 3 ft (1 m) alligator along the banks of the Bronx River. In January 1935, teenagers captured and killed a 125 lb (57 kg) alligator found in a manhole at East 123rd Street. In May of 1937, a barge captain lassoed a large alligator in the East River. In August 1982, a 26-inch-long (0.66 m) alligator was sighted in a Westchester reservoir and in July, 1997, a four-foot-long (1.2 m) alligator was encountered in Kissena Lake, Queens. More recently, in June, 2001, an alligator was spotted in the Harlem Meer in the northeastern section of Central Park but was likely a mistaken sighting of a large snapping turtle, which are *bona fide* residents of New York City's sewer system (large individuals have been reported fairly regularly at the intake grates of the city's sewage treatment plants). Alligators are not restricted to New York City; a live alligator was captured near a public swimming beach on Thompson's Lake, Albany County in 1983 and a youngster was pulled out of a ditch in Pulaski (near Lake Ontario) by one of us (G. Johnson) in 1993. The good news is that New York's climate all but ensures that alligators released in the summer will die in the following winter (source: archives of *The New York Times*).

Figure 2.1. *Coelophysis* was an ostrich-like predator (4.7 ft. [1.5 m]) that hunted the mudflats, lake shores, and rivers of New York some 200 million years ago, eating amphibians and smaller plant- and animal-eating reptiles that were stuck in the mud or too slow to escape the dinosaur's "numerous sharp knife-like teeth designed for slashing and severing flesh" (Fisher 1981). (New York State Museum.)

A prominent, although now extinct group of reptiles—dinosaurs—almost certainly wandered New York State in the past. Two sets of fossil footprints probably made by the three-toed *Coelophysis* are known, one from Rockland County and the other from Long Island (figure 2.1). As yet, no fossils of the bodies of dinosaurs have been found in New York. Most rocks of Mesozoic age (when the dinosaurs lived, about 65 to 240 million years ago) that might have contained such fossils have been repeatedly "bulldozed" by glaciers and obliterated throughout the region.

Similarities between Amphibians and Reptiles

One similarity between amphibians and reptiles is that both obtain body heat necessary to function from sources outside their bodies. Often, the animals are termed "cold-blooded," a characterization that is technically incorrect because amphibians and reptiles can (and often do) raise their body temperatures to "warm-blooded" levels by basking in sunlight. The correct term is "ectothermic," which suggests that amphibians and reptiles must position themselves strategically in the environment to warm themselves sufficiently to become active or otherwise must remain inactive for long periods, as most do during the long New York winters.

Being ectothermic gives reptiles and amphibians some distinct advantages. For one, it permits many to have small bodies. If a bird or mammal is too small, heat loss becomes prohibitive because their bodies have too much surface area relative to volume to retain much body heat. But for "herps," which do not need to keep body temperatures high and stable to survive, this is not an issue. Although some "herps" such as snapping turtles are large-bodied, most are in fact quite small (<10 g) and much smaller than most vertebrate animals. Being small-bodied permits "herps" to exploit a myriad of ecological niches unavailable to larger-bodied, endothermic vertebrates, such as tiny tunnels in the soil and leaf litter, cracks in rocks, the insides of decaying logs, and bark fissures.

Being ectothermic also lets amphibians and reptiles put all the energy that is not frittered away staying warm directly into growth and reproduction; hence, they can become exceedingly numerous (e.g., Burton and Likens 1975b, Petranka and Murray 2001, Davic and Welsh 2004). The eastern red-backed salamander may well be, for example, the most abundant terrestrial vertebrate animal in New York State. A typical density is about 1,660 individual salamanders per acre (4,100/ha) of mature forest (P. K. Ducey and A. R. Breisch, unpublished data). Given that 62% of New York State is forested, there may be some 35,894,311,000 (36 billion) eastern red-backed salamanders in the leaf litter. Much of this layer is too young to support healthy salamander populations, yet only about 20% of salamanders are likely to be at the soil surface and "countable" at any given time (Bailey et al. 2004). Who knows how it all adds up, but suffice it to say that there are likely tens of billions of these salamanders lurking in the soils of the forests of the state. Moreover, although many amphibians and reptiles are small, their collective weight adds up. This means that amphibians make important contributions to animal "biomass" and predator–prey connections in many ecosystems. For example, woodland salamanders are important conduits of nutrients being cycled within the forest, particularly calcium (Burton and Likens 1975a). Because they consume so many invertebrates that fragment leaf litter they slow significantly decomposition and the release of carbon dioxide to the atmosphere (Wyman 1998).

Differences between Amphibians and Reptiles

Beyond the commonality of being ectothermic, the differences, rather than similarities, between amphibians and reptiles are more striking. Indeed, modern reptiles are more closely related to birds and mammals than they are to modern amphibians (Laurin and Reisz 1995). Most reptiles, for example, produce a few eggs with shells (like birds), usually well provisioned with yolk, and lay these eggs in dry soils. Some even give birth to live offspring. Reptiles also have dry, scaly skin and respire primarily through their lungs.

Amphibians, in contrast, must remain in moist environments and most return to water to breed. Their eggs are fragile structures—mere embryos in jelly envelopes typically cast into the water in vast numbers. Amphibian skins are generally so permeable that much gas and water exchange occurs directly through the skin (whereas the tough skin of reptiles results in most reptilian respiration occurring across the membranes of the lung). The dependence of amphibians on both land and water underpins the term amphibious used to describe them (*amphi*=both and *bios*=modes of life).

3

New York's Environment as Habitat for Amphibians and Reptiles

New York State covers 49,108 sq. mi. (127,189 km²) and extends from sea level along Long Island Sound to 5,344 ft. (1,600 m) in the Adirondack Mountains (figure 3.1). This area spans almost 5° of north–south latitude and 8° of east–west longitude. The state occurs in a humid temperate region, with average temperatures of 16–34°F (–9 to 1°C) in January and 66–77°F (19–25°C) in July. Precipitation is evenly distributed through the year, and much of the state receives about 40 in. (102 cm) annually. This variation in climate, topography, and vegetation generates the striking diversity of amphibians and reptiles of the state.

New York's complement of amphibians and reptiles represents a convergence of species with affinities to more southern, midwestern and northern regions. For example, the state is the northern limit of the hellbender, marbled salamander, tiger salamander, red salamander, long-tailed salamander, Wehrle's salamander, eastern spadefoot, northern cricket frog, southern leopard frog, eastern mud turtle, bog turtle, eastern fence lizard, and copperhead. It is also the eastern extreme for the tiger salamander, massasauga, queen snake, and western chorus frog. One species reaches its southern range limit in New York: the mink frog. These peripheral species are complemented by a large number of species that are widely distributed across the entire state. These include the spotted salamander, eastern red-backed salamander, northern two-lined salamander, eastern newt, bullfrog, spring peeper, green frog, wood frog, pickerel frog, snapping turtle, painted turtle, and common gartersnake. Other widespread species

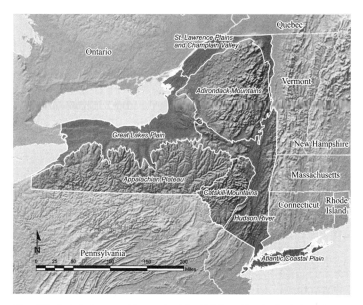

Figure 3.1. Ecological zones and topography of New York State. Elevation is relative to the highest point, Mt. Marcy in the northeastern Adirondack Mountains at 5,344 ft. (1,629 m), and the lowest, sea level along the margin of the Atlantic Coastal Plain. Data sources: New York State Gap Analysis Project (for ecological zones) and US Geological Survey EROS Data Center, April, 2003, North America Shaded Relief: National Atlas of the United States, Reston, Virginia (for topography).

include the northern water snake and eastern milk snake (missing from parts of northern New York) and the American toad (absent only from Long Island).

This chapter describes the major ecological zones found in New York: Atlantic Coastal Plain, Appalachian Plateau, Great Lakes Plain, Hudson and Mohawk Valleys, Catskill Mountains, St. Lawrence Plains/Champlain Valley, and Adirondack Mountains (see figure 3.1) as well as the herpetological specialties of each. "Ecozones" are referred to in the species accounts and are based on those recognized by the New York State Department of Environmental Conservation (Dickinson 1979, Will et al. 1982). Similarly, other identifiers are mentioned often in the species accounts so we also provide maps for these: rivers and lakes (figure 3.2), counties and cities (figure 3.3), and major habitat associations (figure 3.4).

Figure 3.2. Major lakes and rivers of New York State. Data source: Streams and Waterbodies of the United States, National Atlas of the United States, March, 2005.

Figure 3.3. Counties and major cities of New York State. Data sources: Census 2000 US Gazetteer Files, 2002, US Census Bureau (for cities); County Boundaries of the United States, National Atlas of the United States, June, 2005 (for counties).

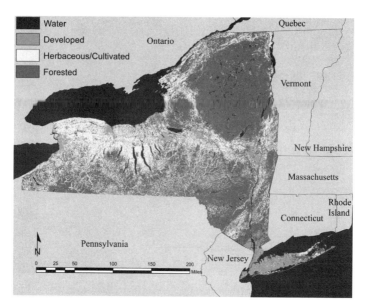

Figure 3.4. Land cover of New York State. "Water" includes both fresh and marine water bodies, "herbaceous/cultivated" includes primarily pasture and cropland, "developed" represents primarily suburban and urban areas, and "forested" is dominated by trees. Data source: National Land Cover Dataset 1992, US Geological Survey, January 1, 1997, Sioux Falls, South Dakota.

Ecological Zones of New York State and Their Herpetofauna

Atlantic Coastal Plain

This zone is represented primarily by Long Island and Staten Island (see figure 3.1; figure 3.5). The zone has very low relief, typically less than 200 ft. (60 m). Climate is strongly moderated by the ocean, and soils are mostly derived from glacial drift. Soils are therefore generally "poor" and sandy, with natural vegetation dominated by scrub oak and pines. Much of the vegetation in the zone, with the exception of eastern Long Island, has been "urbanized" (see figure 3.4). Nevertheless, because of its distinct climate and ecosystems, the region remains a stronghold for several species, including the eastern mud turtle, eastern box turtle, and tiger salamander. Moreover, large populations of diamond-backed terrapins occur in salt marshes and estuaries. This is the only part of the state where sea turtles appear, typically stranded on the beaches. Notably, Long Island Sound is also a

Figure 3.5. The Atlantic Coastal Plain. Queens Co., New York. (Russell Burke.)

vital nursery area for young Kemp's ridley seaturtles (see Chapter 6 box: Sea turtles in New York State).

Appalachian Plateau

This zone (see figure 3.1; figure 3.6) represents a vast swath of the State, covering the hilly regions of much of central and western New York to the Pennsylvania border. The zone extends from west of the Catskill Mountains through the southern end of the Finger Lakes region to the Allegheny Hills. Elevations are typically between 1,000 and 2,000 ft. (300–600 m). The region's hilly nature in combination with its deeply carved valleys results in a topography that supports fewer wetlands than are found in other parts of the state. Northern hardwood forests are the predominant vegetation, covering about one third of the region, with hemlock (*Tsuga canadensis*) prominent in stream valleys. Most of the remainder of the land is in agriculture, although much of grassland component has been abandoned and is slowly reverting to forest. The Appalachian Plateau is a stronghold for many notable species, including the long-tailed salamander, slimy salamander, Wehrle's salamander, hellbender, short-headed garter-snake, and coal skink.

Figure 3.6.   The Appalachian Plateau. Wyoming/Livingston Co., New York. (James P. Gibbs.)

Great Lakes Plain

This zone (see figure 3.1; figure 3.7) extends along the plains of
Lake Erie and Lake Ontario and includes land at the eastern end of
Lake Ontario. The region remains mostly below 800 ft. (240 m), except for the Tug Hill Plateau at the extreme eastern end of Lake
Ontario, which reaches almost 2,000 ft. (600 m). Northern hardwood forests cover only about one fifth of the area, and these are
highly fragmented by agriculture, mainly dairy farms and orchards,

Figure 3.7. The Great Lakes Plain. Jefferson Co., New York. (James P. Gibbs.)

except for the Tug Hill region, which remains heavily forested (see figure 3.4). Notably, salamander communities tend to be relatively impoverished in this region, possibly because much of the remaining forest is young and heavily fragmented, making it difficult for salamanders to repopulate. Specialties of the Great Lakes Plain include the spiny softshell, northern map turtle, massasauga, and bog turtle.

Hudson and Mohawk Valleys

This zone (see figure 3.1; figure 3.8) consists of plains and hills surrounding the Hudson River valley (about 50% of the area being forest comprised of oak–northern hardwoods) and extending west into the Mohawk River valley (where some 20% of the landscape is forest, primarily northern hardwoods). The Hudson River valley is a stronghold for bog turtle, Blanding's turtle, timber rattlesnake, copperhead, common five-lined skink, and northern cricket frog. One notable area, the Albany Sand Plains, is dominated by oak and pine. The Albany Sand Plains is "a northern outpost for southern species" (Stewart and Rossi 1981) and hosts eastern spadefoot, Fowler's toad, box turtle, eastern wormsnake, and eastern hog-nosed snake.

Figure 3.8. The Hudson River Valley. Englewood Cliffs, New Jersey. (James P. Gibbs.)

Catskill Mountains

This zone (see figure 3.1; figure 3.9) contains numerous peaks over 3,000 ft. (900 m) elevation that form the headwaters of the Delaware River. The region ends abruptly to the north at the Heldeberg Escarpment, a favorite study area of one of New York's preeminent herpetologists, Sherman C. Bishop (Bishop 1926, 1941). Most of the area is heavily forested with spruce and fir at the upper elevations and mixed hardwoods at the lower elevations. Large areas are protected as part of either the Catskill State Park or the New York City watershed. Amphibian and reptile diversity is low at the higher elevations, but the southern lowlands bordering the Delaware River and its tributaries are host to many species, including timber rattlesnakes, eastern racers, and eastern ratsnakes.

St. Lawrence Plains/Champlain Valley

This zone (see figure 3.1; figure 3.10) is composed of lowlands less than 700 ft. (200 m) fringing the Adirondack region to the north and east. The St. Lawrence Plains are made up of fragmented forests of northern hardwoods, expanses of swamplands, and extensive shrub land on abandoned farmlands with a harsh northern climate. The Champlain Valley has a more moderate climate and more

Figure 3.9. The Catskill Mountains. Delaware Co., New York. (James P. Gibbs.)

Figure 3.10. St. Lawrence Plains and Champlain Valley. Jefferson Co., New York. (James P. Gibbs.)

productive and extensive agriculture. Specialties of the region are scattered populations of Blanding's turtle, western chorus frogs, and populations of eastern ratsnakes isolated from southern populations in the state. Mink frogs also extend into this zone from the Adirondack region.

Figure 3.11. The Adirondack Mountains. St. Lawrence Co., New York. (James P. Gibbs.)

Adirondack Mountains

This zone (see figure 3.1; figure 3.11) is extremely mountainous, with many peaks over 4,000 ft. (1,200 m). This results in a colder, harsher winter than much of the rest of New York. Most of the area remains heavily forested, primarily in spruce, fir, and northern hardwoods, with the western portion of this ecozone containing numerous lakes and large peat lands. Because of the severity of the climate, many reptile species common over other parts of the state are absent from all but the periphery of the region. The Adirondack region is the stronghold of the mink frog in the state.

Habitat Associations of New York's Amphibian and Reptiles

The physical features in each ecological zone generate a mix of habitat types for amphibians and reptiles. Topography, geology, and climate determine the hydrology, soil type, and the plant community association that develops at a particular site, that is, the "habitat." Together these environmental factors have generated more than 172 natural ecosystem types in the State (Reschke 1990) that amphibians and reptiles can inhabit. In this book, we have simplified this ecological diversity into 12 primary aquatic/wetland and 11 upland types (tables 3.1 and 3.2). To give you a sense of the species you will typically encounter in different habitats in the various parts of New York State, we have provided a cross-listing of species by region and habitat type to depict typical region-specific suites of species expected to occur in particular ecosystem types for amphibians (table 3.1) and reptiles (table 3.2).

Within a given habitat association, the community of amphibians and reptiles that becomes established depends on three factors. The first is whether a species can tolerate the environmental conditions present. Few species can, for example, survive the long winters and short summers in the Adirondack Mountains, even though all requisite habitats may be present. The second is whether all of a species' habitat needs are met at a particular site. Many mole salamanders, for example, need both mature forest for adults to live in and vernal pools for breeding in and will not persist long without both. The third is whether a species was able to reach the site historically or reinvade it in more recent times after forests have returned. Hellbenders, for example, may well be able to thrive in rivers of the Great Lakes Plain region but were never able to cross into them from the south where the species arose.

It is important to note that a rapidly expanding human population has modified these associations (see figure 3.4), often dramatically. Moreover, New York's landscape is continually changing. Forests currently occupy fully 62% of the landscape (Alerich and Drake 1995), and have recovered remarkably from 1900 when only about 25% of the land was forested. Currently the nonforested part of the state is comprised of cropland (14%), pasture (4%), and suburban and urban areas (20%) (see figure 3.4).

From the perspective of reptiles and particularly amphibians, one dramatic and extremely harmful change that is not likely to change soon is wetland loss. Between the 1780s and 1980s New York lost 60% of its wetlands (Dahl 1990). Reversion of abandoned farmland and currently increasing beaver populations since the mid-twentieth century have resulted in modest recovery to wetland habitats in some areas of the state where urban and suburban sprawl has not yet extended. Another profound change is forest and pond succession. As New York State undergoes rapid increases in forest cover, closed-canopy ponds are becoming more prevalent, to the benefit of such species as wood frogs but to the detriment of American toads, northern leopard frogs, spring peepers, and others (Skelly et al. 1999, Werner and Glennemeier 1999, Halverson et al. 2003). Hence, "open

Table 3.1.

Occurrence of Native Amphibians by Region and Habitat Type within New York State

Common Name	Region												
	Atlantic Coastal Plain	Appalachian Plateau	Great Lakes Plain	Hudson and Mohawk Valleys	Taconic Highlands	St. Lawrence Plains/ Champlain Valley	Adirondack Mountains	Large rivers	Small rivers	Streams	Seeps	Vernal pools	Swamp
Salamanders													
Hellbender		✻						✻	✻				
Mudpuppy		✻	✻	✻		✻		✻	✻				
Jefferson salamander		✻	✻	✻	✻	✻	✻					✻	
Blue-spotted salamander	✻	✻	✻	✻	✻	✻						✻	
Spotted salamander	✻	✻	✻	✻	✻	✻	✻					✻	✻
Marbled salamander	✻			✻	✻							✻	
Tiger salamander	✻											✻	
Eastern newt	✻	✻	✻	✻	✻	✻	✻						
Northern dusky salamander		✻	✻	✻	✻	✻	✻			✻	✻		
Allegheny mountain dusky salamander		✻	✻	✻		✻	✻			✻	✻		
Northern two-lined salamander	✻	✻	✻	✻	✻	✻	✻			✻	✻		
Long-tailed salamander		✻											
Spring salamander		✻	✻	✻		✻	✻			✻			
Four-toed salamander	✻	✻	✻	✻	✻	✻	✻						✻

Habitat																
Peatland	Beaver pond	Salt marsh/marine	Pond/marsh	Reservoir/lake	Wet meadow	Urban	Suburban	Pine barrens	Deciduous forest	Coniferous forest	Alpine	Abandoned field	Row crop	Orchard	Mines and quarries	Rocky outcrops/slopes
									✻	✻						
									✻	✻						
	✻								✻	✻						
									✻							
								✻	✻							
	✻		✻	✻					✻	✻	✻					
									✻	✻						
									✻	✻						
									✻	✻						

Table 3.1. (continued)

Common Name	Atlantic Coastal Plain	Appalachian Plateau	Great Lakes Plain	Hudson and Mohawk Valleys	Taconic Highlands	St. Lawrence Plains/Champlain Valley	Adirondack Mountains	Large rivers	Small rivers	Streams	Seeps	Vernal pools	Swamp
Eastern red-backed salamander	✻	✻	✻	✻	✻	✻	✻						
Northern slimy salamander		✻	✻	✻	✻							✻	
Wehrle's salamander		✻											
Red salamander		✻		✻							✻		
Toads and Frogs													
Eastern spadefoot	✻			✻								✻	
American toad		✻	✻	✻	✻	✻	✻						
Fowler's toad	✻			✻									
Northern cricket frog				✻									
Gray treefrog	✻	✻	✻	✻	✻	✻	✻						
Western chorus frog			✻			✻						✻	
Spring peeper	✻	✻	✻	✻	✻	✻	✻					✻	✻
Bullfrog	✻	✻	✻	✻	✻	✻	✻						
Green frog	✻	✻	✻	✻	✻	✻	✻						✻
Pickerel frog	✻	✻	✻	✻	✻	✻	✻						✻
Northern leopard frog		✻	✻	✻	✻	✻	✻						✻
Mink frog		✻				✻							
Wood frog	✻	✻	✻	✻	✻	✻	✻					✻	
Southern leopard frog	✻												✻

Habitat																
Peatland	Beaver pond	Salt marsh/marine	Pond/marsh	Reservoir/lake	Wet meadow	Urban	Suburban	Pine barrens	Deciduous forest	Coniferous forest	Alpine	Abandoned field	Row crop	Orchard	Mines and quarries	Rocky outcrops/slopes
									☼	☼						
									☼	☼						
									☼	☼						☼
								☼	☼							
	☼		☼				☼		☼	☼		☼		☼		
	☼		☼				☼	☼	☼							
	☼		☼													
	☼		☼						☼	☼						
					☼							☼				
	☼		☼	☼			☼	☼	☼	☼						
	☼		☼	☼				☼								
☼	☼		☼	☼												
	☼		☼		☼							☼				
	☼		☼		☼							☼				
	☼		☼													
									☼	☼						
	☼		☼		☼							☼				

Table 3.2.

Occurrence of Native Reptiles by Region and Habitat Type within New York State

Common Name	Atlantic Coastal Plain	Appalachian Plateau	Great Lakes Plain	Hudson and Mohawk Valleys	Taconic Highlands	St. Lawrence Plains/ Champlain Valley	Adirondack Mountains	Large rivers	Small rivers	Streams	Seeps	Vernal pools	Swamp
Turtles													
Snapping turtle	※	※	※	※	※	※	※	※	※				
Eastern mud turtle	※												
Stinkpot	※		※	※	※	※							
Painted turtle	※	※	※	※	※	※	※						※
Spotted turtle	※		※	※	※							※	
Wood turtle		※	※	※	※	※	※			※			
Bog turtle			※	※	※								
Blanding's turtle				※	※	※						※	※
Diamond-backed terrapin	※												
Northern red-bellied cooter	※												※
Eastern box turtle	※	※		※	※					※			
Pond slider	※												※
Seaturtles													
Loggerhead	※												
Green seaturtle	※												
Hawksbill seaturtle	※												
Kemp's ridley seaturtle	※												
Leatherback seaturtle	※												

Habitat																
Peatland	Beaver pond	Salt marsh/marine	Pond/marsh	Reservoir/lake	Wet meadow	Urban	Suburban	Pine barrens	Deciduous forest	Coniferous forest	Alpine	Abandoned field	Row crop	Orchard	Mines and quarries	Rocky outcrops/slopes
	✿		✿	✿			✿									
			✿	✿												
			✿	✿												
	✿		✿	✿			✿									
	✿		✿		✿											
					✿			✿								
✿					✿											
	✿		✿													
		✿														
	✿		✿	✿		✿	✿									
									✿			✿				
	✿		✿	✿		✿	✿									
		✿														
		✿														
		✿														
		✿														
		✿														

Table 3.2. (continued)

Common Name	Atlantic Coastal Plain	Appalachian Plateau	Great Lakes Plain	Hudson and Mohawk Valleys	Taconic Highlands	St. Lawrence Plains/ Champlain Valley	Adirondack Mountains	Large rivers	Small rivers	Streams	Seeps	Vernal pools	Swamp
Softshell Turtles													
Spiny softshell		✷	✷					✷					
Lizards													
Eastern fence lizard	✷			✷									
Italian wall lizard	✷												
Coal skink		✷	✷										
Common five-lined skink				✷	✷	✷							
Snakes													
Eastern wormsnake	✷			✷									
Eastern racer	✷	✷		✷	✷								
Ring-necked snake	✷	✷		✷	✷	✷	✷						
Eastern ratsnake		✷	✷	✷	✷	✷							
Eastern hog-nosed snake	✷			✷	✷								
Milksnake	✷	✷	✷	✷	✷	✷	✷						
Northern watersnake	✷	✷	✷	✷	✷	✷	✷						
Queen snake		✷							✷	✷			
DeKay's brownsnake	✷	✷	✷	✷	✷	✷	✷						
Red-bellied snake		✷	✷	✷	✷	✷	✷						
Short-headed gartersnake		✷											
Eastern ribbonsnake	✷	✷	✷	✷	✷	✷							

Habitat																
Peatland	Beaver pond	Salt marsh/marine	Pond/marsh	Reservoir/lake	Wet meadow	Urban	Suburban	Pine barrens	Deciduous forest	Coniferous forest	Alpine	Abandoned field	Row crop	Orchard	Mines and quarries	Rocky outcrops/slopes
				✵												
								✵	✵					✵	✵	
					✵	✵										
									✵						✵	✵
									✵						✵	✵
									✵							✵
					✵							✵			✵	
									✵	✵		✵				
									✵			✵				✵
								✵								
							✵					✵				
	✵	✵	✵													
						✵	✵		✵	✵					✵	
									✵							
												✵				
												✵				

Table 3.2. (continued)

Common Name	Region												
	Atlantic Coastal Plain	Appalachian Plateau	Great Lakes Plain	Hudson and Mohawk Valleys	Taconic Highlands	St. Lawrence Plains/ Champlain Valley	Adirondack Mountains	Large rivers	Small rivers	Streams	Seeps	Vernal pools	Swamp
Common gartersnake	✿	✿	✿	✿	✿	✿	✿						
Smooth greensnake	✿	✿	✿	✿	✿	✿	✿						
Copperhead				✿	✿								
Timber rattlesnake		✿		✿	✿	✿							
Massasauga			✿										✿

land" species are giving way to those more closely associated with forests (see Chapter 8 box: "Are Amphibians Declining in New York State?"). Last, the seemingly inexorable trend toward more urbanization is problematic for the herpetofauna; consistently negative associations occur between reptile and amphibian abundance and diversity and urban development (Knutson et al. 2000, Gibbs et al. 2005). This said, amphibians and reptiles manage to "hang on" in some unlikely places (see box: "The Native Herpetofauna of New York City").

The Native Herpetofauna of New York City

New York City is a seemingly endless expanse of wall-to-wall apartment buildings, skyscrapers, factories, and other creations of asphalt, steel, and concrete. Yet in the green patches and watery spots that remain, a diversity of native amphibians and reptiles persists. During the period from 1990 to 1999, the "Herp Atlas" recorded 32 native species of amphibians and reptiles and 3 introduced species within the five boroughs of New York City. The New York City Department of Parks and Recreation has also recorded a surprising suite of amphibians between 2000 and 2005: spotted salamanders from

	Habitat															
Peatland	Beaver pond	Salt marsh/marine	Pond/marsh	Reservoir/lake	Wet meadow	Urban	Suburban	Pine barrens	Deciduous forest	Coniferous forest	Alpine	Abandoned field	Row crop	Orchard	Mines and quarries	Rocky outcrops/slopes
	✩						✩		✩	✩		✩				
												✩				
									✩							✩
									✩							✩
✩									✩							

Queens and Staten Island; northern dusky salamanders from Manhattan and Staten Island; northern two-lined salamanders from the Bronx, Queens, and Staten Island; eastern newts and red salamanders from Staten Island; and eastern red-backed salamanders from all boroughs. For frogs, "NYC Parks" made observations of Fowler's toads, spring peepers, and wood frogs from Queens and Staten Island; green frogs and bullfrogs from the Bronx and Staten Island; and grey treefrogs and southern leopard frogs from Staten Island (E. Pehek, personal communication). Wetlands in such seminatural areas as Pelham Bay and Van Cortlandt Park contain thriving populations of snapping and painted turtles. Notably, a 35-lb. (16-kg) female snapping turtle was recently struck by a car on Central Park's West Drive at 76th Street (*New York Post*, June 26, 2003). In addition, New York City is home to a large population of diamond-backed terrapins that paddle along its shorelines.

One notable species is missing: the northern cricket frog, which was last reported on Staten Island in the 1970s. And Rattlesnake Brook in what is now Seton Falls Park in the Eastchester section of the Bronx alludes to a former haunt of this species. The New York City government has been trying to reverse some losses by reintroducing many species, including eastern box turtles, to Staten Island parks as part of "Project X" (*The Buffalo News*, September 7, 1998). "NYC Parks" has been actively restoring habitat critical for herps in the City such as Twin Fields kettle pond, one of the marshes fed by Rattlesnake Brook in Seton Falls Park, the floodplain of the Bronx River in the Bronx Forest section, the Alder Brook wetland in Riverdale Park, and many acres of salt marsh. The Twin Fields pond has been colonized by Fowler's toads, Alder Brook wetland has green frogs, and terrapins are using some of the restored salt marsh (E. Pehek, personal communication). In summary, although the current diversity of native "herps" is reduced from that reported 50 years ago (Kieran 1959), New York City is still home to an impressive array of native amphibians and reptiles.

4

Salamanders: Species Accounts

Salamanders are secretive creatures, almost entirely nocturnal, and little known to most of us (figure 4.1). Not tremendously social creatures, they communicate with one another mostly via chemical compounds secreted within the soil where they spend most of their lives. Salamanders are intriguing because along with slender bodies, long tails, and front and hind legs of similar size, they sometimes possess eye-grabbing coloration. The colors of some species include bright reds, garish yellows, and neon orange, which advertise their considerable toxicity to potential predators. Speck (1923) relates a tale of 18 men in a lumber camp in Maine who died after having drunk from a pail of water into which a salamander had crawled. Although the veracity of this tale is questionable, medical journals have reported deaths of humans in the Pacific Northwest that were caused by eating newts (e.g., Brodie 1982). Even the name "salamander" is steeped in intrigue; it derives from an Arab-Persian word meaning "born of fire." The belief that moist-skinned salamanders are born of fire is at first implausible. But upon tossing an old log on the fire while camping, you might see panicky salamanders making a quick exit, and you can thereby appreciate the probable origins of the myth.

By and large, salamanders in New York State are creatures of the soils, litter, and fallen timber of mature forests and wooded streamsides. Otherwise reclusive creatures, they can be seen in abundance on the ground surface during heavy, nighttime rains in spring, summer,

Figure 4.1. Eft stage of the eastern newt, one of the most widespread salamanders in New York State. (Neg./Trans. no. 335622, American Museum of Natural History Library.)

and fall. Some species emerge from the soil to travel to breeding sites, others to forage on the ground surface, and still others to explore new territory.

Salamanders have complex life cycles that generally include three stages: egg, larva, and adult. The mating and courtship patterns that initiate the life cycle are particularly interesting. With the exception of hellbenders, all salamanders in New York have internal fertilization involving the external placement of a spermatophore. Males court females with complex rituals and attempt to entice females to pick up the sperm packets (spermatophores) that sit on gelatinous stalks that males attach to the ground or the bottom of a breeding pool. In some species, such as spotted salamanders, large groups of males ("congresses") gather in vernal pools (figure 4.2) to court females. The unused spermatophores can be seen on the bottom of pools the next morning following a night of courtship (see figure 4.2). Females then lay fertilized eggs in clumps on pond bottoms or in moist refuges under leaves or rocks, depending on the species.

Salamander larvae hatch from these eggs and are of two distinct types: pond-type and stream-type (figure 4.3). Salamander larvae are entirely predaceous and carnivorous, consuming aquatic invertebrates,

Figure 4.2. A "congress" of male spotted salamanders gathered in a vernal pool to court females. Note the spermatophores attached to leaves (white dots). Onondaga Co., New York. (Aaron C. Jacobsen.)

including large numbers of mosquito larvae and larvae of other amphibians (In contrast, frog larvae are known as "pollywogs" or "tadpoles" and are primarily grazers that scrape algae off submerged surfaces or filter-feeders that collect material in a mucous net.)

Some notable exceptions to this basic salamander life history occur. Eastern red-backed salamanders and many other members of the family Plethodontidae lay eggs under rocks or rotten logs on land, with larval development completed within eggs that hatch into tiny juveniles barely 0.75 in. (2 cm) long. Eastern newts are also an exception, with a typical aquatic egg and larval stages but follow with a terrestrial "eft" stage that lasts 2–7 years. At the end of this prolonged juvenile stage the efts transform back into a more aquatic, adult form and remain in or close to a pond for the rest of their lives. The hellbenders, which remain fully aquatic even after they lose their external gills at about 1.5 to 2 years of age, and mudpuppies, which have a 6-year larval period and retain their external gills even as fully reproductive adults, are at the other end of the spectrum. A particularly confusing group of salamanders, including the hard-to-distinguish Jefferson salamanders, blue-spotted salamanders, and related unisexual taxa, have the ability to produce fertile hybrids with two, three, or even four sets of chromosomes (see the Jefferson Salamander, Other Intriguing Facts).

Figure 4.3. Salamander larvae consist of two types: pond-type larvae (A) have large gills, a high tail fin, and very thin limbs; and stream-type larvae (B) have small gills, a low tail fin, and heavier limbs. (A, Twan Leenders; B, Suzanne L. Collins, the Center for North American Herpetology.)

Another characteristic of salamanders is their longevity: salamanders typically live for a decade or more in the wild, whereas few frogs survive that long (most less than 5 years). Even the tiny and abundant eastern red-backed salamander has a generation time of about a decade in length (Hairston 1983). The hellbender is the champion in terms of longevity, with a record in captivity of at least 55 years.

Key characteristics for distinguishing among the salamanders and newts of New York State are depicted in figure 4.4. Because terrestrial salamanders often lose parts of their tails to predators, we report their sizes as snout vent lengths (SVL=distance from the tip of the snout to the anterior angle of the vent). However, for aquatic larvae and fully aquatic adult salamanders, which show less variation in tail size, we use total lengths (distance from the tip of the snout to the tip of the tail).

Figure 4.4. External characteristics useful for classifying salamanders and newts. Adult salamanders are measured from the tip of the snout to the anterior angle of the vent (snout-to-vent length [SVL]) or to the posterior angle of the vent (standard length). (B.M. Glorioso.)

New York's eighteen native species are distributed among five families. These include two wholly aquatic families: the giant salamander family or Cryptobranchidae, with one member, the hellbender, and the waterdog family or Proteidae, also with one member, the mudpuppy. Members of the family Salamandridae are called newts by North Americans and often have rougher skin and lack distinct grooves along their sides. New York has one native species—the eastern newt.

One particularly large family in New York is the mole salamanders, or Ambystomatidae, which have stout bodies and limbs and blunt heads; there are five species. The mole salamanders are so-named because they are subterranean and have a capacity for burrowing. But the most species-rich family (in New York and worldwide) is the Plethodontidae, or lungless salamanders, which do indeed lack lungs, respiring instead through their moist skins and the lining of their mouths. Lungless salamanders also possess a groove between the nostril and upper lip, known as the nasolabial groove, that transports waterborne compounds by capillary action from the ground into the nose, thereby transferring chemical cues left by other salamanders (figure 4.5).

"Herp Atlas" records indicate particular "hot spots" for salamander diversity in the Hudson River valley and southern Catskill Mountain regions and at scattered locations in western New York on the Appalachian Plateau, where 10 to 12 species may occur in areas as small

Figure 4.5. Nasolabial grooves distinguish the lungless salamanders (family Plethodontidae) and are used to transport waterborne chemical cues left by other salamanders from the ground to the nose via capillary action. (Frank T. Burbrink.)

as a few hundred acres. With nearly 5% of the world's total (18 of 430), New York can play a significant role in global salamander conservation efforts.

Hellbender
Cryptobranchus alleganiensis [Plate 1]

Quick Identification

An enormous, brown salamander of Appalachian Plateau rivers with highly folded skin and short stocky legs

Description

Hellbenders are, in terms of bulk, the largest salamanders in the Western Hemisphere. Adults reach total lengths of 29 in. (74 cm), although most are 18–24 in. (46–61 cm). The eel-like two-toed amphiuma (*Amphiuma means*) and greater siren (*Siren lacertina*) of the southeastern United States are known to grow considerably longer but are far less robust. Hellbenders are characterized by broad flat heads and bodies, with tails that are laterally compressed and keeled. Along each side of the animal there are fleshy irregular folds beginning at the rear of the head and extending to the base of the tail. Short stocky legs, with five toes on the hind legs and four toes on the forelegs, allow hellbenders to walk along the stream bottom. A pair of tiny, dark eyes and a large mouth are characteristic. The adults do not possess external gills but have a gill cleft on each side. These clefts are hidden by folds of skin—hence the generic name: *Cryptobranchus*, which means hidden gills. Hellbenders are usually brownish in color, but this can vary from yellowish brown to almost black. Most of these salamanders also have numerous, irregular, dark blotches on their bodies.

Habitat

Hellbenders occur in oxygen-rich rivers and larger streams, that is, with little or no siltation, cold and fast-flowing water, and average depths of 1–3 ft. (0.3–1 m). Places to hide, such as large, flat rock slabs (20–40 in. [50–100 cm]) largest diameter) or, less often, waterlogged boards and timbers, are essential. Deep gravel beds appear to be critical for larvae (Nickerson et al. 2003).

Natural History

Hellbenders are a fully aquatic species (although there are a few records of hellbenders on land close to streams during damp evenings). They respire primarily through their highly folded skin and frequently rock back and forth to replenish the water at the skin surface (Guimond and Hutchison 1973, Harlan and Wilkinson 1981). Hellbenders typically crawl along river bottoms at night and use their keeled tail for rapid swimming when necessary. They are sedentary (Peterson 1987), with small home ranges (typically 1,000–3,000 sq. ft. (100–300 m²) for such large animals (Hillis and Bellis 1971). Their diet consists mainly of crayfish (Mays and Nickerson 1973), with fishes, earthworms, and insects as important supplements (Swanson 1948) that are seized primarily by rapidly opening the jaws and suctioning the prey into the mouth (Cundall et al. 1987). What few fish hellbenders consume are mostly minnows and suckers; fishermen have wrongly persecuted hellbenders for preying on game fishes such as trout. Hellbenders may also eat carrion.

Hellbenders are the only salamander in New York that reproduces via external fertilization (shedding sperm onto eggs deposited outside the female's body). Mating occurs in August and September, and eggs are deposited in nests excavated by the male under large rocks within streams. Females in Pennsylvania lay 200–500 eggs (Hulse et al. 2001). Several females may mate with the same male and deposit their egg masses under the same rock, which is guarded by the male who may compensate for his labors by ingesting some of the eggs. The incubation period lasts 10–12 weeks depending on water temperature (Bishop 1941). The larval hatchlings are about 1.25 in. (3 cm) long, and may take 5 to 6 years to become adults, by which time they will have attained a length of about 12 in. (30 cm) (Bishop 1941). Adults may survive for more than 30 years (Taber et al. 1975).

Status and Distribution

In New York (map 4.1) hellbenders occur in the Allegheny River and its major tributaries (Allegany, Cattaraugus, and Chautauqua Counties) and the Susquehanna River and its large tributary, the Unadilla River and some of its feeder streams (in Broome, Chenango, and Delaware Counties). There is also a positive identification, along with photographs, of a hellbender captured in the Delaware River in Sullivan County in 1990. Hellbenders are listed as a species of Special Concern in New York and are clearly less common than they once were. Hellbenders are threatened by habitat destruction as well as dams, gravel mining, stream siltation, poor water quality, declining

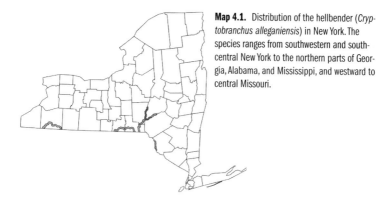

Map 4.1. Distribution of the hellbender (*Cryptobranchus alleganiensis*) in New York. The species ranges from southwestern and south-central New York to the northern parts of Georgia, Alabama, and Mississippi, and westward to central Missouri.

crayfish populations, indiscriminate anglers, and illegal take for the pet trade.

Other Intriguing Facts: Where Are the Young Hellbenders?

In some parts of the hellbenders' range, including New York, herpetologists are finding only large adult hellbenders in recent years, despite extensive searching. Smaller hellbenders may simply be difficult to capture or they may hide in currently unknown microhabitats. Alternatively, lack of small hellbenders may indicate that little or no reproduction is occurring in many locations, and that as the older adults gradually die, the populations of hellbenders at these sites will go extinct. Researchers are working to determine which of these explanations is true. Similar, perplexing declines have occurred elsewhere in the species' range (Wheeler et al. 2003).

Mudpuppy (Common Mudpuppy)
Necturus maculosus [Plate 2]

Quick Identification

A large salamander with flat head, small eyes, and gilled adults found in rivers and lakes throughout New York State except in the southern tier counties and on Long Island.

Description

One of New York's two fully aquatic salamanders (along with the hellbender), mudpuppies keep many larval traits throughout life. Total length is 8–13 in. (20–33 cm), maximum 19.1 in. (48.6 cm). Adults have two external gill slits; three large, branching external gills on each side of the head; lip folds to help capture aquatic prey; a short, laterally compressed tail; and smooth skin. The head is flattened and widens behind the small eyes. The legs are short and sturdy, with four toes on all feet. Adult color is generally brown-gray with variable blackish spots scattered across the trunk, a dark horizontal band through the eye, and a pale to mottled venter. The gills, usually red and bushy, constantly move on the sides of the head. Males differ from females by having two, rear-facing papillae on the cloaca and develop a greatly swollen cloacal region during the mating season. Larval mudpuppies are distinctively patterned; they are nearly black on the sides and along the mid-back and have a yellow band running dorsally along each side from the head to the tail. Four toes on the hind feet distinguish mudpuppies from all salamanders in New York except the four-toed salamander, which has small larvae. The scientific name derives from *nektos* or swimming and *oura* or tail, referring to the aquatic existence, and *maculosus* or full of spots, referring to the somewhat spotted back and sides.

Habitat

Mudpuppies can be found in many aquatic situations in New York, including its largest waterways, deep cold lakes, and shallow, weedy ponds, as well as clean, fast-flowing streams and warm, barely moving rivers. Even in the deepest lakes, mudpuppies probably spend most of their time in the shallower, weedier portions where food and hiding places are most abundant.

Natural History

All life stages of the mudpuppy occur in the water (Bishop 1926, 1941). Adults mate primarily in the fall and females store sperm until depositing eggs in late spring. Eggs (usually 70–120 per nest) are laid singly but are closely grouped and attached to the undersurface of stones, logs, or other fixed objects in shallow water (usually less than 1.5 ft. [0.5 m] deep). The female stays in the excavated area beneath the eggs until they hatch about 2 months later into larvae just over 0.8 in. (2 cm) in length. Mudpuppies reach sexual maturity at 6–8 in. (16–20 cm) in length in about 5 years.

Map 4.2. Distribution of the mudpuppy [common mudpuppy] (*Necturus maculosus*) in New York. Elsewhere the species occurs throughout the Great Lakes and St. Lawrence River drainage basin, as well as the drainage basins for the Allegheny, Ohio, lower Missouri, Arkansas, and Mississippi Rivers.

Adults and larvae are predators on a wide variety of aquatic arthropods, annelids, mollusks, other salamanders, fish, and their eggs (Bishop 1941, Harris 1959). Mudpuppies are preyed upon by larger fish, aquatic birds, snapping turtles, northern watersnakes, and possibly otters and mink. Fisherman using worms or fish as bait or dip netting for smelt occasionally catch mudpuppies. Unfortunately, because of myths about mudpuppies being either poisonous or damaging to game fishes, fisherman often kill these harmless, interesting animals.

Status and Distribution

In New York mudpuppies are present in Lake Ontario and Lake Erie; the St. Lawrence River; Lake Champlain; and the rivers, streams, and ponds interconnected within their drainage basins (map 4.2). Mudpuppies are also reported from the Mohawk, Allegheny, and upper Hudson Rivers and their connected waterways, including the barge canals throughout the state. Recent evidence suggests mudpuppies are native to the Hudson River valley rather than having dispersed there through the canal system as has often been presumed (Schmidt et al. 2004). Mudpuppies appear to be common in some bodies of water, but studies of population sizes and conservation status have not been reported for New York State. Large numbers of mudpuppies are killed indirectly in lamprey and other pest fish control efforts (e.g., Boogaard et al. 2003), particularly in Lake Champlain tributaries, and also by type E botulism outbreaks in Lake Erie (see Chapter 8 box: Mudpuppy: A rash of mysterious deaths). In the St. Lawrence River, mudpuppies are burdened with polychlorinated biphenyls (PCBs) (Bonin et al. 1995).

Other Intriguing Facts: How Mudpuppies "Breathe"

For obtaining oxygen, adult mudpuppies have several options that are used in varying combinations depending on the situation (Miller and Hutchison 1979, Ultsch and Duke 1990, Brainerd et al. 1993). Mudpuppies possess prominent external gills, specialized organs with many blood capillaries and extensive surface area, which can efficiently extract oxygen from the water. Like all modern amphibians, mudpuppies also have a thin skin with numerous capillaries that allows for breathing through the skin. Finally, mudpuppies have lungs that can be filled by gulping air at the water's surface. Studies suggest that this final mechanism may only play a role in the warmest, most stagnant waters.

Jefferson Salamander
Ambystoma jeffersonianum [Plate 3]

Quick Identification

A large, robust and broad-headed salamander with a long tail, long toes, and slate to brownish gray ground color with light flecking on the sides (similar species: blue-spotted salamander).

Description

Jefferson salamanders are large, moderately robust salamanders with long tails and exceedingly long toes. The ground color is slate gray to brownish gray, usually with some flecking of silver or blue-silver along the lower sides, tail, and limbs. Flecking can be faint or absent in some larger New York individuals. Adult snout-to-vent length (SVL) is 2.5–4 in. (6–10 cm). Newly transformed juveniles are grayish or greenish brown with varying amounts of yellow, tan, and silver flecks. Larvae are pond-type, have bushy gills, long, thin limbs, and a broad tail fin that extends far forward over the back. Large larvae are generally light brownish green with some dark spotting and mottling.

Jefferson salamanders have fewer spots and less blue tint than blue-spotted salamanders in addition to being generally larger and having a broader head and longer toes. The lack of nasolabial grooves (see figure 4.5), fewer light dorsal spots, and possession of robust limbs allows you to easily distinguish Jefferson salamanders from northern slimy salamanders. In contrast, distinguishing between Jefferson salamanders and the unisexual *Ambystoma* is often impossible on appearance alone (see Other Intriguing Facts). The scientific name honors Jefferson College, Pennsylvania.

Habitat

Jefferson salamanders are most often found in large tracts of upland, deciduous, and mixed deciduous–coniferous forests with abundant stumps and logs, but sometimes they also occur in bottomland forests bordering disturbed and agricultural areas (Thompson et al. 1980). Small mammal tunnels such as those made by woodland shrews, which the salamanders co-opt for burrows, are critical (Faccio 2003). Breeding occurs mainly in temporary ponds and semipermanent wetlands, particularly near forests (Guerry and Hunter 2002, Porej et al. 2004), with the pool bottom in emergent vegetation, shoreline in forest, slightly turbid waters, and cool water temperatures (Thompson et al. 1980). Fish-free ponds are preferred, but some populations breed in flooded wetlands bordering ponds or rivers with fish.

Natural History

Jefferson salamander adults are quite subterranean, so they are rarely seen outside of their breeding migrations. In New York these breeding migrations occur early in the year (early March through April depending on elevation, latitude, and weather) during rainy nights, with Jefferson salamanders the first amphibian to breed at many localities. Generally, males (identified by their swollen vents and more laterally compressed tails) arrive at the breeding sites a few days before females (visibly filled with eggs), and mating occurs in the water from within a few days to 2 weeks at any particular site (Douglas 1979, Kumpf and Yeaton 1932). Eggs are attached to sticks or vegetation in water in small loose masses containing 20–30 eggs, with individual females laying 100–300 eggs per season. Eggs hatch in 4–6 weeks into aquatic larvae that metamorphose into terrestrial juveniles between mid-July and the end of August.

Larvae feed on aquatic invertebrates (including mosquito larvae), tadpoles, and other salamander larvae (Smith and Petranka 1987). In turn, they are preyed upon by predaceous diving beetles, larval dragonflies, larger salamander larvae, snakes, and, in some places, fish. Adults eat a wide variety of earthworms, mollusks, and insects and other arthropods (Judd 1957). For antipredator defense, Jefferson salamanders have heavy concentrations of granular glands along the top of the tail, back, and neck, which produce noxious and sticky secretions that repel some potential predators. To entice predators to strike at the tail of these salamanders instead of their heads (thereby ensuring that the predator gets a mouthful of secretions), Jefferson salamanders, like blue-spotted and marbled salamanders, undulate their tails at the first sure sign of imminent peril (e.g., the touch of a snake's tongue, a shrew's whisker, or a bird's beak [Ducey and Brodie 1983; Ducey 1988]).

Status and Distribution

Jefferson salamanders are broadly distributed across south-central New York, but they are absent from the lake plain of Lake Ontario and the St. Lawrence River and from much of the Adirondack plateau (map 4.3). Distribution is spotty (e.g., Bishop 1941). Like many other animals living in the forests of the northeastern United States, Jefferson salamanders are affected by acidification of breeding ponds (Rowe et al. 1992, but see Cook 1983), with fewer egg masses found at sites with lower pH (Freda and Dunson 1986), high sulfate concentrations, and high aluminum concentrations (Horne and Dunson 1994). In New York, breeding is most successful in ponds with a pH of 5–6 (Pough and Wilson 1977).

Other Intriguing Facts: The "Jeff" Complex

About 40 years ago scientists first took note of populations of Jefferson-like salamanders that were more heavily spotted, somewhat smaller-sized, and almost exclusively female (now called "unisexual" forms). Research has shown that these salamanders were the results of past (and possibly present) hybridization between blue-spotted and Jefferson salamanders (Sessions 1982). Moreover, the unisexual forms have additional sets of chromosomes that are not present in the parent species (Uzzell 1964, Bogart 1982). The unisexuals were originally divided into two "species": the silvery salamander (containing two sets of chromosomes from the Jefferson salamander and one set from the blue-spotted salamander) and the Tremblay salamander (containing two sets of chromosomes from the blue-spotted salamander and one set from the Jefferson salamander). Scientists now understand that the situation is more complex. Unisexual forms are found with a variety of chromosome numbers (from two to five sets), may possess uneven mixtures of genes from the parent species (suggesting continued

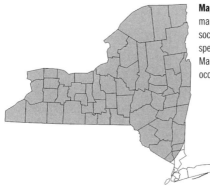

Map 4.3. Distribution of the Jefferson salamander (*Ambystoma jeffersonianum*) and associated hybrids in New York. Elsewhere the species occurs from New England south to Maryland and west to Illinois. In Canada, it occurs only in Ontario.

genetic exchange), and may also contain genes and chromosomes from small-mouthed salamanders (*Ambystoma texanum*) and tiger salamanders in some parts of the range (Bogart et al. 1987, Kraus et al. 1991). The unisexuals occur commonly in western and central New York, living in the same areas as either Jefferson or blue-spotted salamanders (Bogart and Klemens 1997, Cameron et al. 1998). During spring, mating occurs between the unisexuals and males of the parent species but the genes from the males are only rarely incorporated into the developing eggs of the unisexuals (Bogart et al. 1989). Reproduction in the unisexual salamanders is parthenogenetic and has challenged many scientists' notions of just what constitutes a biological "species" (Bogart and Klemens 1997).

Blue-spotted Salamander
Ambystoma laterale [Plate 4]

Quick Identification

A mid-sized, broad-headed salamander with bluish-black ground color and blue-silver spotting and flecking on the back, legs, tail, and sides (similar species: Jefferson salamander).

Description

Blue-spotted salamanders have slate gray to bluish black ground color with distinctly blue-silver spotting and flecking on the back, legs, tail, and heaviest along the sides. Adult SVL is 2–3 in. (4–8 cm). The belly is usually fairly dark. During the breeding season, males are more brightly colored and have more swollen vents and more compressed tails than either females or males outside of the breeding season. Newly metamorphosed blue-spotted salamanders are grayish or greenish brown, often with silver and yellow flecking. Blue-spotted salamanders differ from Jefferson salamanders by having more blue flecking, a smaller body size, and shorter toes, and they differ from northern slimy salamanders by having blue-silver instead of silver-white spots and by lacking nasolabial grooves (see figure. 4.5). It is often impossible to distinguish between blue-spotted salamanders and unisexual forms of *Ambystoma* (see Jefferson Salamander, Other Intriguing Facts) based on external appearance alone. The scientific name *laterale* ("pertaining to the side") refers to the blue spots on the salamanders' sides.

Habitat

Blue-spotted salamanders are found in damp deciduous and deciduous-coniferous forests containing temporary ponds across a wide range of elevations in New York and often where soils have high sand or loam content. They tolerate habitat disturbance in some suburban areas (Klemens 1993). Breeding occurs in small, fish-free ponds, particularly those adjacent to forests (Guerry and Hunter 2002) but also flooded wetlands at the edges of lakes.

Natural History

Blue-spotted salamanders are another mole salamander with an early spring breeding migration (March or April, depending on latitude and elevation) that often occurs before snow is completely gone from the forest floor and before the ice has cleared from the pond surfaces. Breeding occurs in the water over a 1–2-week period (Kumpf and Yeaton 1932), and females lay up to 300 eggs in loose masses of 10–20 eggs (Gilhen 1984) attached to twigs or resting on the bottom (Uzzell 1967). Larvae are rapacious predators on many invertebrates and larval amphibians (Brodman et al. 2003). Metamorphosis occurs in July and August, depending on rainfall and temperature. Juveniles hide beneath logs and stones at the water's edge for about a week before migrating into the forest. During migrations among ponds, blue-spotted and other mole salamanders transport pea clams that attach to the salamanders' toes (Davis and Gilhen 1982).

Although all members of the genus *Ambystoma* disappear beneath the ground for most of the year, blue-spotted salamanders are the species most likely to be found directly beneath rocks or logs in late spring, early summer, and autumn. Because blue-spotted salamanders are not powerful diggers, they often use the burrows of other animals. When they come into contact with a predator, adults and juveniles elevate and undulate their tails, drawing the initial attack of the predator to the tail (Brodie 1977) where there are concentrations of granular glands containing noxious secretions that may repel the attacker. If a portion of the tail is eaten during an attack, blue-spotted salamanders, like all salamanders, will regenerate a new tail.

Blue-spotted salamanders are part of the group of salamanders involved in past and present hybridization resulting in the unisexual *Ambystoma* taxa (see full description under Jefferson Salamander, Other Intriguing Facts).

Status and Distribution

Blue-spotted salamanders occur throughout most of New York State, including Long Island, except for parts of central New York and the southern tier of counties bordering Pennsylvania (map 4.4). The only pure lineages of blue-spotted salamanders may occur on eastern Long Island (Bogart and Klemens 1997). Although locally abundant, the species distribution is spotty in New York. However, ascertaining the actual distribution of this species is confounded because of difficulties distinguishing it from others in the "Jefferson complex." Blue-spotted salamanders do not readily occupy restored or created wetlands (Lehtinen and Galatowitsch 2001). Larvae of blue-spotted salamanders provide valuable mosquito control (Brodman et al. 2003).

Other Intriguing Facts: Association with Vernal Pools

Blue-spotted salamanders rely primarily on temporary ponds (vernal pools) and seasonally flooded areas for reproduction. Such sites contain plenty of food for the developing larvae and generally have fewer large predators (especially fish) compared to permanent bodies of water. However, breeding in such areas engenders some risk, because in dry years these ponds may dry up completely before the salamander larvae have had time to metamorphose. Another potential problem is that humans do not usually appreciate the value of these sites to the salamanders. They often take steps to "improve" vernal pools by changing water flow patterns or adding fill to prevent flooding, by dredging to make the ponds permanent, or by adding fish. Such actions have significant negative impacts on blue-spotted salamanders and other vernal pool–breeding amphibians.

Map 4.4. Distribution of the blue-spotted salamander (*Ambystoma laterale*) and associated hybrids in New York. Elsewhere the species occurs throughout New England (except Rhode Island), the Great Lake States, and Atlantic Canada.

Spotted Salamander
Ambystoma maculatum [Plate 5]

Quick Identification

A medium-sized, broad-headed salamander with blue-black body overlaid by distinct rows of large yellow spots along sides of back and tail.

Description

It is impossible to mistake the spotted salamander for any other salamander in New York. The two rows of large yellow spots on a black ground color along the back and tail are truly distinctive. Spotted salamanders have sturdy limbs, broad heads, and fairly long tails attached to thick bodies. The lower sides and belly may be dark or light gray, often with small white spots. In parts of the range, the spots on the back of the head are orange instead of yellow, but this is rare in New York. During the breeding season, males can be recognized by their swollen vents. Adults have an SVL of 3–4.5 in. (7.5–10 cm). The larvae are pond-type, are darker above than below with no strong markings except near the tail tip, and may reach about 3 in. (7.5 cm) before metamorphosis. The scientific name *maculatum* means spotted.

Habitat

Spotted salamanders live in moist soil areas in mixed deciduous, bottomland, or upland forests in New York (Wyman 1988). It is important that the environment has an abundance of small mammal tunnels, which spotted salamanders adopt as burrows (Faccio 2003, Regosin et al. 2003a). Most spotted salamanders breed in fish-free ponds, where larval survival is highest (Ireland 1989, Egan and Paton 2004). Ponds with extensive coverage by shrubs and bottom vegetation for egg attachment sites are preferable (Egan and Paton 2004), but flooded swamps along slow rivers and gravel pit ponds may also serve as breeding sites. In addition, the species will readily adopt constructed ponds (Petranka et al. 2003). Spotted salamanders may be found in suburban and agricultural areas as long as forest covers more than about 30% of the landscape (Gibbs 1998b, Guerry and Hunter 2002, Porej et al. 2004). Spotted salamanders are frequently reported in winter in homes with fieldstone cellars.

Natural History

Like other members of the genus *Ambystoma*, adult spotted salamanders are subterranean most of the year. Spotted salamanders can dig but depend heavily on tunnels in the forest floor made by small mammals, particularly short-tailed shrews (*Blarina brevicauda*) (Madison 1997). Adults regularly eat earthworms, snails, spiders, isopods, and a wide variety of insects, and they occasionally feed on eastern red-backed salamanders (Ducey et al. 1994). Adults have been shown to be aggressive in defending their tunnels, biting other spotted salamanders that come too close (Ducey and Ritsema 1988, Ducey and Heuer 1991). Spotted salamanders are themselves sometimes preyed on by wolf spiders (Rubbo et al. 2003), snakes, birds, shrews, and other small mammals. Concentrations of granular glands at the back of the head and along the dorsal edge of the tail produce sticky, distasteful secretions that repel many would-be predators (Brodie et al. 1979).

Mating occurs in early spring, soon after edges of breeding ponds are ice free, but often a week or so after Jefferson or blue-spotted salamanders have mated. Individuals generally return to the same ponds each year (Whitford and Vinegar 1966, Sexton et al. 1986), finding them in part by their characteristic smell. The salamanders use either wind- or water-borne olfactory cues associated with seepage of pond water into the adjacent land (McGregor and Teska 1989). Males generally arrive at the ponds several days to over a week before the females (Baldauf 1952). Depending on the weather, courtship and breeding may occur over a period of several days to several weeks (Breder 1927). Some 70% of egg clutches near Ithaca, New York, exhibited multiple paternity (Myers and Zamudio 2004), although the first male mating sires most of the offspring (Tennessen and Zamudio 2003). After mating, females lay 50–250 eggs in a mass that rapidly absorbs water and may swell to the size of a grapefruit. The eggs' heavy jelly coat makes it difficult for insects, fishes, tadpoles, newts, and turtles to seize and ingest the eggs. The egg masses are firm. Some have a milky appearance. Notably, many also have a greenish hue from a symbiotic alga (*Oophilia ambystomatis*) that grows on the eggs and apparently harvests carbon dioxide generated by the developing embryos while in exchange provides them with oxygen (Bachman et al. 1986, Pinder and Friet 1994; see Chapter 5, Wood Frog, Other Intriguing Facts). The eggs hatch in 20–60 days, and the larvae metamorphose several months later during late summer. Larvae are carnivorous and eat a variety of aquatic insect larvae and other aquatic invertebrates. In New York adults may emigrate up to 360 ft. (120 m) from breeding sites to overwinter in small mammal burrow systems, which provide them with protection from severe temperatures (Madison 1997). Individuals may live for more than 20 years. Adults can be plagued with leeches. Curiously, leeches attach to the forelimbs and exploit the salamanders primarily for mobility within and between ponds and also for gathering food particles expelled by the salamander during feeding, not removing blood meals from the salamanders (Khan and Frick 1997).

Status and Distribution

Spotted salamanders occur throughout the state, including less developed portions of Long Island (map 4.5). However, because ever-increasing numbers of these salamanders die each year as they cross highways during their breeding migration, conservation biologists are concerned about this species' prospects. Moreover, this species is sensitive to acidification of its breeding ponds, which kills or deforms embryos and slows growth of larvae (Clark 1986, Portnoy 1990)—a particular issue in the parts of the state that receive heavy acid inputs, for example, the Adirondack and Catskill regions. Reproduction is highest in ponds with pH 7–9 in New York (Pough and Wilson 1977), where the species is also sensitive to acidification of soils (Wyman 1988). The insecticide carbaryl is particularly lethal to spotted salamanders (Boone and James 2003). Reproduction is reduced near roadsides,

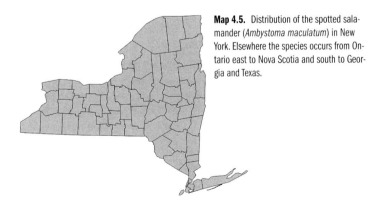

Map 4.5. Distribution of the spotted salamander (*Ambystoma maculatum*) in New York. Elsewhere the species occurs from Ontario east to Nova Scotia and south to Georgia and Texas.

possibly because deicing salts used in highway maintenance contaminate roadside vernal pools (Turtle 2000).

Other Intriguing Facts: Mating Strategies

During the breeding season there are generally more male than female spotted salamanders present in ponds at any one time. This skewed sex ratio leads to competition among the males for opportunities to mate. By visiting ponds at night during light rains you can often spot groups of a dozen or more males near a single female (see figure 4.2). The males nudge and gently bump the female and each other depositing spermatophores on the pond bottom. A female, stimulated by the interaction with a male, positions her vent over a spermatophore and removes the sperm-containing cap. You should look for large numbers of whitish spermatophores attached to leaves and sticks under the shallow waters of breeding ponds following a night of heavy rains in early spring (see figure 4.2). Some males deposit their spermatophores on top of the spermatophores of other males, increasing their chances of inseminating the female. This so-called spermatophore capping has evolved as a form of sexual competition (Arnold 1976).

Marbled Salamander
Ambystoma opacum [Plate 6]

Quick Identification

A striking, fall-breeding mole salamander of forests "marbled" with white or grayish cross-bands from head to tail tip on a black body.

Description

One of New York State's most striking salamanders, this salamander is "marbled" with white or grayish cross-bands on a black background from head to tail tip. Cross-bands are variable and may converge or remain distinct from one another. Marbled salamanders are medium-sized mole salamanders ranging from 1.75 to 3 in. (4–7.5 cm) in SVL and have 11–13 costal grooves. Cross-bands on the male are described as silvery-white whereas those on the females are silvery-gray. Both sexes have black bellies. Larvae are pond-type and characteristically brownish-gray with numerous golden-flecks and often rows of light spots along each side. The scientific name *opacum* derives from shaded, dark, or obscure and refers to the color pattern.

Habitat

Marbled salamanders are found in upland and floodplain, deciduous forests with suitable wet depressions for breeding. The species seems to prefer forests with dry, friable soils and well-drained slopes as long as there are moist areas (streams, seeps) nearby (Bishop 1941). It breeds in temporary, "autumnal" pools that flood in the fall, remain inundated during the winter and spring, and dry during the summer. Marbled salamanders use constructed pools for breeding but clearly prefer older ones (more than 30 years) (Merovich and Howard 2000). Migratory routes include intermittent streambeds (Gibbs 1998a).

Natural History

Marbled salamanders are unique among mole salamanders in New York because they breed in the fall, mating and laying eggs on land near small ponds in forests. Males migrate to breeding sites in late summer or early fall followed shortly thereafter by females. Courtship is initiated by the male and takes place either before males and females arrive at the breeding site or at the time of their arrival (Noble and Brady 1933). Females can store sperm for up to a month after mating (Sever at al. 1995). Males nudge other salamanders until a receptive female responds and retrieves a spermatophore that he has deposited. Females lay 50–200 or more eggs singly in a shallow nest that she has constructed under leaf litter or woody debris in dry or partially dry depressions (Petranka and Petranka 1981, Jackson et al. 1989). Nest attendance is important to egg survival (Petranka 1990); females remain coiled around the eggs, periodically turning them until rains fill the depression and flood the nest, whereupon hatching is quickly initiated (Kaplan and Crump 1978). Hatching success is highly variable from year to year (Stenhouse 1987).

The larvae grow slowly beneath the ice throughout the winter, feeding mainly on large zooplankton (Petranka and Petranka 1980, Branch and Altig 1981) and occasionally on their own kin (Walls and Blaustein 1995); however, they apparently recognize their siblings and are less aggressive toward them (Walls and Roudebush 1991). By spring, the larvae have generally grown large enough to feed on the newly hatching larvae of other salamanders, their main prey (Stenhouse et al. 1983). The strategy of the marbled salamander thus seems to be to get a "jump" on their major prey—the amphibian larvae—by breeding much earlier than the other amphibians. Notably, predation by marbled salamanders on other amphibian species can be so strong that it affects which species may persist in a local area (Cortwright and Nelson 1990).

Marbled salamander larvae undergo metamorphosis in May through July (Paton and Crouch 2002); their size and fitness at this point has a strong influence on first-year survival (Scott 1994). On land, adults and juveniles are fossorial for the most part but can be seen on the ground surface after heavy rains, looking for snails, slugs, earthworms, and a wide variety of small arthropods (Bishop 1941, Hulse et al. 2001). Terrestrial adults are aggressive, repelling other marbled salamanders from favored tunnels and feeding areas (Ducey 1989, Ducey and Heuer 1991). Even on land, marbled salamanders recognize their siblings (Walls 1991). The adults face a broad spectrum of predators, including snakes, birds, and small mammals. Marbled salamanders are protected from shrews by distasteful skin secretions (DiGiovanni and Brodie 1981). By arching and undulating their tails at the start of an attack, the salamanders lure predators into attacking their secretion-filled tails (Brodie 1977).

Status and Distribution

In New York State, marbled salamanders are found only in the extreme southeastern part of the state: from the Catskill Mountains to the Hudson River valley and on Long Island (map 4.6). Numbers

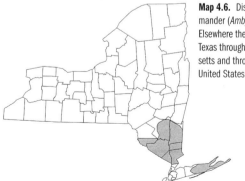

Map 4.6. Distribution of the marbled salamander (*Ambystoma opacum*) in New York. Elsewhere the species occurs from eastern Texas through southern Illinois to Massachusetts and throughout most of the eastern United States except Florida.

have become greatly reduced by habitat fragmentation, especially on western Long Island and Westchester County, although the species is still relatively common elsewhere. The species is listed as a one of Special Concern in New York.

Other Intriguing Facts: Escaping the Egg

Marbled salamander embryos possess a fascinating mechanism that triggers hatching in response to flooding of the nest. As the nest is submerged in water, the bodies of the embryos demand more oxygen than can pass through the egg membranes from the water. Such oxygen stress, which is termed hypoxia, triggers glands in the developing embryo's snout (known as "hatching glands") to release enzymes that dissolve the egg, thereby freeing the embryo from its capsule and permitting it to become a free-swimming larva in the newly flooded pool (Petranka et al. 1982).

Tiger Salamander (Eastern Tiger Salamander)
Ambystoma tigrinum [Plate 7]

Quick Identification

A robust-bodied salamander of Long Island with strong legs, long keeled tail, broad head and yellow chin, and numerous yellow or tan irregular spots or blotches on a dark brownish-black body.

Description

As New York's largest terrestrial salamanders, tiger salamanders are robust-bodied with a long, laterally compressed tail, a broad head, and strong legs. The ground color is a dark brownish-black, covered by numerous yellow or tan irregular spots and blotches of various sizes and shapes scattered on the head, limbs, trunk, and tail. There is yellow under the chin and along the lower sides. SVL is generally 3.5–5.5 in. (9–13 cm), which results in some individuals reaching total lengths more than 12 in. (30 cm). Males have swollen vents and more compressed tails during the breeding season. Tiger salamanders differ from spotted salamanders by having yellow under the chin and on the sides, and by their yellow spots being scattered (not in rows) on the back. The larvae are pond-type (see figure 4.3), greenish-gray with some irregular dark spotting, with long gills, large tail fins, and a broad head. The scientific name derives from "tiger" and refers to the tiger-like coloration of most individuals.

Habitat

Throughout their range, tiger salamanders live in bottomlands, old fields, mixed woodlands, and marsh edges. Soils must be suitable for burrowing or already have extensive small mammal–created burrow systems (Madison and Farrand 1998). These salamanders favor breeding ponds that receive direct sunlight (i.e., not woodland ponds with a heavy canopy), but will otherwise inhabit a variety of temporary to permanent ponds, including farm ponds. Although adult salamanders have been found more than 1,640 ft. (500 m) from breeding ponds, most remain within 820 ft. (250 m) (Madison and Farrand 1998).

Natural History

Adult tiger salamanders are subterranean and are only rarely seen on the surface outside of their breeding migrations. Studies have shown that individual salamanders occupy limited home ranges, staying within the same 32–107 sq. ft. (3–10 m^2) for months at a time. Strong diggers (even possessing hardened toe-tips for digging), tiger salamanders also use the burrows of other animals when available (Semlitsch 1983). These salamanders migrate from their underground tunnels to breeding ponds in early spring, often as soon as the pond edges are ice-free. Within the breeding ponds, males scan for mates from clear areas of the pond (Madison 1998) and may be aggressive, pushing other males. When a male encounters a female, he may physically guide her away from competing males (Arnold 1976). Females lay their eggs in loose masses of 20–100 eggs attached to plants and sticks (Howard et al. 1997). Eggs hatch in 3–6 weeks, and larvae grow to a large size (more than 3 in. [7.6 cm]) before they metamorphose in late summer.

Larvae eat invertebrates, frog tadpoles, and the larvae of other salamanders, and they are preyed upon by herons, northern watersnakes, and fish. Tiger salamander larvae also help control mosquito populations in ponds (Brodman et al. 2003). Adults feed mainly on earthworms and arthropods but will eat other salamanders, frogs, small snakes, and newborn mice. The adults produce noxious secretions from granular glands that repel some predators, which include birds, snakes, and small mammals. The salamanders are able to elevate their tails and lash their predators with considerable force (Brodie 1977).

Status and Distribution

In New York, tiger salamanders are found only on Long Island, primarily in Suffolk County (map 4.7). Currently, these salamanders are listed as an Endangered in New York State.

Other Intriguing Facts: Road Mortality

Tiger salamanders, like other members of the genus *Ambystoma*, face a major threat—road mortality—of which tiger salamanders seem particularly sensitive (Porej et al. 2004). Adults live beneath the ground, often a considerable distance from their breeding ponds. During spring migrations, when the adults must walk to the ponds and back across the surface of whatever ground separates the two habitats, the adult salamanders suffer mortality from predators and automobiles. Sometimes along short stretches of highway, dozens to hundreds of dead tiger salamanders can be seen on rainy nights (Clevenger et al. 2001). One potential solution, tried with some success in a few places around the country, is to create wildlife walkways that pass under busy roads adjacent to breeding ponds and wetlands (see Chapter 11, Conservation Case Studies: Amphibians Cross Here: New York State's First "Herp" Tunnel).

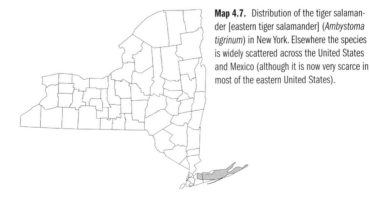

Map 4.7. Distribution of the tiger salamander [eastern tiger salamander] (*Ambystoma tigrinum*) in New York. Elsewhere the species is widely scattered across the United States and Mexico (although it is now very scarce in most of the eastern United States).

Eastern Newt (Red-spotted Newt)
Notophthalmus viridescens [Plate 8]

Quick Identification

Adults in ponds: green with a few black-bordered red spots, yellow bellies, and a tail fin; efts (juveniles) on land: bright orange-red, with rough dry skin and a thin bony tail.

Description

Eastern newts are probably New York's most familiar salamander. The brightly colored juvenile newts (called "efts") are often seen walking about on the forest floor on moist days in summer and autumn. Adults are commonly seen in ponds, lakes, rivers, and pet shops. Adults, which are nearly fully aquatic, are olive-green with a yellow belly, numerous tiny black dots, one row of two to seven small, bright red spots on each side, and a laterally compressed tail. SVLs are 1.75–2.75 in. (4.5–7 cm). Compared to females, males have larger hind limbs and a more apparent tail fin that expands during the breeding season and recedes thereafter. During breeding, males also develop black, rough patches inside their thighs and at the hind toe tips for holding females during mating. Efts vary from bright red-orange to a drab olive-orange above and orange or yellow-orange below. Efts have rough, dry skin, a thin bony tail, and, like adults, a single row of black-edged, red spots on each side. The aquatic larvae are small and thin with a pale greenish-brown color, a row of light spots on the sides, a dark line through each eye, and a blunt snout. Efts may be confused with small red salamanders at first glance. However, efts differ from the red salamanders in lacking nasolabial grooves (see figure 4.5) and costal grooves (see figure 4.4) , and in having rough skin, orange bellies, and a characteristic row of black-bordered, red spots on each side of the back. The scientific name refers to *noto* or mark and *ophthalmus* or eye, referring to the eye spots on sides and back or possibly black marks within the actual eye, and *viridescens* or slightly green, referring to the greenish color of most adults.

Habitat

Adult eastern newts can be found in almost any pond, lake, or slow-moving river with relatively unpolluted water. Favored habitats are ponds or flooded bottomland swamps with dense aquatic vegetation

that are surrounded by forest but not fully shaded by the forest
canopy. Usually denizens of the shallow edges of ponds, eastern
newts have been reported from depths of 40 ft. (13 m) in Lake George
(George et al. 1977). Adult newts are quick to colonize new habitats,
and large numbers of adults are often seen in beaver ponds and man-
made impoundments (Petranka et al. 2003). Efts occur in forests of
any type at almost any elevation but most commonly in deciduous
and mixed forests. Surprisingly sensitive to habitat fragmentation,
eastern newts disappear from the landscape when forest cover de-
creases below about 70% (Gibbs 1998b).

Natural History

Eastern newts have a more complex life cycle than the other salamanders of New York (see Other Intriguing Facts). In late spring, each female lays some 200–350 eggs singly in the water, attached to and often
wrapped in aquatic vegetation or fallen leaves (Bishop 1941). The eggs
hatch in 3 to 5 weeks into aquatic larvae, and the larvae spend 2–3
months in the water. There they feed mostly on microcrustaceans and
insect larvae (Hamilton 1940) before metamorphosing into terrestrial
juveniles in late summer, often at a small size. This so-called "eft"
stage typically lasts for 2–3 years (Bishop 1941), although it may extend
to more than 7 years (Healy 1974), during which time efts wander
extensively. A second metamorphosis occurs as efts transform into
adults, which are principally aquatic. Many, if not most, adults remain
in the water the rest of their lives. In some populations in New York
and elsewhere, adults may actually spend much time terrestrially each
year (Noble 1926), leaving ponds in summer and not returning to the
water until the following spring. Other reported variations in the life
cycle of some populations include skipping the terrestrial eft stage and
either transforming directly into an aquatic juvenile or partially transforming into a gilled subadult, which occurs only rarely in New York
(mainly on Long Island, e.g., Healy 1974).

Adults eat aquatic insects, crustaceans, mollusks, and the eggs and
larvae of other amphibians. The diet may include large numbers of
mosquito larvae during the summer. In Lake George, New York, researchers have observed eastern newts eating perch eggs (George et al.
1977). Studies near Cooperstown, New York, indicate that terrestrial
efts and adults eat largely the same foods and feed on earthworms,
mollusks, and arthropods (especially springtails, mites, and fly larvae) found within the leaf litter (MacNamara and Harman 1975,

MacNamara 1977). Newts may serve as intermediate hosts for fresh-water mussels by transporting their larvae (Van Snik Gray et al. 2002).

On uplands, efts and adults prefer moist substrates (Wyman 1988) and avoid desiccation during dry periods by moving into shade, re-ducing activity, and huddling (Rohr and Madison 2003). Adults and efts receive some protection against predators from their skin secre-tions, which contain a number of toxins, including tetrodotoxin (the same class of toxins found in puffer fishes that occasionally cause problems to sushi eaters) (Brodie 1968). These secretions cause many predators to avoid newts altogether, reject them after tasting, or vomit after swallowing one; some newts have sufficient toxins to cause the death of predators. Efts are particularly toxic (some 10× more so than adults; Brodie 1968), but both efts and adults use similar special-ized defensive postures when they come in contact with predators (Howard and Brodie 1971, Ducey and Dulkiewicz 1994). The aquatic larvae are eaten by some aquatic insects (Formanowicz and Brodie 1982) and *Ambystoma* larvae, and aquatic adults may be eaten by some aquatic insects, snapping turtles, and some birds. In addition, both adults and efts are eaten by gartersnakes. Leeches plague many aquatic adults (Gill 1978); in response, the adults produce chemical secretions with antileech properties (Pough 1971).

Status and Distribution

Newts are found throughout New York State wherever suitable habitat occurs (map 4.8). Numerous anecdotal reports describe shifting patterns of land use that have reduced or exterminated once

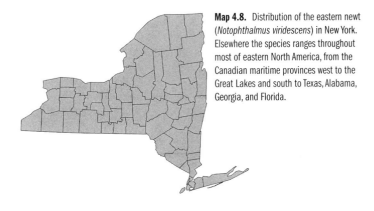

Map 4.8. Distribution of the eastern newt (*Notophthalmus viridescens*) in New York. Elsewhere the species ranges throughout most of eastern North America, from the Canadian maritime provinces west to the Great Lakes and south to Texas, Alabama, Georgia, and Florida.

dense populations of newts, but these reports are poorly documented. Because of their wandering nature, eastern newts are among the amphibians most vulnerable to habitat fragmentation and forest loss (Gibbs 1998b, Guerry and Hunter 2002). Low concentrations of commonly used insecticides, such as endosulphan, disrupt pheromone systems of newts (Park et al. 2001). Newt populations are also reduced by fish introductions to newt breeding ponds (Smith et al. 1999).

Other Intriguing Facts: Change, and Change Again

Eastern newts must endure two major changes in their structure and behavior. Like many other salamanders, eastern newts undergo a major metamorphosis from an aquatic larval stage into a terrestrial juvenile, a process that involves significant changes in many aspects of their breathing apparatus, feeding structures, and skin. The larvae lose their gills (which work only in water) and must rely more fully on their lungs as efts. The thick skin developed by the efts also reduces the percentage of respiration that occurs through the skin. The feeding apparatus changes from one based on catching swimming invertebrates using suction to a system in which the tongue flops out of the mouth to catch crawling prey. During the first metamorphosis, the skin fills with poison glands and thickens into a waterproof barrier that keeps the efts from drying out while wandering the forest's floor. After a few years, the efts begin to mature sexually and pass through a second metamorphosis into aquatic adults. This time the modifications are less extreme: switching to a thinner, less toxic skin; returning to a dependence on suction feeding; and reacquiring tail fins (especially in males) for more efficient swimming in their new, aquatic medium.

Northern Dusky Salamander
Desmognathus fuscus [Plate 9]

Quick Identification

A generally brownish salamander of streams and seeps, with variable dorsal colors, relatively large hind limbs, and light line extending from eye to rear of jaw, whose tail has a keeled upper edge giving it a triangular shape in cross-section (similar species, Allegheny Mountain Dusky Salamander).

Description

The northern dusky salamander is a small- to mid-sized streamside salamander with hind legs larger than the front, usually a light line from the eye to the rear angle of the mouth (both characteristics of all members of this genus), and a tail with a dorsal keel. Presence of a tail keel can be determined by gently rolling the tail between thumb and forefinger—a keeled tailed does not roll smoothly. Color pattern is extremely variable; many northern dusky salamanders have a broad light dorsal stripe (some shade of brown or tan) with wavy edges and containing dark spots and markings. Some individuals are greenish gray with lighter spots on back. Others are dark brown with a few light flecks on the sides and almost no other distinguishable markings. Nasolabial grooves are present. The SVL of adults is 1.5–3.25 in. (4–8 cm). Newly transformed individuals often have somewhat irregularly alternating light spots (tan, yellow, or reddish) along back that may become fused into a wavy stripe. Larvae are stream-type (see figure 4.3); they are greenish-gray with light dorsal spots. It is possible to distinguish this species from northern two-lined salamanders by the lack of yellow under the tail. Distinguishing between New York's two native dusky salamanders is much more difficult (see Other Intriguing Facts). The scientific name derives from *desmos* or ligament and *gnathos* or jaw, referring to the bundle of ligaments holding the jaw, and *fuscus*, referring to dark and swarthy—hence "dusky."

Habitat

Northern dusky salamanders prefer streams and seeps within mature deciduous and mixed forests with undisturbed banks. These salamanders seem to be most abundant in areas where a heavy canopy allows little light to reach the forest floor and substrates are nonacid and moist (Wyman 1988). The salamanders are located beneath logs or stones within seeps and along the edges of streams, with most individuals found within a few feet (one meter) of water.

Natural History

Northern dusky salamanders mate on land near stream edges in spring and fall (Bishop 1941). A female puts 12–40 eggs into a depression or cavity under leaves, logs, stones, or mosses directly adjacent to the stream or seepage (Krzysik 1979, Hom 1987). She remains with the eggs until they hatch 50–80 days later, leaving only occasionally at night to feed. Clutches untended by females suffer high mortality (Juterbock 1987). The larvae crawl into the water and remain there for 7–11 months before metamorphosing into terrestrial juveniles.

Adults often move only a few meters along a stream over many months (Barbour et al. 1969a, Ashton 1975). Northern dusky salamanders are mostly nocturnal and can be observed moving over rocks along the stream edge searching for food (mainly insects, amphipods, snails, and worms) on cool, moist nights between late spring and mid-autumn. In winter in central New York, they are active in shale banks in seepage areas, moving upward during warmer periods and downward during colder periods (Hamilton 1943). The adults and juveniles are fast runners and good jumpers. Northern dusky salamanders must rely on these escape abilities (as well as some defensive biting) because their skin secretions are less toxic than those of other species. However, like many species, dusky salamanders release portions of their tails when grabbed by a predator and then regenerate nearly identical copies of the missing portions over a few months. Dusky salamanders are eaten by birds, small mammals, snakes, and larger salamanders.

Status and Distribution

Northern dusky salamanders are found throughout much of the state (map 4.9), with the exception of Long Island (except its westernmost end) and portions of the Great Lakes/St. Lawrence River

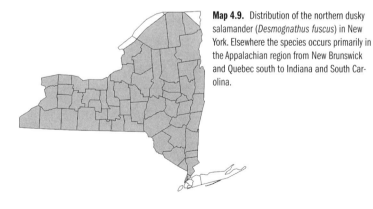

Map 4.9. Distribution of the northern dusky salamander (*Desmognathus fuscus*) in New York. Elsewhere the species occurs primarily in the Appalachian region from New Brunswick and Quebec south to Indiana and South Carolina.

Plain (where it seems not to have yet repopulated following extensive deforestation and sedimentation of waterways in the region over the past two centuries). Northern dusky salamanders, two-lined salamanders, and eastern red-backed salamanders are the few salamanders that persist in heavily urbanized areas; northern duskies, for example, are not uncommon on Staten Island. Northern dusky salamanders are probably absent from high elevations in the Adirondack Mountains, perhaps because they are sensitive to soil acidity and, by extension, acid rain (Wyman 1988). However, definitive studies of their altitudinal distribution have not been performed.

Other Intriguing Facts: Discriminating among the "Desmogs"

Distinguishing between northern and Allegheny mountain dusky salamanders in the field in New York is a major challenge, even for professional herpetologists. The two species have similar body sizes and shapes, and although both have a range of color patterns, the two species share many of the same patterns. Probably the most used distinguishing feature concerns the shape of the tail: northern dusky salamanders have a keeled dorsal edge on the tail making it triangular in cross-section, whereas Allegheny mountain dusky salamanders generally have a tail that is round in cross section. When an Allegheny mountain dusky salamander regenerates a broken tail, however, it often has a dorsal keel. To make the situation worse, genetic evidence suggests that hybridization occurs between these species (Karlin and Guttman 1981), including in New York (S. Broyles and P. Ducey, unpublished data) and Pennsylvania (Hulse et al. 2001). Such hybrids show some mixture of physical characteristics of each species.

Allegheny Mountain Dusky Salamander (Mountain Dusky Salamander, Allegheny Dusky Salamander)
Desmognathus ochrophaeus [Plate 10]

Quick Identification

A generally brown salamander of streams and seeps, with variable dorsal coloration, relatively large hind limbs, light line extending from eye to rear of jaw, with a tail that is round in cross-section (similar species, northern dusky salamander).

Description

Allegheny mountain dusky salamanders are small- to mid-sized salamanders of streams and woodlands with a light line from the eye to the rear angle of the mouth, hind legs distinctly larger and more robust than the front legs, and a tail that is round in cross section. Color pattern is extremely variable, individuals in New York often have a light (tan, yellow, orange), broad stripe from the head onto the tail having dark borders, somewhat straight sides, and containing some dark markings. Many other individuals throughout the state are nearly completely dark brown or black (e.g., specimens from Chautauqua County; Schueler and Schueler 1977), with some light flecking on the sides. Nasolabial grooves (see figure 4.5) are present. Adults are 1.25–2.75 in. (3–7 cm). Newly metamorphosed individuals have a red or orange stripe with dark borders along the back and tail. Allegheny mountain dusky salamanders can be distinguished from northern two-lined salamanders by having white under the tail instead of yellow and are usually differentiated from northern dusky salamanders by their round tails (but see Northern Dusky Salamander, Other Intriguing Facts). Juvenile Allegheny mountain dusky salamanders can be distinguished from small eastern red-backed salamanders by the dusky's shorter trunks, different leg sizes, and light line beneath the eye. The scientific name derives from *ochros*, or yellow and pale, and *phaeos*, or light, and it refers to the bright coloration of some individuals.

Habitat

Allegheny mountain dusky salamanders are most often found in mixed deciduous forests that contain streams and seeps. They can be found in brooks and streams within small towns and cities throughout upstate New York. More terrestrial than northern dusky salamanders, Allegheny mountain dusky salamanders may often be found under logs or stones on the forest floor far from water. In winter they retreat under mosses and rocks at springs, small streams, and seeps.

Natural History

Allegheny mountain dusky salamanders are abundant in New York, reaching highest densities along streams, where they establish home ranges and remain within a few meters for months at a time (Holomuzki 1982). Other individuals move away from streams into surrounding forests, living and foraging within the leaf litter and beneath logs and rocks. Allegheny mountain dusky salamanders feed on earthworms, snails, and a wide range of arthropods (Keen 1979). Laboratory studies show that Allegheny mountain dusky salamanders are aggressive toward members of their own species and other salamanders that approach too close, possibly defending territories (Smith and Pough 1994).

Despite being common, much uncertainty remains regarding reproduction in this species. Mating reportedly occurs in both spring and fall. Egg laying occurs primarily in late spring to early summer, although some clutches are laid in mid to late summer (e.g., Keen and Orr 1980). Females deposit eggs in clusters of 8–20 eggs in small depressions beneath logs or rocks on the banks of seeps or streams, or within the beds of temporarily dry seeps. Females remain with eggs until they hatch, usually 7–10 weeks later. Nests of eggs near hatching have been found in New York in March, however, suggesting that at least some females lay eggs in fall and remain with them over the winter. The eggs hatch into aquatic larvae that remain in streams 1–10 months before metamorphosing into small terrestrial juveniles. Forester (1977, 1979, 1981, 1984) has provided details about the reproductive biology of Allegheny mountain dusky salamanders.

Status and Distribution

Allegheny mountain dusky salamanders are found throughout New York State except on the St. Lawrence River plain, areas east of the lower Hudson River, and Long Island (map 4.10).

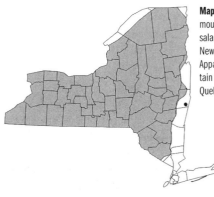

Map 4.10. Distribution of the Allegheny mountain dusky salamander [Allegheny dusky salamander] (*Desmognathus ochrophaeus*) in New York. Elsewhere the species occurs in the Appalachian, Allegheny, and Adirondack mountain regions from Kentucky through southern Quebec.

Other Intriguing Facts: Escaping Predators

Because of their small size, abundance, and relative lack of distasteful skin secretions (Brodie et al. 1979), Allegheny mountain dusky salamanders are potential prey for many mammals, birds, snakes, and larger salamanders. Despite the many threats, population sizes remain high in many places because these salamanders have a broad spectrum of structural and behavioral defenses. Probably most important, they avoid detection by remaining hidden under cover during the day and by having color patterns that help to camouflage them against the substrate. The considerable variation in color that exists among individual salamanders within populations may reduce the foraging success of birds by preventing the birds from developing a reliable search image or by confusing them about the true identity of the salamanders (Brodie 1981). If predators do detect these salamanders, the amphibians can run fast and jump well. If actually seized by a predator, Allegheny mountain dusky salamanders can lose pieces of their tails and escape while the predator is distracted by the writhing tail fragment. Many Allegheny mountain dusky salamanders survive predation attempts by spring salamanders only through tail autotomy (Formanowicz and Brodie 1993). If all of these defenses fail, a salamander may resort to biting (Brodie et al. 1989). Although the mouth and teeth are so small that little damage can be inflicted, the biting can startle a predator or make it difficult for the predator to swallow the salamander.

Northern Two-Lined Salamander
Eurycea bislineata [Plate 11]

Quick Identification

A small to mid-sized and yellowish brown salamander with two dark brown stripes running the length of the body and tail. It is often found near cold, fast-running brooks.

Description

The northern two-lined salamander is a small- to mid-sized salamander with a long, thin trunk and thin, small legs that lives in cold, fast-running brooks. The tail is narrow, equal or greater than the length of the trunk, and is laterally compressed. These salamanders are yellowish brown with two dark brown stripes running dorsolaterally the length of the body and tail (usually breaking into spots on the tail).

Small dark spots are lightly scattered on the trunk, tail, and limbs. The underside of the tail and trunk is bright orange-yellow. Nasolabial grooves are present and most individuals have 13–16 costal grooves. Adults are 1.5–2.5 in (3–6 cm) in SVL. The larvae are elongate, with stream-type morphology (see figure 4.3), short legs, and a row of light spots on each side. Unusual adult male northern two-lined salamanders with extra broad heads (referred to as "Morph A" males) are found occasionally in New York, as well as in other parts of the range (Petranka 1998). The scientific name derives from *bis*, or twice, and *lineata*, or lined, referring to two dorsal stripes.

Some Allegheny mountain and northern dusky salamanders in New York look like northern two-lined salamanders. However, both "dusky" species have larger hind limbs, a heavier trunk, white coloration under the tail, and usually a light line from behind the eye to the corner of the mouth, which the northern two-lined salamander lacks. Four-toed salamanders have a tan dorsal color but differ from northern two-lined salamanders in having distinctly white undersides and round tails.

Habitat

Northern two-lined salamanders are most abundant along small streams in deciduous forests. In New Hampshire, scientists have found that key features associated with presence of northern two-lined salamanders in streams there were lack of brook trout, higher water temperature, and higher pH (Barr and Babbitt 2002). Northern two-lined salamanders are also found along larger streams, rivers, and clear lakes. In New York, northern two-lined salamanders are the only streamside salamanders that can frequently be encountered beneath stones along waterways that lack a forest canopy cover. Moreover, adults and newly metamorphosed juveniles have been found more than 330 ft. (100 m) from the nearest running water. In winter, northern two-lined salamanders sometimes can be found aggregated under rocks in springs and seeps (Ashton and Ashton 1978). Quite atypically, large numbers of adult and larval northern two-lined salamanders have been observed in lakes at depths to 54 ft. (18 m) in New York (Lake Minnewaska in the Shawangunk Mountains; Bahret 1996).

Natural History

Mating occurs streamside from fall through spring and the eggs are generally laid from May to July. Females usually attach and then attend to hatching 12–36 eggs to the underside of a flat stone in flowing water. Eggs have been reported attached to rocks at depths of more than 30 ft. (10 m) (Bahret 1996). In late summer, the eggs hatch after 30–70 days or more (Bishop 1941) into aquatic larvae that remain in the streams for 2–3 years (Hudson 1955), eating a variety of aquatic invertebrates. Although some larvae can be seen resting in quiet pools, many are found in shallow areas where water rapidly percolates through loosely packed stones and pebbles.

In parts of New York, densities of northern two-lined salamanders can be quite high at certain times along particular portions of streams in less disturbed habitats. Searches along the same stretches of stream at different times of the year, however, may yield few adults. Although definitive studies have not been completed, these apparent swings in abundance are probably due to a combination of some individuals moving deeper into the talus of the streambed and surrounding banks and others moving away from the streams altogether and living in the nearby forest floor. Adult and larval northern two-lined salamanders eat a wide range of small arthropods, worms, and mollusks. Adults have also been reported to eat fish embryos and fry. Predators of northern two-lined salamanders include fish, spring salamanders, snakes, birds, and small mammals.

Status and Distribution

The northern two-lined salamander is found throughout the state (map 4.11). Notably, northern two-lined salamanders are found in quite highly populated areas, including many small upstate towns and cities.

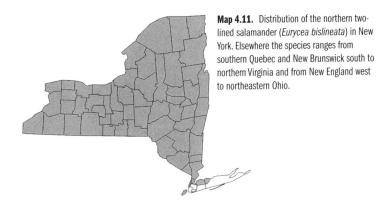

Map 4.11. Distribution of the northern two-lined salamander (*Eurycea bislineata*) in New York. Elsewhere the species ranges from southern Quebec and New Brunswick south to northern Virginia and from New England west to northeastern Ohio.

Other Intriguing Facts: Avoiding Being Eaten

Northern two-lined salamanders, potential dinner for a large number of forest and streamside predators in New York, are protected by a suite of defenses. Depending on the type of predatory encounter, these salamanders may remain cryptically immobile, posture boldly, or run like "heck" (Ducey and Brodie 1983). Because many predators overlook an unmoving salamander, immobility is an effective means of reducing the chances of predation. However, once detected by a feeding predator (as when touched by a snake's tongue), northern two-lined salamanders rely on their impressive speed (Ducey and Brodie 1983; Dowdy and Brodie 1989). This apparent "running" actually involves rapidly bending the trunk from side to side, creating an erratic, bounding movement that is effective for eluding both predators and lethargic herpetologists. If actually bitten by a bird or shrew, northern two-lined salamanders may posture by coiling the body, tucking the head under the cloaca, and elevating and undulating the tail (Brodie 1977), thereby drawing additional strikes to the tail, which can be autotomized easily. The broken tail segment may occupy the predator long enough for the salamander to escape.

Long-Tailed Salamander (Longtail Salamander)
Eurycea longicauda [Plate 12]

Quick Identification

A slender salamander with orange ground color and black blotches on body and black vertical bars on the tail, with the tail accounting for about 60% of its total length.

Description

Long-tailed salamanders are beautiful, moderately-sized salamanders (SVL 2–3.25 in. [5–8 cm]). They are quite slender, with a laterally compressed tail that is proportionately long, often accounting for about 60% of total length. Their legs are long and slender. The ground color is a striking orange or yellowish-orange, and black spots and blotches cover the body, tail, and sides of the head. The blotches on the tail tend to form more or less vertical bars. Larvae are stream-type and fairly dark in dorsal coloration with light bellies. Long-tailed salamanders can be distinguished from northern two-lined salamanders by having a more orange ground color, distinctly vertical dark bars along the tail, and much longer legs. The scientific name refers to *longus*, or long, and *cauda*, or tail.

Habitat

Long-tailed salamanders are often found in deciduous and mixed forests containing cool streams or seeps or along the edges of more open habitat bordering such forests. They appear to favor sites that contain moist soils and numerous cover objects like flat stones, bark, logs, or other detritus. Although adults may be occasionally be found away from streams, they are most common in the moist areas immediate to running water. These salamanders show no strong preference for substrate pH (Mushinsky and Brodie 1975).

Natural History

Adult long-tailed salamanders are overwhelmingly terrestrial, even though there are a few reports of adults in ponds. Like most salamanders, they spend the daylight hours under cover and may move about the forest floor on cool, moist nights in search of the small insects, spiders, and isopods, centipedes and earthworms that make up their diets (Anderson and Martino 1967). Adults use caves and deep rock fissures in fall and winter, when available (Bell 1955).

There is much still to be learned about the reproductive behavior of long-tailed salamanders, and we know of no studies of their reproduction in New York. Elsewhere, mating occurs in the fall, and egg-laying takes place in winter or spring attached to the undersides of stones along the edges of subsurface seepages or streams. Throughout their range and depending on temperature, eggs of

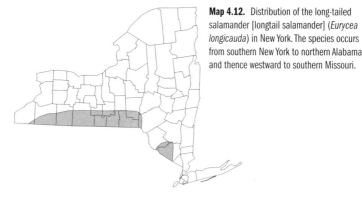

Map 4.12. Distribution of the long-tailed salamander [longtail salamander] (*Eurycea longicauda*) in New York. The species occurs from southern New York to northern Alabama and thence westward to southern Missouri.

long-tailed salamanders hatch in 1–3 months, and larvae usually metamorphose in 3–6 months following hatching (Petranka 1998). However, the larvae in some areas may spend the entire winter in the water, not transforming until the next spring some 12 months after hatching.

Status and Distribution

In New York State, the long-tailed salamander has recently been found in a limited numbers of sites (map 4.12) on the Appalachian Plateau (Cattaraugus through Broome counties) and in the Hudson River valley (Orange and Sullivan Counties). In addition to these sites, it is reported to have historically occurred in Albany, Chemung, and Ulster Counties. The species is in an apparent but unexplained decline in range and numbers and has been listed as a species of Special Concern in New York State.

Other Intriguing Facts: Tail Autotomy and Regeneration

When a predator grabs onto the end of the tail of a long-tailed salamander, the salamander contracts muscles that cause the tail to break along specific lines. Separation between two tail vertebrae occurs closer to the body than the point of skin separation, allowing the extra skin to fold in and protect the broken end of the tail. This, together with valves in the blood vessels, results in little blood loss, a limited chance of infection, and quick healing. The piece of the tail that is released wiggles and writhes about, maintaining the attention of the predator while the salamander escapes. Within less than a week, new tissue is visible at the end of the tail. Salamanders, unlike lizards, grow tails that are nearly identical to the originals. New tails contain new muscles and vertebrae and can wave and undulate, restoring the salamander to full functioning in a few months.

Spring Salamander (Northern Spring Salamander, Purple Salamander)
Gyrinophilus porphyriticus [Plate 13]

Quick Identification

A robust salmon-pink and mottled salamander with distinctive light line running from the eye to the nostril that is found mostly in cool streams.

Description

Spring salamanders are robust animals with a long trunk and relatively short, thick legs and tails. These salamanders are the largest members of the family Plethodontidae in New York. Adult SVL length is 3–4.75 in. (7.5–11 cm). Their tails, which are muscular at the base, are laterally compressed into a paddle distally, giving these salamanders the ability to swim short distances across swift current. The smooth, almost translucent skin ranges from salmon pink to orange-tan with darker mottling on the dorsal surface. A distinctive light line runs along a ridge from the eye to the nostril. Larvae are stream-type (see figure 4.3) with a pale tan coloration under darker reticulations. Occasionally, albino forms are found in New York (e.g., Chenango County, Ferriero et al. 1998). Older larvae may have an orange or pink tinge. Adults have nasolabial grooves and 17–19 costal grooves. There is no external sexual dimorphism in this species. The scientific name derives from *gyrinos*, or tadpole, and *philos*, or fond of, referring to the multi-year larval phase, and *porphyros* or purple, referring to the dorsal body color.

It is possible to distinguish spring salamanders from red salamanders by the light line from the eye to the nostril found only in the spring salamanders. Red salamanders are also more clearly red rather than pink or tan-orange. Separating spring salamanders from the eft stage of eastern newts is even easier. Spring salamanders have costal grooves, nasolabial grooves (see figure 4.5), fat tails, and smooth skin—all features lacking in efts.

Habitat

Spring salamanders are most commonly found in rocky brooks, seeps, springs, and streams well shaded by trees. Although the salamanders may move over ground (and across roads) during nights of heavy rain in spring and fall, they are found near running water most of the time. Spring salamanders are much less abundant in isolated streams and streams with brook trout (Lowe and Bolger 2002), the fingerlings of which outcompete larvae for resources (Resetarits 1995). The salamanders seem particularly averse to disturbed environments and are rare in streams within logged or polluted areas (Lowe et al. 2004).

Natural History

During the day, spring salamanders stay under large stones or deep beneath talus within seeps and creeks. Spring salamanders move through tunnels and crayfish burrows, and among wet rocks, coming to the surface only on cool, wet nights. Their large body size and reliance on respiration through the skin (like all members of the Plethodontidae, they lack lungs) restricts them to moist, oxygen-rich microenvironments. Spring salamanders may remain active in streams all winter. Adults have an enormous gape and, although eating some earthworms and insects, are major predators on other salamanders. This predation can influence which species of smaller-bodied salamanders occur in a given area (Hileman and Brodie 1994, Grover and Wilbur 2002). Spring salamanders themselves may fall prey to fish, larger snakes, and small mammals.

Because of their secretive habits, much remains to be learned about breeding in this species. Mating occurs in the fall, and possibly in the spring, but the salamanders lay eggs later in the spring and summer (Bishop 1941). Females attach 20 to more than 100 eggs to the underside of large stones deep underground in flowing water. It is believed that the females attend the eggs until hatching. The eggs hatch during late summer, and the larvae will remain in the streams for 3–5 years. The larvae stay in running water within the rocky layers of the stream bottom for about 3 years (Bishop 1941), moving about quiet waters at night. By the time they metamorphose, larvae are 4–5 in. (10–13 cm) in total length.

Map 4.13. Distribution of the spring salamander [northern spring salamander] (*Gyrinophilus porphyriticus*) in New York. Elsewhere the species occurs in and around the Appalachian Mountains and north to the Adirondack Mountains, southern Quebec, and Maine.

Status and Distribution

Because spring salamanders are difficult to locate, our knowledge of their current distribution and densities is somewhat limited. Spring salamanders are quite common in many creeks in central New York but are only rarely found in many streams in the Adirondack Mountains and do not appear to occur east of the Hudson south of Rensselaer County (map 4.13). It is believed that environmental changes caused by sedimentation from logging, residential development, acid rain, and other pollution may be reducing their range and numbers (Lowe et al. 2004).

Other Intriguing Facts: Salamander Eaters

Although analyses of stomach contents show that the diet of spring salamanders in the northeastern United States is largely invertebrates (Petranka 1998), both adults and larvae regularly feed on other salamanders in the streams of New York. During the day, adults remain in subterranean tunnels or crayfish burrows and ambush invertebrates or small salamanders that stray too close. On cool, moist nights, spring salamanders rise from their underground lairs and move about the shallow riffles, seeps, and splash zones along streams to stalk their prey (Formanowicz and Brodie 1993). Using a combination of visual, tactile, and chemical senses, they detect and follow smaller salamanders before striking. Their victims are usually dusky and northern two-lined salamanders, as well as smaller members of their own species. Potential predation by large spring salamanders may be a major reason why newly metamorphosed streamside salamanders often leave the stream area and move into the surrounding forests for the early part of their lives (Hileman and Brodie 1994, Grover and Wilbur 2002).

Four-toed Salamander
Hemidactylium scutatum [Plate 14]

Quick Identification

A small salamander with a reddish brown back flecked with dark spots, a distinctly white and spotted belly, a tail with obvious constriction ringing its base, and four toes on each hind foot. It occurs most often in swamps often associated with *Sphagnum* moss.

Description

Four-toed salamanders are small, somewhat unusual salamanders and denizens of New York's woodlands and swamps. Adults are reddish brown, bronze, or tan dorsally, flecked with small dark spots, and primarily grayish on the sides. The venter is distinctly opaque white with irregularly scattered black spots. The skin is rougher or more granular in appearance than other local members of this family. The snout is blunt and a mid-dorsal groove is present along the trunk. The tail is usually somewhat longer than the body and has an obvious constriction ringing its base. Adults have an SVL of 1–1.75 in. (2.5–4.5 cm). The common name of this species refers to the four toes on each hind foot (instead of the usual five found in all other New York salamanders except mudpuppies). Compared with females, males are slightly smaller, have a mental gland under the chin, show overhanging teeth in the upper jaw, and are usually less reddish than females. Larvae are aquatic and pond-type (see figure 4.3), with a fairly uniform coloration actually composed of numerous flecks of browns, gold, greens, and orange. Darker spots often form a "Y" on the back of the head. The scientific name derives from *hemi*, or half, and *daktylion*, or fusion of digits, referring to reduced number of digits on each hind foot, and *scutatum*, referring to costal grooves that appear covered with shield-like plates.

Habitat

Four-toed salamanders are found in moist forests of all kinds as long as they contain small ponds, seepage areas, bogs, or swamps. Although they are often found associated with sphagnum mosses, moisture levels appear to be more critical than the species of mosses present.

Natural History

Four-toed salamanders mate in the fall among and beneath leaves, plant roots, and logs on the forest floor. Females migrate to the edges of ponds, slow-moving creeks, and flooded swamps in mid-spring and choose nest sites hidden beneath mats of mosses or plant roots just overhanging the water's edge (Bishop 1941). In New York, females lay an average of 25 eggs (Gilbert 1941) and usually remain at the nest until eggs hatch some 4–6 weeks later (Bishop 1941). The exact numbers of eggs laid by any female is difficult to estimate because several females may lay eggs at the same site. Females often skip breeding between years, likely because of limitations on food available to form eggs (Harris and Ludwig 2004). The hatchlings are aquatic larvae that wiggle from the nest and drop into the water, their movement often aided by heavy rains. The larvae remain in the water until metamorphosis in mid- to late-summer at a size of 0.75 in. (2 cm). Little is known about the ecology of the larvae and juveniles. Most adults, and presumably juveniles, live terrestrially beneath logs, stumps, and stones adjacent to the water's edge to more than 300 ft. (100 m) into the forest. In Pennsylvania, four-toed salamanders eat primarily springtails, ants, and larvae of small flies (Hulse et al. 2001).

Four-toed salamanders, although having skin secretions that repel some predators, are food for a wide variety of snakes, larger salamanders, birds, and mammals. When first contacted by a predator, this species will coil its trunk, tucking its head under its tail, and sometimes lift and undulate its tail. If the predator bites the tail, four-toed salamanders autotomize the entire tail from the constriction at its base (other local salamanders autotomize only portions of the tail) often with little provocation (Bishop 1941). The separated tail continues to undulate, distracting the predator while the salamander escapes. Moreover, eggs of four-toed salamanders contain a chemical repellent in the jelly layer (Hess and Harris 2000), which may explain why these salamanders often safely abandon their nests.

Status and Distribution

Four-toed salamanders have a patchy distribution across New York State (map 4.14). They appear to be difficult to find in many areas and locally abundant in only a few. They formerly occurred on Staten Island (Rumph 1979).

Map 4.14. Distribution of the four-toed salamander (*Hemidactylium scutatum*) in New York. Elsewhere the species is scattered across the eastern half of the United States and southeastern Canada.

Other Intriguing Facts: Communal Nests

After laying eggs in a secluded crevice within a moss mat just above a pond edge, female four-toed salamanders usually remain curled up with their eggs. Nest guarding probably increases egg survivorship by reducing losses due to predation and infection. Occasionally, several females place their eggs together. Such communal nests usually contain eggs from two to five females (Breitenbach 1982), although a nest in Michigan was reported to contain the eggs of more than 30 females. Usually only one female remains with the joint nest; scientists are studying why some females leave and others remain.

Eastern Red-Backed Salamander (Northern Redback Salamander)
Plethodon cinereus [Plate 15]

Quick Identification

An extremely abundant small salamander of mature woodlands with a "salt and pepper" belly and either a brick-red stripe along back and tail (all parts of New York) or a dark unstriped back (figure 4.20b [increasingly common moving southward in New York]).

Description

Eastern red-backed salamanders (commonly known as "redbacks") are small, slender salamanders with short legs and a round tail of about equal length to the body. Adults are 1.25–2.25 in. (3.0–5.5 cm) in SVL. The hind limbs are only slightly larger than the forelimbs. Males have a square-shaped snout; females have a more rounded one. Nasolabial grooves are present. Individuals of the most common color morph have a brick-red or red-orange stripe that runs along the dorsal surface of the trunk and tail, dark gray sides, and a mottled ("salt and pepper") belly. Individuals referred to as "leadbacks" or "lead phase" are also common in many areas (particularly in southern parts of New York). This morph lacks the dorsal stripe and has a uniform blackish-gray color with silvery or gold flecks dorsally and the typical mottled belly. Many populations contain a mixture of the two color morphs (Lotter and Scott 1977) plus low numbers of individuals with stripes of other shades of red, orange, pink, or even white. Some populations in Connecticut and Massachusetts contain individuals that are nearly completely bright red with only a few black blotches on the tail; this color morph ("erythristic") is rare in New York. The morphs have a genetic basis that is likely maintained by temperature-dependent selection. Black morphs seem to experience higher mortality in colder sites (Lotter and Scott 1977, Moreno 1989). The erythristic morphs, with their bright red coloration, are partially protected from some predators because of their resemblance to efts (Brodie and Brodie 1980). The scientific name refers to *plethore*, or full of, and *odon* teeth, referring to the number of vomerine and prevomerine teeth, and *cinereus*, or ash-colored, referring to the dorsal color of the lead-backed phase (the morph of the first specimen described).

Habitat

Eastern red-backed salamanders are found in greatest density in deciduous and mixed forests with heavy canopy cover and a well-developed soil organic layer. These salamanders occur in lower densities within coniferous forests and forests disturbed by human activity as long as the canopy is partially complete; the soil is not too acidic; and the forest floor contains leaf litter, logs, and stones to provide hiding places for the salamanders and their prey (Wyman 1988). Eastern red-backed salamanders show little preference for the type of object under which they take refuge (Bennett et al. 2003). They seem to be rare or absent in areas either too wet or too dry, that is, sites with occasional flooding or sandy soils.

Natural History

The eastern red-backed salamander is likely the most abundant salamander in New York State's forests. Counts of individuals within the leaf litter and under surface debris have commonly found (0.5–1.0 individuals/m²) at many localities within the state (as is typical elsewhere in its range, e.g., in Michigan, Heatwole 1962; or New Hampshire, Burton and Likens 1975b). Because most of the individuals within a population are deep beneath the forest floor and are missed during these surveys, population sizes of red-backed salamanders are likely much higher than these figures imply.

Eastern red-backed salamanders live out their entire life cycle on land. Mating occurs in fall and possibly spring (Bishop 1941), and females lay eggs during the summer (July and August). A female lays 3–17 light- to dark-yellow, miniature eggs in grapelike bunches in a small cavity under a log or stone (Test and Heatwole 1962) and guards the eggs (Highton and Savage 1961) until they hatch about 30 days later into terrestrial juveniles that resemble miniature adults.

Eastern red-backed salamanders feed on a wide variety of small arthropods (especially mites and beetle and fly larvae), earthworms, and mollusks that live on the forest floor (Wyman 1998). During rainy nights, some eastern red-backed salamanders may scale low vegetation to search for food (Jaeger 1978). The salamanders, in turn, are prey for many larger animals, including birds (Brodie and Brodie 1980), snakes, small mammals, larger salamanders, and even beetles. Eastern red-backed salamanders have skin secretions that are distasteful to some predators (Brodie et al. 1979) and sticky enough to thwart others (Arnold 1982, Gall et al. 2003). When attacked, they also drop their tails, which by vigorously wriggling, attract predators away from the escaping body (Lancaster and Wise 1996). The abundance of eastern red-backed salamanders, together with their roles as predators on smaller animals and prey for larger animals, results in their having a significant impact on the nutrient cycling and overall health of forest ecosystems in which they live (Wyman 1998).

Status and Distribution

Eastern red-backed salamanders are found throughout New York wherever mature forests are present (map 4.15), even in urban areas (Gibbs 1998b) as long as closed forest canopy and thick leaf litter layer on the soil surface are retained. However, the species is particularly sensitive to reduced soil moisture and acidification (Wyman 1988,

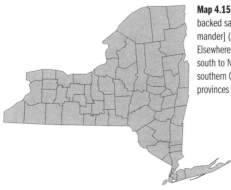

Map 4.15. Distribution of the eastern red-backed salamander [northern redback salamander] (*Plethodon cinereus*) in New York. Elsewhere the species occurs west to Missouri, south to North Carolina, and ranges north from southern Quebec and the Canadian maritime provinces to Minnesota.

Sugalski and Claussen 1997); thus, it is vulnerable to changes in forest health caused by climate change, timber harvest, and acid deposition. The striped morph ("redbacks") predominates in the north and the unstriped morph ("leadbacks") increasingly predominates (to about 50% of populations) in the southern part of the state. Populations on Long Island are particularly variable, with redbacks predominating on the western end of the island and leadbacks on the eastern end (Williams et al. 1968). Leadbacks may have increased in frequency during the Pleistocene glacial advances due to geographic isolation and drier ecological conditions on the island, with redbacks later recolonizing the west end of the island.

Other Intriguing Facts: Aggressive Defense of Territories

Adult eastern red-backed salamanders defend small areas on a forest floor against other members of their species (Jaeger 1984), and the details of these interactions have been the subject of considerable research (Mathis et al. 1995). The salamanders mark their territories with pheromones (Jaeger and Gergits 1979) and greet intruders with aggressive posturing and biting (Jaeger 1984). Males may permit females and juveniles within their territories at certain times (Jaeger et al. 1995b). Larger individuals tend to have better territories (i.e., with more secure cover and higher quality food [Mathis 1991]). Females, when choosing mates, tend to select males that have been eating higher quality food (Walls et al. 1989, Jaeger et al. 1995a, Maerz and Madison 2000).

Northern Slimy Salamander
Plethodon glutinosus [Plate 16]

Quick Identification

A large woodland salamander with nasolabial grooves and silvery-white flecking on its sides, tail, and back upon a slate gray to black base color.

Description

The northern slimy salamander is a fairly large woodland salamander that has a dark, slate gray to black base color with distinctive silvery-white flecking (heavy in some) on the sides, tail, and back. The SVL of adults is 2.25–3.5 in (5.5–9 cm). The round, robust tail is about the length of the body and may appear lighter than the trunk because of the large amounts of white secretions stored in the granular glands beneath the skin of the tail. The venter is also dark although the undersides of the throat and feet are lighter. Males have a light-colored mental gland about 0.2 in. (0.5 cm) in diameter under the chin; otherwise the sexes are similar. There is no larval stage, and the juveniles have the same color pattern as adults. The presence of nasolabial grooves (see figure 4.5) and a black color distinguish northern slimy salamanders from blue-spotted and Jefferson salamanders. Unstriped eastern red-backed salamanders have a more elongate trunk, much smaller legs, and no bright spots. The scientific name refers to *glutinosus*, or full of glue, in reference to the species' sticky secretions when molested.

Habitat

In New York, this fully terrestrial species inhabits upland mixed forests with thick canopies and many rocks and logs on the forest floor. Northern slimy salamanders are most common on heavily forested slopes dominated by hardwoods and extensive rocky outcrops, with shale or talus that may serve as critical overwintering habitat (Bishop 1941).

Natural History

Northern slimy salamanders mate terrestrially during the spring and fall, and they lay eggs in cavities underground or within rotting logs and stumps during early summer. Much remains to be studied about reproduction and development of these animals in New York, but females likely breed every other year, laying 10–40 eggs, which they probably guard until hatching. In mid- to late-summer, the eggs hatch into juveniles less than 1 in. (2.5 cm) in length that are a miniature version of the adults. It may take 4–5 years before these salamanders reach sexual maturity.

Adult and juvenile northern slimy salamanders spend most of the time underground in crevices beneath the forest floor and in talus slopes. In New York during spring and fall, some individuals can be found just beneath stones or logs during the day and others can be seen at the mouths of crevices or on the forest floor on rainy nights. Studies suggest that northern slimy salamanders remain within small (6–15 ft. [3–5 m] diameter) home ranges for months at a time but achieve surprisingly high densities in parts of their range (Semlitsch 1980). Foods include many arthropods, earthworms, and terrestrial mollusks (Davidson 1956). Individuals may show aggression toward other members of their species that move too close.

Status and Distribution

New York populations (map 4.16) represent the northern limit of the range except for an isolated population in New Hampshire. Within New York, these salamanders are found from the westernmost counties to the Connecticut border but typically only south of the Mohawk River. Northern slimy salamanders have not been reported in the northern parts of the Great Lakes/St. Lawrence River plains, Adirondack Mountains and their foothills, or Long Island. Throughout the range, these salamanders are abundant in some areas but rare or absent in more disturbed sites.

Other Intriguing Facts: One Species Or Many?

Originally, the specific name *Plethodon glutinosus* was applied to animals ranging from Texas and Oklahoma to Florida to New York. Recent studies examining their proteins and DNA, however, have indicated that many of the populations across this range are distinct genetically (Highton et al. 1989). Such studies have resulted in some scientists breaking apart the one original species into about 15 separate taxa. Although a few of these new species designations are now well supported, experts disagree about how many of the other 13 are distinct enough to warrant their own species name. Regardless of the outcome of the studies and discussions, northern slimy salamanders in the mid-Atlantic states retain the name *Plethodon glutinosus*.

Map 4.16. Distribution of the northern slimy salamander (*Plethodon glutinosus*) in New York. The species occurs from Alabama to Illinois to New York.

Wehrle's Salamander
Plethodon wehrlei [Plate 17]

Quick Identification

A slender salamander of the Allegheny region with dark coloration and whitish spots on the animal's lower sides and a tail that is moderately long and round in cross section (figure 4.22).

Description

Wehrle's salamanders are long slender salamanders and the SVL of adults is 2–3 in (5–7.5 cm). The tail is round in cross section and up to 50% of the total length. The forelegs and hind legs are well developed and of about equal size, and the toes on the hind foot are, to some extent, webbed. The color of these salamanders varies from dark brown to (more often) a dark slate gray—almost black. Along the lower sides there are usually a few whitish spots or flecks. The belly is uniformly gray and noticeably lighter in color than the dorsum. The throat is light, almost white. Wehrle's salamanders differ from northern slimy salamanders in having a lighter ground color and generally less spotting. The scientific name honors naturalist Richard W. Wehrle, who collected the first specimen.

Habitat

Although they have been found in valleys, Wehrle's salamanders usually frequent the more uphill sections of the forests within their range. These forests are usually, but not exclusively, mixed deciduous forests. Wehrle's salamanders avoid clearcut areas (Duguay and Wood 2002) and seek cover under flat rocks, and occasionally, under logs or bark (Hall and Stafford 1972). These salamanders use fairly dry habitats compared to most salamanders (Bishop 1941). However, when the ground becomes too dry, Wehrle's salamanders penetrate deeper into the soil by following the interstices between subsurface rocks.

Natural History

The natural history of Wehrle's salamanders is not well documented (Hall and Stafford 1972). Terrestrial mating likely occurs in September and October in New York State. Females lay the eggs in clusters in deep underground cavities in early spring, and immature juveniles emerge in late spring or early summer. Males likely do not mature until the fourth year and females not until the fifth. Densities in suitable habitat can be moderately high, that is, one per 110 sq. ft. (10 m²). Wehrle's salamanders are typically active during the night. On wet, foggy and dark days, however, they have been seen in the open on the surface of the ground. In Pennsylvania, they feed mostly on weevils, insect larvae, centipedes, spiders, and orthopterans, and particularly, the introduced European strawberry weevil (Hall 1976).

Status and Distribution

Wehrle's salamanders occur in peripheral populations in New York in the western Appalachian Plateau where it borders Pennsylvania (map 4.17). Because this creature is, like most salamanders, quite secretive and typically occupies terrain that is somewhat remote from brooks and roads, it is not frequently encountered. Thus, it has been considered to be uncommon. However, it is likely quite common and living on most hills within its range.

Other Intriguing Facts: A Dryness Specialist

Wehrle's salamanders can evidently survive evaporative water loss to a greater degree than can other salamanders of the genus *Plethodon*. In some studies, *P. wehrlei* showed a critical activity point of 36%, which represents the percent body weight loss caused by desiccation that the animal could endure. Such desiccation resistance enables Wehrle's salamanders to function in drier (higher) sites than the other species. This habitat specialization may, among other things,

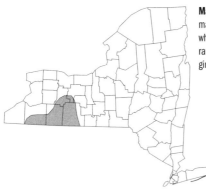

Map 4.17. Distribution of the Wehrle's salamander (*Plethodon wehrlei*) in New York. Elsewhere the species has a small geographic range, occurring mainly in Virginia, West Virginia, and Pennsylvania.

reduce competition for food with the other salamanders that prefer moister situations.

Red Salamander
Pseudotriton ruber [Plate 18]

Quick Identification

A stunning salamander with moist, smooth skin that is orange-red to bright coral red with small, scattered black spots; similar species: "eft" stage of the eastern newt (see Plate 8).

Description

One of New York's most spectacular salamanders, the red salamander is bright coral red to orange-red with small, scattered black spots as young adults. The dark markings increase, and the base color subdues with age so that older individuals appear to have extensive dark mottling over reddish purple. The venter of adults is light pinkish red. Red salamanders are robust-bodied with smooth skin; short, sturdy legs; and a short, thick tail that is greatly compressed laterally on its distal half. The snout is short and rounded and the iris of the eye is yellow. The SVL of adults is 2–4 in. (5–10 cm). Larvae are stream-type (see figure 4.3) with black markings mottled over a brown base color. Some young may begin to show red pigmentation before metamorphosis, whereas others may not develop the adult color until more than a month after metamorphosis. The scientific name probably derives from *pseudes*, or false, and *triton*, the original term for newt (hence to "false newt" referring to its superficial appearance to the red eft), and *ruber*, or red.

Red salamanders may be confused only with spring salamanders and the eft stage of eastern newts. The efts lack nasolabial grooves, lack costal grooves, have granular skin, and have thin bony tails. Spring salamanders can be distinguished by a light line and ridge from the eye to the nostril and a generally more orange or purple color.

Habitat

Red salamanders live near streams, springs, ponds, and bogs in hardwood, conifer, or mixed forests. Red salamanders are occasionally found in open meadows and ditches with cold running streams or beaver ponds. Although adults spend much time terrestrially, they are also aquatic many months of the year.

Natural History

Most red salamanders spend the summer and early fall beneath logs, stones, and leaf litter, or within burrows in forests. Courtship and mating occurs during this time (Organ and Organ 1968). Females migrate into streams or ponds to lay eggs in mid-autumn, attaching 50–80 eggs to the underside of a rock in shallow water. It is believed that females remain with the eggs until they hatch in 8–10 weeks. The larvae seem to prefer the slower parts of streams, often those areas with many plants and a muddy bottom. Red salamanders remain in the water about 3.5 years before metamorphosing into terrestrial juveniles at 3–4 in. (7.5–10 cm) total length. Most adult males and females spend the late fall, winter, and early spring in the water. Red salamanders eat the usual assortment of worms, arthropods, and mollusks, but they also feed on other salamanders, particularly eastern red-backed salamanders (Petranka 1998). Little information is available concerning the predators of red salamanders.

Status and Distribution

In New York, red salamanders are most often found in the lower Hudson River valley from Albany south, on Staten Island, and within a few western counties that border Pennsylvania (map 4.18). They are absent from Long Island. Red salamanders are by no means common in New York, although robust populations exist at some sites.

Other Intriguing Facts: Toxic Skins

Like most amphibians, red salamanders have a suite of defenses helping to protect them from predators. Red salamanders have a habit of

Map 4.18. Distribution of the red salamander (*Pseudotriton ruber*) in New York. The species has its southern limit in northern Florida, western limit in central Kentucky, and northern limit in New York.

staying hidden most of the time, possess skin glands that produce noxious secretions, and use behaviors that draw a predator's strike to the tail (containing concentrations of glands). These salamanders are also protected by their coloration. The gaudy red color may function as a warning signal easily learned by predators—those that have had a previous encounter with a poisonous red eft, or even with another somewhat noxious red salamander, are likely to avoid attacking bright red salamanders of any kind (Howard and Brodie 1971, Brandon and Huheey 1981).

5

Frogs and Toads: Species Accounts

Most of New York's 14 species of frogs and toads are reclusive creatures, often lurking for much of the year unnoticed underground, in old logs, in wet areas, or in trees. On warm spring and summer nights, however, frogs and toads emerge from their refuges in great numbers and converge on pools and ponds where they advertise loudly for mates (figure 5.1). Examples are the spring peeper's signature "peep" or the bullfrog's "jug-o-rum." Other less familiar species produce a wide range of snores, clucks, quacks, clicks, trills, bleats, and whistles.

Noisy mating choruses in the spring and early summer (see table 5.1 for species-specific seasonal calling patterns) initiate a fascinating and complex life cycle. The first stage is the egg, often produced in the thousands each year by individual females. Males clasp females from behind in a behavior called "amplexus" (see figure 5.1) and dribble sperm on the eggs as the female extrudes them into the water. The eggs (see figure 5.1) hatch quickly (a few days to a month), particularly if the water is warm, into the second stage—aquatic larvae commonly known as a tadpoles (see figure 5.1). Tadpoles are typically herbivorous, rasping algae and other organisms attached to submerged surfaces. Tadpoles grow rapidly to avoid the constant threats posed by predators, especially aquatic insects and fishes, and, in some species, by desiccation of their rapidly evaporating breeding ponds.

The transition between the tadpole stage and the third, or adult stage, is called "metamorphosis" and involves a quick conversion of a tadpole to a juvenile frog. It is one of the true wonders of nature:

Figure 5.1. Complex life cycle of frogs and toads illustrated here by the American toad: (A) male calling as part of courtship display; (B) female and male in amplexus prior to moving to water where the male (smaller toad, top) will deposit sperm on the eggs as they are extruded by the female (larger toad, bottom); (C) characteristic double and coiled strings of eggs deposited by the female; and (D) tadpole just prior to metamorphosis into a terrestrial "toadlet." (A: Victor S. Lamoureux; B: B.M. Glorioso; C: Victor S. Lamoureux; D: Twan Leenders.)

over just 1 to 3 weeks, an elongate, swimming herbivore and gill-breather with a tail and long, coiled intestine transforms into stout terrestrial carnivore with legs, lungs, a short intestine, and no tail. The entire life cycle (egg to adult) generally begins early in the warm season and may extend for just weeks (spadefoots) to several years (bullfrogs), but it is usually concluded in a single spring and summer.

As few as about one in 1,000 eggs survives to become a breeding adult frog or toad (e.g., Berven 1990). Even as adults, life spans of frogs also tend to be short. Female wood frogs, for example, typically breed for just a single season before they die (Berven 1990). Curiously, the number of adult frogs hopping around is often determined more by the survival of tadpoles in their highly restricted breeding pools than survival of the adults. Thus, the number and quality of breeding ponds in an area can be the most important factor determining frog abundance.

The frogs and toads native to New York are members of four families. Most are members of the Ranidae, also known as the pond frogs,

Table 5.1.
Seasonality of Calling by Frogs and Toads in New York State[a]

Species	Region								
	Northern			Eastern, Western, and Central			Southern		
	Early	Middle	Late	Early	Middle	Late	Early	Middle	Late
Northern Cricket Frog	—	—	—	—	—	—	May 27	Jun 24	Jul 8
American Toad	Apr 26	May 24	Jul 23	Apr 11	May 2	Jun 6	Mar 29	Apr 24	Jun 1
Fowler's Toad	—	—	—	—	—	—	May 1	May 17	Jun 27
Eastern Gray Treefrog	May 7	Jun 2	Aug 1	Apr 26	May 27	Jul 25	May 4	Jun 11	Aug 21
Spring Peeper	Apr 14	May 5	Jul 27	Mar 29	Apr 22	Aug 2	Mar 18	Apr 14	Aug 3
Western Chorus Frog	Apr 1	Apr 21	May 2	Mar 26	Apr 11	Apr 25	—	—	—
Bullfrog	May 1	Jun 6	Jul 1	May 15	Jun 15	Jul 17	May 15	Jun 18	Jul 12
Green Frog	May 2	Jun 15	Jul 18	May 17	Jun 17	Jul 25	May 13	Jun 15	Jul 25

Table 5.1. (continued)

Region

Species	Northern			Eastern, Western, and Central			Southern		
	Early	Middle	Late	Early	Middle	Late	Early	Middle	Late
Pickerel Frog	Apr 2	May 2	Jul 8	Apr 4	Apr 29	May 15	Apr 3	May 3	Jun 25
Northern Leopard Frog	Apr 1	Apr 21	May 26	Mar 29	Apr 17	May 8	—	—	—
Southern Leopard Frog	—	—	—	—	—	—	Mar 22	Apr 1	May 15
Mink Frog	May 17	Jun 18	Jul 24	—	—	—	—	—	—
Wood Frog	Apr 9	Apr 21	May 25	Mar 26	Apr 4	Apr 20	Mar 7	Mar 28	Apr 14

[a]Based on 10,261 reports of vocalizing frogs from the New York State "Herp Atlas" in 1990–1999. Early, middle, and late calling dates conform to earliest 10%, 50%, and 90% of reports received, respectively. Only species for which more than 10 reports were available were analyzed (eastern spadefoots were too rare anywhere for inclusion). The northern region includes Oswego, Oneida, Herkimer, Fulton, and Warren Counties and northward. The southern region includes Sullivan, Ulster, and Dutchess Counties and southward. All other counties fall within the eastern, central, and western regions.

the "ranids" or "true frogs." These frogs are found throughout the world (except in Antarctica) and are highly adapted for aquatic life. They have long, strong hind legs and webbed toes that facilitate jumping and swimming (and that make them difficult to catch and hold). Bullfrogs are a familiar member of this family. Another prominent family is the Hylidae, mostly diminutive climbers with sticky toe pads, including three groups: the tree frogs (*Hyla*), the cricket frogs (*Acris*), and the chorus frogs (*Pseudacris*). The tree frogs, aptly named, dwell mostly in tree canopies, foraging in tree holes and among the branches. Cricket frogs and chorus frogs dwell lower to the ground, favoring bushes and thickets.

Toads in New York are represented by two families: the Bufonidae and the Pelobatidae, which both spend most of their time on or in the ground. Despite the popular perception that frogs and toads are distinct amphibians, they are merely members of different frog families. These are the main distinctions: (1) most frogs have moist, smooth

Figure 5.2. External characteristics useful for classifying toads, such as this American toad. (James P. Gibbs.)

skin, whereas most toads have dry, warty skin; (2) bufonid toads have no teeth but frogs and pelobatids have rows of tiny teeth on their upper jaws; (3) toads have short hind legs and amble or hop, whereas most frogs have long hind legs and jump; and (4) toads have poison glands on the shoulders (the "parotoid glands") but frogs do not (figure 5.2). The bufonids or "true toads," such as the American toad, are the most common and more familiar toads in New York. Only one pelobatid occurs in the state, a distinctive and rare kind of toad—the eastern spadefoot; it has "spades" on its back feet (hardened surfaces) for digging burrows.

Frogs and toads are the most diverse group of amphibians, with some 4,370 species worldwide (Pough et al. 2004). New York is neither frog- nor toad-rich, with a maximum 8 to 10 of its 14 species total occurring in any given area. The highest diversity in the state occurs in the St. Lawrence River Plain, where the ranges of the western chorus frog and mink frog coincide with ranges of the more widespread species.

Identifying New York's frogs and toads is straightforward based on external features (figures 5.2 and 5.3). These include skin texture, which may be (1) moist or dry and (2) smooth, granular, or warty. The

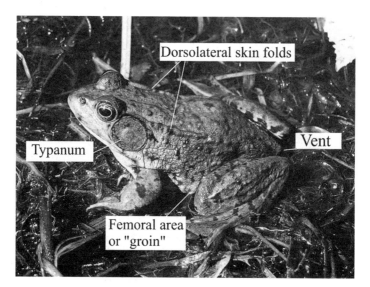

Figure 5.3. External characteristics useful for classifying frogs. Lengths of toads and frogs (such as this male green frog) are measured from the tip of the snout to the posterior end of the body above the vent (called the standard length). (James P. Gibbs.)

presence of glandular ridges of skin—the dorsolateral folds that extend from behind the eyes down each side of the back—can be diagnostic, as well as the extent of webbing between the toes of the rear feet and the presence of swollen discs on the ends of toes. Features frequently used to distinguish toads are L-shaped ridges called cranial crests, which occur between and slightly behind eyes, as well as the parotoid glands on each shoulder (see figure 5.2).

Eastern Spadefoot
Scaphiopus holbrookii [Plate 19]

Quick Identification

A squat, plump toad with smooth skin and few warts; eyes with vertical pupils; and a sickle-shaped spade on each hind foot used for digging in sandy habitats between the Albany area and Long Island.

Description

Eastern spadefoot is a squat, plump toad with smooth skin with small, scattered warts. Eyes are protuberant and golden, with vertical pupils. A sickle-shaped, prominent dark ridge (spade) is present on the underside of each hind foot. Two irregular, light-colored lines usually extend down the back. The tympanum is obvious. A bony hump, usually present between the eyes of most frogs and toads, is absent. These toads lack parotoid glands. The standard length is 2–2.5 in. (4.5–5.5 cm), with a maximum length of 2.75 in. (7.3 cm). Males have dark throats whereas females have light-colored ones. Females hang their eggs in strings of some 2,500 upon submerged stems of emergent plants, usually grasses. Tadpoles are bronze with transparent undersides and short, rounded, finely spotted tails. The voice of an adult eastern spadefoot is a coarse "wank, wank, wank . . ." The scientific name derives from *skaphis*, or spade, and *pous*, or foot, referring to adaptation of hind foot for digging, as well as honoring John E. Holbrook, a prominent early North American herpetologist.

Habitat

Most commonly found on well-drained, loose, and sandy soil. Vegetation overlying such soils may be open forest, brushy areas, meadow, or even crops. These toads are extremely terrestrial and visit temporary, rain-formed pools only to breed.

Frogs and Toads

Natural History

Breeding occurs whenever intense rainstorms trigger toad emergence from their burrows, typically in June and July but as early as March and as late as September. Mating is highly "explosive" and may last only a few days (e.g., on Long Island; Burnley 1973). Male eastern spadefoots arrive at breeding pools earlier than females, calling, searching pools for females, and jousting with other males. After finding a mate, female eastern spadefoots lay eggs that hatch in 1–7 days (Richmond 1947). Tadpoles often form dense aggregations and metamorphose just 14–60 days after hatching, then become diurnal and forage at their natal pond's edge.

Making good use of their foot spades, these toads spend large amounts of time in the burrows they dig (often 3–6 ft. [1–2 m] belowground). Burrows are used during extended dry spells in the warm season as well as during winter. Even during moister periods of the warm season, these toads emerge only sporadically; they surface at night, usually after heavy rains, when they feed on insects, particularly caterpillars and adult beetles (Whitaker et al. 1977). Many vertebrates, including northern watersnakes, European starlings, and common grackles, eat eastern spadefoots (Palis 2000). The toads' primary defense is quickly burrowing into soft soil. Adults are thought to live at least 5 years.

Status and Distribution

In New York State, eastern spadefoots are found in two regions with extensive sandy soils (map 5.1): on Long Island and on the pine barrens near Albany as far north as Saratoga County (Tierney and Stewart

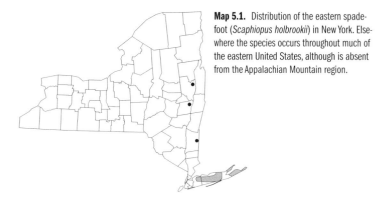

Map 5.1. Distribution of the eastern spadefoot (*Scaphiopus holbrookii*) in New York. Elsewhere the species occurs throughout much of the eastern United States, although is absent from the Appalachian Mountain region.

2001), which represents the known northern limit of the species. In addition, the species has recently been discovered in the Dover Plains area intermediate between Albany and New York City. It is absent elsewhere in New York, in part because the specialized sandy habitats these toads require are uncommon and, where they occur, these habitats are so readily converted to residential developments, the substrates of which (lawns, driveways) impede burrowing (Jansen et al. 2001). The eastern spadefoot is listed as a species of Special Concern in New York State.

Other Intriguing Facts: The Spade of Spadefoots

Eastern spadefoots make efficient use of their digging apparatus, digging holes in a corkscrew fashion. They shuffle their feet to loosen the earth beneath them, turn their bodies, and shuffle again, repeating the process while descending into the ground; the digging is often surprisingly rapid if the toads feel threatened. Farmers cultivating fields and construction workers excavating the ground have found eastern spadefoots up to 6 ft. (2 m) belowground, dormant and curled up inside a cocoon. Eastern spadefoots make this cocoon by secreting a mucouslike fluid around their bodies, which hardens to form a protective, moisture-retaining chamber critical for survival in the dry, sandy soils. Only heavy rains penetrate to the depths eastern spadefoots hibernate and soak and soften their cocoons sufficiently to permit the toads to uncurl and climb back to the surface, ready for their explosive mating season.

American Toad
Bufo americanus [Plate 20]

Quick Identification

A stout, rough-skinned toad, usually reddish brown to light brown in color, with one to two warts per dark spot on back, spots on belly, and parotoid glands that usually do not touch the cranial crests. It is common throughout New York State except on Long Island.

Description

The standard length of the American toad is 2–3.5 in. (5–9 cm), with a maximum length of 4.5 in. (11.1 cm). Females are generally larger than males and develop a reddish-brown color during the breeding season, when they are distinctly more prickly to the touch. Males have a dark throat and have enlarged thumb pads for clasping females during the breeding season. Eggs are laid in long, double-strings (see figure 5.1) comprising 4,000–12,000 eggs total, looped loosely around submerged aquatic plants. Tadpoles are ink-black with flecked, oval bodies and bicolored, rounded tails. The call of the male toads call is a high whir, sustained for 30 seconds or more—a stunningly beautiful call for such a warty creature. You can imitate this call by simultaneously whistling and humming. The American toad is easily confused with another toad, Fowler's toad. To distinguish them, first look at the dark spots on the toad's back. American toads usually have one to two warts per spot, whereas Fowler's toads have three to five warts per spot. Next turn the toad over. American toads have spots on their bellies but Fowler's toads do not. Last, note that the parotoid glands on the shoulders of American toads usually do not touch the cranial crests located behind the eyes but do on Fowler's toads. If you find a toad that does not easily fit either description, keep in mind that American and Fowler's toads occasionally hybridize where their ranges overlap (Green and Parent 2003), producing offspring intermediate in appearance. The scientific name derives from the ancient name *bufo* for toad, as well as the species' widespread distribution in North America.

Habitat

American toads are not particular about habitat (Kolozsvary and Swihart 1999), although they favor more open than forested landscapes (Guerry and Hunter 2002). In New York State, American toads thrive most in regions with more pasture, more deciduous and mixed forest, less evergreen forest, and less urban land (Gibbs et al. 2005). They mainly require shallow waters that last long enough (2–3 months) to rear their tadpoles; ponds, ditches, lakes, marshes, and wet meadows suffice (Babbitt et al. 2003). They occasionally occur in brackish waters of tidal marshes on the Hudson River (Kiviat and Stapleton 1983). American toads are found in suburban backyards, golf courses, gravel pits, fields and meadows, as well as deep forests, even at high elevations, and just about anywhere except urban areas and the marine shore. A survey of alpine amphibians in the Adirondack Mountains found American toads and red efts to be the only amphibian species at elevations greater than 4,500 ft. (1,370 m) (G. Johnson, unpublished data).

Natural History

American toads breed in New York from April to July, with breeding peaking in April and May (see table 5.1). The breeding period in any locale is often brief, from two weeks to only a few days. Males gather to form "choruses," alternating calling and jockeying among themselves for opportunities to clasp females entering ponds. Larger males usually win contests, but in New York, small males may sneak matings by sitting with their cloacas pressed to those of males and females already in amplexus (Kaminsky 1997). Smaller toads also tend to skip calling to swim about within "choruses" of larger, calling toads in an attempt to intercept females (Forester and Thompson 1998). American toads generally avoid pools already occupied by wood frogs to avoid predation on their tadpoles by the larger wood frog tadpoles. Eggs are quite distasteful and hatch quickly, usually in less than a week. Tadpoles form dense schools, appearing like ink clouds in shallow water, that confuse predators and stir up food-rich sediments. Metamorphosis into "toadlets" occurs after 1–2 months.

American toads are mostly active during the early evening hours, feeding on insects and other small invertebrates, as well as slugs and earthworms (Hamilton 1930). They usually remain in moist burrows during the day. When threatened, they may inflate themselves, thereby appearing larger and also reducing a predator's ability to swallow them; however, the hog-nosed snake, a toad-specialist predator, has sharpened rear teeth that puncture inflated toads. Most notably, American toads are covered with warts that secrete, sometimes explosively, a

Map 5.2. Distribution of the American toad (*Bufo americanus*) in New York. Note absence from Long Island. Elsewhere the species occurs over most of the eastern half of the United States, as well as southeastern Canada.

sticky white substance that nauseates many potential predators. The secreting cells are concentrated into large parotoid glands on the nape of the toad's shoulders—the precise location where predators tend to bite down on their prey. These steroid-based toxins are not harmful on human skin (and do not cause warts) but do irritate mucous membranes, so be careful of touching your eyes or lips with your fingers. These secretions do little to protect toads from another form of mortality—infection by fly larvae (Bolek and Coggins 2002). Young toads also can change their ground colors modestly (after 15 minutes or so) and move to substrates with a background color that best matches their body color to become more inconspicuous to potential snake predators (Heinen 1994). In addition, when picked up by humans, American toads often void their bladders of harmless fluid.

Status and Distribution

American toads are nearly ubiquitous in New York State (map 5.2); however, they are notably absent from much of Long Island, the primary domain of Fowler's toads. Populations in central, western and northern New York remained largely stable from 1970 to 2000 (Gibbs et al. 2005).

Other Intriguing Facts: Sibling Recognition

Although we tend to think of toads as unsophisticated creatures, American toad tadpoles possess an uncanny ability to recognize their sisters and brothers. Such sibling recognition is quite an accomplishment, given that a set of siblings might initially number a thousand or more, and several hundred thousand toad tadpoles may carpet the bottom of a typical breeding pond immediately after hatching. Siblings not only recognize each other but prefer to swarm together. Cannibalism is a factor in their survival, and grouping together may ensure that a tadpole's closest neighbors are better intentioned than the average neighbor (Waldman 1985).

Fowler's Toad
Bufo fowleri [Plate 21]

Quick Identification

A stout, rough-skinned toad, greenish or gray in color, with three to four warts on each dark spot on the back; a creamy unspotted belly;

and parotoid glands that usually contact the cranial crests. It is found commonly on Long Island and scattered elsewhere in the southern part of the state (similar species; American toad).

Description

Fowler's toads are somewhat variable in color but most often are gray with greenish tints and have three or four warts within each dark spot on the back. They have no spots on the underside and usually their parotoid glands contact the cranial crests. The standard length of Fowler's toads is 2–3 in. (5–7.5 cm), with a maximum length of 3.75 in. (9.5 cm). Males are smaller than females and have a darkly tinged vocal pouch. (If in doubt about identification, also consult the account for the American toad, with which the Fowler's toad is often confused.) Females lay eggs in double strings some 9 ft. (3 m) in length, comprising up to 8,000 eggs total, draped upon submerged vegetation in shallow water. Tadpoles are difficult to distinguish from those of the American toad and are black with red flecking. The call has been described as "the bleat of a sheep with a cold" or a nasal "w-a-a-h," which lasts about one to two seconds and contrasts distinctly with the melodious trill of the American toad. The scientific name honors Samuel Fowler, a member of the US House of Representatives, 1833–1837.

Habitat

Fowler's toads frequent lowlands, particularly dry, sandy woodlands, rocky and poorly vegetated sites, and river flood plains with sandy soils. Breeding occurs in shallow pools, including marshes, borrow pits, and ditches with semipermanent water. Like American toads, Fowler's toads occur in disturbed habitats and are common in some suburban areas (e.g., many parts of Long Island).

Natural History

Fowler's toads are active for a fairly short period during the warm season, from May to September. Breeding activities tend to be more prolonged (mid-May through July) than in American toads and usually occur several weeks after American toads have completed breeding (see table 5.1). Males form choruses on warm, damp nights and call from land or in shallow water. Females rove through these choruses to choose mates. Eggs hatch quickly, in just 2–5 days, hastened by the warm water temperatures favored by these toads for egg laying.

Frogs and Toads

Tadpoles metamorphose into toadlets in about 35 days. Like other toads, Fowler's toads usually remain hidden by day in burrows or dense vegetation, and they actively hunt at night, particularly at dusk and dawn, for insects, mainly ants and beetles (Bush and Menhinick 1962). Artificially lit areas are favorite hunting areas. After feeding, they seek warm locations to facilitate digestion (Willers and Siegert 2001). In New York, Fowler's toads use depressions and holes created by nest excavations of diamond-backed terrapins for refuges and perhaps hibernation sites (Bossert et al. 2003). They overwinter on Long Island in loose sand at depths up to 6 ft. (1.8 m; Latham 1968c). A variety of vertebrate animals prey upon Fowler's toads, such as herons and ducks, garter and eastern hog-nosed snakes, raccoons and skunks. Fowler's toads defend themselves with toxic skin compounds, mostly secreted from parotoid glands, by inflating themselves, by withdrawing their limbs, or by seeking refuge in burrows underground.

Status and Distribution

In New York State, Fowler's toads can be locally abundant. They occur mostly in southeastern part of the state (map 5.3), with a stronghold on Long Island and the lower Hudson River valley. Populations extend north, with concentrations in the Albany Pine Bush and Saratoga and Warren Counties. There is also a peripheral population on the state's western border with Pennsylvania. Occurrence elsewhere in the state may be misidentifications or released animals.

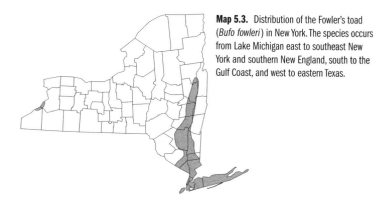

Map 5.3. Distribution of the Fowler's toad (*Bufo fowleri*) in New York. The species occurs from Lake Michigan east to southeast New York and southern New England, south to the Gulf Coast, and west to eastern Texas.

Other Intriguing Facts: Mate Selection

Communication between male and female Fowler's toads during mating is fascinating (Sullivan 1983). Females prefer large males and rely exclusively on the quality of a male's call to discriminate male size. The calls are affected by a male's size in conjunction with his body temperature. Larger males produce calls that are deeper and longer than those of smaller males. Warmer males produce shorter, higher calls than do colder males, thereby presenting females with a perplexing problem: discriminating between a warm, large male and a cold, small male. As it turns out, larger males exclude the smaller males from colder parts of breeding ponds, and thereby make their calls even deeper, slower, and more appealing. The smaller toads are relegated to the pond banks, where they remain much warmer, producing higher, faster calls, and sounding distinctly puny. Smaller toads are not completely eliminated from mating, however, because they are also in the best position to intercept and clasp females entering the pond before the females find the larger males they are seeking (Sullivan 1983).

Northern Cricket Frog
Acris crepitans [Plate 22]

Quick Identification

A tiny frog of the state's lower Hudson River valley with small dorsal warts, a dark, triangular mark between the eyes, brown-to-green base color on back and a light belly.

Description

The northern cricket frog is the smallest frog in New York: its standard length is 0.5–1.5 in. (1.5–3.5 cm). Most of the New York specimens we have measured in the field were less than 1 in.(2.5 cm) at maturity. All have many small warts dorsally, a light belly, and a dark triangle pointing backward between the eyes. Overlaying the brownish to greenish background color, northern cricket frogs exhibit a variety of color patterns. The dorsal pattern can vary from subtle browns or grays to stripes of brilliant reds or greens. The throat of the male is yellow during the breeding season.

The northern cricket frog's decidedly non-froglike call has fooled many casual listeners to think they are hearing a chorus of insects. Although northern cricket frogs have the jumping ability and size of a field cricket, it is the frogs' metallic chirping sound that gives the species its common name. The call starts out as a slow "click, click, click" that is repeated more rapidly for half a minute or so. The sound can be imitated by tapping together two pebbles or by slowly rotating a ratchet wrench, which, with a little practice, can elicit a response from a nearby male. The scientific name derives from *akris*, or locust, referring to the insect-like song, and *crepitans*, or clattering, referring to the repetitious clicking call.

Habitat

Breeding occurs in permanent, open, sunny, shallow ponds with dense vegetation. Although further south in their range, northern cricket frogs are found in a variety of pond habitats, they seem to be habitat specialists in New York State, where they are found in a few, rather distinct wetlands. Generally water lilies are present, as are floating mats of vegetation consisting of mosses and other aquatic plants that give the appearance of sparsely vegetated mud flats in the middle of the ponds. Northern cricket frogs are sometimes found in small, slow-moving streams and in upland areas surrounding their breeding ponds. Elsewhere in their range, northern cricket frogs prefer moist (muddy) substrates near shelter items (especially rocks) and the water (Smith, G.R. et al. 2003).

Natural History

Northern cricket frogs emerge in late March or early April, but unlike spring peepers, whose breeding call is heard soon after they emerge, northern cricket frogs forage quietly for 6–8 weeks. Chorusing finally begins in mid-May and lasts until mid-July, making these little frogs among the last to breed in New York (see table 5.1). Although calling does occur during the day, the strongest choruses are heard on warm, humid nights. Males seem to prefer to call from the base of ferns or other plants rooted on the floating mats, but they also call while floating on the surface of the water or from lily pads. Intense interactions, include wrestling bouts, occur between calling males (Burmeister et al. 2002). In New York, a chorus of 50 males is considered to represent a large population.

A female can produce 200–400 eggs, but the eggs are rarely seen because they are laid singly or in small clusters attached to vegetation below the surface. The tadpoles, which emerge from the eggs within a few days, are generally bottom feeders. If you are fortunate enough to find one, the tadpole can be identified by the black tip on its tail. As the tadpoles approach metamorphosis near the end of their first summer, they are more readily found swimming on the surface near the shore. The new metamorphs transform when they are just barely 0.5 in. (12 mm) long. It is believed that some individuals reach sexual maturity by the year following metamorphosis and that most only survive for one or maybe two breeding seasons in the wild. With this type of life history, it is not surprising that small populations "wink out" following a poor recruitment year. Adult northern cricket frogs eat mostly terrestrial arthropods (Labanick 1976).

In southern states, cricket frogs are reported to overwinter in mud flats surrounding ponds, whereas in Indiana and Ohio, they hibernate in crayfish burrows and cracks of pond banks, where the wet soil buffers against freezing of the soil (Irwin et al. 1999). We have observed northern cricket frogs moving away from the ponds in September and October and toward the ponds in the spring. Presumably the frogs are going to or returning from their overwintering retreat sites, which may be 330 ft. (100 m) or more from the pond.

Status and Distribution

Historically, northern cricket frogs were found on Long Island, Staten Island, and in the lower Hudson River valley. By 1930, Long Island populations had disappeared, although occasionally a local naturalist reports having heard a chirp of a northern cricket frog but was not able to locate one. Northern cricket frogs have not been reported from Staten Island since the 1970s. Today, only a handful of populations remain (map 5.4), most of them on private land, in Orange, Ulster, and

Map 5.4. Distribution of the northern cricket frog (*Acris crepitans*) in New York. Elsewhere the species occurs from southern New York to the Florida panhandle west to Texas and southeastern New Mexico, and north to South Dakota, Wisconsin, and Michigan.

Dutchess Counties. These populations are at the northern limit of this subspecies' range. Recent studies suggest the species may be particularly vulnerable to pesticides (Knutson et al. 2004). The northern cricket frog was listed as a Threatened species in 1983 and was elevated to Endangered in 1999. The type locality of the northern cricket frog is in Nassau County, where it was first discovered by James DeKay and later described in his *Zoology of New York* in 1842.

Other Intriguing Facts: Cricket Frog Locomotion

Although the northern cricket frog is in the tree frog family (Hylidae), this species is not much of a climber. The northern cricket frog has small toe pads compared to the gray tree frog and spring peeper, and rarely is found more than a few inches above the surface. It is, however, a fantastic jumper, leaping as high as 3 ft. (1 m). It can also jump as far as 4 ft. (1.2 m) — some 50 times its body length — fleeing from danger with repeated jumps across the surface of the water. The extensive webbing between the toes of its hind feet also makes it an excellent swimmer (Blem et al. 1978).

Gray Tree Frog
Hyla versicolor [Plate 23]

Quick Identification

Stout, tree-dwelling frogs with rough skin and dark blotches on the back over base color of gray in adults to light green in juveniles, a light spot with a dark edge beneath each eye, a yellowish tinge to the groin, and toes with large, adhesive discs.

Description

These stout, tree-dwelling frogs are frequently heard but not often seen. The standard length is 1.5–2 in. (3–5 cm), with a maximum length of 2.5 in. (6 cm). Adults have rough skin with dark blotches on the back and a base color that can range from gray to light green, whereas immatures are lime-green. Toes are tipped with large, adhesive, mucous-secreting discs that facilitate clinging to tree bark and are only partially webbed. A light spot with a dark edge occurs beneath each eye. The undersides are white and granular — a texture that may assist adhering to vertical bark. Females have light-colored throats, whereas males have dark gray or black throats and an orange tinge to the backs of their thighs and groin. Eggs are bi-colored (gray above and white beneath), laid singly or in clusters of 10–40 attached to submerged vegetation. Tadpoles are green or black and have tails with high, orange or scarlet, darkly blotched fins. Because gray tree frogs are cryptic, arboreal, and generally difficult to find, their voice is the most frequent indicator of their presence; a hearty trilling issues from trees—usually, but not always, near wetland breeding areas. The scientific name derives from *Hylas*, the lost companion of Heracles, who called Hylas' name repeatedly but in vain, and *versi*, or variable, referring to the frogs' ability to change color.

Habitat

Gray tree frogs frequent moist, deciduous woodlands, especially those with swamps and shrubby wetlands, but they also occur in sandy, pine barrens habitats. Breeding occurs mostly in semipermanent wetlands, usually beaver ponds and red maple swamps but sometimes standing water in pasture ponds and even swimming pools. Preferred breeding areas have dense emergent and scrub or shrub vegetation bordered by forest, although the tree frog is clearly a habitat generalist (Kolozsvary and Swihart 1999).

Natural History

Gray tree frogs appear after early spring rains and are active well into the autumn months. Breeding can be prolonged and extend up to 2 months, usually between mid-May and late July, later than many other frogs in New York (see table 5.1). Males, perched in vegetation surrounding ponds and swamps, defend calling spots vigorously. Females navigate around wetlands and assess potential mates by the quality of the male's calls. Males call between 500–15,000 times per hour—an extremely energetically costly activity for such a small, ectothermic animal. Consequently, males steadily lose weight during the breeding season and often skip the chorus every few nights to feed and resuscitate themselves. Adult gray tree frogs also travel up to 660 ft. (200 m) within a breeding season to multiple breeding ponds (Johnson and Semlitsch 2003). Females climb to and nudge the male of their choosing, and then they depart in tandem to enter a wetland and lay eggs over a 4–5-hour period. Sneaky males often lurk near calling males, trying to intercept incoming females or to usurp a calling site when it is vacated by a male for mating. Each female lays about 2,000 eggs in batches of 50 or so (Wright and Wright 1949). Hatching occurs in 2–5 days. Exposure to predators induces larvae to develop relatively deep tail fins and short bodies for quicker escapes (Relyea and Hoverman 2003). Surviving tadpoles metamorphose after 1–2 months, usually in July or August. Adults are mostly nocturnal, foraging in trees on gnats and flies; aphids; caterpillars; spiders; mites; termites; and beetles and other invertebrates, particularly those associated with moist cavities, bark, and weeping wounds of trees (Ralin 1968). Individuals can change color and flatten themselves against tree bark to minimize the casting of shadow, thus mimicking lichen-covered tree bark, the primary haunt of the frogs, their prey, and their predators. New York–based studies indicate that gray tree frogs emit a "bark" that startles predators and also possess noxious skin secretions (Brodie and Formanowicz 1981); this noxiousness is perhaps advertised by the yellow or orange patches in the groin region characteristic of this species. Gray tree frogs survive New York winters using a cryoprotectant, glycerol, produced in response to freezing of their peripheral tissues, such as toes (Layne and Jones 2001).

Status and Distribution

Gray tree frogs are widespread in New York (map 5.5), although they are conspicuously absent from the western Catskills region (for unknown reasons). Vulnerability to both wetland loss and forest loss make this species rare in some parts of the state. Gibbs et al. (2005) reported that populations were stable to increasing in central, western, and northern New York State between 1970 and 2000.

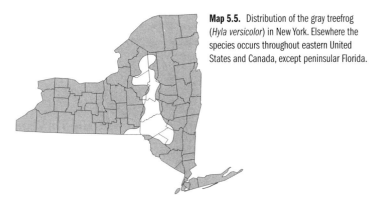

Map 5.5. Distribution of the gray treefrog (*Hyla versicolor*) in New York. Elsewhere the species occurs throughout eastern United States and Canada, except peninsular Florida.

Other Intriguing Facts: Sorting Out the Tree frogs

A related species, Cope's gray tree frog (*Hyla chrysoscelis*) is virtually identical in appearance and also occurs to an unknown extent in New York State. The gray tree frog and the Cope's gray tree frog, long thought to be the same species, are now known to be distinguishable in the field by their calls (the calls of the Cope's gray tree frog are somewhat faster) or in the laboratory by their chromosome number (with the tetraploid *H. versicolor* having twice as many chromosomes [48], as the diploid *H. chrysoscelis* [24]). But no systematic surveys of the two species have been conducted in New York State, and most records of gray tree frogs are assumed to be *H. versicolor*.

Western Chorus Frog
Pseudacris triseriata [Plate 24]

Quick Identification

A small, brown frog with three dark brown stripes down its back, usually encountered in wet fields early in spring issuing a call like a fingernail dragged along the teeth of a plastic comb.

Description

These small, brown, secretive frogs have three dark brown stripes down the back that are often broken or discontinuous. The standard length is 0.5–1.5 in. (2.0–4.0 cm). A dark facial mask and white line on the upper lip also characterize the species. The belly is white. Toe discs are poorly developed and the hind feet are webbed only at the base of the toes. Males have tan-colored, mottled vocal sacs during the breeding season and are slightly smaller than females, which have white throats. These frogs are sometimes confused with spring peepers, which have an imperfect X-shaped pattern on their back, or northern cricket frogs, which have many warts, highly webbed feet, and alternating light and dark bars on the upper jaw. Eggs occur in a cylindrical mass of 25–75 attached to submerged vegetation. Tadpoles are plump and dark brown to mouse gray, bronze-colored underside, with clear tail fins with dark flecks. Western chorus frogs are more often heard than seen in early spring near ditches and ponds associated with agricultural areas, issuing an upwardly rising call that sounds like a fingernail dragged along the teeth of a plastic comb.

The scientific name derives from *tri*, or three, and *seriata*, or lines, referring to dark lines on dorsum.

Habitat

Western chorus frogs are secretive frogs of grasslands, meadows, and forest edges, usually found in damp meadows and shallow pools with low shrubs and grasses (Kolozsvary and Swihart 1999). For breeding, they strongly prefer temporary wetlands (Skelly 1996), including pools, flooded fields, and ditches. Populations thrive in regions of New York State with less acid soils and in areas with more pasture, less cultivated grasses, and less forest of all types (Gibbs et al. 2005).

Natural History

Not often observed, western chorus frogs spend much of the warm season underground or lurking in dense grass. They emerge from hibernation in crayfish holes and other underground shelters in very early spring, usually in New York State in mid-March, only slightly after wood frogs and spring peepers have emerged. At this time, breeding ponds may still be partially iced over (this species is freeze-tolerant; Swanson et al. 1996). Early arrival at breeding ponds is facilitated by hibernating nearby such ponds. Breeding tends to be highly synchronized and concentrated on just three to five nights in any given year (Whitaker 1971). It may persist until June (see table 5.1), with males calling mostly at night from emergent and woody vegetation near or in breeding pools. Females lay about 500–1,500 eggs in many small egg masses (Wright and Wright 1949). Eggs hatch in 5–10 days. Larvae increase tail fin and tail muscle size in the presence of dragonfly (*Aeshna*) predators (Smith and Van Buskirk 1995). Tadpoles transform to froglets 2–3 months later. Foods include beetles and their larvae, spiders, ants, caterpillars, and amphipods (Whitaker 1971). These frogs are difficult to observe and study because of their small size, camouflage, and tendency to jump into water at the slightest provocation. Furthermore, their calling is often obscured by more abundant and vocal spring peepers breeding in the same habitats.

Status and Distribution

In New York State, western chorus frogs occur in low-lying parts of western regions, along the eastern shore of Lake Ontario, and along the St. Lawrence River plains lowlands and south to Lake Champlain (map 5.6). These localities represent part of the northeastern extent of the species' range. Recent genetic analysis by Moriarty and Cannatella (2004) suggests that the geographically distinct populations of chorus frogs in western and northern New York may in fact represent different species. During 1970–2000, populations declined in northern New York State (Gibbs et al. 2005), as well as elsewhere throughout the Great Lakes region (Weeber and Vallianatos 2000) because of wetland loss, forest expansion, and other unknown factors. Western chorus frogs are sensitive to nitrate pollution from agricultural fertilizer (Hecnar 1995) and droughts (Shepard and Kuhns 2000). In addition, they are susceptible to infection by introduced aquatic "chytrid" fungi (Rittmann et al. 2003), a factor identified in amphibian declines elsewhere.

Other Intriguing Facts: Awkward Transition

Western chorus frogs provide a good example of the perils of being an amphibian, that is, undergoing the transition between two distinct life forms: aquatic and terrestrial. The transition itself is quite hazardous. At some point during the conversion of a tadpole that propels itself through water by means of a tail to a frog that moves through air by jumping, western chorus frogs reach a point where they are poorly adapted to either aquatic or terrestrial life. Tadpoles with budding limbs are poor swimmers, and froglets with tails still attached are poor hoppers. It's no wonder that predators such as common gartersnakes focus on these easy-to-pick-off intermediate forms and why natural selection has ensured that this risky transition phase is brief (Smith, D.C. 1987).

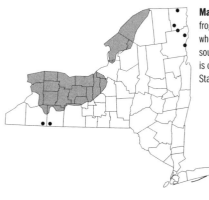

Map 5.6. Distribution of the western chorus frog (*Pseudacris triseriata*) in New York. Elsewhere the species occurs in northern Vermont, southern Quebec, and southern Ontario, and it is otherwise widespread in the central United States.

Spring Peeper
Pseudacris crucifer [Plate 25]

Quick Identification

A small, dark-skinned frog with an imperfect "X" on its back frequently he and emitting "peep" calls in spring throughout New York State.

Description

Spring peepers are quite small, often heard, and seldom seen. The standard length of 0.5–1.5 in. (2–3 cm), with a maximum length of 1.5 in. (3.7 cm). The skin is smooth and tends toward brown but can verge on gray or green. The most distinctive feature is an imperfect "X" on the back, a feature that lends the species its Latin species name of *crucifer* or "one who bears a cross." A dark patch surrounds the eye and the underside is cream-colored. The waist is narrow and limbs slender and delicate. The toes are appended by small round disks and joined with extensive webbing on the hind feet. The females are typically larger than the males, who have much darker throats. The eggs are brown above and cream colored beneath, nearly microscopic, and attached individually to submerged plants. The tadpoles are distinctive, although tiny, with relatively foreshortened bodies, tan-colored above and bronze beneath, and high, speckled dorsal fins. Spring peepers are an aptly named harbinger of spring emerging during the first rains of the year and emitting a distinctive loud, rising, and high-pitched "peep." Long considered a member of the tree frog genus (*Hyla*), they are genetically more closely related to the chorus frogs (Hedges 1986), hence the recent switch of their genus name to *Pseudacris*.

Habitat

Spring peepers are habitat generalists, occurring in wooded areas, meadows, sandy coastal and pine barren habitats, and lawns. They are fairly tolerant of human disturbance and manage to persist in many suburban areas (Gibbs 1998b, Zampella and Bunnell 2000). For breeding, spring peepers use almost any semipermanent pool with an abundance of light (Babbitt et al. 2003, Halverson et al. 2003). All that is required is standing vegetation, which gives the males a place to call from, and submergent vegetation, which harbors the tadpoles. Such areas include marshes, ponds, alder-filled ditches, swamps, and gravel pits. In New York State, populations thrive at higher elevations, on less acid soils, and in areas with less row cropping, less developed land, less cultivated grasses, less evergreen forest, more mixed forest, less open water, and less marsh (Gibbs et al. 2005).

Natural History

Spring peepers are active from March through October. Their breeding season extends from March through May and is fairly prolonged (see table 5.1). Breeding activity at any given pond lasts about a month, although it often peaks in just over a 2-week period. Males defend small territories of patches of raised vegetation, from which they produce their familiar mate advertisement call, usually 15–25 times per minute. Often males call in tandem while carefully synchronizing calls to prevent overlap (Rosen and Lemon 1974). Trespassing males trigger the less familiar aggressive trilling, which attentive human listeners of spring peeper choruses can often hear beneath the din of the "peeping." Females navigate the choruses and choose males based on call volume and rapidity, nudging a chosen male and departing the calling site with him in tandem to search out egg deposition sites. Noncalling, "satellite" males often lurk in choruses, attempting to intercept females (Lykens and Forester 1987). Fertilization can be time-consuming, because each amplected female may extrude up to 900 eggs over several hours. During this time satellite males may move into preferred calling sites. Eggs are nearly microscopic and not easily found, even in densely occupied breeding ponds. Eggs hatch within a week, and metamorphosis follows 2–3 months later, with froglets retaining their tails on land for several days after emerging. Three distinct size classes are often evident in populations: new metamorphs and 1-year-olds, first-time breeders (2-year-olds), and older breeders (3- and 4-year-olds, Lykens and Forester 1987).

Primarily nocturnal, spring peepers are most active rainy or humid nights and overcast, damp, and cool days in early autumn, when they feed upon a wide variety of small invertebrates. After breeding, spring peepers retreat to the uplands and defend small foraging territories that encompass moist beds of mosses, stumps, debris, or logs. They can also be found in leaf litter. Other animals, including ribbon snakes and northern watersnakes, and other, larger frogs, consume

Frogs and Toads

spring peepers. Wood frogs, green frogs, and bullfrogs occasionally stalk and eat calling peepers. The spring peeper's small size, cryptic ground coloration, and ability to quickly shift skin color permit them to remain undetected despite being locally abundant outside the breeding season.

Status and Distribution

Spring peepers are found throughout New York State (map 5.7). Surveys in central, western, and northern New York State indicate a stable to increasing population between 1970 and 2000 (Gibbs et al. 2005). Notably, organochlorine pesticides (dichlorodiphenyltrichloroethane [DDT], dichlorodiphenyldichloroethylene [DDE], dichlorodiphenyldichloroethane [DDD], and dieldrin) have shown significant tissue accumulations in spring peepers in Ontario even 26 years postapplication (Russell et al. 1995).

Other Intriguing Facts: Frozen Peepers

Consider the plight of the spring pepper as winter approaches. These frogs weigh just a few grams and have no internal means to regulate their body temperatures. Spring peepers hibernate in shallow soil often overlain with snow. When they freeze, their bodies become stiff and white, their eyes become opaque, and their breathing and heart beating stop. Formation of ice crystals within their bodies could cause tremendous damage to internal organs, just as frost heave destroys asphalt. But spring peepers survive the long months of freezing temperatures by producing their own antifreeze. Glycogen in their livers is converted to large amounts of

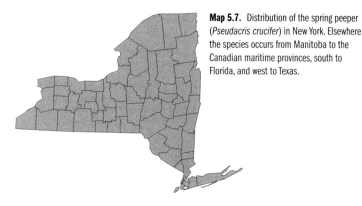

Map 5.7. Distribution of the spring peeper (*Pseudacris crucifer*) in New York. Elsewhere the species occurs from Manitoba to the Canadian maritime provinces, south to Florida, and west to Texas.

glucose that is dispersed to cells throughout the spring peeper's body. The glucose lowers the freezing point of the frog, slows the formation of ice crystals, and helps maintain water balance inside the frog. The whole process is triggered by the freezing of the toe tips and may occur in just minutes. This remarkable physiological ability to survive freezing temperatures persists well into the spring breeding season (to help guard these creatures against occasional freezing bouts) but then shuts down for the summer (Layne and Kefauver 1997).

Bullfrog
Rana catesbeiana [Plate 26]

Quick Identification

A large frog with a dull green, mottled exterior and a small skin fold curving from the eye downward around the rear of the tympanum (not along the side of the body as in other similar frogs), often heard calling "jug o' rum" on warm summer nights.

Description

The largest frogs in New York State, bullfrogs are green with varying amounts of darker mottling dorsally and have a small skin fold that curves from the eye around the rear of the eardrum. Standard length of bullfrogs is 3.5–6 in. (9–15.0 cm), with a maximum length of 8 in. (20.3 cm). Conspicuously absent are the long skin folds along the sides of the back (present in all other New York frogs of the genus *Rana*). In females, the tympanum is about the size of the eye and the throat is white, whereas in males, the tympanum is considerably larger than the eye and the throat may be suffused with yellow during the breeding season. The eggs are black and white, with some 12,000–20,000 per clutch, laid in mat-like surface films up to 2 ft. (0.6 m) in diameter (Ryan 1980). The tadpoles can attain large sizes (to 5.7 in. [14.5 cm]), and they are bullet-shaped and olive-green in color, with head, body, and tail with diffuse spots, bellies light-colored with a bronze-iridescence on the venter, and tails quite muscular. The bullfrog's resonant call on warm summer nights of "jug o' rum" has a somewhat bull-like quality that gives the frog its common name. The scientific name honors early naturalist Mark Catesby.

Habitat

Bullfrogs frequent the banks, edges, and shallows of warmer, permanent waters (Babbitt et al. 2003) such as ponds, lakes, marshes, swamps, and slow-moving stretches of streams and rivers. Within these habitats, patches of emergent, floating, or submerged vegetation are preferred, providing cover for both adults and larvae. The species is quite compatible with suburban and agricultural landscapes (Zampella and Bunnell 2000).

Natural History

Bullfrogs overwinter under water in warm, shallow areas and remain active throughout the winter, often remaining exposed on the pond bottom (Stinner et al. 1994). Bullfrogs are usually encountered in New York State from late April through October, breeding later than most frogs, only after water temperatures have warmed fully to summer levels, mostly in June and July (see table 5.1). Males remain silent for up to a month prior to initiating calling (once water temperatures have warmed sufficiently; Oseen and Wassersug 2002) and exhibit aggressive defense of fixed territories rich in aquatic plants. Notably, male bullfrogs vocalize while partially submerged, which permits sound to propagate through both air and underwater (Boatright-Horowitz et al. 1999). Curiously, the much larger eardrums of males may facilitate sound production rather than sound reception, as is usually assumed (Purgue 1997). Intense contests occur between males for territories with good egg deposition spots; this is the basis upon which females choose males (Howard 1978). Hatching of eggs generally occurs in 4–20 days. A notable feature of bullfrog metamorphosis is that it can occur between 4 months to 3 or more years after hatching. Thus, any large tadpoles encountered during winter on pond bottoms or under the ice in New York State are likely bullfrogs (although greenfrogs are another possibility). Sexual maturity is reached in 4–5 years (Shirose et al. 1993), with maximum ages of adults likely 10 years.

Bullfrogs are voracious sit-and-wait predators on insects, crayfish, minnows, and other frogs, including bullfrogs. Larger adults may even take rodents, hatchling turtles, ducklings, and snakes. Tadpoles are mostly vegetarian, snipping the tips off aquatic plants and rasping submerged surfaces, but they do scavenge dead fish. Many vertebrate animals, including humans, heavily prey upon bullfrogs, which are the primary source of "frog legs" in New York State. Bullfrogs' only means of defense are their powerful back legs, which permits them to quickly jump away from a predator's reach.

Status and Distribution

Widespread and abundant throughout New York State (map 5.8), bullfrogs readily occupy created wetlands (Adams 2000), although residential development and clearing of shoreline vegetation have reduced habitat in some areas. Bullfrogs are considered "small game" in New York and can be collected with a license. Bullfrogs have evidently declined in Ontario (Berrill et al. 1992), possibly due to increased predator populations, loss of wetland habitats, overharvesting, poaching, acidic deposition, and contaminants. This species is disproportionately sensitive to the insecticides fenitrothion and the herbicides triclopyr and hexazinone, which are used in forest management in eastern North America (Berrill et al. 1994). Bullfrogs are unlikely in waters acidified to pH less than 4.0 (Grant and Licht 1993).

Other Intriguing Facts: Voracious Predator

Owing to their voracious food habits, bullfrogs can have a powerful influence on the number and type of other frogs present in a wetland. The impact on green frogs is particularly pronounced; after a local bullfrog extinction at Point Pelee, Ontario, green frog populations quadrupled (Hecnar and M'Closkey 1997). Not only do bullfrogs eat large numbers of green frogs and their tadpoles, bullfrog tadpoles also are better competitors for the foods that green frog tadpoles need. These voracious habits make bullfrogs a major pest where introduced outside their normal range, notably on the west coast region of the

Map 5.8. Distribution of the bullfrog (*Rana catesbeiana*) in New York. Elsewhere the species is native to the central and eastern United States and the southern portions of Ontario and Quebec but has been introduced to many areas in the western United States and elsewhere around the globe.

United States, Europe, and even parts of Asia and South America. In these regions, escapees from bullfrog farms have devastated native frog populations (Flores-Nava 2000, Banks et al. 2000).

Green Frog
Rana clamitans [Plate 27]

Quick Identification

A long-legged, highly aquatic frog, usually green or bronze, with a skin fold that extends from the eye two-thirds of the way down the sides, and spots on folded legs that "fit nicely" into stripes (similar species; bullfrog throughout New York and mink frog in northern New York).

Description

Green frogs are large frogs with long hind legs for jumping and swimming. The standard length is 2.5–3.5 in (5.5–9 cm), with a maximum length of 4.25 in. (10.8 cm). Coloration of green frogs is variable, but usually green, brown, bronze, or rarely blue, often with dark mottling that may be extensive. The dark spots on the rear legs form stripes when the legs are folded. Green frogs have a skin fold that is often golden and that extends from the eye two-thirds of the way down along each side of the back. The underbelly is white, overlain by a dark pattern of lines and spots. Toe webbing extends to the second joint of the fourth toe but does not reach the fifth toe. Male green frogs have yellow throats during the breeding season, and tympanic membranes are usually larger than the eye. Green frog eggs are black and white and deposited in a jelly mass of 1,500–5,000 eggs attached to vegetation, but partly floating upon the water's surface. Green frog tadpoles are elongate (reaching more than 6 cm, 2.5 in), olive-green, with tails covered in irregular dark spots and an acute tip. Calls of green frogs sound like the plucking a loose banjo string; they are often heard as single notes but are sometimes issued in a series of two or three notes of diminishing intensity. The frog emits a loud squeak as it leaps from danger; thus its name *clamitans*: the frog that exclaims or cries loudly.

Identification may be difficult. Green frogs can closely resemble young bullfrogs but are distinguished by the skin fold that extends from the eye down the back. Green frogs also can be confused with mink frogs, but spots on folded legs of green frogs align to form stripes. Moreover, the webbing on the hind feet of mink frogs extends to the tip of the fifth toe and to the last joint of the fourth toe but on the green frog does not reach tip of fifth toe and barely extends to the second joint of the fourth toe. Northern leopard frogs may be a further source of confusion, but the skin folds along the back extend only about two-thirds down in green frogs, often becoming interrupted before they terminate, versus extending all the way to the groin in northern leopard frogs.

Habitat

Green frogs are denizens of permanent waters, which include ponds, marshes, lake fringes, and sometimes streamsides (Babbitt et al. 2003). In Quebec, shrubby areas have been identified as critical to the green frog (Courtois et al. 1995). At the landscape scale, ponds associated with forest are more likely to be used by green frogs than those associated with agriculture (Guerry and Hunter 2002). Adults generally reside in deeper waters by day, moving to shorelines to feed at night, whereas subadults remain on shorelines night and day. Adults may occupy temporary pools on uplands, and intermittent streams used as movement corridors but require permanent water for breeding, where tadpoles can overwinter under silt and dead vegetation. They usually do not wander far from some water source.

Natural History

Green frogs are active from March through November, with an extended calling period, from May to August (see table 5.1); females can lay two egg masses in one season (Wells 1976). Calling activity is closely associated with water temperature (Oseen and Wassersug 2002). Males defend small, often densely vegetated territories along the water's edge. Choice of mates by females is largely a matter of the quality of egg-laying sites within the male's territory, which, in New York State, is a combination of shallow water, dense emergent vegetation, and heavy submergent vegetation (Wells 1977). Receptive females back toward males to initiate amplexus, and both then engage in egg deposition and fertilization, during which time the male's territory may be usurped by another male. Eggs hatch in 3–5 days. Females who lay eggs prior to July 21 in New York are able to produce a second clutch in the same year (Wells 1976). Tadpoles eat mainly algae, especially diatoms, but also take small crustaceans and fungi. Tadpoles metamorphose in 3 months to 2 years, depending on envi-

Frogs and Toads

ronmental temperature and food supply, and thus regularly overwinter as tadpoles. Predators include wood turtles (Ernst 2001), herons, turtles, snakes, raccoons, fish, and particularly bullfrogs (Courtois et al. 1995, Hecnar and M'Closkey 1997), from which green frogs escape by jumping swiftly into the water and submerging themselves for extended periods. Adults feed by choosing a foraging perch and intercepting passing prey, although they sometimes stalk out-of-reach prey. Foods are mainly flies, terrestrial beetles, grasshoppers, and caterpillars, depending on what is locally and seasonally available. In New York State, larger adults focus on other frogs (especially other green frogs), their own shed skin, spiders, crayfish, and fish (Hamilton 1948).

Green frogs are thought to live to 5 years. They may overwinter in the muck at the bottom of wetland breeding sites; however, in New York, they apparently more often leave breeding ponds and travel long distances (up to 900 ft. [300 m]) to overwinter in streams on hillsides or other areas with cold, running, well-oxygenated waters (Lamoureux and Madison 1999). Before moving to overwintering sites, green frogs make repetitive forays to areas near pond edges where food is more abundant in order to replenish fat reserves exhausted during breeding and thereby prepare for overwintering (Lamoureux et al. 2002).

Status and Distribution

Green frogs are widespread in New York State and are among its most common frogs (map 5.9). Although they can thrive in human-dominated areas, lakeshore development that does not protect the

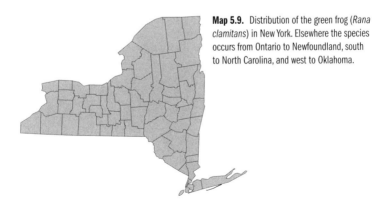

Map 5.9. Distribution of the green frog (*Rana clamitans*) in New York. Elsewhere the species occurs from Ontario to Newfoundland, south to North Carolina, and west to Oklahoma.

quality of breeding habitats can result in lower abundance of adult green frogs (Woodford and Meyer 2003).

Other Intriguing Facts: A Tadpole's Life

The daily life of the green frog tadpole is a complicated one, mostly spent lurking quite inactive on the wetland bottom, slowly but continuously rasping the surfaces of submerged vegetation. Why remain so inactive? Particularly while it is small, a tadpole's activity is strongly influenced by a deadly predator—dragonfly larvae, which rapidly dismember and consume any tadpoles they can seize. The effect of dragonflies is so great that they do not need to kill to alter the lives of small green frog tadpoles. Laboratory experiments with caged dragonfly larvae and green frog tadpoles housed in the same dish indicate that the tadpoles remain so inactive and eat so little that they fail to grow, even though the dragonfly larvae are physically restrained. Chemical cues in the water likely alert the tadpoles to the presence of the predator and cause them to freeze. Curiously, adult green frogs are an important predator on adult dragonflies—an ironic reversal of roles between predator and prey (Peacor and Werner 2000).

Pickerel Frog
Rana palustris [Plate 28]

Quick Identification

A spotted frog with rectangular spots on a tan-colored back and orange or yellow inside the hind legs and groin, similar species: northern leopard frog, southern leopard frog).

Description

Pickerel frogs are far more common in New York State than many appreciate—they are frequently mistakenly identified as leopard frogs. To identify a pickerel frog, note the rectangular spots on their tan-colored back (occasionally the spots blend to form more elongate rectangles), which distinguishes it from the northern leopard frog with its more circular spots. If you have a frog in hand or can peer beneath it when it hops or swims, also note that a distinguishing feature of pickerel frogs is yellow or orange tinge inside the hind legs and groin. A subtle feature is a light stripe extending along the jaw. The standard length is 2.0–3 in. (4.5–7.5 cm), with a maximum length of 3.5 in. (8.7 cm), which is somewhat smaller than that of the northern leopard frog. The eggs are brown and yellow, laid in firm, almost spherical jelly masses of 2,000–3,000 eggs each. Tadpoles (up to 3 in. [7.5 cm]) have dark green backs covered with small yellow and black spots and a dark tail usually twice the length of the body. The adult's call is a steady, low-pitched croak when issued above water or a rolling snore when issued below water, often likened to a rusty hinge of a door opened slowly. Recent work suggests that males have at least three different calls, one advertising to females, and two others used in male-male interactions (Given 2005). The common name may stem from its popularity as bait for fishing for pickerel or, alternately, because its coloration is reminiscent of the flanks of pickerel. The scientific name derives from *palustris*, or "of the marsh."

Habitat

Pickerel frogs live in slow, shallow moving waters with dense vegetation, such as swamps, meadows, streams, bogs, and fens. After breeding, they become quite terrestrial for the remainder of the warm season, moving into fields, meadows, and damp woods.

Natural History

Pickerel frogs have a long period of seasonal activity, which extends from April to October, with breeding occurring usually in April and May (see table 5.1). Males aggregate in small areas of still waters and call sporadically both from elevated mounds of vegetation or from in the water among submerged vegetation for 4–6 weeks (Paton and Crouch, 2002). Because mating females are extremely skittish, little is known of their mating biology. Eggs tend to be laid in areas not heavily occupied by fish, often in high densities (Wright and Wright 1949). Hatching occurs in 11–21 days. Tadpoles grow for 2–3 months, metamorphosing in July or August when body lengths have reached 1 in. (2.5 cm). Pickerel frogs are nonspecialists and eat a variety of terrestrial invertebrates, mainly insects; including beetles, caterpillars, true bugs, and ants; as well as spiders; harvestmen; sow bugs; and mites; and aquatic animals; including snails, crayfish, amphipods, and isopods. Pickerel frogs are often the last frogs to enter hibernation before winter, and they can be seen swimming beneath the ice. The frogs overwinter in the muck on pond bottoms.

Map 5.10. Distribution of the pickerel frog (*Rana palustris*) in New York. Elsewhere the species occurs throughout most of the eastern United States except in the extreme southeast.

Status and Distribution

The pickerel frog is widespread in New York State (map 5.10). It can tolerate acidic waters to about pH 4 (Dale et al. 1985).

Other Intriguing Facts: Distasteful Frogs

Most vertebrate animals tend to avoid preying on pickerel frogs because these frogs produce a distasteful skin secretion, purportedly of sufficient strength to kill other frog species placed in the same container. However, green frogs and bullfrogs appear to be unaffected by pickerel frog toxins. Common gartersnakes, a major frog predator that regularly scout pond edges for frogs, do apparently find pickerel frogs unpalatable, as do shrews and some fishes (Formanowicz and Brodie 1982, Holomuzki 1995). The orange groin coloration is thought to advertise this toxicity to predators. Moreover, like mink frogs, pickerel frogs produce a distinctive odor, described as "like that of alfalfa sprouts or the inside of a latex glove" (Grant 2001), which may be an olfactory warning to potential predators.

Northern Leopard Frog
Rana pipiens [Plate 29]

Quick Identification

A common frog of grassland areas with an elongate body, a slightly pointed snout, and brown, gray, or green background color overlain by two or three rows of "roundish," dark spots with light borders (similar species: pickerel frog, southern leopard frog).

Description

Northern leopard frogs are perhaps the most common frogs of grassland areas in New York State. Look closely at the large spots: northern leopard frogs have two or three rows of roundish, dark spots with light borders that lie between the dorsolateral folds that extend from the eye to the pelvic region. The background color can be green, tan, or gray and the underside is pure white. The standard length is 2–3.5 in (5–9 cm), with a maximum length of 4.5 in (11.1 cm). Northern leopard frogs are frequently confused with the pickerel frogs, which have a less streamlined body, shorter legs, irregularly square spots arranged in distinct rows, and a yellow tinge to the groin. Female and male northern leopard frogs can be difficult to distinguish, except during the breeding season, when males have swollen front thumbs and females, engorged with eggs, may appear fatter. Females lay their eggs in flattened oval-shaped clusters of 2,000–4,000 eggs attached to submerged vegetation. Tadpoles are large (up to 3.3 in. [8.4 cm]), dark brown with fine gold spots and a tail that is lighter in color than the body. The coiled gut of the tadpole can be readily observed through the translucent belly skin. When disturbed, adult northern leopard frogs leap across the ground in a characteristic zigzag pattern to the safety of water or to a place where they remain motionless in vegetation. The mating call of males is a low, guttural snore, lasting about 3 seconds, followed by several nasal clucks. The scientific name derives from *pipiens*, or peeping, likely because the original collector heard spring peepers while collecting the first northern leopard frog and wrongly concluded that the peeping sound came from the northern leopard frog.

Habitat

Northern leopard frogs use a variety of habitats throughout New York State, but are most common in grassy habitats near marshes and ponds, along the borders of lakes, and along slowly moving streams in less forest regions (Guerry and Hunter 2002). They breed in temporary and permanent bodies of water, including ponds, marshes, lakes, and streams. Populations thrive in parts of the state at lower elevations and in areas with less acid soils, access to open water, more marsh, less swamp, and some pasture (Gibbs et al. 2005).

Natural History

Northern leopard frogs are active in New York State from about March through October, with breeding activities peaking in April through May (see table 5.1). Males aggregate at egg laying sites (shallow and exposed waters with extensive submergent vegetation), and females then choose among males based on male call quality (Merrell 1977). Eggs (some 1,000–5,000 eggs per mass) are often laid in communal nesting sites in shallow water (generally less than 65 cm). Hatching occurs in 10–20 days and metamorphosis some 60–80 days after hatching. Breeding can occur 1 year after hatching for some males, although 2 years is more typical. Because northern leopard frogs cannot withstand freezing, they overwinter in the muck of lake and pond bottoms. In Vermont, large numbers have been recorded hibernating under water with northern map turtles (Ultsch et al. 2000). Northern leopard frogs take a variety of prey; Linzey's (1967) study of the stomachs of 463 frogs near Ithaca, New York reported a preponderance of insect larvae and vegetable matter; large numbers of beetles; and smaller amounts of grasshoppers, crickets, worms, bugs, leafhoppers, and spiders. Tadpoles glean algae and detritus off submerged surfaces. Many vertebrates prey on northern leopard frogs, particularly gartersnakes, pike, pickerel, and bass, and bullfrogs.

Status and Distribution

Northern leopard frogs are still widespread in lower elevations of the New York (map 5.11), although their distribution is scattered in the Catskill and Adirondack Mountains. They are strikingly absent from the extreme southeastern portion of the state, including Long Island—the

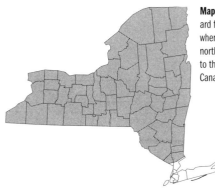

Map 5.11. Distribution of the northern leopard frog (*Rana pipiens*) in New York. Elsewhere the species is widely distributed across northern sections of the United States, except to the West Coast, and northward through Canada to the Arctic Circle.

domain of the southern leopard frog—although the two species overlap in the lower Hudson River valley, where more surveys are needed to resolve their range limits (Klemens et al. 1987). In New York State, the species experienced puzzling declines in the 1970s and 1980s, as they have elsewhere in the eastern and midwestern United States, possibly because of a widespread epidemic of unknown origin. Numbers are now stable if not recovering in western, central, and northern New York (Gibbs et al. 2005). Males can display a high incidence of deformities (hermaphroditism), possibly related to exposure to the commonly used pesticide Atrazine (Hayes et al. 2003). Northern leopard frogs are also susceptible to road mortality (Carr and Fahrig 2001) because they are particularly mobile during the summer and fall and must make-making long migrations to breeding ponds and hibernation sites.

Other Intriguing Facts: Competition

Northern leopard frogs prefer warm, open ponds for breeding because their larvae are poorly adapted to foraging on the types of algae and plants that grow in ponds underneath tree canopies, where they simply do not find much to eat (Werner and Glennemeier 1999). Another factor is that wood frogs, which thrive in closed canopy ponds, outcompete northern leopard frog tadpoles for food and sometimes even eat the smaller, more slowly growing northern leopard frog larvae. Dissolved oxygen concentrations also tend to be lower in closed-canopy compared with open-canopy ponds; northern leopard frogs also have difficulty coping with this factor. These local interactions have wider significance for the overall abundance of northern leopard frogs in New York because forests have been steadily recovering in the state, thus converting many open ponds to closed ponds. This thereby reduces northern leopard frog numbers over the long term (Werner and Glennemeier 1999, Gibbs et al. 2005).

Mink Frog
Rana septentrionalis [Plate 30]

Quick Identification

Pond frogs largely restricted to the Adirondack and Tug Hill Plateaus with olive-gray backs that are darkly and uniformly mottled and markings on the back legs that run parallel with rather than across the long axis of the legs (similar species: green frog).

Description

Mink frogs, with their green to olive-gray backs and extensive dark mottling, resemble green frogs, but the leg markings of mink frogs are less likely to form neat stripes on the folded rear legs. Mink frogs are so named because of the musky, mink-like odor (some say more like crushed scallions) that they impart when disturbed, so if you have a frog in the hand, sniff it. Also, inspect the hind feet. The webbing on a mink frog extends to the last joint of the fourth toe and to the tip of the fifth toe (but rarely passes beyond the second joint of the fourth toe and never reaches the tip of the fifth toe in the green frog). Last, turn the frog over—the mink frog's belly region is grayish white and occasionally with pale yellow on the sides and chin. Dorsolateral folds are typically (although not always) absent. Tympanum diameter in females is relatively smaller in females than males. The standard length is 2–3 in. (5–7.6 cm). Tadpoles are less than 4 in. (10 cm) long and share the greenish, darkly mottled coloration of adults, and the tails of the tadpoles are slightly paler but still mottled and have acute tips. The females lay eggs in globular masses of up to 500 eggs that swell in aggregate to 3–6 in. (7.5–15 cm) in diameter. Initially attached to submerged vegetation, the eggs often drop to the bottom. The call of the mink frog is perhaps best described as "cut-cut-cut-ghur-r-r," and it is higher, more rapid, and much sharper than the banjo string call of the green frog. The scientific name derives from *septentrionalis*, or northern, referring to a distribution restricted to higher latitudes, that is, primarily in Canada.

Habitat

Mink frogs occur in cold northern lakes, ponds, and streams with open, shallow waters dotted with lily pads and fringed with emergent vegetation (Courtois et al. 1995). These frogs are vulnerable to desiccation and rarely occur on land except during heavy rains. They hibernate in the mud at the bottom of permanent waters. Only by wading into water lily-rich lakes and ponds of northern New York State are these frogs typically encountered.

Natural History

Mink frogs spend much of their time sitting on lily pads, floating half-submerged among floating plants, or lurking in the vegetation fringe along shorelines. At Cranberry Lake in New York's Adirondack region, they remain in a "head-up" position attempting to intercept insects active at the water's surface (Kramek 1976). Mink frogs eat more aquatic insects than other frogs in the same habitats, mainly dragonflies, damselflies, aquatic beetles, waterbugs and water striders (Shrwart and Sandison 1972). Vegetation, such as duckweed, is accidentally ingested. Breeding occurs from June to early August (see table 5.1). Males gather in shallow areas throughout the breeding season to form temporary choruses that females visit only briefly for mating. Otherwise, females and subadults remain in shallow, peripheral, and often temporary pools of water throughout the warm season. After hatching, tadpoles rasp algae from the surface of submerged logs, rocks, and plant stems for an entire year and transform into froglets during June to August when they have reached an SVL of 0.4–0.8 in. (1.1–1.7 cm). Males reach maturity 1 year after metamorphosis and females at 1–2 years (Shirose et al. 1993). Despite these frogs' rank smell, wood ducks, great blue herons, mergansers, raccoons, giant water bugs, and leeches prey upon adults and tadpoles.

Status and Distribution

The mink frog is found on the Tug Hill plateau and in the Adirondack region and northward along the St. Lawrence River plain (map 5.12). Quite common in its geographically restricted habitats, the mink frog is known as the "frog of the north" because it has the most northern southerly limit of any frog in the state.

Map 5.12. Distribution of the mink frog (*Rana septentrionalis*) in New York. Elsewhere the species occurs in the eastern and central United States and Canada above about 43° north latitude.

Other Intriguing Facts: Why the "Frog of the North?"

Many have speculated about what might restrict mink frogs to northern latitudes (Schueler 1975). The mostly widely accepted explanation relates the mink frog's globular egg mass to its preference for permanent bodies of water. Most pond- and lake-breeding frogs lay their eggs singly, in strings, or in spreading mats, such that oxygen in the water can easily diffuse into each egg. But the globular nature of the mink frog egg mass impedes the diffusion process of oxygen to the eggs in the interior of the mass, which often die in the more poorly oxygenated, warmer, and southerly waters of the state. Colder, more northerly waters are usually sufficiently oxygenated to diffuse throughout the egg mass and sustain all the embryos (Hedeen 1986).

Wood Frog
Rana sylvatica [Plate 31]

Quick Identification

A tan-colored frog of forests with dark patches around the eyes, prominent dorsolateral folds, and undersides that are white or cream and unmottled whose hoarse, "duck, duck, duck" call is heard in early spring.

Description

The wood frog is generally tan-colored with a "raccoon mask" of dark patches around the eyes, prominent dorsolateral folds, and undersides that are white or cream and unmottled. During early spring breeding season, males may darken considerably while the plumper females may verge on beige-pink. The standard length is 1.5–3.0 in. (3.5–7 cm), with females slightly larger and consistently lighter colored. The eggs are black and white in bluish, transparent masses of 500–2,000 eggs, attached to sticks below the water's surface, often deposited in large aggregations. Tadpoles have high fins and are rotund, with back and sides dark brown or black and undersides pinkish in color and fairly transparent; the internal coil of intestines is quite visible. Adult males emit a series of short, hoarse "duck, duck, duck" calls audible at only a short distance in early spring. The scientific name derives from *sylvatica*, or amidst the trees.

Habitat

An aptly named denizen of close-canopied forests, wood frogs prefer mature, deciduous forests with dark and moist conditions on the forest floor (Wyman 1988). In New York State, the species thrives at higher elevations and in regions with less pasture, more deciduous and mixed forest (particularly if more than 30% remains forested, Gibbs 1998b), and less evergreen forest, and more swamp (Gibbs et al. 2005). Breeding is primarily in fish-free wetlands, such as in cold, clear waters of temporary (vernal) pools, and, less often, in beaver meadows, small permanent ponds, swamps, bogs, and fens (Babbitt et al. 2003, Egan and Paton 2004).

Natural History

Wood frogs are freeze-tolerant (Brooks et al. 1999) and often first emerge when patches of snow are still on the ground during first hard rain following winter. Breeding activities are intense over just a 3–4 night period in March and early April (see table 5.1). Scientists hypothesize that such "explosive" or synchronized breeding is an adaptation to reduce cannibalism by ensuring that all larvae are approximately the same size and hence unable to eat one another (Petranka and Thomas 1995). It may also be a result of the short duration of the temporary pools in which wood frogs breed. Males float on the surface of a breeding pool, calling, jousting with other males, intercepting females, and clasping not just females but occasionally other males, spotted salamanders, or even sticks. Females often dump egg masses communally, perhaps to decrease predation and minimize drying of eggs if pool levels drop and egg masses become stranded and to increase egg temperatures to hasten development (Seale 1982, see below). Eggs hatch in 2–4 weeks, depending on water temperatures. Tadpoles rasp algae and detritus from submerged surfaces, sometimes consuming newly hatched or weakened tadpoles, decaying plants, and dead invertebrates, before metamorphosing into froglets after 2–3 months by July and August in the northeastern United States (Paton and Crouch 2002). Juveniles and adults often remain still on the forest floor, especially near moist glades, seizing mostly small flies, gnats, beetles, caterpillars, spiders, snails, and slugs, until about October. Burrows and holes are used for shelter and protection from many woodland vertebrate predators, particularly gartersnakes and raccoons and occasionally waterfowl, against which wood frogs have few defenses other than long legs that permit a strong hop, camouflage, and mildly toxic skin secretions (Formanowicz and Brodie 1982). In Massachusetts, densities can reach up to 240/acre (600/ha), with males overwintering on land closer to ponds than females (Regosin et al. 2003b). The numbers of adults found in uplands is thought to be determined by numbers of tadpoles surviving to metamorphose from nearby breeding ponds (Berven 1990).

Status and Distribution

In New York, wood frogs are widespread in landscapes with mature forest cover (map 5.13). Wood frogs are susceptible to local extinction caused by loss of vernal pool breeding areas and forest clearing and housing developments of adult habitats adjacent to vernal pools. Acidification of breeding pools (wood frogs cannot tolerate waters with pH less than 4; Grant and Licht 1993) may also reduce reproduction in the Adirondack and Catskill regions. In central, western, and northern New York, wood frog populations were stable to increasing between 1970 and 2000 (Gibbs et al. 2005), evidently benefiting from the gradual reforestation of the state (Werner and Glennemeier 1999) in regions not being converted to urban areas.

Other Intriguing Facts: Symbiosis

Wood frog egg masses are fascinating to study. The eggs act like tiny lenses that concentrate the sun's rays and increase egg temperatures several degrees above that of the surrounding water. The cumulative

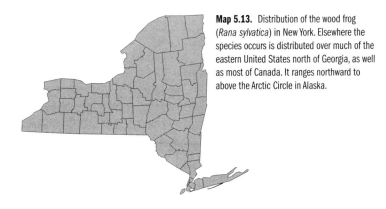

Map 5.13. Distribution of the wood frog (*Rana sylvatica*) in New York. Elsewhere the species occurs is distributed over much of the eastern United States north of Georgia, as well as most of Canada. It ranges northward to above the Arctic Circle in Alaska.

Frogs and Toads

effect of many hundreds of thousands of eggs in communal egg masses can be substantial. The solar heating also promotes the formation of tiny water currents through the eggs masses, which increase the availability of oxygen to developing embryos (Waldman 1982). Oxygen availability may also be increased by a symbiotic alga, *Oophila amblystomatis*, that grows on the egg masses. The alga is thought to provide oxygen for the frog embryos in exchange for carbon dioxide and waste nutrients that the embryos are trying to eliminate. In addition, the alga provides a food source for the tadpoles when they first hatch. These mechanisms help wood frog tadpoles grow a little more quickly in the race to metamorphose before their shallow breeding pools dry by mid-summer (Pinder and Friet 1994).

Southern Leopard Frog
Rana sphenocephala [Plate 32]

Quick Identification

A medium-sized frog with an unbroken dorsolateral fold from the eye to the pelvic region, heavy round spots, and a light marking on the center of the tympanum. It is largely restricted to Long Island (similar species: see northern leopard frog).

Description

Quite similar in appearance to the northern leopard frog, the southern leopard frog can be distinguished by a light marking on the center of the tympanum; few dark spots on its side; and spots that are smaller, often elongated, and that generally lack a light border. The head is also somewhat longer and more pointed than that of the northern leopard frog—hence the scientific name, which derives from *sphenos*, or wedge, and *kephalos*, or headed. Occasionally, in sandy habitats, all spotting is lacking. The standard length is 2–3.5 in. (5.0–9 cm), with a maximum length of 5 in. (12.7 cm). The females deposit the eggs in irregular masses of 3,000–5,000 eggs attached to plant stems. Tadpoles are dark brown to olive with gold flecking, an iridescent and transparent belly, and a tail lighter than body with transparent fins and fine dark markings. The call of southern leopard frogs is a low-pitched, guttural croak, similar to but rendered more slowly than that of the northern leopard frog; it is followed by two or three clucking sounds, sounding much like a wet finger rubbed against an inflated balloon.

Habitat

Preferring moist meadows, the southern leopard frog may be found in many types of permanent and semipermanent wetlands, even in slightly brackish marshes. During the summer, the frogs prefer vegetated or weed-encroached areas away from the water where shade is prevalent. It sometimes ventures far from wetland habitats in the late summer and finds shade under grasses or small shrubs and moisture in pools and puddles on the uplands.

Natural History

Southern leopard frogs are alert and skittish and capable of making long, quick leaps, disappearing rapidly into water or dense vegetation when feeling threatened. In New York State, breeding occurs primarily from March through June (see table 5.1). Males call from floating vegetation mostly between midnight and daylight. Females attach their flattened egg clusters to vegetation in shallow water, where they are vulnerable to caddisfly predation (Richter 2000). Females frequently deposit their egg masses communally, likely to take advantage of a "temperature effect" afforded by sharing conductive heat gathered during the day from the warm air, heat from solar radiation captured by the eggs acting as black bodies, as well as some metabolic heat of the developing embryos (Caldwell 1986). Hatching occurs in 7–12 days. Tadpoles usually transform to the adult stage in 2–3 months, a process hastened if predators are present (Saenz et al. 2003), although some tadpoles from late hatching eggs may overwinter as tadpoles. Tadpoles frequently lose the tips of their tails, without lasting consequences, possibly as a means of warding fish and newt predators away from the tadpole's vital organs. Dense vegetation at the bottoms of wetlands is key to tadpole survival and avoidance of predation. Because southern leopard frogs breed in rather shallow waters that are prone to drying, massive mortality of tadpoles from desiccation is common. After metamorphosis, froglets can dig burrows to escape desiccation (Parris 1998). During spring and fall, these frogs remain near water but travel considerable distances on the surrounding uplands during summer, particularly to forage in grassy areas. Adults forage primarily on beetles, but prefer more soft-bodied arthropods, such as caterpillars and spiders, when available. Hibernation occurs in the muck of wetland bottoms.

Status and Distribution

In New York State, the southern leopard frog occurs only in the extreme southeastern counties and on Long Island, areas of the state with the densest human settlement (map 5.14). The cluster of records in central New York is associated with the Seneca Army Depot and is almost certainly the result of releases of animals (a popular focus of school biology laboratories). Loss of breeding sites threatens this species, but if sufficient wetland habitat is retained, this species can thrive in suburban settings. Given its limited range and threats to its breeding habitat, the southern leopard frog is listed as a species of Special Concern in New York State. The species is also at the northern edge of its range in the state.

Other Intriguing Facts: When and Where to Breed?

Female southern leopard frogs face a complex dilemma when they first emerge in spring and are ready to mate—where to lay their eggs. The problem relates not just to the obvious issue of which ponds are nearby and the likelihood that the ponds will remain flooded long enough for tadpoles to metamorphose. In addition, which other species might also choose to breed in a particular pond affects females. Southern leopard frogs grow most quickly when alone in a pond or when they breed much later than toads. The best time to lay eggs depends on whether toads are present at the time of hatching, which is quite difficult to predict. The comings and goings of toads and the risks of premature drying of ponds thus make breeding in southern leopard frogs something of a lottery (Alford and Wilbur 1985).

Map 5.14. Distribution of the southern leopard frog (*Rana sphenocephala*) in New York. The species occurs southward from New York to the Florida Keys and west to Kansas.

6

Turtles: Species Accounts

Everybody recognizes a turtle for its most distinctive feature—its shell (figure 6.1). Remarkably, turtles and tortoises first evolved more than 200 million years ago and have changed little since then. Thus, they represent an ancient lineage of "creatures who are entitled to regard the brontosaur and mastodon as brief zoological fads" (Gilbert 1993). The shell is composed of two parts: an upper domed section, or carapace, and a lower belly plate, or the plastron. Building the shell is no trivial matter, so turtles tend to delay reproduction in favor of building the shell early in life, often maturing reproductively only after a decade or more of growth. But once the shell is developed, it confers effective protection against most predators and continuous reproduction for many decades. Until recently, precisely because of their shells, adult turtles suffered relatively little predation. Only a few mid- to large-sized mammals, such as wolves, could tackle them. The situation has changed dramatically, however, and mortality of adults caused by collectors and automobiles is now a serious threat to turtles in New York (see Wood Turtle, Other Intriguing Facts). Cars and collectors aside, turtles can indeed attain great longevity because of their shells. For example, an old eastern box turtle found in 1926 on Long Island had the date 1878 carved on its shell (Townsend 1926). Another found on Long Island in 1926 carried the date 1884 (Nichols 1939) (see Eastern Box Turtle, Other Intriguing Facts).

Reproduction in turtles involves internal fertilization and prolonged sperm storage by females in many cases (Gist and Congdon

Figure 6.1. Wood turtle, a formerly abundant riparian zone turtle in New York State. (Neg./Trans. no. 16727, American Museum of Natural History Library.)

1998). Sperm storage may permit females to sample sperm from multiple males or simply to secure sperm while a male is available (an infrequent event in the case of the more solitary turtles). Because of the males' rigid shell, copulation can be tricky, and they must rest their plastrons tenuously on the carapace of the females. As a result, males of many species have a distinct concavity in their plastron to facilitate this delicate balancing act.

Reproduction in turtles may involve migrations of considerable distances from wetlands to lay eggs on land (figure 6.2). After warm rains in late spring and early summer, we often witness primeval-looking, female snapping turtles emerging from wetlands, as they have done for millions of years, tottering onto highways in search of a patch of warm, dry, loose soil in which to lay eggs. Another quite remarkable feature about reproduction in turtles is that their sex is largely determined by the temperature of the nest in which they develop (Ewert and Nelson 1991). Females are generally produced at higher temperatures and males at lower temperatures, but many other patterns occur. Of New York's turtles, only the wood turtle and spiny softshell are known to have genetic sex determination (the sort we are most familiar with). Hatchlings emerge usually in late summer, although some overwinter in the nests to emerge in spring (figure 6.3).

Despite its obvious advantages, the shell imposes constraints on turtles. Locomotion is a ponderous undertaking and involves tilting

Figure 6.2. Egg laying can be somewhat problematic for turtles (such as this eastern box turtle), given the fixed, narrow openings to their shells. (William Capitano.)

back and forth while moving one or sometimes two limbs, leaving the others fixed as supports. Because ribs are fused with the shell, breathing is accomplished by specialized musculature that sloshes the internal organs back and forth to draw air in and out of the lungs. Lastly, rigid shells mean that turtles must remain on the ground or in the water, thereby excluding themselves from the wealth of resources available in trees that many other reptiles as well as amphibians exploit. Notably, one native turtle does scale small trees and shrubs with branches that overhang the water to bask—if a turtle plummets from the sky into your canoe in New York State, it is most likely a stinkpot.

The non-marine turtles of New York are represented by 12 species in four families: Chelydridae—the snapping turtles, Emydidae—the pond turtles, Kinosternidae—the mud and musk turtles, and Trionychidae—the softshells (table 2.2). Aquatic turtles generally have webbed feet and

Figure 6.3. Young snapping turtles recently hatched from their eggs. (Neg./Trans. no. 38601, American Museum of Natural History Library.)

relatively flatter shells than terrestrial turtles, facilitating movement through water. At the extreme are softshell turtles, which have extremely flat shells, soft skin and no scales—they look like leathery dinner plates. A few aquatic turtles, such as the stinkpot, more often walk on the bottom than swim and have shells more domed than more prolific swimmers, such as painted turtles.

The marine turtles of New York are short-term but not uncommon visitors. They are most frequently encountered when they become stranded on sandy beaches on Long Island (see box: Sea Turtles in New York State). Marine turtles are represented by three

Figure 6.4. A wood turtle showing the external characteristics of the shell useful for identifying turtles, including the plastron and the locations of the vertebral, pleural, and marginal scutes and nuchal scute on the carapace. (Ariana Breisch.)

species in the Cheloniidae and one species in the Dermochelyidae. They are the only New York reptiles that migrate to warmer climes in winter.

Lastly, New York has a few turtles that are not easily categorized ecologically. These species, such as the wood turtle and Blanding's turtle (both in the family Emydidae), regularly move between upland and wetland sites (often encountering many hazards in between) and are best considered semiaquatic. Characteristics useful for distinguishing among turtles are depicted in figure 6.4.

New York's severe winters and short, cool summers limit turtle reproduction and growth, such that only a handful of species are able to persist in the higher latitudes and elevations of the State. Only two species are widespread in the state: painted turtles and snapping turtles. This said, New York supports about 6% of the approximately 285 species of turtles on earth—a significant fraction of global turtle diversity.

Sea Turtles in New York State

Because we usually associate sea turtles with coral reefs in far off tropical places, you might be surprised to learn that (1) there are large numbers of sea turtles in New York waters and (2) New York waters are vital to the survival of some species. To give you a sense of the numbers of sea turtles that ply the state's waters, consider Latham (1969), who reported encountering 103 dead sea turtles washed up on 3 miles of beach near Orient, Long Island after a cold spell in November 1924. Research conducted since the 1980s by Steve Morreale, Vincent Burke, Ed Standora, and others also has revealed a predictable annual occurrence of these creatures in Long Island Sound. Four species occur fairly regularly: the loggerhead, green, Kemp's ridley, and leatherback sea turtles (figure 6.5). Some of these turtles are immense—Latham (1969) reported a 150-pound loggerhead caught in a fish trap in Orient in 1931.

Although sea turtles are paddling around Long Island Sound throughout the warm season and the early part of winter, they are usually observed when temperatures suddenly drop to less than 46°F (8°C) in November and December. Some become hypothermic and, unable to propel themselves, float around like drift wood until they fetch up on beaches, sometimes dead but often alive. Winds in the region prevail from the northwest, so virtually all strandings occur on the north side of Long Island, particularly along its eastern end (Burke et al. 1991).

Kemp's ridleys are by far the most common species in Long Island Sound, accounting for about three-fourths of all strandings. Notably, nearly all the Kemp's ridleys encountered were juveniles. Kemp's ridleys when small appear to spend their time far out to sea, but when they reach 8 in. (20 cm) in length they head to richer feeding grounds in near-shore waters. Long Island Sound appears to be among the most important of all areas for Kemp's ridleys along the entire stretch of coastline that they occupy from the Gulf of Mexico to New England. Adults seem to escape from the area before the cold strikes, so they are not stranded as often as juveniles, which either get caught by mistake or linger and take risks in order to continue to reap the bounty of the Sound.

What is so special about Long Island Sound for marine turtles? The abundance of walking crabs. Crabs by far predominate in the turtles' diet (as determined by scientists, who hold captured turtles in pens for 48 hours and examine the feces the turtles produce); however, the turtles also take mollusks, algae, and a small amount of natural and human-generated debris (Burke and Standora 1993). By preserving these rich feeding grounds, New York State plays a vital role in conserving the entire Kemp's ridley species.

Figure 6.5.   A leatherback turtle captured near Block Island, 1905, similar to those that still ply Long Island Sound. (Neg./Trans. no. 3996, American Museum of Natural History Library.)

It is also important to limit pollution in Long Island Sound for the sake of all sea turtles. Some 11 of 15 dead leatherback sea turtles that washed up on Long Island beaches during a 2-week period in the early 1980s had plastic bags blocking their stomach openings, most with 4–8 quart-sized bags and one with 15 such bags. The turtles mistake the transparent floating bags for jellyfish, one of the favorite meals of leatherback sea turtles.

In the accounts that follow, we report turtle size as carapace length, the straight line distance from the anterior edge to the posterior edge of the carapace.

Snapping Turtle (Common Snapping Turtle)
Chelydra serpentina [Plate 33]

Quick Identification

A turtle with a massive head, dark carapace with serrated or jagged posterior edge, narrow, t-shaped plastron, and tail with saw-toothed keels.

Turtles

Description

Snapping turtles are large, freshwater turtles characterized by massive heads and powerful, oversized jaws. The carapace is generally dark, ranging in color from brown to dark green and even black, and it is often mottled with algae and mud. The carapace has three rows of slightly keeled and backward pointing scutes that give its margin, particularly the posterior carapace, a heavily serrated appearance. The distinctly small and cruciform plastron is light in color, ranging from yellowish to tan, and unpatterned. The tail is often as long as the carapace with saw-toothed keels. Tubercles protrude from the neck and chin like a stubbly beard. The head, neck, and legs are often gray to black. Occasionally, albino individuals occur (Saumure and Rodrigue 1998). Wild specimens range up to 45 lb. (20 kg), whereas captive specimens can exceed 75 lb. (34 kg). Carapace length is 8–14 in. (20.5–36 cm), with a maximum length of 19.4 in. (49.4 cm). Males, which have an anal opening posterior to the carapace rim, are typically larger than females (which have an anal opening that intersects the carapace rim). The scientific name derives from *chelys*, or turtle; *hydros*, or water serpent, referring to the aquatic nature of genus; and *serpentina*, or snakelike, referring to the snakelike neck.

Warning: These turtles are aptly named. Although tranquil under water, on land they "snap" in self-defense and can easily mangle your fingers. This aggressiveness likely compensates for their puny plastron, which provides little physical protection to the vulnerable underside of the turtle. Despite advice to do so, never pick up a snapping turtle by the tail—in doing so you can sever its spinal cord! Instead, pick it up firmly by the rear flanges of the carapace and hold it away from your body (figure 12.3).

Habitat

Snapping turtles can be found in almost every freshwater habitat within their range but seem to prefer slow-moving, shallow waters with muddy substrates. They are highly aquatic and prefer to rest in warm shallows, often buried or partially buried in the mud, with only their eyes and nostrils exposed. Snapping turtles may also live in the shallow regions and margins of deep lakes and rivers and in estuaries and, occasionally, in salt marshes. In northern New York, nesting occurs in sparsely vegetated, thinly soiled areas, including forest clearings, bare soil banks, road embankments, and hayfields and pastures (Petokas and Alexander 1980).

Natural History

Snapping turtles mate from April to November, and females may retain viable sperm for several years (Galbraith et al. 1993). In New York, peak nesting occurs in June and is about equally divided between early morning and evening hours (Petokas and Alexander 1980), when gravid females lumber up from water to find sandy or loamy soils for their nests, often along roadsides. At Cranberry Creek marsh in Jefferson County, snapping turtles typically lay 25–50 spherical eggs approximately 1.25 in. (30 mm) in diameter (Petokas and Alexander 1980). These eggs are deposited in a flask-shaped cavity 4–7 in. (10–18 cm) deep. Each egg is directed into place by alternating movements of the hind feet so that the eggs are neatly stacked within the nesting cavity. Nests are usually within 82 ft. (25 m) from water and 13 ft. (4 m) above water (Petokas and Alexander 1980). Nests are occasionally placed in ant mounds (Burke et al. 1993). Incubation takes 9–18 weeks (depending on weather and climate), and hatching may occur from August to October. In colder parts of the State, hatchlings may overwinter in the nest to emerge in the spring (e.g., in Vermont; Parren and Rice 2004). Nest temperatures higher than 84°F (29°C) produce predominately females, whereas lower temperatures produce predominately males. Most nests are destroyed by predators before the eggs can hatch. Some 95% of nests in northern New York were destroyed, mostly by raccoons (*Procyon lotor*), leaving just two to three of 42 nests found to produce hatchlings in any given season (Petokas and Alexander 1980). Exiting nests is a hazardous time for hatchings, mostly because of the risk of drying. Some hatchlings leave nests quickly, minimizing exposure to predators, but increasing their water loss and risk of desiccation. Others wait in nests for moderate air temperatures and precipitation, increasing exposure to predators but limiting water loss (Kolbe and Janzen 2002). Snapping turtles have been reported to reach sexual maturity at about 20.0 cm in carapace length at approximately 14 years of age. Mature males are sometimes observed in combat, thrashing in the shallows, possibly delineating territories (for a vivid account from Long Island, see Latham 1968a).

Snapping turtles bask mostly in shallow water and much less frequently on logs or rocks, although in the colder, northern parts of

New York they may engage in a high frequency of "out of water" basking (e.g., high on rocks, which they plummet off when disturbed). Subadults may move overland to new wetlands, especially in rainy periods, resting in seemingly unlikely places such as vernal pools. Evidently this species has a cleaning symbiosis with painted turtles, which derive a nutritional benefit by removing chlorophytic algae and leeches from snapping turtles, which in turn benefit by having parasites removed (Krawchuk et al. 1997). Snapping turtles most commonly forage in the evenings or at night. Active foraging may be more common in juvenile turtles, whereas older, larger individuals may rely more on lying in wait to ambush prey at the bottom of a water body. "Snappers" are omnivorous, feeding on almost anything that can fit into their large mouths. Intensive studies by Pell (1940) in New York and New Jersey indicated that plant matter was 53% of diet by volume, with crayfish the most important animal prey. Diet also includes invertebrates, fish, amphibians, turtles, snakes, young birds, small mammals, and carrion. Snapping turtles are often maligned by sportsmen who contend the turtles take a heavy toll on fish and waterfowl populations, but scientific studies to date indicate that predation on game fish or birds has a negligible effect on the populations of the supposedly predated species (Coulter 1957). This said, snapping turtles do indeed eat birds. In Cranberry Creek marsh, Jefferson County, snapping turtles have ambushed adult ring-billed gulls, by clamping down on the posterior of birds sitting on the water surface (Petokas 1981). On the New York side of Lake Ontario, snapping turtles ambush migrating shorebirds (Pryor 1996). Although

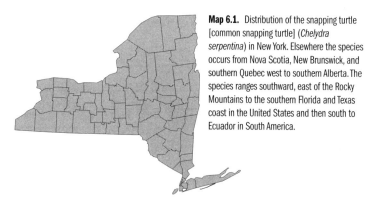

Map 6.1. Distribution of the snapping turtle [common snapping turtle] (*Chelydra serpentina*) in New York. Elsewhere the species occurs from Nova Scotia, New Brunswick, and southern Quebec west to southern Alberta. The species ranges southward, east of the Rocky Mountains to the southern Florida and Texas coast in the United States and then south to Ecuador in South America.

snapping turtles are relatively invulnerable to predation, sometimes adults are killed in large numbers by otters (Brooks et al. 1991). Hatchlings are freeze-tolerant (Packard et al. 1999), and adults overwinter on pond bottoms (Meeks 1990).

Status and Distribution

Snapping turtles are abundant and quite widespread in New York (map 6.1). They even occur in some estuaries in the state (e.g., the Hudson River; Kiviat 1980), although studies on Long Island indicate that they cannot maintain fluid balance in marine situations (Kinneary 1993). Each year in New York, large numbers of subadults and especially nesting females are killed on roads (Steen and Gibbs 2004), especially in mid-June during the nesting season (Haxton 2000). Nevertheless, snapping turtles may persist in suburban and urban areas, although in many cases they predate the arrival of the residential development. Snapping turtles have a high tolerance for polluted waters, including areas subject to oil spills (Saba and Spotila 2003). Historically, snapping turtles were prized for their edible flesh and eggs, but these are top predators so polychlorinated biphenyl (PCB) loads, particularly in liver and fat, are often well above consumption guidelines, particularly in the Great Lakes region (de Solla and Fernie 2004) and the Akwesasne, Mohawk Territory of the St. Lawrence River (de Solla et al. 2001).

Other Intriguing Facts: Should We Harvest Snappers?

Many people are surprised to learn that snapping turtles are still taken in substantial numbers from the waters of New York State for commercial purposes. They are usually even more surprised when they learn the reason for the industry: food. Although some New Yorkers might find the notion of eating an algae-covered, leech-infested reptile that not only emits a nasty odor when handled but can also snip off your fingers repulsive, many folks in the southern United States would disagree. In fact, commercial plants that pack turtle meat are still found in states such as Mississippi (although about one-fourth of the purported "turtle meat" sold actually is alligator meat; Roman and Bowen 2000). The southern states are the main destination for many of New York State's harvested snappers, after a long and bumpy ride stacked in the back of a truck. Others make their way to the New York City area, where they are consumed locally or are flown to markets in China and Southeast Asia. In 1998, the

Turtles

World Wildlife Fund estimated that 150,000 live snapping turtles
were exported from the United States to other markets. Whether
such harvest of a native reptile should continue, essentially unmoni-
tored and benefiting a small group of trappers working to satisfy the
quirky appetites of people thousands of miles away, is a issue deserv-
ing more scrutiny.

Eastern Mud Turtle
Kinosternon subrubrum [Plate 34]

Quick Identification

A rare turtle with a smooth, oval carapace; a dark-colored plastron
with two well-developed hinges; a dark brown head with yellow mottling; and a nail-tipped tail. It is restricted to Long Island and Staten
Island.

Description

The carapace of eastern mud turtles is smooth, unkeeled, and oval
in shape, and it varies in color from plain brown, yellowish to olive,
or even black. There are 11 marginal scutes on each side of its carapace (most freshwater turtles have 12). The plastron is yellow to
brown and has two well-developed hinges. The head is typically dark
brown with yellow mottling. Both sexes have nail-tipped tails. The
male's tail is much larger than the female's with the cloacal opening
beyond the rear margin of the carapace, and there is a patch of
rough scales on the inner surface of the male's rear legs. Common
carapace lengths are 3.0–4 in. (7–10 cm), with a maximum length of
4.9 in. (12.4 cm). Hatchlings are 0.7–1.1 in. (1.7–2.7 cm) and have two
faint stripes on each side of the head and neck. The hinge in the
plastron is poorly developed and mottled with orange. The scientific
name derives from *sub*, or below, and *rubrum*, or red, referring to the
red-orange plastron of the hatchlings.

Habitat

Eastern mud turtles are found in freshwater and brackish water wetlands. Marshes, small ponds, water-filled ditches, creeks, and swamps
serve as habitats. The turtles prefer shallow, quiet waters with a soft
bottom and emergent vegetation. Muskrat lodges are a favorite retreat. On Long Island and adjacent islands, eastern mud turtles are

found in brackish marshes and ponds dominated by giant reed grass (*Phragmites australis*).

Natural History

Eastern mud turtles emerge from hibernation in New York in April and are active until September or early October (Nichols 1947). Surprisingly, the turtles are quite terrestrial and depart drying wetlands in late spring and may stay on land until early the following spring. During the summer, they may spend long periods buried under damp humus at the edge of wetlands. In New York, eastern mud turtles burrow into a dry sandy hillside or under leaf litter at the edge of the wetland to spend the winter. Hibernation is also known to occur underwater in soft mud.

Breeding occurs shortly after spring emergence, and nesting in northern areas occurs in June. Females deposit one to eight (typically four to five) bluish or pinkish elliptical eggs in a shallow cavity in sandy soil or vegetative debris. Walls of muskrat and beaver lodges are occasionally used as nesting sites. Females undertake prolonged nesting forays (averaging 9 days in one study; Burke et al. 1994), with the departure and return to wetlands triggered by rain events. Although one or two clutches of eggs are laid each season in northern areas, three or four clutches may be laid during the warm season in the south. Predation rates can be high (typically greater than 80%; Burke et al. 1998). Eggs incubate for about 3 months and hatchlings may emerge in late summer, although they often overwinter in the nest until the following spring (Nichols 1947). Eastern mud turtles are typically bottom feeders, probing the soft substrate for crustaceans, aquatic insects, snails, and algae. Depending on locality and conditions, sexual maturity is reached in 4–8 years. A long-lived species, survivorship in males is greater than in females (Frazer 1991). One captive individual acquired as an adult lived for 38 years.

As is the case for other turtles, predators, including crows, raccoons, skunks, weasels, opossums, foxes, and coyotes, take a large proportion of the eastern mud turtle's eggs and hatchlings. Blue crabs, fish, eastern hog-nosed snakes, and northern watersnakes also eat hatchlings. Being small turtles, even adults are not predator proof; raccoons, canids, and bald eagles take them.

Turtles

Status and Distribution

New York's few populations of the eastern mud turtle (map 6.2) on Long Island and islands in Peconic Bay represent the eastern extreme of the species' range (Craig et al. 1980). This species is relatively common in the southern parts of its range, but in New York local populations have been reduced by wetland alteration and destruction. In New York, the eastern mud turtle is listed as an Endangered species and is likely the state's rarest turtle. The frenetic development on Long Island has increased mortality to turtles on roads and destroyed wetland habitat as well as upland nesting and hibernation sites; this has seriously eroded the species' hold on the northernmost end of its range. Collection for the pet trade also has reduced local populations.

Other Intriguing Facts: Feisty Turtles

Eastern mud turtles are feisty creatures. One report of an encounter between two turtles described a 10-minute head-to-head jousting match that ended with one turtle walking away. The other turtle then followed in pursuit and bit the escaping turtle on its left hind leg. Once freed, the bitten turtle had lost its leg at the knee joint and the researcher observed the other turtle had the severed limb in its mouth. Eastern mud turtles are often found in nature with missing limbs that are usually ascribed to encounters with predators and machinery. Perhaps turtles themselves account for some of them!

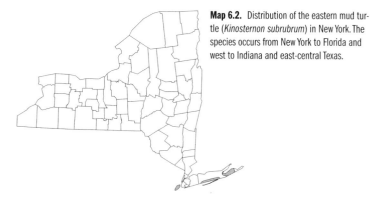

Map 6.2. Distribution of the eastern mud turtle (*Kinosternon subrubrum*) in New York. The species occurs from New York to Florida and west to Indiana and east-central Texas.

Stinkpot (Common Musk Turtle)
Sternotherus odoratum [Plate 35]

Quick Identification

A small turtle that lurks on the bottoms of wetlands with a smooth, high-domed carapace, a single hinge on front portion of plastron, two yellow stripes extending backward from its pointy snout (one above and one below the eye), and barbels on the chin and throat.

Description

The stinkpot often looks at first glance like an oval, algae-covered stone. If not obscured by a mantle of algae, the smooth, high-domed carapace appears brown, gray, or black. The plastron is small, light brown to yellow, with patches of skin between the scutes along the centerline. Only the front portion of the plastron is hinged. Two yellow stripes extend backward from the turtle's pointy snout, one above and one below the eye, to the neck. The stripes fade with age. Barbels extend from the chin and throat. Males have a thick tail that ends in a blunt nail and two small patches of rough scales on the inner surface of their rear legs. The carapace has a central keel (which diminishes with age) and is black with small white spots along the edge of the shell. The carapace length is 2–4.5 in. (5.0–11.5 cm), with a maximum length of 5.4 in. (13.7 cm). Hatchlings are 0.7–1.0 in. (1.9–2.5 cm) in length. The scientific name derives from *sterno*, or chest; and *thairos*, or hinged, referring to the hinged plastron; and *odoratus*, referring to the strong odor produced by the turtles' musk glands.

Habitat

The stinkpot's favorite haunts are slow-moving, muddy-bottomed rivers and big streams, and the shallow, weedy coves of natural lakes and impoundments found along a long watercourse (e.g., Sutton and Christiansen 1999). Stinkpots do not wander far from their aquatic habitats, so they are not often found in isolated water bodies. They generally avoid brackish waters but do occur in the slightly salty Onondaga Lake near Syracuse.

Turtles

Natural History

In New York, stinkpots are active from late March until October. They overwinter underwater in muskrat lodges or in the soft mud below a sunken log or other debris. They court and mate underwater in April and most nesting occurs in the first two weeks of June. Females can store viable sperm for months (Gist and Congdon 1999). Females lay two to nine elliptical, glossy white, brittle eggs in a shallow nest constructed in the side of a muskrat lodge, in a rotting stump, or under other shoreline debris (Finkler and Schultz 2003). Despite wide variation in female size, egg size is remarkably consistent in stinkpots because of constraints imposed by the fixed width of the gap between the rear parts of the carapace and plastron (Clark et al. 2001). Eggs hatch in August or September. Young stinkpots grow quickly. Males may reach sexual maturity in 3–4 years, although females develop more slowly and may take 6–10 years or longer to mature, depending on local conditions. Populations tend to be male-biased, possibly because of higher female mortality (Edmonds and Brooks 1995, Smith and Iverson 2002).

Stinkpots are highly aquatic. They bask cryptically in shallow weedy waters, which rapidly heat up on sunny spring days. Here stinkpots appear as a lump on a thick mat of emergent vegetation with only the center of their shell exposed. Often the carapace is draped with algae. However, stinkpots have strong claws and do occasionally climb onto partially submerged logs or even onto the branches of trees, which overhang water, to sun themselves (Nickerson 2000); they have been known to tumble into passing canoes.

Although inconspicuous, stinkpots are occasionally seen slowly walking along the bottom, poking their snouts into clumps of algae or the mud. They feed on algae festooned with small snails, crustaceans, and microinvertebrates. They also eat leeches, worms, aquatic insects, crayfish, small fish, and tadpoles, as well as carrion (Ernst 1986). Crows and raccoons take a high percentage of stinkpot eggs. Otters, mink, weasels, herons, northern watersnakes, bullfrogs, and bass consume hatchlings and adults. Occasionally, a bald eagle becomes a stinkpot feeding specialist; the eagle's nest contains a collection of cleaned stinkpot shells. Once a stinkpot was found dead with its head clamped inside a pond mussel shell (Plummer and Goy 1997). Stinkpots are surprisingly long-lived. The Philadelphia Zoo kept one for more than 54 years, and stinkpots are known to live in the wild for at least 28 years. Stinkpots are capable navigators. When a group was released 1 mile (1.6 km) from their capture point in Byram Lake in Westchester County, New York, some returned in less than a day.

Status and Distribution

In New York, stinkpots occur in the Great Lake drainages, the Hudson River and many of its tributaries, and on Long Island. Stinkpots are generally absent from higher elevations such as the Appalachian Plateau and the Adirondack Mountains (map 6.3). Stinkpots are locally common in New York. Unfortunately, development of lake shorelines and removal of aquatic "weed beds" has affected populations. Stinkpots, too, fall victim to the baited hooks of fishermen. Perhaps because of the turtle's pugnacious behavior or the misguided belief that they harm fish populations, their captors often kill them as nuisance animals or cut them free to die a slow death from the stainless steel hook remaining in their throat.

Other Intriguing Facts: The "Stink" of Stinkpots

The stinkpot, also known as "Stinking Jim," has four musk-producing glands whose tiny, pinpoint orifices may be seen on the underside of the marginal scutes of the carapace. Freshly captured individuals often produce a drop of the yellowish musk from each of the glands. Although the foul-smelling fluid does not appear to be a effective predator repellent, it is pungent enough to earn the species its scientific, common, and colloquial names, and to occasionally discourage a kid from taking it home.

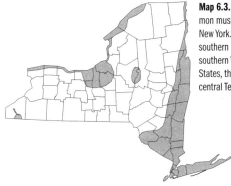

Map 6.3. Distribution of the stinkpot [common musk turtle] (*Sternotherus odoratum*) in New York. Elsewhere the species occurs from southern Maine, southeastern Ontario, and southern Wisconsin southward to the Gulf States, through peninsular Florida, and to central Texas.

Turtles

Painted Turtle
Chrysemys picta [Plate 36]

Quick Identification

A common and widespread aquatic turtle with a smooth, dark and somewhat flattened carapace that is oval in shape, yellow or red markings on the marginal scutes; and skin that is black to olive with stripes of red and yellow on the neck, legs, and tail.

Description

Painted turtles are common fresh water turtles with an average carapace length of 4.5–6 in. (11.5–15.0 cm), and maximum length of 7.50 in. (19.0). The carapace is somewhat flattened, smooth, unkeeled and oval in shape, and its color ranges from olive to black with yellow or red borders between the scute seams and red bars or crescents on the marginal scutes. The plastron is not hinged and is yellowish to orange in color, with varying patterns of black or dark pigment. The skin is black to olive with stripes of red and yellow on the neck, legs, and tail. The striping patterns of the head area are variable, but a typical pattern is two wide yellow stripes running up either under-side of the chin to enclose a narrower yellow stripe, meeting at the jaw. Relative to females, males have noticeably longer front-limb claws and smaller, more vertically compressed shell dimensions. Males are smaller, and they also have longer tails and anal openings on tail posterior to the margin of the carapace. The scientific name is derived from *khrysos*, or golden; *emys*, or turtle, referring to the yellow stripes on head of all members of this genus; and *picta*, or painted, referring to the delicate shell pattern.

Habitat

Painted turtles occur in nearly all permanent freshwater wetlands in New York. However, the turtles prefer slow-moving, shallow water systems such as ponds, marshes, lakes, and oxbows, as well as slow creeks, streams, and rivers. They are most common in clustered wetlands with abundant basking sites, much aquatic vegetation, and ample surrounding nesting habitat (Marchand and Litvaitis 2004). The turtles may enter slightly brackish waters.

Natural History

Painted turtles are among the first turtles to emerge from their aquatic hibernacula in the spring, usually in March when they can be observed basking communally on half-submerged logs. Painted turtles may remain active into early November at which time they reenter winter hibernacula within muskrat dens or in wetland sediments. During the warm season, painted turtles are mostly active by day, returning to safe havens or remaining in a semisubmerged basking position throughout the night. Although overland movements of females are confined almost exclusively to the nesting season, male painted turtles may travel between aquatic habitats during the spring and early summer as water bodies fill and dry. In one pond in New York, turtle densities of 9.7/acre (24.0/ha) were reported (Bayless 1975).

Courtship and mating occur from March through mid-June, and females can store sperm for several months or more. Sperm storage by females may facilitate production of multiple clutches of eggs each year, which occurs even in northern populations. Many clutches are fathered by multiple males, with the latest male having precedence in paternity over those preceding (Pearse et al. 2002). Nesting activity peaks in June and early July, with females seeking out sunny nesting sites in sandy or loamy soil. Females dig a 10-cm deep cavity into which they deposit 3–15 oval-shaped, white eggs. Hatching typically occurs in 10–12 weeks, with peak hatching in August and September, although hatchlings may overwinter in the nest. Both adults and hatchlings are freeze-tolerant (Packard and Packard 2002).

Painted turtles forage primarily along the bottom of a wetland among clumps of aquatic vegetation, and they are active day or night (Rowe 2003). Studies in New York suggest that adults are omnivores and eat a wide range of plants and animals, whereas juveniles, intent on growing quickly, feed mainly on insects and crustaceans (Raney and Lachner 1942). Painted turtles apparently engage in a symbiotic relationship with snapping turtles (Krawchuk et al. 1997) by feeding on leeches and algae that plague the snapping turtles. Because sex is temperature determined, females can evidently affect the sex of their offspring by placing their nests in more shaded (cooler) or open (warmer) areas (Janzen 1994). This said, long-term studies in painted turtle populations on Long Island indicate that adult sex ratios are 1:1

(Zweifel 1989). Sexual maturation occurs when plastron length reaches 2.75–3.75 in. (7.0–9.5 cm), or by the age of 3–7 years depending on how fast the turtle grows. Painted turtles may live for 40 years or more.

Status and Distribution

Painted turtles are likely the most abundant turtle in New York (map 6.4) and are surpassed only by snapping turtles in their ability to persist in disturbed and polluted habitats (Saba and Spotila 2003). Painted turtles thrive in reservoirs, impounded areas, and artificial ponds, the recent creation of which has contributed much habitat for the species. Painted turtles often nest in artificially open and cleared areas, such as railroad beds, lawns, cultivated fields, and even roadway margins with loose soil. They present no threat to game fish, although many become hooked and are subsequently killed by fishermen. In New York, sex ratios in populations near roadsides may become male-biased, perhaps due to loss of nesting females on roads (Steen and Gibbs 2004); providing alternate nesting habitat away from roads can reduce such mortality (Baldwin et al. 2004).

The relationships and distribution on subspecies of this turtle (*C. picta marginata, C. picta bellii, C. picta dorsalis, C. picta picta*) have been debated for decades based on the extent of patterning on the plastron and the degree of misalignment of scutes on the carapace. However, recent analyses based on genetic data suggest that the subspecies are not distinct taxa (Ultsch et al. 2001).

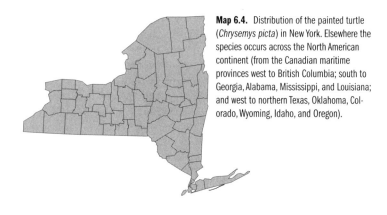

Map 6.4. Distribution of the painted turtle (*Chrysemys picta*) in New York. Elsewhere the species occurs across the North American continent (from the Canadian maritime provinces west to British Columbia; south to Georgia, Alabama, Mississippi, and Louisiana; and west to northern Texas, Oklahoma, Colorado, Wyoming, Idaho, and Oregon).

Other Intriguing Facts: Turtle Courtship

Courtship in painted turtles involves quite a bit of underwater ballet. The female uses pheromones to attract the typically much smaller male who pursues her, overtakes her, and then spins around to face her. The male has long foreclaws, with which he then strokes the female's head and neck. If the female is receptive, she counters by stroking his outstretched forearms with her shorter foreclaws. The male then swims away a short distance but returns quickly for more mutual bouts of foreclaw stroking. If both parties retain interest, the female sinks quickly to the bottom of the pond, the male swims behind, and they copulate. At any point, the larger female can break the courtship sequence and disregard the male. Peering into a pond, you will often see a large, disinterested female surrounded by several small males, each jockeying expectantly for a prime position in front of her to initiate courtship.

Spotted Turtle

Clemmys guttata [Plate 37]

Quick Identification

A small turtle with a black carapace sprinkled with bright yellow spots.

Description

Perhaps New York's most handsome freshwater turtle, this turtle has been termed the "polka dot turtle" because of its distinct yellow dots spread over a black carapace. Some spotted turtles lack spots or they may become darkly stained from water and sediment. The plastron is yellow to orange with a large black blotch on the outside edge of each scute (although the markings may be obscured by heavy stain in older individuals). The rich satin black head and neck have orange and yellow spots, too. Adult males have a concave plastron; long tail; brown eyes; and a tan, brown, or dark gray chin. Females can be identified by their flat plastron, shorter tail, orange eyes, and yellow chin. The carapace length is 3.5–4.5 in. (9–11.5 cm), with a maximum carapace length of 5 in. (12.7 cm). Hatchlings are 0.9–1.4 in. (2.4–3.6 cm) long and resemble adults (3.5–5.4 in., 9–13.6 cm). The scientific name derives from *klemmys*, or tortoise, and *guttata*, or spotted.

Turtles

Habitat

In the northeastern United States, spotted turtles typically use vernal pools in spring; upland forest for dormancy during part of the summer; and wet meadows, forested swamps, or sphagnum bogs for overwintering (Litzgus and Brooks 2000, Milam and Melvin 2001, Joyal et al. 2001). Most of the spotted turtle's aquatic haunts have similar qualities—shallow, clear water, with a muddy substrate. Winter retreats include abandoned muskrat and beaver lodges and burrows, beaver dams, cavities under the roots of flooded shrubs and trees, and flooded sections of stonewalls that cross wetlands.

Natural History

Spotted turtles are quite tolerant of cold water and normally emerge from their winter quarters in March or early April. Notably, spotted turtles have been observed basking among snow patches in midwinter during bouts of unusually mild weather. The best time to observe spotted turtles is in the spring, when they bask in full sunlight early in the morning and then while they prowl about warm shallows in search of spotted salamander and wood frog egg masses, tadpoles, snails, slugs, worms, small crustaceans, and aquatic insects (Hulse et al. 2001). In late May or early June, spotted turtles seem to disappear as shallow wetlands begin to dry out. Spotted turtles burrow into wetland muck or depart for safe haven in sunny fields where they disappear under thatch, often for weeks. Egg-carrying females then move up to several hundred yards (several hundred meters) from their retreats to their nest sites (Milam and Melvin 2001, Joyal et al. 2001) during early June. Females lay two to seven elliptical eggs in a cavity dug in grass or sedge tussocks, sphagnum moss, or loamy soils in a sunny location. Incubation takes about 7–12 weeks, depending on the warmth of the nest. Hatchlings appear in August or September, or the following April, after overwintering in the nest. Young that escape predation may grow rapidly during the first years of life but then more slowly as they approach sexual maturity at 10–15 years of age (Litzgus and Brooks 1998). When fall rains arrive, spotted turtles move to their winter retreats where temperatures remain stable and slightly above freezing (Litzgus et al. 1999). Spotted turtles typically hibernate in groups at the same site year after year (Litzgus et al. 1999, Haxton and Berrill 1999), occasionally with bog turtles and snapping turtles. Despite their diminutive size, spotted turtles are a long-lived species—wild and captive specimens have reached more than 40 years of age. Members of a wild population in Ontario averaged a minimum of 30 years of age (Seburn 2003). Densities in Massachusetts reach 0.4 adults/acre (1.4/ha; Milam and Melvin 2001).

Status and Distribution

In New York spotted turtles are found on the Great Lakes Plains south of Lake Ontario and east of Lake Erie, the lower Hudson River valley, and on Long Island (map 6.5). They are also abundant in some areas east of Lake Ontario in Oswego, Lewis, and Jefferson Counties. Spotted turtles inhabit wetlands below 700 ft. (213 m); thus, the species is not typically encountered on the Appalachian Plateau, the Catskill Mountains, or the Adirondack Mountains.

Spotted turtles are declining throughout their range. It is listed as a species of Special Concern in New York, where it suffers from habitat fragmentation, wetland draining, suburban development, invasive wetland plants, and heavy highway mortality (e.g., Lewis et al. 2004). Soaring predator populations—especially crows, raccoons, and coyotes—have also taken their toll. Commercial collection for the pet trade is a serious problem (Levell 2000).

Other Intriguing Facts: Mobile Turtles

Spotted turtles are remarkable navigators. They know their habitats well and may suddenly head for a distant vernal pool hundreds of yards away to take advantage of a food supply—drowned slugs and worms—brought by a heavy downpour. Some males have wanderlust,

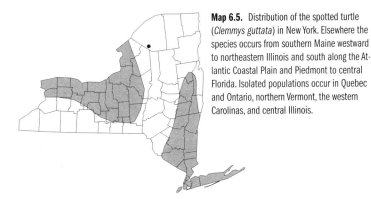

Map 6.5. Distribution of the spotted turtle (*Clemmys guttata*) in New York. Elsewhere the species occurs from southern Maine westward to northeastern Illinois and south along the Atlantic Coastal Plain and Piedmont to central Florida. Isolated populations occur in Quebec and Ontario, northern Vermont, the western Carolinas, and central Illinois.

especially in springtime, and may travel more than a mile to other wetlands in search of females. Nevertheless, spotted turtles are faithful to their hibernacula and may share the same retreat with a large number of their kin for many years.

Wood Turtle
Glyptemys [Clemmys] insculpta [Plate 38]

Quick Identification

A large brown turtle that has a dark-colored carapace with a midline ridge and dark skin except under the chin, throat, tail and forelimbs, where it is often yellow, orange, or reddish.

Description

The wood turtle is a large turtle; the average carapace length is 5.5–8 in. (14–20 cm), with a maximum carapace length of 9.2 in. (23.4 cm). The black or brown carapace is highly sculptured (hence its species name, *insculpta*, or "sculpted") and somewhat flattened overall, although it has a slightly keeled appearance. The plastron is mostly yellow except for large black blotches along the posterior, outer corners of each scute (these blotches uniquely identify individuals). The skin is dark brown to black except under the chin, throat, tail and the underside of the forelimbs which are yellow, orange or red. Males have tails that are thicker and longer than those of females. In males, the vent extends past the posterior margin of the carapace. Males also display a more concave plastron and prominent scales on the anterior surface of the forelimbs. Considered for many years as the largest member of the genus *Clemmys*, wood turtles have recently been placed with bog turtles in a newly created genus, *Glyptemys*, on the basis of genetic affiliation (Parham and Feldman 2000).

Habitat

Wood turtles have large home ranges that typically include riverside or streamside habitats bordered by woodlands or meadows (Compton et al. 2002, Arvisais et al. 2002, 2004). Within activity areas, wood turtles tend to occupy open sites close to water with low canopy cover (Compton et al. 2002), and they may use agricultural land (Kaufmann 1992a). Wood turtles bask extensively along stream banks, particularly in the early and late portions of the activity season, and they hibernate in creeks (Kaufmann 1992b). These turtles occasionally inhabit tidal fresh water areas in the Hudson River (Kiviat and Barbour 1996).

Natural History

Wood turtles consume mostly animal material, specifically earthworms, snails and slugs, insects, amphibians (tadpoles and adults), mice, carrion, as well as some filamentous algae, moss, grass, willow and alder leaves, berries, and fungi (Ernst 2001, Walde et al. 2003). These turtles are typically active only by day (Ernst 2001), from March to April through October and November. In New York, aggressive interactions occur between males on land (Barzilay 1980), although wood turtles are not considered territorial (Kaufmann 1992b). Wood turtles do not mature sexually until 14–18 years of age. Nesting occurs from May through early July, with females laying 4–12 elliptical eggs in sunny areas with well-drained yet somewhat moist and loose soil that is free of debris and not prone to flooding. Predators take most nests, and up to 60% of adults are injured in any population (Brooks et al. 1992); this is a particular problem in agricultural areas due to encounters with machinery (Saumure and Bider 1998). Hatching occurs from September to October (hatchlings are not known to overwinter in the nest). Once emerged, hatchlings may disperse overland considerable distances before establishing a permanent home range. Densities in suitable riparian habitat can reach 1.8/acre (4.42 /ha, Ernst 2001). Daily movements are usually less than 425 ft. (100 m), although females may travel up to 0.6 mi. (1 km) to nest (Ernst 2001). Unlike most turtles, this species has genetic sex determination (Ewert

Turtles

Map 6.6. Distribution of the wood turtle (*Glyptemys insculpta*) in New York. The species occurs throughout eastern North America, from Nova Scotia and southern Quebec southward through New England, New York, Pennsylvania, northern New Jersey, northern Maryland, northern Virginia, and northeastern West Virginia. It ranges westward into Ontario, north and central Michigan, Wisconsin, and eastern Minnesota and Iowa.

and Nelson 1991). In New York, wood turtles suffer from parasitism by *Placobdella* leeches, especially during the winter months when the animals are highly aquatic, but infestation declines in summer as turtles remain dry for longer periods (Koffler et al. 1978).

Status and Distribution

Although widely scattered through New York (map 6.6), wood turtles are most common in the Hudson River Valley. The species is listed of Special Concern. Once widespread, wood turtle populations have suffered from overcollection for the pet trade (for which this species is avidly sought; Levell 2000), road mortality and others factors that are not well understood.

Other Intriguing Facts: Going, Going, Gone . . .

Just how vulnerable are wood turtle populations? One herpetologist, Steve Garber, spent 20 years studying a wood turtle population on land controlled by the South Central Connecticut Regional Water Authority. On 2,471 acres (1,000 ha), he marked some 133 turtles. For the first decade of his study, populations remained stable and healthy. But in 1983, when the Authority began issuing access permits to hikers, the turtles began to disappear almost immediately. Garber investigated whether road mortality, predation, or disease might be the cause of the decline, but the problem turned out to simply be hikers taking the turtles home. By 1991, only 14 turtles remained, and by 1992 the population had dropped to zero. Scientists can marshal impressive data and statistics on the subject of the sensitivity of turtle populations to overharvest, but this anecdote gets right to the point (Garber and Burger 1995).

Bog Turtle (Muhlenberg's Turtle)
Glyptemys [Clemmys] muhlenbergii [Plate 39]

Quick Identification

A small turtle with bright yellow or orange blotch on each side of the head and neck.

Description

The bog turtle is New York's smallest turtle. The carapace length is 3–3.5 in. (7.5–9 cm), with a maximum carapace length of 4.5 in. (11.4 cm). A bright yellow or orange blotch on each side of the head and neck is characteristic. The carapace is domed and somewhat rectangular, often with prominent rings on the scutes, although in older individuals or those that burrow in coarse substrates, shells may be smooth and polished. Although generally black, the carapace sometimes has a chestnut-colored, sunburst pattern on each scute. The plastron lacks a hinge and has cream and black blotches. The scientific name honors Rev. Gotthilf Heinrich Ernst Muhlenberg, who collected the first specimen.

Habitat

In New York, bog turtles are found in open, early successional habitats such as wet meadows or open calcareous fens generally dominated by sedges or sphagnum moss. Despite their name, they are not known to inhabit acidic bogs. Other habitat features are cool, shallow, slow-moving waters; deep, soft, muck soils; and tussock-forming, low-lying, herbaceous vegetation. In Virginia, bog turtles favor wet meadow, smooth alder, and bulrush, and they avoid dry meadows and streams (Carter et al. 1999).

Natural History

In New York, bog turtles emerge from hibernation (often spent communally in an abandoned muskrat lodge or other burrow with other bog turtles and spotted turtles) by mid-April when air and water temperatures exceed 50°F (10°C). These turtles also use soft mud within spring-fed rivulets for hibernation. They are extremely secretive but can be seen basking in the open, often on hummocks in early spring. Highly mobile turtles, bog turtles often use multiple wetlands in a given year (Carter et al. 2000, Morrow et al. 2001). They eat what they can find but prefer slugs, worms, and insects, and they sometimes take seeds, plant leaves, and carrion (Barton and Price 1955, Bury 1979). Mating activities occur primarily in the spring (Barton and Price 1955) but also in the fall, often focused in or near the hibernaculum. In early to mid-June, the female lays a clutch of two to four eggs in nests that are usually located inside the upper part of an unshaded tussock. The eggs hatch around mid-September. Some young turtles spend the winter in the nest, emerging the following spring. The adults enter hibernation in late October. Sexual maturity may be reached as early as 8 years or as late as 11 years. Longevity may extend to 30 years.

Turtles

Status and Distribution

In New York, more than half of 74 known, historic bog turtle locations still contain apparently suitable habitat, but only one-fourth of these support extant populations; these are primarily in the southeastern part of the state (Klemens 2001). Most remaining locations are also in southeastern New York. However, few populations occur in Seneca and Oswego Counties (map 6.7). The US Fish and Wildlife Service (USFWS) listed the bog turtle as Threatened in 1997, and the species has been included in Appendix I of the Convention of International Trade in Endangered Species since 1975. In New York, the bog turtle is listed as Endangered. Unfortunately, illegal collection continues, threatening this long-lived, slowly reproducing turtle, even though collection without a permit is prohibited in all states where it occurs. Invasive plant species can also reduce habitat quality for this species (Morrow et al. 2001). Habitat conservation efforts should focus on slowing ecological succession and habitat loss and not altering wetland hydrology (Carter et al. 1999).

Other Intriguing Facts: Reasons for Decline

Populations of bog turtles are in decline for a number of reasons. In New York, development and natural succession are the major threats to bog turtle habitat. As sites deteriorate, bog turtles normally move out of their old sites to find new areas that fire, beavers, agriculture, or other environmental factors may have created the open wet meadow type habitat that the turtles prefer. But development, especially roads, residential, and commercial and reservoir construction, inhibits the

Map 6.7. Distribution of the bog turtle (*Glyptemys muhlenbergii*) in New York. The species occurs in scattered colonies from New York and Massachusetts south to southern Tennessee and Georgia.

ability of the species to move to new locations. Consequently, new populations are not being established as old sites deteriorate. Contamination by pesticides, agricultural runoff, and industrial discharge may also affect populations as well as the turtle's invertebrate food supply. Like other ectothermic species, bog turtles require habitats with a good deal of solar penetration for basking and egg incubation, but plants such as purple loosestrife and common reed can quickly invade such areas, resulting in the loss of critical basking and nesting habitat.

Blanding's Turtle
Emydoidea [Emys] blandingii [Plate 40]

Quick Identification

A mid- to large-sized turtle with a bright yellow throat and a smooth, elongated, helmet-shaped, brown to black carapace containing cream or tan squiggles and streaks.

Description

Whether it is seen poking its head out of the water for a look about or basking on a distant log, the bright yellow throat of Blanding's turtles is a dead giveaway. It has a smooth, elongated, dark carapace, domed to a helmet-shape, that is decorated with cream or tan squiggles and streaks. Its plastron is ivory-yellow with brown-black blotches on the outer rear edge of each scute. Like an eastern box turtle, Blanding's turtles have a hinge, which allows the front lobe of the shell to close and protect the head and front limbs from predators. The head is rather flat. The upper jaw is notched in front, which coupled with the bright yellow lower jaw and the slight upward curve of the jawline, gives a "smiley face" impression. Blanding's turtles have an unusually long neck; this serves as a periscope when they are in shallow water or exploring deep pockets underwater for prey. The plastron may exceed the length of the carapace. The carapace length is 5–7 in. (12.5–18 cm), with a maximum carapace length of 10.75 in. (27.4 cm). Hatchlings are 1.1–1.4 in. (2.8–3.5 cm) long. The scientific name honors Dr. William Blanding, who first located the species.

Habitat

Key habitat characteristics for Blanding's turtles in New York are (1) both shallow (12 in. [30 cm]) and deep (48 in. [120 cm]) pools connected by channels; (2) tree canopy open or absent; (3) tree fringe present; (4) a dense cover of shrubs, forbs, and grasses dispersed as hummocks and tussocks throughout the wetland; and (5) coarse and fine organic debris (Kiviat 1997, G. Johnson unpublished data). Nesting habitat may be some distance from wetlands and includes plowed agriculture fields, pastures, lawns, and road berms. In northern New York, a radiotelemetry study of 18 Blanding's turtles indicated that home ranges averaged 62.8 acres (0.254 km²) (Jensen 2004). During the hot summer months, turtles remain in wetlands or retreat to forested uplands, where they burrow under leaf litter, sometimes at surprisingly large distances from wetlands (Joyal et al. 2001). Their hibernacula are located in vernal pools, shrub swamps, and ponds.

Natural History

Blanding's turtles are active from early April to October or November. They may move around under the ice in winter as well. Courtship and breeding activity take place in shallow water and commence shortly after emergence from the winter retreats. Fewer than half of the adult females in a population may nest in a given year. Nesting females travel up to 0.6 mi. (1 km) overland to find a suitable sunny spot for deposition of their eggs (Joyal et al. 2000). Clutch size varies from 6 to 21 eggs (Joyal et al. 2000). Predators take most eggs before hatching (Congdon et al. 2000). Hatchlings emerge from nests from August to October after 8–17 weeks of incubation, and shrews occasionally eat them (Standing et al. 2000). Blanding's turtles

Map 6.8. Distribution of Blanding's turtle (*Emydoidea blandingii*) in New York. Elsewhere the species is primarily a midwestern, ranging from southwestern Quebec and southern Ontario west to Minnesota and Nebraska, and south to central Illinois, with isolated populations in Nova Scotia, southern Maine, southeastern New Hampshire, and eastern Massachusetts.

feed in water and on land, and in water, they ambush and stalk their prey. Crayfish are a favorite food item of adults. The turtles also consume tadpoles, frogs, small fish, leeches, aquatic insects, snails, slugs, worms, berries, and leaves. When prey are within reach of the long neck, the turtle thrusts its head forward. At the last instant, the turtle's large mouth and cavernous throat open, causing water and prey to be sucked in. During the hot days of summer, Blanding's turtles feed at night.

Status and Distribution

Blanding's turtles occur in northern and eastern New York (map 6.8) where they are found mainly in the St. Lawrence drainage in Jefferson and St. Lawrence Counties (Petokas and Alexander 1981, Johnson and Wills 1997) and in the Great Lakes Plain in Niagara County. There is also an enigmatic population in the lower Hudson River valley in Dutchess County and one recently discovered in Saratoga County. Isolated records on map 6.8 are almost certainly released animals, which have caused significant confusion in determining the true range of Blanding's turtles in New York.

Blanding's turtle is listed as a Threatened species in New York. Residential development and the associated loss of vernal pools and marshlands, along with development in ancient travel corridors between the turtle's wetland habitats and between these wetlands and their nesting areas, are the leading reasons for this species' decline (Kiviat and Stevens 2003). Populations are sensitive to very small reductions in adult survival (Congdon et al. 2000). Once thriving populations have vanished in recent years. This species is also sought after for the pet trade (Levell 2000).

Other Intriguing Facts: Older Than We Think . . .

Long-term studies of a Blanding's turtle population in southern Michigan (Congdon et al. 1993) showed that sexual maturity was not reached until the turtles were 14–20 years of age. These are long-lived turtles and may reach 50 or 70 years of age, or older, in the wild. Investigators calculated that more than 93% of the adults and at least 72% of the juveniles greater than 1 year of age had to survive each year to maintain a stable population. Thus, if predation, road mortality, disease, winter-kill, or incidental collection were to increase losses beyond these narrow limits, population decline is extremely likely.

Turtles

Northern Map Turtle (Common Map Turtle)
Graptemys geographica [Plate 41]

Quick Identification

An aquatic turtle with a keeled carapace that is covered by map-like network of dark bordered yellow-orange lines and circles.

Description

The northern map turtle's common name is derived from the network of dark-bordered yellow-orange lines and circles on its gray brown or olive carapace that has the appearance of a topographical map. (Older individuals often have a uniformly dark shell.) The carapace is smooth with a keel down the midline, and the rear edge is flared and serrated. The plastron of the adult northern map turtle is plain yellow and fades to a cream color in older adults. The border of scutes of the plastron may have dark markings in small individuals. Fine yellow, orange, or greenish lines accent the head, neck, and legs, and a light blotch — often oval or triangular in shape — is seen behind the eye. Females are decidedly larger than males, and the head of females is wide and their carapace is broad and has a low keel. In contrast, males have a relatively narrow head and an oval carapace with a distinctive keel. The carapace length for males is 3.5–6.5 in. (9–16 cm) and for females 7–11.0 in. (18–27.5 cm). Hatchlings are 1.1–1.3 in. (28–34 cm) long and patterned like the adults. The scientific name is derived from *graptos*, or inscribed; *emys*, or turtle; and *geographica* or "world map," referring to topographic map-like patterns on back of carapace.

Habitat

This species is a "big water" turtle, meaning that, in New York it is primarily found in bays and inlets of Lake Ontario and in large rivers, preferring those stretches that are slow moving and have soft bottoms and good basking sites. In Minnesota, northern map turtles are associated with the presence of open sandy areas, uniform channel bottoms, and gravel substrates (DonnerWright et al. 1999). Large northern map turtles prefer deep sections of rivers, whereas smaller individuals prefer slow and shallow areas. Northern map turtles use large toppled trees, logs, exposed rocks, and sandbars for basking, preferring those sites that are not connected to the shoreline. In backwaters and lakesides, they bask on large muskrat lodges.

Natural History

Northern map turtles overwinter under submerged logs, in mud at the bottom of deep pools, or in beaver or muskrat burrows. The turtles require hibernacula with well-oxygenated water (Reese et al. 2001), where they can avoid lactic acid buildup from anaerobic respiration over the long winter (Crocker et al. 2000), which may be the reason these turtles are mainly found in rivers and large lakes rather than in small ponds and swamps. Northern map turtles typically reuse the same hibernaculum between years and range as far as 9 mi. (15 km) from it (Graham et al. 2000). Northern map turtles emerge in April and may be seen basking in some numbers on warm sunny days (Gordon and MacCulloch 1980). These turtles are alert and quick to desert their basking sites for deep water when disturbed; when one departs, the rest quickly follow. Mating occurs in the spring and fall, with nesting occurring from late May through early July. Occasionally, females produce a second clutch in a season. Nesting usually takes place in early morning or late afternoon. Females return to former nesting sites, looking for unshaded sand or soft-soil locations to dig their flask-shaped nest cavity. A clutch may contain 6–20 oval, flexible-shelled eggs. Eggs hatch and emerge in August or September but hatchlings in late nests may overwinter in the nest cavity and escape the following spring. Males take about 3–5 years to mature, although females need some 10–14 years to reach sexual maturity. Diets of males and females differ. Female with their massive head and powerful jaws with wide crushing surfaces in the mouth are well designed to smash large snails, freshwater clams, and crayfish. Diminutive males (typically much younger than females) take aquatic insects, small snails and crustaceans. Raccoons are the most significant predator on northern map turtle nests, whereas herons and large fish prey on hatchlings.

Status and Distribution

In New York, northern map turtles are known from the south shore of Lake Ontario, the St. Lawrence River, the Lake Champaign and Hudson River valleys, and the Niagara River (map 6.9). The turtles may also be present in the Delaware River in New York (they are found in the Delaware Water Gap National Recreation Area just south of the state line).

Northern map turtles are wary and are quick to retreat when approached. However, the turtles cannot escape the waterfront development that destroys nesting habitats or the increased traffic that causes mortality in females who are traveling in search of a suitable nesting area. Occasionally, northern map turtles are killed by speedboat propellers or mortally wounded by the hooks of bait fishermen. Northern map turtles have disappeared from waterways where the food chain has collapsed because of pollution and habitats simplified from channelization (Vandewalle and Christiansen 1996).

Other Intriguing Facts: Odd Bedfellows

Northern map turtles sometimes choose odd companions with which to spend the winter. In the Lamoille River in Vermont, an aggregation of more then 36 northern leopard frogs was found in a northern map turtle hibernaculum. The frogs were sometimes lurking under the turtles. Turtles do not feed during the winter, so the frogs likely did not feel threatened. Were they all seeking companionship over the long winter? Probably not. Both the frogs and turtles prefer to overwinter submerged in a secure, oxygen-rich microenvironment, which is difficult to find, and likely merely tolerated, if even noticed, one another's presence (Ultsch et al. 2000).

Map 6.9. Distribution of the northern map turtle [common map turtle] (*Graptemys geographica*) in New York. Elsewhere the species occurs from southern Quebec; the Great Lakes region; and central Minnesota southward to central Alabama, eastern Kansas, and Arkansas. Scattered populations exist in the northeastern United States.

Diamond-backed Terrapin (Diamondback Terrapin)
Malaclemys terrapin [Plate 42]

Quick Identification

A medium-sized turtle of estuaries and salt marshes with distinct concentric grooves on each scute and light colored skin covered with dark flecks.

Description

These medium-sized turtles inhabit brackish water of estuaries and salt marshes. Occurrence in or near salt marshes may be one of the most helpful clues in identifying diamond-backed terrapins. Their carapace ranges in color from gray to light brown to black, and it is broad and keeled with noticeable concentric grooves on each scute. Posterior marginal scutes are slightly upward curled and somewhat serrated. The skin is typically light colored but may range from white to gray, and it is covered with dark flecks. The plastron lacks a hinge and may be yellow, green, or black. The feet are strongly webbed, and the hind limbs are strikingly large. The head is egg-shaped, protruding from a narrower neck. Many individuals have dark, mustache-like markings on the face. Color variation may be extensive. Males are dramatically smaller than females; the carapace length is 4–5.5 in. (10–14 cm) for males and 6–9 in. (15.0–23.5 cm) for females. Females also often have noticeably shorter tails and proportionally larger heads than males. The scientific name is derived from *malakos*, or soft, *clemmys*, or turtle, referring to the skin of this turtle, which is softer than that of other turtles. Terrapin is a Native American word for turtle.

Habitat

Diamond-backed terrapins commonly inhabit coastal salt marshes, bays, estuaries, and tidal creeks. Juveniles seem to spend their first few years of life within and beneath tidal debris near the shoreline. This species is able to tolerate the polluted waters surrounding New York City. Most nesting occurs in shrub land, dune and mixed-grasslands; exposed sand along trails or beaches are heavily used (Feinberg and Burke 2003).

Turtles

Natural History

Diamond-backed terrapins in New York emerge from late April to early May after spending the winter in small marsh creeks, where they hibernate individually or in small groups on the bottom under water, buried atop creek banks and beneath undercut banks (Johnson and Yearicks 1981). Terrapins remain active throughout the summer months and may not reenter hibernacula until November or December (ocean waters retain summer heat well into autumn). Apart from nesting activities, diamond-backed terrapins are diurnal. They are carnivorous and often pursue their prey, targeting a variety of mollusks, crabs, and other marine invertebrates. Limited by the small size of their mouths, terrapins as often "crop" the legs off oversized crabs (Davenport et al. 1992). Importantly, terrapins are a vital component of the marsh food web by helping to control the abundance of periwinkles (grazing snails), thereby preventing conversion by periwinkles of perhaps the most productive grasslands in the world to barren mudflats (Hurd et al. 1979, Silliman and Bertness 2002).

Male terrapins attain sexual maturity at 3 years of age, whereas females may not mature until 6 years of age. Consequently, sex ratios in some adult populations are often heavily male-biased (Lovich and Gibbons 1990), although the bias can be reversed in areas where crabbing occurs due to the greater vulnerability of males' drowning in crab pots (Roosenburg et al. 1997). Mating in terrapins occurs most often in April or May. During the height of mating, terrapins may form large breeding aggregations with many heads visible bobbing above the water's surface. Courtship may last for hours, and mating occurs in water. On Long Island, nesting begins in June and extends into July (Feinberg and Burke 2003), at which time the females leave the water, especially at high tide and on warm days to nest nearby in soil not threatened by tidal inundation (Burger and Montevecchi 1975). Females lay 4–15 pinkish leathery eggs (New York average : 10.9 eggs/clutch) and at least two clutches in a given year (Feinberg and Burke 2003). Hatching peaks in September, but hatchlings may not emerge from late-deposited clutches until early spring. Recently, nest predation is reportedly extensive. Of 2,053 nests monitored in 1999 at Gateway National Recreation Area on Long Island, New York, some 92% were predated primarily by raccoons, which also kill nesting females (Feinberg and Burke 2003). Nest predators also include Norway rats (Draud et al. 2004). Ghost crabs kill hatchlings (Arndt 1994).

Status and Distribution

In New York, the range of diamond-backed terrapins is largely confined to Long Island, including the brackish waters of the New York City metropolitan area (map 6.10). These turtles also penetrate far up the Hudson River (to Tivoli Bay; Simoes and Chambers 1999). Diamond-backed terrapins have recovered from near extinction due to overharvest in the early 1900s but face many renewed threats and an uncertain future (see Chapter 11: Conservation Case Studies). Although nest protection efforts are important, protection of juveniles and adults at sea is equally or perhaps more so (Mitro 2003). Enforcing the use of redesigned crab pots that prevent drowning of terrapins is particularly needed (Tucker et al. 2001); terrapin-friendly crab pot designs already exist and evidently do not reduce crab catches (Cole and Helser 2001, Roosenburg and Green 2000). Mercury contamination is an issue for both terrapins and the humans who might eat them (Burger 2002).

Other Intriguing Facts: "Eggectomies"

"Eggectomies" are postmortem surgeries to salvage eggs from diamond-backed terrapins killed during nesting migrations on roads. Eggs are taken from road-killed female turtles by cutting through the skin just anterior to the hind legs. From this location, the oviduct is reached and

Map 6.10. Distribution of the diamond-backed terrapin [diamondback terrapin] (*Malaclemys terrapin*) in New York. Elsewhere the species range extends from Massachusetts along the Atlantic Coast to Florida and westward along the Gulf Coast into Texas.

then opened to remove the eggs. After rinsing, the recovered eggs are placed in containers for incubation. The Wetlands Institute of Stone Harbor, New Jersey, in collaboration with Stockton College and SUNY at Cortland, has incubated hundreds of eggs in this manner, releasing the young terrapins after they reach a critical size. These compassionate efforts can make an important contribution to terrapin conservation by saving a valuable clutch of eggs, but unfortunately there is little mitigation possible for the loss of the life of a mature adult female that could have produced more than 30 similar such clutches had she not been flattened on a road.

Northern Red-bellied Cooter (Eastern Redbelly Turtle)
Pseudemys rubriventris [Plate 43]

Quick Identification

A large pond turtle with a dark carapace and dark skin of the head and neck, which is covered with bright yellow stripes but lacks a marking behind eye. It has been, introduced throughout New York and is especially common on Long Island.

Description

This large pond turtle (9–14 in. [24–35 cm]) has a dark brown to black carapace. The plastron is reddish to orange-yellow with no markings. Marginal scutes have vertical, red-colored bars. Dark brown skin of head and neck is covered with bright yellow stripes. The northern red-bellied cooter is often confused with pond sliders but, unlike them, has no marking behind eye.

Habitat

Northern red-bellied cooters inhabit lakes and ponds with sandy or muddy bottoms and aquatic vegetation. They live in marshes and rivers with little current and abundant deepwater basking sites (especially logs).

Natural History

Little is known of the biology of northern red-bellied cooters in large part for two reasons: (1) they are wary, leaving basking sites at the slightest disturbance, and (2) they are difficult to capture in standard meat-baited traps because adults are largely herbivorous (Hulse et al.

2001). The turtles are active in the northeast from May through October (Babcock 1971), lay 8–35 or more eggs in June and July in nests often distant (up to 820 ft. [250 m]) from water (Mitchell 1974), and overwinter on pond bottoms (Graham and Guimond 1995).

Status and Distribution

Northern red-bellied cooters currently have a scattered distribution in central parts of New York State as well as Long Island, resulting from illegal releases of unwanted pets (map 6.11). An isolated, native, and endangered population also occurs in Massachusetts, and this has been the subject of intensive recovery efforts, including head-starting of young turtles (Haskell et al. 1996). In New Jersey, this species is fairly tolerant of water pollution (Saba and Spotila 2003).

Other Intriguing Facts: Native Turned Exotic?

Northern red-bellied cooters are usually reviled as an exotic species in New York State and an unwanted intrusion to its native herpetofauna. But at one time this species was likely native to the southern New York. It was extirpated by turtle hunters who had shifted their attentions in the late-1800s to northern red-bellied cooters in the northern part of the species range in response to depletions of terrapin populations (Hulse et al. 2001). Because most current records of northern red-bellied cooters in New York fall outside the estimated historical range of the species in New York, the species is now best regarded as an introduced form.

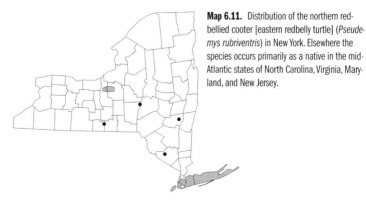

Map 6.11. Distribution of the northern red-bellied cooter [eastern redbelly turtle] (*Pseudemys rubriventris*) in New York. Elsewhere the species occurs primarily as a native in the mid-Atlantic states of North Carolina, Virginia, Maryland, and New Jersey.

Eastern Box Turtle
Terrapene carolina [Plate 44]

Quick Identification

A medium-sized turtle with a highly domed, double-hinged shell and variable patterns of yellow, orange, or olive markings on a dark brown or black scutes, and blunt feet with four toes on the hind feet.

Description

The eastern box turtle is a small- to medium-sized, mostly terrestrial species most often found on or near moist soils. The carapace length is 4.5–6 in. (11.5–15.0 cm), with a maximum carapace length of 7.8 in. (19.8 cm). The shell is highly domed. Scutes forming the carapace have variable patterns of yellow, orange, or olive markings on a dark brown or black background. The plastron has two transverse hinges that allow the turtle to shut both lobes of the plastron tightly (hence the common name "box" turtle). The feet are blunt, and each hind foot has four toes. Males usually have red eyes and a depression on the hind lobe of the plastron to facilitate perching on females' carapaces, whereas females have yellowish-brown eyes and no depression on plastron. Males also have longer, thicker tails than females. The scientific name derives from *terrapene*, a Native American word for turtle, and the Carolina region where the turtle was originally found.

Habitat

Eastern box turtles live in open and logged-over woodlands, meadows, pastures, old fields and powerline cuts. The species seems to prefer habitat with sandy, well-drained soil, often near ponds or streams.

Natural History

Eastern box turtles are strictly diurnal and forage most actively in early morning for slugs, earthworms, wild strawberries, and mushrooms. These turtles also eat a variety of fruits and increase seed germination rates and disperse seeds (Braun and Brooks 1987). On Long Island, eastern box turtles have a particular preference for fungi, especially *Russula* (Latham 1968b). The turtles do not roam far if habitat conditions are stable; an individual may spend its entire life in an area the size of a football field, and some individuals have been found at sites where they were marked decades previously (Stickel 1950). Although largely terrestrial, eastern box turtles may soak in mud or water for hours at a time, especially during the hottest periods of the summer. During drought conditions, they burrow under logs or vegetation, or migrate to wet areas. When sudden summer rains arrive, eastern box turtles may appear in large numbers. Courtship is often prolonged, and females can store sperm for extended periods; perhaps their small home ranges mean that these turtles infrequently encounter one another. Nesting occurs mostly in June, when females lay four to seven round white eggs in sunny, sandy, or loamy soils. Hatching normally occurs in September and October, although hatchlings may overwinter in the nest. Eastern box turtles have extended hibernation periods in the soil and are only active typically from May through October. The species is freeze-tolerant (Storey et al. 1993). Eastern box turtles reach sexual maturity at 5–10 years and live to 30–40 years, with some individuals approaching the century mark (Stickel 1978).

Status and Distribution

In New York, eastern box turtles are most commonly encountered in the Hudson River valley. They are scattered throughout the Appalachian Plateau and still locally common, although declining, in many parts of Long Island (map 6.12). Elsewhere in the central and western New York, occurrence is spotty, most likely the result of released pets but possibly remnant populations of a species once far more widely distributed before decimations by Native Americans and

Turtles

Map 6.12. Distribution of the eastern box turtle (*Terrapene carolina*) in New York. Elsewhere the species occurs throughout the eastern North America from southern Maine south through Florida and west to Michigan, Illinois, eastern Kansas, Oklahoma, and Texas.

early European settlers (Adler 1970). Eastern box turtles are listed of Special Concern in New York State. Although eastern box turtles respond favorably to land clearing, they suffer from overcollection (Levell 2000) and road mortality, which has resulted in long-terms declines of the species in many parts of its range (Hall et al. 1999). On Long Island, a positive relationship evidently exists between organochlorine pesticide pollution and the level of bacterial infections in eastern box turtles (Tangredi et al. 1997).

Other Intriguing Facts: A Centenarian Box Turtle

John Treadwell Nichols (1883–1958), of the American Museum of Natural History, marked nearly 1,000 eastern box turtles on his Long Island estate, some of which are still alive and well. Nichols marked each turtle by etching his initials, the date, and a unique number to each turtle's shell with a penknife (see figure 1.1). He paid his children five cents for each marked turtle and three cents for each unmarked turtle they collected while he was away from the estate. Turtles were kept in the window wells of the estate until Nichols' return, when he would mark and then release them at the estate's flagpole. One of Nichols' marked turtles was discovered September 16, 2002 (Plate 44). The turtle in question, "JN21/21," was approximately 20 years old at the time of its first marking in 1921. Nichols' field notes indicate the turtle was about the same size when he found him more than 80 years earlier. Many of Nichols' turtles are still being discovered 60 to 70 years later in the same locations Nichols once found them.

Pond Slider (Slider, Red-Eared Slider, Yellowbelly Slider)
Trachemys scripta   [Plates 45 and 46]

Quick Identification

Two subspecies that have been widely introduced into urban and suburban ponds, particularly on Long Island: a red-eared slider has a red stripe behind the eye, a yellow plastron with black striping, and a green to brown body with yellow stripes (Plate 45) whereas a yellowbelly slider has a yellow blotch behind the eye, vertical yellow bars on costal scutes, and a yellow plastron with dark spots on anterior scutes (Plate 46).

Description

Both subspecies of pond sliders are medium-sized pond turtles (5–8 in. [12–20 cm]). Females are typically larger than males. Red-eared sliders (*Trachemys scripta elegans*) have a red stripe behind the eye (which fades with age). The plastron is yellow with black striping. The carapace and the body are green to brown with yellow stripes, which can become dull brown with age. Yellowbelly sliders (*Trachemys scripta scripta*) have a yellow blotch behind the eye. The carapace has vertical yellow bars on the costal scutes. The plastron is yellow with dark spots on the anterior scutes.

Habitat

Pond sliders prefer quiet, deep fresh water that has a muddy bottom and abundant vegetation. The turtles are occasionally found in moving waters, and they bask on rocks, logs, vegetation, and sometimes on banks (Dundee and Rossman, 1989).

Natural History

Pond sliders excavate their nests along banks (Packard et al., 1997). Clutch size varies from 2 to 19 eggs and is typically between 7 and 13 (Tucker and Janzen, 1998). Eggs hatch in approximately 68–70 days (Dundee and Rossman, 1989). Females may lay up to three clutches per season. Hatchlings may overwinter in nest (Packard

Turtles

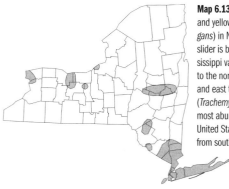

Map 6.13. Distribution of the red-eared slider and yellowbelly slider (*Trachemys scripta elegans*) in New York. Elsewhere the red-eared slider is believed to naturally occur in the Mississippi valley from northern Illinois and Indiana to the northern Gulf of Mexico, west to Texas, and east to western Alabama. Yellowbelly sliders (*Trachemys scripta elegans*) are perhaps the most abundant turtle in the southeastern United States and occur along the coastal plain from southeastern Virginia to northern Florida.

et al., 1997). The turtles are omnivorous; however, juveniles tend to be more carnivorous, whereas older specimens tend to be more herbivorous (Dundee and Rossman, 1989). Sexual maturity is reached at 2–5 years, and adults live for 50–75 years (Dundee and Rossman, 1989).

Status and Distribution

Pond sliders occur commonly on Long Island and are scattered elsewhere in New York State (map 6.13). The two subspecies constitute so-called "cooter colonies" now reproducing in urban and suburban water bodies in the state (notable breeding populations occur in Lake Ronkonkoma and the Bronx River). Populations are also sustained by continuous releases of pet trade animals. This species is an major component of the international trade in pet turtles, with about 6 million pond sliders exported from the United States each year since 1988 (Schlaepfer et al. 2005). Pond sliders have been so widely released that the native range of these turtles is now not fully known.

Other Intriguing Facts: Interactions with Native Turtles

Despite how commonly pond sliders are introduced to ponds and lakes of urban and suburban New York, we know little about their effects on native turtles. But research in Europe on the effects of red-eared sliders on one of Europe's few native turtles, the European pond turtle (*Emys orbicularis*) suggests that the introduced turtles can be a problem (Cadi and Joly 2003). The researchers examined competition for basking sites. Being ectothermic, basking sites can be a crucial resource to turtles, especially in early spring when turtles are attempting to recover from hibernation and jump-start their physiologies for reproduction during the short, temperate zone warm season. Both the introduced and native turtles preferred the same basking resource—places in the safe zone of open, deep water. The bad news is that the sliders outcompeted the native turtles for preferred basking sites. The same behavioral asymmetry may be occurring between pond sliders of "cooter colonies" in New York and native species, such as painted turtles. This possibility is worth examining further to better understand the impacts of "cooters" on native turtles.

Loggerhead
Caretta caretta [Plate 47]

Quick Identification

Occasionally stranded on Long Island, a large, reddish-brown turtle with two pairs of prefrontal plates on the conspicuously large, block-like head.

Description

The carapace length of this reddish-brown turtle is 31–45 in. (79–114 cm), with a maximum carapace length of 48 in. (122 cm) or more, and a weight of about 300 lb. (136 kg). Both the loggerhead and Kemp's ridley seaturtles have five or more costal scutes on each side between the vertebral and marginal scutes. The vertebral scutes of the loggerhead's carapace are slightly keeled. The loggerhead has two pairs of prefrontal plates on the conspicuously large, blocklike head. The plastron is yellow to cream-colored, often with two low ridges, and the skin is reddish brown, similar to the color of the carapace. Males have long tails extending beyond the posterior edge of the carapace. *Caretta* is a contraction of the term "carey" for a type of tur-tle and Latin "etta" for little.

Habitat

Within its range, loggerheads inhabit warm waters on continental shelves and areas among islands. These turtles prefer estuaries, coastal streams, and salt marshes.

Natural History

Loggerheads wander extensively throughout the Atlantic, Pacific, and Indian Oceans, usually far out in the open ocean, but occa-sionally entering into bays, lagoons, salt marshes, and mouths of large rivers. The loggerhead's powerful jaws are well suited to eating hard-shelled prey. Loggerheads are omnivorous, feeding on crabs and other crustaceans, mollusks, jellyfish, sponges, and sometimes fish and eelgrass (invertebrates seem to be their most important food source; Burke et al. 1993). Occasionally in Long Island Sound, the turtles eat sea horses (*Hippocampus erectus*) (Burke and Stan-dora 1993).

Turtles

Most nesting occurs north of the Gulf of Mexico and Caribbean Sea in temperate waters, although some individuals nest in the western Caribbean. Loggerheads also nest along the southeastern US coast, with 90% of nests occurring in Florida. Females breed every 2–3 years and leave the water to lay their eggs on beaches at night above the high tide mark. An individual may nest up to seven times in a single season, laying 100–125 eggs every 2 weeks or so. The eggs hatch in 55–65 days; the hatchlings emerge at night to spend their first year among mats of *Sargassum* weed and other flotsam. Sexual maturity is reached in 10–15 years, and the estimated maximum lifespan is 30 years.

Status and Distribution

The loggerhead is perhaps the most common of the sea turtles and the only one that still regularly nests on the US Atlantic coast—on beaches from New Jersey to Texas. Loggerheads are found nearly globally, preferring temperate and subtropical waters. In the western Atlantic, they range from the Canadian maritime provinces south to Argentina. In New York, the species occurs in Long Island Sound and is occasionally stranded on its beaches. It is listed as a Threatened species in New York State and is also considered Threatened by the federal government.

Other Intriguing Facts: Modern Hazards

Loggerheads are regularly caught in commercial fishing gear around Long Island, but their numbers shift annually for unclear reasons. In most years loggerheads are the dominant species of marine turtle captured (about 20 per year), constituting one-half to three-fourths of captures of all such turtles. But some years their numbers drop, perhaps due to changes in Gulf Stream eddies. A big conservation concern in the region is changing modes of fishing. Traditionally "pound nets" open to the surface, which entrap but do not drown turtles, have been used. More recently, "fish pots," in which the entire net structure is submerged, are being used, which prevents entrapped marine turtles from surfacing to breathe. Balancing the needs of New York's struggling commercial fishing industry and the welfare of loggerheads is a continual challenge.

Green Seaturtle (Green Turtle)
Chelonia mydas [Plate 48]

Quick Identification

Occasionally stranded on Long Island, a large olive to brown turtle with a broad, smooth, heart-shaped carapace.

Description

The adult green seaturtle is named for the greenish color of its fat or "calipee" used for soup stock, not its shell color. This turtle is a medium to large: it has a carapace length of 36–48 in. (90–122 cm), with a maximum carapace length of 60.4 in. (153 cm). Giant specimens may reach 750 lb. (340 kg). The color is olive to brown, occasionally black. The carapace is broad, smooth, and heart-shaped, and it may be blotched or patterned with radiating yellow, brown, or black streaks. The plastron is white or yellow, and the bridge between the plastron and the carapace has four large, poreless scutes. The darkly colored scales of the head and flippers are often edged in yellow. Males have a large prehensile tail, which is tipped with a heavy, flattened nail. Hatchling green seaturtles are 1.5–2.3 in. (3.9–5.9 cm) in length and weigh about 0.6–1.2 oz. (18–35 g). The scutes of the carapace are brown to dark green, and those of the head and flippers are black; all of these scutes are edged in white. The scientific name derives from *chelone*, or tortoise, and *mydas*, or wetness, referring to the aquatic habitat of this turtle.

Habitat

Green seaturtles may be seen from coastal shallows to open seas. They feed in protected shallow waters with extensive pastures of sea grasses and algae and take shelter in nearby reefs or rocky places. Although they are most often encountered along the coast, they may also be seen crossing deep water to a distant nesting site. Hatchlings and small juveniles drift with the pelagic *Sargassum* weed mats between the Americas and Africa.

Natural History

The age at which green seaturtles reach sexual maturity varies from population to population, and estimates range from less than 10 years to more than 50 years. Females nest every 2–4 years, with most nesting

Turtles

occurring every 3 years. Females have a strong fidelity to their nesting beach and may deposit up to seven clutches at 2-week intervals in a given season. They prefer beaches with little surf and a gentle slope and may nest in sections of the beach that are exposed to full sun rather in those that are completely shaded. The nest temperature determines the hatchlings' sex: cooler nests produce more males, warmer ones more females. Clutch size ranges from fewer than 50 to more than 200 eggs, with typical nests containing 100–120 eggs. The incubation period is normally 50–55 days. The first hatchlings do not head for the surface but rather wait for their nest mates to hatch. Then they collectively work upward, the sandy roof falling and filling the spaces their collapsed eggs left behind. Hatchlings emerge at night to avoid the lethally hot daytime beach surface but face a host of ghost crabs and birds waiting to prey upon them as the hatchlings scramble to the sea. There fish predators abound. Few young turtles survive their journey to the *Sargassum* weed flotillas. Those that do spend a year or more adrift foraging on small invertebrates before they join other green seaturtles on the sea grass pastures. Adult green seaturtles are the only marine turtles that derive their main sustenance from plant material. This primarily herbivorous diet leaves the turtles with little vitamin D. For this reason, green seaturtles are also the only marine turtles known to leave the water (other than to nest) to bask on shore, which they may do to acquire vitamin D through the action of sunlight irradiating sterols in their skin's surface.

Status and Distribution

Green seaturtles are chiefly a resident of tropical Atlantic, Pacific, and Indian Ocean waters. This said, the species does range north and southward into temperate environs. In the western North Atlantic, green seaturtles occur from Massachusetts to the Florida Keys and the Bahamas. The species also resides in the Gulf of Mexico and the Caribbean basin. Occasionally, juveniles are found in Long Island Sound (Morreale et al. 1992). Most often they are seen in New York in the fall as cold-stunned stranded turtles on beaches (see box: Sea turtles in New York State). Green seaturtles are listed as Threatened under the federal Endangered Species Act (ESA), with populations in Florida and west coast of Mexico designated as Endangered. Stranded green seaturtles in New York should be reported to the Riverhead Foundation Research and Preservation hotline number: (516) 369-9829.

Color Plates

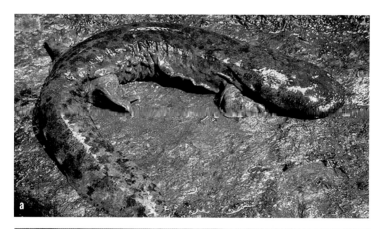

Plate 1
Hellbender
Cryptobranchus alleganiensis [page 54]

a Enormous (most 18-24 in., 46-61 cm total length), brown salamanders with highly folded skin and short, stocky legs.

b Adults have fleshy irregular skin folds beginning at rear of head and extending to base of tail.

Plate 2
Mudpuppy
Necturus maculosus [page 57]
A large aquatic salamander with flat head; small eyes; and external gills, even as adults. Total adult length 8-13 in. (20-33 cm).

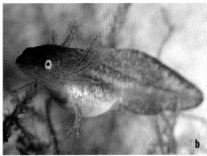

Plate 3
Jefferson salamander
Ambystoma jeffersonianum [page 60]

a Robust and broad-headed, with long
tail; slate to brownish gray ground
color with light flecking on sides;
and exceedingly long toes. Adult
snout-to-vent length 2.5–4 in.
(6–10 cm). Hamilton Co., New York.

b Larvae with bushy gills; long, thin
limbs; and broad tail fin that
extends far forward over back.

c First amphibians to breed at many
localities in New York—often
migrate over snow.

Plate 4
Blue-spotted salamander
Ambystoma laterale [page 63]

a Mid-sized and broad-headed with bluish-black ground color; blue-silver spotting; and flecking on back, legs, tail, and sides. Adult snout-to-vent length 2–3 in. (4–8 cm).

b Shorter body length and toes than Jefferson salamander (Plate 3). Hamilton Co., New York.

Plate 5
Spotted salamander
Ambystoma maculatum [page 66]

a Migrate at night from their terrestrial
burrows to ancestral breeding ponds
prompted by first warm rains of
spring. Columbia Co., New York.

b Rows of large yellow spots truly
distinctive; some populations with
orange spots on head.

c Distinguishing features include broad
head; prominent coastal ridges; and
stout limbs. Adult snout-to-vent
length 3.0–4.5 in. (7.5–11 cm).
Columbia Co., New York.

d Egg masses firm and typically
translucent (top), but some have
milky appearance (bottom). Hamilton
Co., New York.

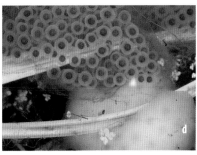

Plate 6
Marbled salamander
Ambystoma opacum [page 69]

a Males "marbled" with white
cross-bands and females with grayish
cross-bands from head to tail tip on
black body. Adult snout-to-vent
length 1.75–3 in. (4–7.5 cm).
b Cross-bands variable and may
converge or remain distinct.
c Newly transformed juveniles are
brown or black with light flecking.
d Larvae are brownish-gray with
numerous golden flecks along each
side.

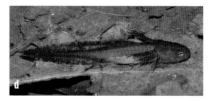

Plate 7
Tiger salamander
Ambystoma tigrinum [page 72]
a Robust-bodied with strong legs; long, keeled tail; and numerous yellow or tan irregular spots or blotches on dark brownish-black body. Snout-to-vent length 3.5–5.5 in. (9–13 cm). Suffolk Co., New York.
b Differ from spotted salamanders (Plate 5) by having yellow under chin and on sides and yellow spots being scattered on back.
c Larvae are greenish-gray with irregular dark spotting and a broad head; some, such as this individual, become cannibalistic.

Plate 8

Eastern newt

Notophthalmus viridescens [page 75]

a Adults green with a few black-bordered, red spots; yellow bellies; and tail fin prominently keeled in males. Adult snout-to-vent length 1.75–2.75 in. (4.5–7 cm). Dutchess Co., New York.

b Efts (juveniles) bright orange-red, with rough, dry skin and thin, bony tail. Delaware Co., New York.

c Males develop black, rough patches inside their thighs and at hind toe tips during breeding season useful for holding slippery females during mating.

d Larvae small and thin with pale greenish-brown color; row of light spots on sides; dark line through each eye; and blunt snout.

Plate 9
Northern dusky salamander
Desmognathus fuscus [page 78]
a Brownish with variable dorsal colors; relatively large hind limbs; and light line extending from eye to rear of jaw. Snout-to-vent length 1.25–3.25 in. (4–8 cm).
b Tail with "keeled" upper edge diagnostic.
c Females remain with their eggs for 1–3 months.

Plate 10
Allegheny mountain dusky salamander (mountain dusky salamander)
Desmognathus ochrophaeus [page 81]

a Generally brown with variable dorsal coloration; relatively large hind limbs; and light line extending from eye to rear of jaw. Snout-to-vent length 1.75–2.75 in. (3–7 cm). Chautauqua Co., New York.

b A round tail in cross section diagnostic (contrast with northern dusky salamander, Plate 9). Hamilton Co., New York.

c New York's two species of dusky salamanders are difficult to distinguish but both have a light line from behind the eye to the corner of the mouth and more robust hind than fore limbs.

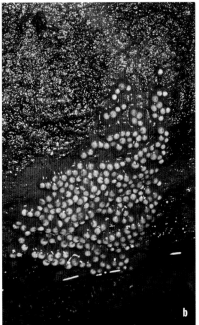

Plate 11
Northern two-lined salamander
Eurycea bislineata [page 84]
a Small to mid-sized; yellowish brown
with two dark brown stripes; bright
yellow-orange under the tail. Snout-
to-vent length 1.5–2.5 in. (3–6 cm).
b Eggs usually attached to underside
of flat stone in flowing water; may be
deposited communally by several
females (as in this case).

Plate 12
Long-tailed salamander
Eurycea longicauda [page 87]
a Orange ground color and black
   blotches on body and black vertical
   bars on tail. Snout-to-vent length
   2–3.25 in (5–8 cm). Cattaraugus Co.,
   New York.
b Tail accounts for about 60% of total
   length.
c Long-tailed salamanders have
   distinctly vertical bars along the
   sides of tail.

Plate 13
Spring salamander (northern spring salamander, purple salamander)
Gyrinophilus porphyriticus [page 89]
a Robust, salmon-pink, and mottled with snout-to-vent length 3–4.75 in (7.5–11 cm).
b Light-colored line extends from eye to nostril.
c Larvae with feathery gills and pale tan coloration under darker reticulations. Tompkins Co., New York.

Plate 14
Four-toed salamander
Hemidactylium scutatum [page 92]
a Reddish brown back flecked with dark spots; constriction at base of tail; and four toes on each hind foot. Snout-to-vent length 1–1.75 in. (2.5–4.5 cm).
b Striking white belly with distinct black spots.
c Females usually remain at nest until eggs hatch.

Plate 15
Eastern red-backed salamander
Plethodon cinereus [page 95]

a Typically with brick-red stripe along back and tail—this "striped" morph is that most commonly encountered in New York. Snout-to-vent length 1.25–2.25 in. (3–5.5 cm).

b Those lacking red stripes along back and tail known as "lead-backs" and increase in frequency moving southward in New York State. Broome Co., New York.

c Occasionally occur in New York as all red or "erythristic" morphs. Chautauqua Co., New York.

d Females lay miniature eggs in grapelike bunch within small cavity and guard them until they hatch. Broome Co., New York.

Plate 16
Northern slimy salamander
Plethodon glutinosus [page 98]
a Large with silvery-white flecking on
sides, tail, and back on slate gray to
black base color (this individual has
regenerated tail). Snout-to-vent
length 2.25–3.5 in. (5.5–9 cm).
Chautauqua Co., New York.
b Even juveniles, such as this
individual, have prominent flecking.
Broome Co., New York.

Plate 17
Wehrle's salamander
Plethodon wehrlei [page 101]
Long and slender with dark coloration
and whitish spots on lower sides. Tail
about half total length; round in cross
section. Snout-to-vent length 2–3 in.
(5–7.5 cm).

Plate 18
Red salamanders
Pseudotriton ruber [page 103]

a Moist, smooth skin orange-red with small, scattered black spots in older individuals. Snout-to-vent length 2–4 in. (5–10 cm). Orange Co., New York.

b Younger individuals have bright coral red skin with small, scattered black spots.

c Preys on other salamanders (note protruding tail of slimy salamander).

d Snout is short and rounded.

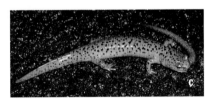

Plate 19
Eastern spadefoot
Scaphiopus holbrookii [page 113]
a Squat and plump with smooth skin and few warts and eyes protuberant with pupils vertical (standard length 2–2.5 in. [4.5–5.5 cm]). Suffolk Co., New York.
b Breeding occurs whenever intense rainstorms trigger toad emergence from their burrows, typically in June and July. Albany Co., New York.
c These toads lack parotoid glands.

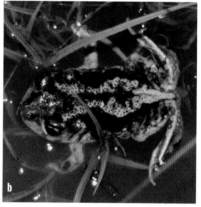

Plate 20
American toad
Bufo americanus [page 115]
a Light-colored individuals encountered. Oswego Co., New York.
b Stout; rough-skinned; and often reddish-brown in color with just one to two warts per dark spot on back and parotoid glands (Figure 5.2) that usually do not touch cranial crests (standard length 2–3.5 in. [5–9 cm]). Franklin Co., New York.
c Belly typically spotted. Onondaga Co., New York.

Plate 21
Fowler's toad
Bufo fowleri [page 118]
a Stout; rough-skinned and greenish or gray in color; with three to four warts per dark spot on back and parotoid glands (Figure 5.2) that usually contact cranial crests. Standard length 2–3 in. (5–7.5 cm).
b Belly creamy and unspotted.

Plate 22
Northern cricket frog
Acris crepitans [page 121]
a Small dorsal warts and red-to-brown-to-green base color on back. Standard length 0.5-1.5 in. (1.5-3.5 cm).
b A dark, triangular, backward-pointing mark between eyes. Orange Co., New York.
c Dorsal color highly variable.

Plate 23
Gray treefrog
Hyla versicolor [page 124]

a Stout with rough skin and dark
  blotches on back over gray base
  color; light spot with dark edge
  beneath each eye; toes with large,
  adhesive disks; and yellow-tinged
  groin. Standard length 1.5-2 in.
  (3-5 cm).

b Young adults and juveniles have
  green base color. Onondaga Co.,
  New York.

c Voice is the most frequent indicator
  of their presence – a hearty trilling
  from trees near ponds.

d Larvae have tails with high, orange or
  scarlet, darkly blotched fins.

Plate 24 *(right)*
Western chorus frog
Pseudacris triseriata [page 127]
Small and brown with three dark brown
stripes (often broken or sometimes
discontinuous) down back. Standard
length 0.5–1.5 in. (2.0–4.0 cm).
Livingston Co., New York.

Plate 25
Spring peeper
Pseudacris crucifer [page 130]
a Small and brown-skinned with an
imperfect "X" on their backs and toes
appended by small, round disks.
Standard length 0.5–1.5 in (2–3 cm).
Hamilton Co., New York.
b Smooth skin tends toward brown but
can verge on gray or green. Hamilton
Co., New York.

Plate 26
Bullfrog
Rana catesbeiana [page 133]

a Large with typically dull green, mottled exterior and without dorsolateral ridges. Standard length 3.5-6 in. (9-15.0 cm). Hamilton Co., New York.

b Variable in color, but lateral skin fold curves from eye downward around rear of tympanum.

c Males have tympanum larger than eye and throat suffused with yellow during breeding season. Hamilton Co., New York.

Plate 27
Green frog
Rana clamitans [page 136]
a Long-legged, usually green or bronze, with skin fold that extends from eye two-thirds of way down sides and spots on folded rear legs that "fit nicely" into cross stripes. Standard length 2.5–3.5 in. (5.5–9 cm). Hamilton Co., New York.
b Bronze coloration common over much of New York. Hamilton Co., New York.
c Lack of yellow pigment can cause bluish base color. Hamilton Co., New York.
d Males (three frogs on left side) have yellow throats during breeding season, and their tympanic membranes are usually larger than eye. Broome Co., New York.

Plate 28
Pickerel frog
Rana palustris [page 139]
a Rectangular spots on tan-colored
  back. Standard length 2.0-3 in.
  (4.5-7.5 cm). Hamilton Co.,
  New York.
b Orange or yellow inside hind legs
  and groin.

Plate 29
Northern leopard frog
Rana pipiens [page 141]
a Elongate body; slightly pointed snout;
and two to three rows of "roundish,"
dark spots with light borders.
Standard length 2–3.5 in (5–9 cm).
Onondaga Co., New York.
b Background color varies from light
brown to this light green.
c Spots are characteristically round (as
opposed to irregularly square in the
pickerel frog).

Plate 30
Mink frog
Rana septentrionalis [page 144]

a Olive-gray back darkly and uniformly mottled. Markings do not run neatly across folded rear legs (contrast with green frog). Standard length 2.0-3.0 in. (5.0-7.6 cm). Hamilton Co., New York.

b Individuals of St. Lawrence River valley and northern Adirondack Mountains characteristically lack dorsolateral ridge and are heavily mottled. St. Lawrence Co., New York.

c On hind foot of mink frog (left), webbing extends to tip of fifth toe and to last joint of fourth toe. On green frog (right), webbing does not reach tip of fifth toe and barely extends to second joint of fourth toe.

Plate 31
Wood frog
Rana sylvatica [page 147]
a Tan-colored with dark patches around eyes and prominent dorsolateral folds. Standard length 1.5–3.0 in. (3.5–7 cm). Oswego Co., New York.
b During breeding season, males darken considerably whereas larger, plumper females verge on beige-pink. Broome Co., New York.
c Eggs black and white and deposited in bluish, transparent masses. Hamilton Co., New York.
d Tadpoles have high fins and are rotund with backs dark brown or black and undersides pinkish in color and fairly transparent. Internal coil of intestines visible.

Plate 32
Southern leopard frog
Rana sphenocephala [page 150]

a Medium-sized with unbroken dorsolateral fold from eye to pelvic region and heavy round spots. Standard length 2–3.5 in. (5.0–9 cm).

b Light marking on center of tympanum diagnostic.

c This species is restricted to Long Island.

Plate 33
Snapping turtle
Chelydra serpentina [page 159]
a Dark carapace with serrated or
jagged posterior edge and tail with
saw-toothed keels. Carapace length
8–14 in (20.5–36 cm). Franklin Co.,
New York.
b Massive head and hooked beak.
Dutchess Co., New York.
c Plastron narrow, "t"-shaped, light-
colored, and unpatterned.

Plate 34
Eastern mud turtle
Kinosternon subrubrum [page 164]
a Smooth, oval carapace and dark
brown head with yellow mottling.
Carapace length 3.0–4 in. (7–10
cm). Suffolk Co., New York.
b Extensive, dark-colored plastron
with two well-developed hinges
(evident on this empty shell).

Plate 35
Stinkpot (common musk turtle)
Sternotherus odoratus [page 167]

a Smooth, high-domed carapace; two yellow stripes extending backward from pointy snout (above and below eye); and fleshy protrusions on chin and throat. Carapace length 2–4.5 in. (5.0–11.5 cm).

b Plastron reduced and brown to yellow with patches of bare skin between scutes along centerline, and front portion hinged.

Plate 36
Painted turtle
Chrysemys picta [page 170]

a Smooth, dark and somewhat
   flattened carapace oval in shape.
   Carapace length 4.5-6 in.
   (11.5-15.0 cm).
b Yellow or red markings on marginal
   scutes.
c Readily identified even at distance by
   pronounced yellow striping beneath
   chin. Columbia Co., New York.
d Hatchlings occasionally encountered.

Plate 37
Spotted turtle
Clemmys guttata [page 173]
a Small to mid-sized with black
   carapace sprinkled with bright yellow
   spots. Carapace length 3.5–4.5 in.
   (9–11.5 cm).
b Spotting occurs on head, limbs, and
   neck. Onondaga Co., New York.
c Hatchlings often have orange
   coloration on plastron. Onondaga
   Co., New York.

Plate 38
Wood turtle
Glyptemys insculpta [page 176]
a Large and brown with dark-colored carapace. Carapace length 5.5–8 in. (14–20 cm).
b Skin dark except under chin, throat, tail, and forelimbs, where often yellow, orange, or reddish.
c Carapace "sculpted" and somewhat flattened overall with slightly keeled appearance.
d Hatching wood turtle with egg tooth prominent.

Plate 39
Bog turtle
Glyptemys muhlenbergii [page 178]
a Small turtle with bright yellow or orange blotch on each side of head and neck. Carapace length 3-3.5 in (7.5-9 cm). Dutchess Co., New York.
b Carapace color can become darkened from staining by organic acids of wetland habitat.
c Typically occur in fens in New York.

Plate 40
Blanding's turtle
Emydoidea blandingii [page 181]
a Mid- to large-sized (5-7 in. [12.5-18 cm]) with bright yellow throat and carapace smooth, elongated, helmet-shaped, brown to black decorated with cream or tan squiggles and streaks.
b Easily identified by bright yellow throat.

Plate 41
Northern map turtle
Graptemys geographica [page 184]
a Keeled carapace covered by topographical maplike network of dark-bordered yellow-orange lines and circles. Carapace length for males 3.5–6.5 in. (9–16 cm) and for females 7–11.0 in. (18–27.5 cm).
b Head and neck have fine yellow, orange, or greenish lines. Often light blotch, oval or triangular in shape, behind eye.

Plate 42
Diamond-backed terrapin
Malaclemys terrapin [page 187]
a Medium-sized with distinct concentric grooves on each scute; skin typically light-colored and covered with dark flecks. Carapace length for males 4-5.5 in. (10-14 cm) and for females 6-9 in. (15.0-23.5 cm).

b Most frequently encountered in New York venturing onto beaches to nest in May and June. Queens Co., New York.

Plate 43
Northern red-bellied cooter (redbelly turtle)
Pseudemys rubriventris [page 190]
Large pond turtles with dark carapace and head and neck covered with bright yellow stripes but lacking marking behind eye. Carapace length 9-14 in. (24-35 cm).

Plate 44
Eastern box turtle
Terrapene carolina [page 192]
a Medium-sized with highly domed, double-hinged shell with variable patterns of yellow, orange, or olive markings on dark brown or black carapace. Carapace length 4.5–6 in. (11.5–15.0 cm).
b Males usually have red eyes. This particular turtle is "JN 21-21" marked by John Treadwell Nichols in 1921 and recaptured as healthy, centenarian in 2002 in Suffolk Co., New York.
c Adult coloration highly variable in New York.

Plate 45
Red-eared slider
Trachemys scripta elegans [page 194]
Red stripe behind eye; yellow plastron
with black striping; and green to brown
body with yellow stripes. Carapace length
5–8 in. (12–20 cm).

Plate 46
Yellowbelly slider
Trachemys scripta scripta [page 194]
Yellow blotch behind eye; vertical yellow
bars on costal scutes; and yellow
plastron with dark spots on anterior
scutes.

Plate 47
Loggerhead
Caretta caretta [page 197]
Large, reddish-brown turtles with
two pairs of prefrontal plates on
conspicuously large, block-like head.
Carapace length 31–45 in.
(79–114 cm).

Plate 48
Green seaturtle
Chelonia mydas [page 199]
Large and olive to brown with broad,
smooth, heart-shaped carapace.
Carapace length 36–48 in.
(90–122 cm).

Plate 49
Kemp's ridley
Lepidochelys kempii [page 201]
Distinctive round-to-heart-shaped
carapace serrated along posterior
margin. Carapace length 23–27.5 in.
(58–70 cm).

Plate 50
Leatherback turtle
Dermochelys coriacea [page 203]
Enormous with barrel-shaped body
covered by leathery skin. Carapace
length 4–8 ft. (1.2–2.4 m).

Plate 51
Spiny softshell
Apalone spinifera [page 205]

a Round, flattened, and leathery with long neck; snorkel-like snout; and flexible rear carapace. Males considerably smaller (5-9.4 in. [12.7-23.9 cm]) than females (7-18.9 in. [17.8-48 cm]).

b Sharp tubercles along leading edge of carapace make softshells painful to handle (they also frequently bite).

c Coloration varies from gray to light brown.

Plate 52
Eastern fence lizard
Sceloporus undulatus [page 212]
a Small gray or brown with sharply
  keeled scales. Snout vent length
  4-7.5 in. (10-18.5 cm).
b Claws aid in traction on inclined
  surface.
c Well camouflaged against tree bark
  and bare rock that it frequents.

Plate 53
Italian wall lizard (ruin lizard)
Podarcis sicula [page 214]
Slender with long tail; head, neck, and
most of upper body generally green with
brownish stripe down middle of back.
Snout vent length 5.5–9.5 in. (14–24 cm).
Nassau Co., New York.

Plate 54
Coal skink
Eumeces anthracinus [page 216]
Two wide black stripes bordered by
narrow yellow or white stripes running
length of body. Snout vent length
5–7 in. (12.5–18.0 cm). Schuyler Co.,
New York.

Plate 55
Common five-lined skink
Eumeces fasciatus [page 218]
a Small with shiny scales and five
light-colored stripes on black or gray
body. Snout vent length 5–8.5 in.
(12.5–21.5 cm).
b Deposit eggs under rocks, logs, in
loose soil, or in rotting stumps.

Plate 56
Eastern wormsnake
Carphophis amoenus [page 221]
Small, shiny, and brown with smooth
scales and pink belly. Total length
8–15 in. (20–38 cm).

Plate 57
Eastern racer
Coluber constrictor [page 223]
a Glossy smooth scales and gray belly. Total length 36–75 in. (90–190 cm).
b Juveniles patterned with wide blotches on gray background.
c Often bask in low shrubs; this individual illustrates distinctly satiny appearance of some eastern racers.

Plate 58
Ring-necked snake
Diadophis punctatus [page 226]
a Small, slender, and bluish-gray with
  shiny smooth scales. Total length in
  New York 10–15 in. (25.5–38.0 cm).
  Catskill Park, New York.
b Distinct yellow ring behind head
  diagnostic. Delaware Co., New York.
c Most New York specimens have yellow
  to yellow-orange bellies.

Plate 59
Eastern ratsnake (black ratsnake)
Elaphe alleganiensis [page 228]
a Large and mostly black with black-and-white checkered belly. Total length commonly to 60 in. (150 cm). Putnam Co., New York.
b Young boldly patterned with series of light, almost white blotches. Orange Co., New York.
c Adept climbers of trees and shrubs.

Plate 60
Eastern hog-nosed snake
Heterodon platirhinos [page 231]
a Upturned snout diagnostic.
b Stocky and medium-sized (total length 20-33 in. [50-84 cm]). Orange Co., New York.
c When threatened, often feign death by rolling onto back, writhing, and going limp.
d Teeth in back of mouth to grip and puncture toads, their main prey. Orange Co., New York.

Plate 61
Milksnake (spotted adder)
Lampropeltis triangulum [page 234]
a Strikingly colored and medium-sized with red or reddish-brown blotches bordered by black on gray to tan body. Total length 24–36 in. (61–90 cm).
b U- or Y-shaped light patch on back of head and neck good field mark in New York.
c Belly scales with checkerboard pattern of alternating gray or white with black. Queens Co., New York.
d Some individuals attain a distinctly grayish hue. Sullivan Co., New York.

Plate 62
Northern watersnake
Nerodia sipedon [page 237]
a Often bask on shrubs or tree roots immediately adjacent to ponds and streams. Total length 24–42 in. (61–107 cm). Columbia Co., New York.
b Diagnostic cross banding and blotches often obscured by heavy staining from organic acids in wetland waters.

Plate 63
Queen snake
Regina septemvittata [page 240]
Relatively small, with dark tan back with yellow stripes on its lower sides. Extremely rare in New York. Total length 15–24 in. (38–61 cm).

Plate 64

DeKay's brownsnake (garden snake, DeKay's snake)

Storeria dekayi [page 242]

a Small and brown-colored with small head and two rows of black dots running lengthwise down back. Total length 9–13 in. (23–33 cm).

b Coloration varies, but rows of black dots consistently present. Onondaga Co., New York.

c One of few snakes common to suburban and urban areas of New York.

Plate 65
Red-bellied snake
Storeria occipitomaculata [page 245]
a Distinctive red belly and three light spots behind head. Total length 8–10 in (20.3–25.4 cm). Franklin Co., New York.
b Gray morph. Columbia Co., New York.
c Belly coloration can verge on orange. Delaware Co., New York.

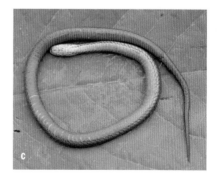

Plate 66
Short-headed gartersnake
Thamnophis brachystoma [page 247]
Small with narrow head slightly broader
than neck and lacking alternating rows
of black spots between stripes. Total
length 10–22 in. (25–56 cm).
Cattaraugus Co., New York.

Plate 67
Eastern ribbonsnake
Thamnophis sauritus [page 250]
a Medium-sized with very slender body;
   three light stripes contrasting clearly
   against dark background; and
   exceedingly long tail. Total length
   45–66 in. (45.7–96.5 cm). Dutchess
   Co., New York.
b Distinct spot of yellow in front of eye.
   Dutchess Co., New York.

Plate 68
Common gartersnake
Thamnophis sirtalis [page 252]
a Small to medium-sized usually with
   at least three light stripes on
   greenish brown background. Total
   length 18–54 in. (46–137 cm).
b Background coloration in New York
   frequently dark brown.
c Found in most habitats, hunting for
   earthworms and other small prey.
   Columbia Co., New York.
d Labial scales are yellowish with black
   edges. Deleware Co., New York.

Plate 69
Smooth greensnake
Liochlorophis vernalis [page 255]
a Small and slender with bright green
sides and back and white underside.
Total length 12–20 in. (30–50 cm).
Columbia Co., New York.
b Typically ground dwellers of grassy
habitats but also adept climbers.
Columbia Co., New York.

Plate 70
Copperhead
Agkistrodon contortrix [page 258]
a Large and venomous with dark cross
   bands in hourglass pattern down
   back and no rattle on end of tail.
   Total length 24-36 in. (61-90 cm).
b Distinctive wide, coppery red head.
   Orange Co., New York.
c Young have bright yellow tail.

Plate 71
Timber rattlesnake
Crotalus horridus [page 260]

a Easily identified by wide head, distinct facial pits, heavily keeled scales, and set of rattles at tail tip. Typical length 36–60 in. (90–152 cm).

b Occur in New York in two color patterns: yellow morph (lower) and black morph (upper).

c Possess two distinct facial pits for sensing warm blooded prey.

Plate 72
Massasauga
Sistrurus catenatus [page 264]
a Medium-sized and gray to brown;
extremely rare in New York. Total
length 18.5–30 in. (47.0–76 cm).
Onondaga Co., New York.
b Distinct facial pit between eyes and
nostrils and rattle at base of tail
(this snake's rattle has been marked
by field researchers).

Image Credits for Color Plates

Plate 1a: Jeffrey Humphries
1b: Jeffrey Humphries
2: Twan Leenders
3a: Nancy E. Karraker
3b: Twan Leenders
3c: Charles Eichelberger
4a: Kenneth Barnett
4b: Nancy E. Karraker
5a: © 2005, David N. Edwards, All rights reserved
5b: Michael Graziano
5c: © 2005, David N. Edwards, All rights reserved
5d: Nancy E. Karraker
6a: Twan Leenders
6b: B. M. Glorioso
6c: Matthew Kull
6d: B. M. Glorioso
7a: Sean T. Giery
7b: B. M. Glorioso
7c: K. Hoffmann
8a: Sean T. Giery
8b: Frank T. Burbrink
8c: B. M. Glorioso
8d: Twan Leenders
9a: Twan Leenders
9b: B. M. Glorioso
9c: US Geological Survey Northeast Amphibian Monitoring and Research Initiative
10a: Twan Leenders
10b: Nancy E. Karraker
10c: Frank Burbrink
11a: Charles Eichelberger
11b: Twan Leenders
12a: Sean T. Giery
12b: Michael Grazian
12c: US Geological Survey Northeast Amphibian Research and Monitoring Initiative
13a: Michael Graziano
13b: Michael Graziano
13c: Twan Leenders
14a: Michael Graziano
14b: B. M. Glorioso
14c: Michael Graziano
15a: US Geological Survey Northeast Amphibian Research and Monitoring Initiative
15b: Victor S. Lamoureux
15c: Twan Leenders
15d: John C. Maerz

16a: Twan Leenders
16b: John C. Maerz
17: M. Watson
18a: Sean T. Giery
18b: Michael Graziano
18c: Jack Hecht
18d: US Geological Survey Northeast Amphibian Research and Monitoring Initiative
19a: Tim Green
19b: Kirstin Breisch
19c: S. Giery
20a: James P. Gibbs
20b: James P. Gibbs
20c: Nancy E. Karraker
21a: Sean T. Giery
21b: Sean T. Giery
22a: B. M. Glorioso
22b: Sean T. Giery
22c: US Geological Survey Northeast Amphibian Research and Monitoring Initiative
23a: Charles Eichelberger
23b: Nancy E. Karraker
23c: Charles Eichelberger
23d: Twan Leenders
24: Kenneth Roblee
25a: Nancy E. Karraker
25b: Nancy E. Karraker
26a: Nancy E. Karraker
26b: B. M. Glorioso
26c: Nancy E. Karraker
27a: Nancy E. Karraker
27b: James P. Gibbs
27c: Nancy E. Karraker
27d: Victor S. Lamoureux
28a: Nancy E. Karraker
28b: B. M. Glorioso
29a: Nancy E. Karraker
29b: Wayne Jones
29c: James P. Gibbs
30a: Nancy E Karraker
30b: Glenn Johnson
30c: Ariana Breisch (left); Jack Hecht (right)
31a: James P. Gibbs
31b: Victor S. Lamoureux
31c: Nancy E. Karraker
31d: Twan Leenders
32a: B. M. Glorioso
32b: US Geological Survey Northeast Amphibian Research and Monitoring Initiative

Other Intriguing Facts: Ancient Mariners

Green seaturtles are remarkable navigators and strong swimmers. Feeding pastures and nesting beaches of some populations may be separated by 620 mi. (1,000 km). Those turtles that nest on Ascension Island in the mid-Atlantic forage along the Brazilian coast, some 1,400 mi. (2,300 km) away. Energy costs of such a sojourn have been calculated at more than 20% of body weight in fat stores. Green seaturtles obviously have an uncanny global positioning system guiding their movements. How do they find a nesting beach on a small island in the middle of the ocean? Although celestial navigation does not hold promise—the turtle's eyesight is too poor to see the stars—other possibilities such as chemical cues and orientation to magnetic fields have not been ruled out.

Kemp's Ridley (Atlantic Ridley)
Lepidochelys kempi [Plate 49]

Quick Identification

The smallest seaturtle, which has a distinctive round to heart-shaped carapace serrated along the posterior margin. It is occasionally stranded on Long Island.

Description

The Kemp's ridley turtle is the smallest marine turtle in New York and the most endangered. The carapace length is 23–27.5 in. (58–70 cm), with a maximum carapace length of 29.5 in. (74.9 cm). The typical weight is 80–110 lb. (36–50 kg). The turtles have a distinctive round to heart-shaped carapace, which is gray-green to black, smooth, keeled, and serrated along the posterior margin. There are five costal scutes on each side of the carapace, with the first in contact with the nuchal scute. In addition, there are four (rarely five) enlarged scutes on the bridge, each with a small pore near the rear margin. The plastron is cream-colored. Hatchlings are 1.5–1.8 in. (3.8–4.6 cm) long, dark gray, with three keels on the carapace and four longitudinal ridges; plastron is white. Kemp's ridley turtles have two pairs of prefrontal plates (green seaturtles have only one pair) and four bridge scutes (loggerheads have only three). The scientific name derives from *lepido*, or scaled, and *chelys*, or turtle; and species epithet honors the species' discoverer, Richard M. Kemp.

Turtles

Habitat

Kemp's ridleys inhabit sheltered shallow coastal environments such as estuaries, bays, and lagoons. In Florida and the Chesapeake Bay, they are closely associated with coastal stands of red mangrove and eelgrass beds, respectively. *Saragassum* and other marine plant mats drifting along coastal currents may provide young turtles with food and shelter. Long Island Sound has been identified as range-wide critical habitat for 2–5-year-old Kemp's ridleys.

Natural History

Kemp's ridleys are predominantly carnivorous, feeding on crabs, fish, jellyfish, squid, snails, clams, starfish, as well as some marine vegetation. In New York, they primarily consume walking crabs (Burke et al. 1993, 1994). Juveniles tend to feed mostly at or near the surface, whereas adults feed primarily at the sea floor within the shallow water areas they frequent. These small marine turtles are especially sensitive to cold water temperatures, which may be a major motivator in seasonal dispersal.

Kemp's ridleys nest in 1–2 year cycles, with sexually mature females laying one to three clutches every season. Females lay clutches that average 110 eggs each at intervals of 20–28 days. The young hatch after 50–70 days, emerging just after dawn and scrambling to the water's edge. The tiny turtles drift with the currents or become associated with rafts of *Sargassum* weed. Sexual maturity is reached at the age of 6 years or more. Longevity in the wild is unknown, but in captivity Kemp's ridleys may live to more than 20 years of age.

Status and Distribution

Adult Kemp's ridleys are primarily residents of the Gulf of Mexico, and they are rarely seen beyond its limits. Juveniles follow the Gulf Stream along the eastern coast of the United States and Canada. Between May and November, the Chesapeake Bay and Long Island Sound are major feeding areas for immature Kemp's ridleys. The species occasionally reaches Newfoundland, Europe, the Azores, and the Mediterranean Sea. In summer and fall, Kemp's ridleys appear in Long Island Sound and along the Massachusetts coast. When fall water temperature plummets below 50°F (10°C), the turtles become stunned and appear as strandings along coastlines where they have gathered (Morreale et al. 1992). The species has been protected in the United States under the ESA since 1973.

Other Intriguing Facts: Conserving the Last Few

Kemp's ridleys suffer from mortality in trawl nets, and the USFWS has issued regulations that require shrimp trawlers on Gulf and southeast coasts to have a turtle excluder device on their nets. The device allows captured turtles and other large marine life to escape. Unfortunately, compliance is not universal, and renegade boats continue to kill turtles. If you discover a stranded Kemp's ridley, contact the Riverhead Foundation Research and Preservation hotline number: (516) 369-9829.

Leatherback Turtle (Leatherback)
Dermochelys coriacea [Plate 50]

Quick Identification

An enormous turtle with a barrel-shaped body covered with leathery skin that is occasionally stranded on Long Island beaches.

Description

The leatherback is the world's largest turtle (4–8 ft. [1.2–2.4 m]). Typically 1,000 lb (500 kg) in weight, they may reach 1 ton (900 kg, Eckert and Luginbuhl 1988). Their scuteless, leathery carapace is black or blue-black and has seven prominent keels running down the teardrop-shaped shell. The shell is dark black, blue, or brown, and speckled with white dots or patches. The plastron is white and has five longitudinal ridges. Its front flippers are enormous. Rear flippers are paddle-like. All flippers are clawless. Males have a concave plastron and a tail longer than their rear flippers. Hatchlings are 2.2–2.5 in. (5.5–6.3 cm) and the keels and flippers are edged in white. The scientific name derives from the Greek for skin and turtle, *dermos* and *chelys*, respectively, alluding to the soft skin covering the shell, and the Latin *corium*, meaning leather.

Habitat

Leatherbacks are pelagic creatures that follows flotillas of jellyfish. They occasionally enter bays and estuaries.

Natural History

Leatherbacks inhabit open waters. Only females come ashore, and then only to nest. In the United States, nesting is uncommon, but it does occur on beaches in Georgia, Florida, and Texas. Females may nest six or more times in a season, depositing 35–150 spherical eggs per clutch, and wait 2–3 years before nesting again. Leatherbacks are jellyfish-eating specialists. Although jellyfish are their main dietary staple, they also consume sea urchins, squid, octopus, fish, snails, algae, and seaweed (Lazell 1980, Grant et al. 1996). They have a unique adaptation for ingesting soft bodied prey—their long esophagus is equipped with numerous backward pointing spines to prevent prey from escaping or being regurgitated by accident. Leatherbacks maintain osmotic and ionic balance while consuming a diet of jellyfish with the help of large, specialized tear glands designed for excreting salt (Hudson and Lutz, 1986). Leatherbacks are unusual among all reptiles in that they can maintain core body temperatures well above water temperatures (Frair et al. 1972). Their large size, thick blubber layer, and countercurrent heat exchangers in the front and rear flippers (Davenport 1997) all favor heat retention from muscular activity, and this enables them to venture into cool temperate waters—to higher latitudes than any other species of marine turtle.

Status and Distribution

Leatherbacks are found in oceans and seas around the world. Leatherback nesting beaches are located in the tropical waters of the Atlantic, Pacific, and Indian Oceans, and the species ventures north in the Atlantic to Nova Scotia, Newfoundland, Iceland, and Norway in the Pacific to Alaska. Similarly, the species ranges into the cold southern waters of the Atlantic and Pacific Oceans to the Cape of Good Hope, Argentina, Chile, and New Zealand. Leatherbacks are occasional visitors to New York waters, most often encountered by deep-sea fisherman or seen stranded on a beach on Long Island. This turtle is listed as Endangered under the federal ESA.

Other Intriguing Facts: Navigating the Deep

Leatherbacks are known for their long distance travel, deep dives, and physiological attributes that allow them to conserve body heat and follow jellyfish into cool temperate waters. Some tagged leatherbacks have been recaptured more than 3,100 mi. (5,000 km) from their original capture point. And they are known to be able to dive to depths greater than 3,280 ft. (1,000 m), perhaps in search of abyssal jellyfish and glowing tunicates.

Spiny Softshell
Apalone spinifera [Plate 51]

Quick Identification

A round, flattened, leathery turtle with a long neck, snorkel-like snout, and flexible rear carapace.

Description

The spiny softshell is quickly identified by its oval or round, flattened, leathery carapace, its long neck, and snorkel-like snout. The carapace lacks scutes, and its hind end is flexible. The front edge of its carapace has short spiny projections—hence the common name. The spiny softshell is olive to light brown. Males and juveniles are decorated with black dots and eye spots and a black line along the margin of the back half of the carapace. Females develop a gray to brown mottled or blotched pattern well before they reach sexual maturity. The white to yellow plastron is relatively small, and its underlying bony elements are visible through the skin. Typically, there are two black-edged yellow stripes on each side of the head. One begins on the tip of the snout and extends back through the eye onto the neck, and the other runs backward from the jaw. The elongated snout has large nostrils each with a ridge extending from the septum. The feet are mottled or streaked with black and yellow, and they are fully webbed. Front feet have three claws, and the hind feet have four. Males are considerably smaller (5–9.4 in. [12.7–23.9 cm]) than females (7–18.9 in. [17.8–48 cm]); have a sandpaper-like skin texture; and a long, thick tail with the anal opening near the tip. Females have a short tail, which is tucked under the edge of their carapace. Hatchlings are 1.2–1.6 in. (3–4 cm) in length and are boldly spotted. The scientific name derives from *apalos*, or soft, and also alludes to the spine-like protrusions on front edge of shell.

Warning: Softshells are pugnacious, quick to bite, and difficult to handle safely.

Habitat

Spiny softshells live in rivers, lakes, reservoirs, and protected bays and river mouths of the Great Lakes. These turtles prefer sites with soft mud or sand bottoms and sparse aquatic vegetation; they avoid

Turtles

areas with rocky bottoms. Mudflats and sandbars are important features of good habitat and are used for basking and nesting. Wind thrown trees with their crowns sticking into deep water are a favorite shelter.

Natural History

Spiny softshells rarely go far from water (Graham and Graham 1997). On sunny wind-free days in late spring and summer, these turtles spend much of their day basking on a steep sloping bank, bar, or floating log. Spiny softshells usually position themselves near the shoreline and facing the water. When startled, they launch themselves into the water in a burst of energy. Spiny softshells are powerful swimmers and are well designed for a rapid escape in their aquatic environment. Winter is spent underwater buried in the soft bottom. They become active in April—often after other local turtle species have emerged. Females nest in June or early July on a sunny morning and may lay a second clutch a few weeks later. In Vermont and Quebec, spiny softshells travel extensively (4.3 mi. [7 km]; Daigle et al. 2002) to particular nesting sites, which are usually close to the water in an open area on a sand or gravel bank or sand bar. Nest site selection, nest cavity construction, egg deposition, closure, and return to water usually occurs in less than an hour. The 9–38 eggs are round and brittle and require 2–3 months of incubation. Hatching occurs in late August or September, but the young may overwinter in the nest and emerge the following spring. Unlike most other turtles, softshells have genetic sex determination, and most nests produce males and females in roughly equal numbers. Males reach sexual maturity in 4–5 years, whereas females take about twice that long.

Spiny softshells may prowl and probe for crayfish, aquatic insects, snails, tadpoles, and small fish in patches of vegetation, crevices, and beneath debris. At other times, softshells settle into the soft mud or sand in shallow water with only their head and neck exposed to ambush passing prey. In this situation, they can simply extend their long neck and snorkel-tipped snout to the surface for a breath of air. Softshells are intolerant of low oxygen conditions (Reese et al. 2003) a constraint that may restrict softshells to large lakes and rivers. In Vermont and Quebec, home ranges consist of spring–summer concentration areas and fall–winter concentration areas with affinity for particular hibernacula (Galois et al. 2002).

Status and Distribution

Spiny softshells are found in the western Allegheny region, Great Lakes plain drainages (particularly Finger Lakes and Gennesee River), and embayments along the southern shore of Lake Ontario (map 6.14). There is an isolated record from the east-central part of the state. Populations likely also occur in Lake Champlain but have yet to be recorded on the New York side (as they have on the Vermont side, as well as the lower Ottawa River in Ontario and along the St. Lawrence River in Quebec). Records from near New York City are likely the result of releases.

Because of the aquatic nature and preference for highly oxygenated water of spiny softshells, these turtles are susceptible to pollution. Lakefront and shoreline development has diminished their aquatic environs and nesting areas in some areas. Raccoons and skunks, which flourish around human habitation, increase levels of nest predation. Increasingly, adult spiny softshells are captured in turtle traps or on strings of baited hooks, for Asian food markets in North America or export to Southeast Asia. Softshells are also killed by bow hunters, vandals with firearms, fishermen who consider them a nuisance, and the propellers of motor boats. A particularly insidious threat is by-catch of softshells in floating aquatic weed harvesters used to clear navigation channels. Spiny softshells are listed as a species of Special Concern in New York.

Map 6.14. Distribution of the spiny softshell (*Apalone spinifera*) in New York. Elsewhere the species occurs in southern Ontario, the central and southeastern United States, and northeastern Mexico.

Turtles

Other Intriguing Facts: How Softshells "Breathe"

Spiny softshells are truly aquatic turtles. Many dive for 20 minutes at a time before taking their next breath, and dives of more than 50 minutes have been recorded. Spiny softshells are also expert at burying themselves in the substrate of the lakes in which they live and are even able crawl beneath the soft bottom. The key to these behaviors is that these turtles are able to respire for long periods below the water's surface via some curious mechanisms. Unlike hard-shelled aquatic turtles that exchange gas primarily across their lungs and need to regularly come up for air, the soft skin of spiny softshells lets them respire directly through the skin. In fact, almost half of the oxygen and nearly all of the carbon dioxide are exchanged directly through the skin while in water. Some particularly important gas exchange sites are the pharyngeal lining of their throat and their cloacal membranes. The pugnacious nature of these creatures may, in turn, be compensation for their soft, sensitive skin that provides them with little physical protection (Stone et al. 1992).

7

Lizards and Snakes: Species Accounts

Lizards and snakes might seem like an odd pair to group together, but they are part of the same evolutionary lineage (Laurin and Reisz 1995). "Limblessness"—a trait seemingly unique to snakes—has in fact evolved repeatedly among snakes and lizards. Although all snakes lack limbs, many lizards do as well (although no legless lizards happen to occur in New York).

An elongate form and lack of limbs constrain snakes in various ways (figure 7.1). In snakes, for example, fitting organs into a long tube has resulted in major anatomical rearrangements, not the least of which is reduction of one lung to a negligible status, with simultaneous elongation of the other to nearly the full length of the body. Although locomotion without limbs might seem difficult, snakes have solved the problem elegantly. Through intricately organized muscles and complex behavior patterns, snakes can move swiftly and quietly over almost any terrain.

An elongate form and lack of limbs also demands modifications to consume prey. All snakes are carnivores, and fitting prey down their gullets has required some modifications. These include highly stretchable skin, a protrusible breathing tube that lets them keep exchanging air despite having a mouth stuffed with prey (see figure 7.11d), and jaws that move independently on either side of the head to assist in swallowing larger prey items. Prey may be secured by direct seizure, constriction, envenomation, or some combination thereof.

Teeth vary among modes of securing prey. Often teeth are numerous, small, and recurved as in the case of common gartersnakes,

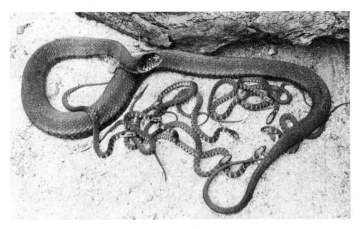

Figure 7.1. A northern watersnake and her newborn young—a species common in unpolluted waters throughout much of New York. (Neg./Trans. no. 16272, American Museum of Natural History Library.)

which take a variety of small-bodied prey. Sometimes they are modified into hypodermic needlelike structures complete with modified salivary glands that provide a pulse of venom on impact, as is the case with rattlesnakes and copperheads.

Snakes that use venoms (figure 7.2) produce a complex soup of proteins that disrupts the nervous and circulatory systems of prey items. In the pit vipers of New York, the major component of venom is hemotoxic; that is, it attacks the blood, destroying blood cells and the walls of small blood vessels, which may lead to internal bleeding. Venoms also often start the process of digestion of the prey, from inside out, whereas the snake's digestive juices work from the outside in, a process that speeds digestion. Lastly, the rear teeth are modified in some forms into cutting devices, as is the case with the eastern hognosed snake, which use their rear teeth to "pop" toads that inflate themselves in an attempt to prevent being swallowed (see eastern hog-nosed snake, Other Intriguing Facts).

Snakes reproduce in a variety of ways. Many lay soft, leathery eggs, but others give birth to live, wriggling young (see figure 7.1). Because they can bask and selectively expose to the sun parts of their bodies containing their internally developing embryos, live-bearing forms are clearly the most successful snakes in northern New York. Many egg-laying species are limited by the simple fact that their eggs do not

Figure 7.2. Venomous snakes of New York, such as this timber rattlesnake, have a thermoreceptive organ called the loreal pit, which is located between the nostrils and eyes, as well as a wedge-shaped head and keeled sales. Catskill Park, New York. (© 2005, David N. Edwards, All rights reserved.)

have sufficient time to develop during the short, cool summers in the northern part of the state. All of New York's few native lizards, for example, are egg layers and they cling to the southern, warmer parts of the state.

New York's three species of native lizards are representatives of two families (the Phrynosomatidae and the Scincidae, or skinks). Of the more than 4,200 species of lizards worldwide, New York supports less than 0.1%. New York has 17 species of snakes in two families: the Viperidae (the copperhead, timber rattlesnake, and the massasauga) and the Colubridae (all remaining species, see table 2.2). Of the approximately 2,900 species of snakes on earth, New York hosts less than 1% of them. Most snake and lizard diversity is concentrated in the warmer, lower lying areas of the state, primarily in the lower Hudson River valley.

We report lizard sizes as snout vent length (distance from the tip of the snout to the cloaca) because lizards often lose all or part of their tails to predators; however we report snake lengths as total lengths (distance from the tip of the snout to the end of the tail).

Eastern Fence Lizard
Sceloporus undulatus [Plate 52]

Quick Identification

A small gray or brown lizard with strongly keeled scales that is restricted to a few sites in extreme southeastern New York.

Description

The eastern fence lizard is the only lizard one is likely to encounter in New York with strongly keeled scales. In fact, fence lizards have scales that are so sharply keeled that they are often called "spiny lizards." They have an SVL of 2–3.4 in. (5–8.6 cm). The species is conspicuously sexually dimorphic. Male eastern fence lizards are grayish brown to almost bronze on the back. They have bellies with sides that are bright pale violet or greenish blue bordered in black, usually with a light stripe down the center. A key field mark for males is the blue throat, usually bordered by black. Females lack the blue throat and are most easily recognized by a series of –seven to nine distinct dark wavy bands running across their backs. Males may have these bands, but, if so, they are indistinct. Females also have a red, yellow or orange patch at the base of the tail and a white belly with scattered black flecks. Both sexes can lighten in color during the hottest part of the day and darken as it becomes cooler. Newborn and young eastern fence lizards are patterned more like adult females. The scientific name derives from *skelos*, or leg, and *porus*, or opening, referring to the pores on the hind legs, and *undulatus*, or having a wavelike dorsal pattern.

Habitat

Eastern fence lizards are creatures of dry, open woods where sunlight is plentiful, and they are more abundant on south-facing hillsides. As their name suggests, fence lizards are often observed on fence posts but are found in brush piles, log piles, bases of trees, and sides of buildings, usually near some protective cover. Across their range, eastern fence lizards are often associated with pine-dominated forests, but in New York they may also be found in oak-hickory and oak-pine communities. Tree boles are the preferred refuge to escape from ground predators and humans. Fence lizards quickly run a few meters up a tree and keep the trunk between their would-be attacker and themselves, peeking out to check the position of their attacker, and making themselves surprisingly difficult to catch. Fence lizards hibernate in underground burrows constructed by other animals, in rotting tree stumps, and in rock crevices.

Natural History

Eastern fence lizards are active from late March to early November, only during the day. These lizards spend the night under bark, in tree cavities, or in rock piles. The breeding season begins soon after emergence from hibernation and may last several weeks. Males occupy discrete territories and defend them from other males. Larger males have larger territories and adapt their territories to intersect with as many female home ranges as possible (Haenel et al. 2003a). One or more females may be found in a male's territory, although females may mate with males outside their home ranges (Haenel et al. 2003b). Individuals learn their territories quite well and return to them following purposeful relocations many meters distant. Courtship is minimal, involving head bobbing and push-ups; once a female signals readiness, copulation is quick. Female eastern fence lizards lay between 6 and 13 eggs in rotting logs or in holes that they construct in moist soil (Tinkle and Ballinger 1972). In the southern portion of their range, eastern fence lizards may produce two or three clutches in a season. Eggs hatch in August and early September. Populations are physiologically adapted to local conditions (Niewiarowski 1995). The diet of the eastern fence lizard is almost entirely arthropods, which are sought both actively and by sitting and waiting for them to pass by.

Map 7.1. Distribution of the eastern fence lizard (*Sceloporus undulatus*) in New York. Elsewhere the species ranges from New Jersey to central Florida and west to Kansas and eastern Texas.

Lizards and Snakes

Status and Distribuion

In New York, eastern fence lizards are restricted to the extreme south-eastern corner of the state (map 7.1). These lizards are not known from Long Island but occur on Staten Island. The species is clearly at the northernmost edge of its distribution in New York. Due to its rarity, the species is listed as "threatened." Elsewhere in their range, these lizards can be abundant.

Other Intriguing Facts: Defending Space

Snakes and turtles rarely exhibit territorial behavior, but it is widespread in lizards and fascinating to watch. The male eastern fence lizard's initial territorial display begins with head bobbing and push-ups for short durations. The displaying individual stands stiff-legged and extends the throat and dewlap, thereby revealing the blue throat (Cooper and Burns 1987). No response on the part of the intruder often brings on a more vigorous performance followed by direct attack. One of the pair eventually leaves the area. These behaviors are innate; hatchlings often perform them (Roggenbuck and Jenssen 1986).

Italian Wall Lizard ("Ruin Lizard")
Podarcis sicula [Plate 53]

Quick Identification

A slender lizard with a tail about the half total length and a head, neck and most of the upper body generally green with a brownish stripe down the middle of the back and white undersides. This lizard is currently restricted to the New York City area and western Long Island.

Description

Adult Italian wall lizards reach between 2.8–4.8 in. (7–12 cm) in SVL, with a tail about equal in length to the head and body. These lizards are variable in color and pattern. The head, neck, and most of the upper body are generally green with a brownish stripe down the middle of the back. Dark markings of various shapes may also be present on the body. The undersides are white with few markings. Males are larger than females.

Habitat

Wall lizards are urban and suburban dwellers, living in and amongst the rubble, debris and vegetation found in city lots.

Natural History

Only a few studies have been conducted on Italian wall lizards in New York. The species is active only from April–October (Burke and Ner 2005). Wall lizards prey mostly on aphids, beetles, and snails (Burke and Mercurio 2002). Wall lizards die if frozen but are able to survive Long Island winters, likely by finding burrows in the soil below the frost line (Burke et al. 2002). House cats eat them and mockingbirds, blue jays, and American crows likely do as well (Burke and Ner 2005).

Status and Distribution

The Italian wall lizard is of European origin. It was introduced in the late 1960s, probably 1967 (Gossweiler 1975), most likely as an accidental escape from a pet shop, to an area in Garden City, Town of Hempstead, Nassau County, Long Island, where it has become permanently established (map 7.2). The species now occurs in Nassau, Suffolk, Kings, Queens, and Bronx Counties (Burke and Ner 2005). Genetic analyses suggest that lizards that colonized Long Island originated near Rome, Italy (Oliverio et al. 2001). This lizard has also surfaced in Philadelphia (where it may have become extinct) and Topeka, Kansas.

Map 7.2. Distribution of the Italian wall lizard (*Podarcis sicula*) in New York. The species is native to Italy, parts of Spain and Turkey, and several Mediterranean islands.

Lizards and Snakes

Other Intriguing Facts: How Far Will They Spread?

To date, natural dispersal aided by further illegal releases by people has permitted Italian wall lizards to expand some 80 miles (130 km) from Garden City, Long Island (Burke and Ner 2005). How far will it go? New York winters, even on relatively mild Long Island, are usually much colder than the native range of these lizards in Italy (Burke et al. 2002). Because the species is not freeze-tolerant, significant geographical gains might be quickly erased by episodic cold winters. But the species somehow manages to find refuge during winter some 10 in. (25 cm) below the soil surface in the frost-free zone (Burke et al. 2002), so further expansion is likely. Although some view the species as a quaint addition to New York's biota, it could become bad news for New York's few, native lizards if Italian wall lizards spread into the Hudson River valley, where the native lizards occur.

Coal Skink
Eumeces anthracinus [Plate 54]

Quick Identification

A small lizard with two wide black stripes bordered by narrow yellow or white stripes running the length of the body.

Description

The coal skink is a small lizard covered with shiny scales. It is one of the so-called four-lined skinks due to the bright yellowish stripes bordering each of two wide dark brown or black lateral stripes running the length of the body. The brown or greenish back may show another faint stripe in some individuals. Unlike the common five-lined skink, there is no pair of converging light stripes on the top of the head. If you turn a coal skink over and examine the undersides of the jaw, you notice a single postmental scale, compared with two such scales in common five-lined skinks. The SVL is 2–2.8 in. (5–7 cm). Sexes are similar, but during the breeding season, males may show a reddish coloration on the sides of the head and along the jaws. Newborn and juvenile coal skinks in New York are dark but otherwise patterned as adults except for blue or dark violet tails. The scientific name derives from *anthrakos*, or coal, referring to the dark dorsolateral color.

Habitat

Coal skinks are found most commonly in moist forested areas near swamps and other wetlands, but they are also found on dry rocky hillsides and shale barrens if water is nearby. Plentiful cover objects, such as loose flat rocks, leaf litter, logs, and boards are important components of their habitat. It is likely that coal skinks hibernate in rock crevices, under hummocks, and similar places that provide access to places below the frost line.

Natural History

Coal skinks breed from April to May in New York (Clausen 1938). Courtship resembles the behaviors of common five-lined skinks, and males bite the necks of females during copulation. Females deposit a clutch of 4–13 (usually 8–9) eggs in June. Nest sites are found under rocks or within rotting logs. Females remain with the eggs and may protect them from potential predators until hatching, which takes 4–5 weeks (Clausen 1938). Age at maturity is about 2 years (Hotchkin et al. 2001).

Coal skinks are believed to be mostly diurnal and feed on small invertebrates, especially spiders, small insects and insect larvae. Coal skinks, in turn, fall prey to many other vertebrates, including carnivorous mammals, birds and snakes. Aside from cryptic coloration, the coal skink's main defense is their surprising quickness and their willingness to give up part of their tail to a predator (see Other Intriguing Facts). It is difficult for an inexperienced person to hand capture a skink—coal skinks dart quickly into small crevices and may even enter the water when chased.

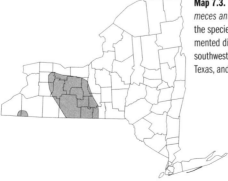

Map 7.3. Distribution of the coal skink (*Eumeces anthracinus*) in New York. Elsewhere the species occurs from with a highly fragmented distribution from western New York southwestward to eastern Kansas, Oklahoma, Texas, and the Gulf Coast states.

Status and Distribuion

The coal skink reaches its northern extent in New York, where it is found in widely scattered locations in the western third of the state (map 7.3). Populations may be locally abundant, but the species is generally uncommon.

Other Intriguing Facts: Tail Loss

Many lizards and salamanders easily part with their tails, especially the most posterior sections, to potential predators. This phenomenon is known technically as "caudal autotomy." In lizards, specialized muscle contractions cause the tail to break along fracture planes (regions of less dense bone) within a region of thinner bone found in many tail vertebrae. Lost tails do regenerate but are shorter and are not supported by vertebrae.

Both species of skinks in New York possess blue-colored tails when they are young. It has been suggested that blue tails serve as an antipredator adaptation by directing a predator's attention to the tail, which tends to contrast sharply with the leaf litter background preferred by these lizards. When the tail is lost, it continues to twitch and writhe, further attracting the predator while the lizard retreats. Alternatively, the blue tails may serve as signals, preventing larger, mature males from acting aggressively toward the juveniles. Interestingly, the blue tails change to a more cryptic brown just as these skinks reach sexual maturity (Vitt and Cooper 1986).

Common Five-lined Skink (Five-Lined Skink)
Eumeces fasciatus [Plate 55]

Quick Identification

A small, shiny-scaled lizard with five light-colored stripes on a black or gray body.

Description

Like all skink species, shiny scales characterize the common five-lined skink, but the species is otherwise quite variable. Young individuals have five thin yellowish or cream-colored stripes running the length of the body against a black background. The young also have bright blue tails. As they age, the tail fades to gray, although females' tails retain a bluish hue. Females usually keep the striping pattern, but older males retain only a trace of it and, more commonly become a uniform brown or olive. Males may also have reddish jaws in spring during the breeding season and have a wider head than similarly aged females. Common five-lined skinks are small lizards; the SVL is 2–3.4 in. (5.0–8.6 cm). The scientific name derives from *fasciatus*, or banded, referring to dorsal stripes of females and young males.

Habitat

Common five-lined skinks are usually found in moist, open-canopy woods with abundant ground cover and leaf litter. In Ontario, they are most plentiful around log piles, slash piles, old buildings, and rock piles (Hecnar and M'Closkey 1998, Howes and Lougheed 2004) and prefer large, thin objects to hide under (Seburn 1993). In New York, they are typically found on talus slopes in mixed deciduous woodlands. Common five-lined skinks are mostly ground dwellers, occasionally climbing dead trees. These skinks hibernate in decaying logs or underground below the frost line.

Natural History

Common five-lined skinks first appear on the surface in mid-April in New York and enter hibernation by early October, but warm spells at either end of this period will extend the active season. Juveniles are active longer in a given year than mature individuals. Most activity is restricted to the ground surface, on rocks, and in woody debris; however, they do scramble up trees and shrubs. A male's home range may be up to 90 ft. (28 m) in diameter, portions of which may be defended from other males. Females restrict their activity to smaller ranges and several females may be found in the territory of a single male (Fitch 1954).

Common five-lined skinks become sexually mature following their second hibernation. They breed in May soon after emergence from winter retreats. A male locates a female by following the pheromone trail she leaves as she moves about. Once two individuals are in visual contact, the males display by tilting their head downward and swaying from side to side. If the other individual does not flee, the male approaches and determines the sex and species from odors by flicking its tongue. Two males may engage in biting and shoving until one yields. A male courts a female briefly and attempts copulation by grasping her and curling his cloaca under hers. Females

Lizards and Snakes

deposit 4–20 eggs in June or July under rocks, logs, in loose soil, or in rotting stumps, where temperatures and moisture levels are stable (Hecnar 1994). Females lay only one clutch per breeding season, and they often remain at the nest site until hatching, particularly if conditions are dry. They may nest communally, perhaps to reduce predation (Hecnar 1994).

Like other skinks, common five-lined skinks are strict carnivores. These skinks feed primarily on insects and other arthropods (Fitch 1954), which they locate primarily by olfaction (Burghardt 1973), but larger individuals may take small vertebrates such as young shrews and lizards, including juveniles of their own species. Predators include many mammals, birds, and snakes. Major defenses used by common five-lined skinks are cryptic coloration, swiftness, and ability to readily give up their tails (Fitch 2003), which are parted with repeatedly during their lives (Cooper and Vitt 1985).

Status and Distribuion

In New York, common five-lined skinks are restricted to the lower Hudson Highlands in the southeastern part of the state and to an isolated population in the uplands near Lake George (map 7.4). Common five-lined skinks are also known from close to the New York border on some of the Thousand Islands of the St. Lawrence River in Ontario. Although not widespread in the state, common five-lined skinks are not given any special protection status in New York. If microhabitats (debris, logs) are maintained in an area, these skinks can tolerate high levels of human disturbance (Hecnar and M'Closkey 1998).

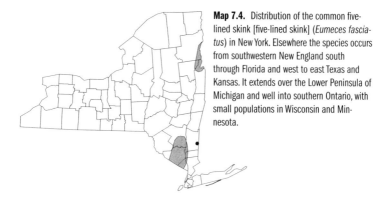

Map 7.4. Distribution of the common five-lined skink [five-lined skink] (*Eumeces fasciatus*) in New York. Elsewhere the species occurs from southwestern New England south through Florida and west to east Texas and Kansas. It extends over the Lower Peninsula of Michigan and well into southern Ontario, with small populations in Wisconsin and Minnesota.

Other Intriguing Facts: Skinks As Parents

With the exception of the birds, alligators, and crocodiles, parental care is limited among reptiles. One exception is the egg brooding observed in many species of skinks. Females of both of New York's skink species engage in this behavior. Why they do this is unclear, but adults might protect the eggs from predators or prevent deterioration in the condition of the nest. Indeed, in one study, when the adults were removed, there was a marked reduction in hatching success. In another, brooding females retrieved eggs moved from their nests. It is not known if females provide any help in the hatching process or beyond, but they leave the nest area soon after the hatchlings emerge. In any event, guarding eggs or simply remaining with the eggs is a considerable investment for the mother skink—it represents time and energy she is not investing to forage for her own welfare (Vitt and Cooper 1989).

Eastern Wormsnake (Eastern Worm Snake)
Carphophis amoenus [Plate 56]

Quick Identification

A small shiny brown snake with smooth scales and a pink belly.

Description

Eastern wormsnakes measure 8–15 in. (20–38 cm) in total length. These snakes possess a cylindrical body, and their scales are quite glossy. The dorsal color is brown (sometimes almost black), whereas the belly and first few adjacent rows of scales are pink to bright red. The eyes are small and the small narrow head is pointed; these are adaptations for a life underground. The tail ends in a blunt spine. The scales are smooth and occur in 13 rows at the middle of the body. The anal plate divided. Young eastern wormsnakes are between 3–5 in. (7.5–12.4 cm) at birth and are more sharply two-toned (brown back, pink belly) than adults. The species name derives from pleasing or lovely, possibly referring to the subtle but nevertheless elegant coloration of this snake.

Lizards and Snakes

Habitat

Eastern wormsnakes are secretive snakes that are usually found in moist forests, often near streams, under objects, or in leaf litter. These snakes may also live in drier forests (McLeod and Gates 1998). Because eastern wormsnakes are especially susceptible to water loss through the skin, they not only select wetter habitats but may also be inactive and burrow deeper in soil during the hot summer months (Barbour et al. 1969b).

Natural History

Eastern wormsnakes are active from March through October, with most intense activity in spring and early fall. Little is known about courtship and mating in this species (Clark 1970). The snakes may mate in spring to early summer; however, some authors believe they mate in fall and store sperm overwinter. Females deposit one to eight eggs in rotting logs and stumps or sawdust piles in late June to early July. Hatching occurs in August or early September.

Eastern wormsnakes feed mainly on earthworms and soft-bodied insects (Barbour 1960). Due to their small mouth, their diet is limited to elongate prey. Several studies have suggested that earthworms are almost the exclusive component of their diet. Because eastern wormsnakes rarely move about on the surface, their major predators include other snakes, shrews, opossums, and leaf-litter foraging mammals. When handled, eastern wormsnakes attempt to burrow between your fingers, and you may feel their sharp-tipped tail. They rarely attempt to bite.

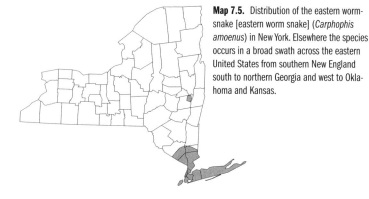

Map 7.5. Distribution of the eastern wormsnake [eastern worm snake] (*Carphophis amoenus*) in New York. Elsewhere the species occurs in a broad swath across the eastern United States from southern New England south to northern Georgia and west to Oklahoma and Kansas.

Status and Distribuion

In New York, eastern wormsnakes are restricted to a few counties in the southeastern corner of the state and Long Island (map 7.5). There are valid historical records from the Albany Pine Bush. Even within their range, eastern wormsnakes are not common in New York and they are a species of "special concern."

Other Intriguing Facts: Fossorial Snakes

Eastern wormsnakes are rarely observed on the soil surface. These snakes possess a suite of morphological adaptations that facilitate living and burrowing below ground, including a narrow head, a body shaped like a cylinder, smooth scales, tiny eyes, and a short tail. But eastern wormsnakes have no unusual burrowing behaviors—they simply locate the path of least resistance in the soil. Eastern wormsnakes investigate potential pathways by pushing their heads forward and moving them up and down or side-to-side in an effort to enlarge the original opening. They painstakingly progress until they reach their destination or hit an impenetrable area, in which case they back up and try elsewhere. Across their range, they are excluded from areas with particularly compact soils.

Eastern Racer
Coluber constrictor [Plate 57]

Quick Identification

A fast-moving large black snake with glossy smooth scales and a gray belly.

Description

The eastern racer is a slender snake that reaches total lengths of 36–75 in. (90–190 cm). In New York, the eastern racer is almost completely black dorsally as an adult, usually with some white scales on the chin and along the throat. The belly tends to be gray or nearly as black as the dorsal surface. The eyes, with their dark brown iris, are ridged above by a bony extension that gives them a fierce aspect. Young racers are strongly patterned with wide brown or red blotches on a gray background. As young racers age, the patterns become harder to distinguish until they eventually disappear. The glossy scales are smooth, are arranged in 17 rows at midbody, and the anal plate is divided. The eastern racer is most commonly confused with the eastern ratsnake, because both are large and mostly black snakes, but closer inspection reveals that eastern ratsnakes tend to be bulkier and have keeled body scales.

Habitat

Eastern racers are terrestrial and are typically found in open woodlands, shrubby grasslands and pastures, old fields, dunes, and along the edges of marshes. During early spring and late fall, these snakes may move to rocky wooded slopes in search of winter retreats.

Natural History

Eastern racers are alert, active, and mostly diurnal snakes with a reputation for a nasty disposition among those who handle serpents. The species does not climb trees but may be found basking in low shrubs or even out in the open. Eastern racers tend to spend inactive periods sheltered under boards and rocks. In New York, these snakes hibernate from mid to late October through early April. They use a variety of overwintering sites, including mammal burrows, rotted stumps, rocky outcroppings and building foundations. Some travel great distances to winter dens and may hibernate communally with other species, including eastern ratsnakes, copperheads, and timber rattlesnakes (Brown and Parker 1976, Rosen 1991).

Eastern racers mate in the spring from soon after emergence until early June. Males mate for the first time in their second year of life, whereas females usually require an additional year until maturity. Males locate females by following the pheromone trails left by the females. Females lay 3–32 large oval white eggs (9–12 most commonly) in late June or early July in old mammal burrows, rotting stumps, piles of leaf litter, sand crevices, and sawdust piles. Several females may nest together (Swain and Smith 1978). Eggs hatch in late August and September, and the young, which hatch at about 12 in. (30 cm) in length, grow quickly.

Eastern racers feed on a wide variety of animals, including insects and other arthropods, lizards, frogs, bird nestlings and eggs, other snakes, and small mammals of many species (Klimstra 1959). Despite their scientific name *constrictor*, eastern racers do not use constriction to overpower their prey. Instead, eastern racers pin struggling prey items to the ground with their mouth and loops of their body and then swallow the prey alive. Eastern racers appear to be most successful in capturing moving prey and often forage with their head and neck elevated off the ground suggesting that vision is important for finding prey. In turn, other snakes, carnivorous mammals, and birds of prey eat eastern racers.

Status and Distribuion

Eastern racers are limited to the southern half of New York State and have recently been reported only from the Catskills, Shawangunks and Hudson Highlands, a few counties in western New York, and on Long Island (map 7.6). Populations of this species in New York are now likely much more fragmented than previously, because the open habitats favored by racers have been converted to residential uses or have reverted to forest.

Other Intriguing Facts: Tail Vibrations

A curious behavior of many snakes, including eastern ratsnakes, eastern hog-nosed snakes, copperheads, and milksnakes, as well as eastern racers, is the tendency to rapidly vibrate their tails when threatened or otherwise annoyed (Greene 1988). On certain substrates, such as dry leaves, the sound of this response is intensified and is sure to get the attention of a potential predator or a human observer. The behavior may imitate the sound of insects and act as a lure to bring potential prey closer for attack. This idea is largely unsubstantiated, especially given that snakes are not known to perform tail vibration in contexts other than defensive ones. More likely the behavior is a signal to potential predators to back off or suffer an attack. It may also represent mimicry

Map 7.6. Distribution of the eastern racer (*Coluber constrictor*) in New York. Elsewhere the species occurs throughout the eastern United States and across the middle Great Plains states and east Texas north to Montana and west to Oregon and California. It is absent from much of the southwest and the north central states.

Lizards and Snakes

of the sound that rattlesnakes produce with their rattles, a snake whose venom provides a powerful incentive for avoidance.

Ring-necked Snake (Ringneck Snake)
Diadophis punctatus [Plate 58]

Quick Identification

A small, slender, bluish-gray snake with shiny smooth scales, a yellow belly, and a distinct yellow ring behind the head.

Description

The most conspicuous feature about this little snake is the bright yellow, orange or cream collar around the neck just behind the head. The generic name *Diadophis* is derived from two Greek words meaning "headband snake" in reference to this ring. In some individuals, the ring is not totally complete at the middle of the back. The belly coloration typically matches that of the ring—most New York specimens tend to be yellow to yellow-orange, sometimes with small dark spots along the midline but more often lacking any pattern. The back color is quite uniformly bluish to slate gray and usually the top of the head is darker than the rest of the back. The maximum total length reported in the literature is 27.5 in. (70.6 cm), but a typical New York adult is 10–15 in. (25.5–38.0 cm). The scales are smooth with 15 rows at the midbody, and the anal plate is divided.

Habitat

Ring-necked snakes are serpents of forests, especially near clearings, canopy gaps, and the edges of wooded areas. They are secretive and require extensive ground cover in the form of flat rocks, logs, and woodland debris. Often several individuals are found under single such objects. They appear to require moist soil (Clark 1967).

Natural History

Ring-necked snakes are active from late March through October, and most foraging and other activities occur at night. Like many reptiles, ring-necked snakes are relatively inactive during the hottest part of the summer. These snakes spend hot spells, as well as the winter months, in mammal burrows, rock piles, and gravel banks, as well as in old wells and stone walls (Blanchard et al. 1979).

Ring-necked snakes lay 2–10 eggs per clutch. There is one valid record of a ring-necked snake producing live young; she apparently retained the eggs in her oviduct until they hatched. Ring-necked snakes have been known to mate in the spring, summer, and fall, and those that mate late in the active season can evidently store sperm over the winter (Fitch 1975).

Plethodontid ("lungless") salamanders and earthworms form the bulk of the ring-necked snake's diet, although small frogs, slugs, beetle grubs, and small snakes are also taken. Because ring-necked snakes spend much time under objects, predation is reduced, but nevertheless these snakes are eaten by other snakes and birds, mammals, and bullfrogs. Ring-necked snakes rarely bite when handled but produce a blend of ill-smelling musk and feces while writhing in your hand. Some ring-necked snakes continually coil and recoil their tails, exposing the brightly colored underside, perhaps as a mechanism to deflect a predator's attention from the head.

Status and Distribution

Ring-necked snakes occur throughout New York, although they are rare or absent from the extreme north and along the southern Lake Ontario floodplain (map 7.7). In many locations, ring-necked snakes are abundant but rarely observed without turning rocks and other surface debris.

Other Intriguing Facts: Social Snakes

Snakes are generally not known as gregarious animals. Outside of the mating season, it is rare to see more that one snake at a time unless you dig them out of their overwintering dens. For at least two reasons,

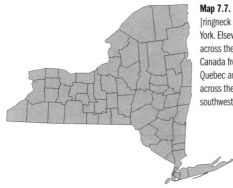

Map 7.7. Distribution of the ring-necked snake [ringneck snake] (*Diadophis punctatus*) in New York. Elsewhere the species is widely distributed across the eastern United States and southern Canada from Nova Scotia through southern Quebec and Ontario to Michigan and south across the Mississippi River states. It occurs southwest into California and Mexico.

Lizards and Snakes

however, it makes sense to find many individuals, often of several species, together in winter retreats. First, suitable hibernacula may be quite rare in the landscape, forcing snakes to be together. Second, grouping behavior may limit water loss when hibernating by reducing the body surface area exposed to air. Curiously, the ring-necked snake is one of the few snakes that may be found together during the active season. It is not uncommon to lift a large flat rock and find three or four or even up to ten individuals coiled there. The reason they do this is not known.

Eastern Ratsnake (Eastern Rat Snake, Black Rat Snake)
Elaphe alleganiensis [Plate 59]

Quick Identification

A large, mostly black snake with a black-and-white checkered belly often found near exposed rocky outcrops in forested regions.

Description

Eastern ratsnakes reach the greatest length of any reptile naturally occurring in New York, and individuals up to 101 in. (256 cm) in total length have been reported. Most are considerably smaller, but specimens of 60 in. (150 cm) are common. Young eastern ratsnakes are much more boldly patterned than the shiny, black adults and have a series of light, almost white blotches. As eastern ratsnakes age, the light blotches on the back become more obscure and disappear altogether in some individuals. The front half of the belly has a distinctive black-and-white checkered pattern, except for the chin and throat, which are plain white or cream-colored. The back half of the belly often appears gray or brown with minimal checkering. The sides appear more flattened than round and form a sharp angle with the flat belly, giving the species a shape like a loaf of bread in cross section. At the middle of the body are 23–27 rows of scales, and the dorsal scales are weakly keeled. The anal plate is divided. In New York, eastern ratsnakes may be confused with eastern racers, which are large, mostly black snakes with smooth scales. Eastern ratsnakes can also be confused with large adult northern watersnakes, which have strongly keeled scales and lightly colored bellies with reddish markings. Young eastern rat snakes and milksnakes may also be confused, but milksnakes have smooth scales and single anal plates.

Habitat

Eastern ratsnakes are active from April to mid-November in a variety of habitats. The snakes may be found in woodlands or the edges of forest-fields, especially where exposed rocky outcrops occur. Old or abandoned buildings in rural areas are favorite haunts, probably because these structures attract rodents (prey). One reason these large snakes are not often encountered by humans is that eastern ratsnakes are excellent climbers and spend much time up in trees (Durner and Gates 1993). They are also accomplished swimmers (McAllister 1995). Eastern ratsnakes hibernate in south-facing openings of rocky outcrops and talus slopes, in unused wells, and even in basements of homes and buildings—in fact, almost anywhere they can escape freezing temperatures. Lack of suitable overwintering sites may be the primary factor limiting the distribution of these snakes.

Natural History

Some studies have suggested eastern ratsnakes reach sexual maturity at about 4 years of age when they are 31–43 in. (80–110 cm) long. Yet recent work in the Frontenac Axis region of Ontario just north of New York has shown that sexual maturity takes between 10 and 12 years (Blouin-Demers et al. 2002). In New York, eastern ratsnakes mate from mid-May in the south through June in the north. They are oviparous and deposit from 5–44 eggs (average 14) following a gestation period of 5–8 weeks. Nest sites include hollow decaying logs and stumps; piles of rotting vegetation; underneath rocks; and in such man-made locales as compost, manure, or sawdust piles. Several females may use nest sites; communal nests are warmer and produce more fit offspring than solitary nests (Blouin-Demers et al. 2004). Eggs are elongate (up to 2 in. [5 cm]) and white, and they hatch in 60–75 days, usually by late August in New York.

As their name implies eastern ratsnakes eat rodents and other mammals as large as squirrels and small rabbits, although the snakes more commonly eat smaller mammals, including shrews, voles, mice, and chipmunks (Weatherhead et al. 2003). These snakes likely even

Lizards and Snakes

have significant economic value: a single adult eastern ratsnake may consume 200 rodents in a single season. Eastern ratsnakes have been reported to thrash their tails in an erratic, whiplike fashion when mammalian prey are detected—this "caudal distraction" may direct the attention of prey away from the approaching head of the snake (Mullin 1999). Birds, especially eggs and nestlings, secured by climbing trees and shrubs are also a major part of eastern ratsnakes' diets (Weatherhead et al. 2003). The snakes also consume lizards, lizard eggs, other snakes, and amphibians. Eastern ratsnakes overpower larger prey by seizing them with the mouth and constricting with one or more coils of the body. In captivity, large eastern ratsnakes have constricted up to three rats at a time. Small or helpless prey are swallowed alive while eggs are taken whole and broken by muscular contractions in the esophagus.

Status and Distribution

Eastern ratsnakes are found south of the Tug Hill Plateau and Adirondack Mountains in New York and as far north as Lake George (map 7.8). An apparently disjunct population occupies the Rideau Lakes district in eastern Ontario and extends onto the New York side of the St. Lawrence River valley in Jefferson and St. Lawrence Counties. Eastern ratsnakes are one of the few reptiles in New York that benefit from forest fragmentation (Blouin-Demers and Weatherhead 2001). Populations tend to undergo synchronized fluctuations caused by large-scale trends in weather (Weatherhead et al. 2002).

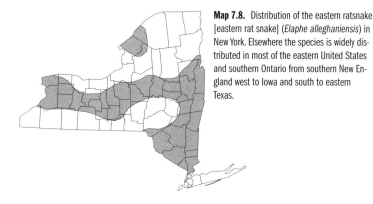

Map 7.8. Distribution of the eastern ratsnake [eastern rat snake] (*Elaphe alleghaniensis*) in New York. Elsewhere the species is widely distributed in most of the eastern United States and southern Ontario from southern New England west to Iowa and south to eastern Texas.

Other Intriguing Facts: Winter Dens

Eastern ratsnakes, like some other snake species, use communal hibernacula, where up to 50 snakes may be found in a single large overwintering site (Prior and Weatherhead 1996). These snakes often share this space with other species, including timber rattlesnakes, eastern racers, milksnakes, northern watersnakes, and common gartersnakes. Interestingly, newborn and juvenile eastern ratsnakes do not appear to use these communal sites; a study in Ontario has shown that the mean age for recruitment of snakes into these sites is 6–7 years. Newborns may overwinter in their nest site, but just where and how the young eastern ratsnakes spend the winter is unknown.

Eastern Hog-nosed Snake (Eastern Hognose Snake, Puff Adder)
Heterodon platirhinos [Plate 60]

Quick Identification

A stocky medium-sized snake with a distinctive upturned snout that typically has dark blotches on a lighter background color. However, nearly black to plain gray individuals are common.

Description

The eastern hog-nosed snake is a striking creature. Because these medium-sized snakes (typical adult total length is 20–33 in. [50–84 cm]) occur in several color varieties, the eastern hog-nosed snake is best recognized by its thick body and flattened, upturned snout. The maximum length is 45.5 in. (115.6 cm). The most common dorsal colors of New York specimens are dark brown blotches on a gray, light brown, or olive to yellowish and red background. Both nearly black and plain gray individuals lacking blotches are also common. A distinct, crooked and dark band between the eyes and a dark band extending backward from the eyes is apparent in well-blotched individuals. Snakes of all color varieties have a pair of darker markings behind the head. The belly is usually lighter than the back and may vary from yellow and cream to light pink, usually with some darker mottling. The dorsal scales are keeled and arranged in 23–27 rows at the middle of the body. The anal plate is divided, and the subcaudal scales are generally lighter than those on the belly.

Lizards and Snakes

Habitat

Eastern hog-nosed snakes occur on wooded hillsides, open pine or deciduous forests, old fields, and beaches (Plummer and Mills 2000). Although these snakes are known to occur in and around marshes and forested bottomlands, a key habitat requirement appears to be sandy or sandy-loamy, well-drained soils (Platt 1969). Eastern hog-nosed snakes hibernate in mammal burrows, under rocks and rotting logs, or in burrows that they dig in sandy soils.

Natural History

Eastern hog-nosed snakes are one of the few New York serpents capable of making their own burrows in loose soil using their unique snouts, but they may also use the burrows of other animals as a retreat or overwintering site (Davis 1946). The snakes are mainly active during the day, but peak activity in the warm summer months is early evenings and mornings. When not on the surface foraging or searching for a mate, eastern hog-nosed snakes spend most of their time underground in loose soil.

Eastern hog-nosed snakes usually mate in April or May, although courtship and copulation have been observed in the fall as well. Males locate females by following the odor trail females leave behind as they move about (Plummer and Mills 1996). As in many snake species, female eastern hog-nosed snakes may mate with more than one male in a season. Females lay 4–42 eggs in loose soil or rotting wood in June or early July. These hatch September or October.

When first encountered, an eastern hog-nosed snake often brings its head and front part of its body up off the ground and inflates a flattened "hood" along its neck and then follows with loud exhalations and close-mouthed strikes. Its tail whips around and repeatedly coils and uncoils. This behavior is remarkably similar to that of some Old World venomous snakes and is the origin of the snake's common name: "puff adder." If this display fails to dissuade a would-be attacker, an eastern hog-nosed snake may roll onto its back while writhing furiously, regurgitating recent meals and defecating, presenting a horrible, smelly spectacle before becoming limp (Platt 1969, Sexton 1979).

Several studies, in both field and laboratory, have demonstrated that eastern hog-nosed snakes have a remarkable preference for toads

(Platt 1969, see Other Intriguing Facts). Young and adults are not sensitive to the toxic secretions of toads (Huheey 1958). Other prey include frogs, salamanders, other snakes, reptile eggs, worms, and insects (Trauth 1982, Mills and Yeomans 1993).

Status and Distribution

Most New York populations are found in the southeastern region of the state and on Long Island (map 7.9). A small population persists in the pine barrens area north of Albany. Lack of sandy soil, toads, and alternative prey for young snakes may limit distribution within the state (Michener and Lazell 1989). The eastern hog-nosed snake is listed as a species of "special concern" in New York State. Efforts to conserve this species by translocating individuals are tenuous, because translocated eastern hog-nosed snakes tend to move more and survive poorly relative to residents (Plummer and Mills 2000).

Other Intriguing Facts: A Toad Specialist

Eastern hog-nosed snakes possess a set of behaviors and adaptations for preying on toads. Their upturned snout undoubtedly facilitates digging for toads once the snake has detected them with its keen sense of small. Their genus name, *Heterodon*, means "different tooth," referring to their large pair of teeth in the back of the mouth. These teeth can be rotated forward somewhat and may help grip captured toads. These teeth may puncture the lungs of toads, which are inflated as a deterrent to predation (Kroll 1976); however, the snakes' jaws alone can deliver sufficient crushing force (Platt 1969). Eastern hog-nosed snakes possess

Map 7.9. Distribution of the eastern hog-nosed snake [eastern hognose snake] (*Heterodon platirhinos*) in New York. The species occurs from Cape Cod and southern New England south to Florida and west to central Texas then north to eastern Minnesota, Michigan and southwestern Ontario. It is absent from much of Ohio, western Pennsylvania, and western New York.

enlarged adrenal glands that produce hormones that provide some resistance to the toxins in the skin of toads (Smith and White 1955). Finally, the saliva of eastern hog-nosed snakes contains compounds that may be toxic to toads and have been known to even cause reactions in hypersensitive humans, including pain, discoloration, and bleeding (McAlister 1963, Grogan 1974, Young 1992)

Milksnake (Milk Snake, Spotted Adder)
Lampropeltis triangulum [Plate 61]

Quick Identification

A strikingly colored, medium-sized snake with red or reddish-brown blotches bordered by black on a gray to tan body commonly encountered near barns and buildings.

Description

Adult milksnakes average 24–36 in. (61–90 cm) but may reach 52 in. (132 cm) in total length. In New York and most of the northern parts of the species' range, the ground color of the back is gray to tan with large red or reddish brown blotches running the length of the body. Blotches are bordered by black and usually appear in three rows (sometimes five), with the lateral rows consisting of smaller spots. A good field mark for New York individuals is the U- or Y-shaped light patch on the back of the neck. The belly scales have a checkerboard pattern of alternating gray or white with black. The smooth scales appear rather shiny—hence the generic name *Lampropeltis*, which is derived from the Greek *lampros*, meaning radiant, and the Latin *pelta*, meaning shield. The scales on the sides and top each possess a pair of apical pits and are arranged in 19–23 rows at midbody. The anal plate is undivided. The blotches on young snakes usually appear a brighter red color than those of adults; otherwise juveniles resemble miniature adults.

Habitat

Milksnakes live in old fields, farmlands, the edges of wet meadows, open or rocky woodlands, lakeshores, the brushy borders of forests, and power line rights-of-way. The snakes are most often encountered by people near barns, sheds, and other outbuildings, although they readily enter garages and houses (particularly kitchen ceilings of old farmhouses) if rodents are present. Piles of firewood and stacks of lumber are favored haunts.

Natural History

Milksnakes are active from mid-April to late October or early November in New York (Wright and Wright 1957) and do most of their active foraging at night. These snakes hibernate, often communally with other species, in rodent burrows, rocky dens, under rotting stumps, or in root cellars and old wells.

Milksnakes lay eggs (from 3 to as many as 23). Often several females gather to deposit eggs at a communal site, possibly because of the lack of availability of suitable egg-laying sites—commonly loose substrates such as sand or sawdust. Eggs incubate for 6–8 weeks, and the young hatch from late August to early September. Outside the breeding season, which occurs from early May through June in New York, milksnakes are rarely found together except in their winter retreats.

Rodents, such as mice and voles, and shrews form the bulk of the milksnake's diet, but milksnakes also take nestlings and eggs of ground-nesting birds and lizards. The snakes use constriction to overpower their prey. Milksnakes are in the "kingsnake" group, so-named because members regularly consume other species of snakes, including smaller individuals of their own species and even rattlesnakes. This is facilitated by an apparent resistance to snake venom (Weinstein et al. 1992).

Map 7.10. Distribution of the milksnake [milk snake] (*Lampropeltis triangulum*) in New York. This species may well have the greatest distribution of any snake and is known from southern Canada to northern South America.

Lizards and Snakes

Status and Distribution

In New York, milksnakes are known from every county, but appear to be absent at higher elevations of the Adirondack Park (map 7.10). Plentiful in some areas, they are relatively secretive and rarely observed abroad on open ground during the day. Milksnake populations have benefited from the expansion of farmland across New York State but may now be declining as abandoned farms revert to forest.

Other Intriguing Facts: Milksnake Myths

No reptile in New York is subject to more myths, tall tales, and misguided notions than the milksnake. Here's an example (Evers 1960):

> The whole thing began when Father came in from the barn one morning in July 1915 with a long face. Bella, our fine Jersey cow, wasn't well, he reported…Charley spotted the cause of Bella's trouble at once. A milk snake was milking the unfortunate cow as she grazed in the pasture by night. Then as dawn broke over Jenny Mountain, the gorged snake would head for the big alder swamp and there the lazy rascal would doze away the day. It was this shameful treatment that had so saddened Bella. In fact, it made her lose her cud.

> Some people refer to these snakes as "copperheads" due to a superficial resemblance to their venomous cousins. Milksnakes are often called "spotted adders" after the venomous serpents of Europe and Asia, perhaps because folks assume any boldly patterned snake is poisonous. Moreover, like many snakes, milksnakes exhibit the unnerving habit of vibrating their tails rapidly like rattlesnakes when annoyed. Milksnakes are, however, quite harmless. In fact, they perform a valuable service to farmers and homeowners by consuming mice and other small mammals that otherwise would damage crops and stored grains. They are present in barns not because they are trying to obtain the milk of cows (something they absolutely do not do), but rather to seek out rodent prey. Probably more worried telephone calls to authorities concerning snakes have come from homeowners who find milksnakes near their dwellings, particularly so in late summer when feisty newborns are moving around in abundance.

Northern Watersnake (Northern Water Snake)
Nerodia sipedon [Plate 62]

Quick Identification

The only dark, relatively large and heavy-bodied snake with brown or reddish-brown cross bands found in aquatic habitats.

Description

Adult northern watersnakes measure from 24–42 in. (61–107 cm) in total length with exceptional specimens reaching 56 in. (144 cm). The coloration and patterns of this species vary, but one of the best field marks is the brown or reddish-brown cross bands and blotches on a tan, brown, or gray background. The front half of the body is typically banded, whereas the back half is blotched. This characteristic pattern is most pronounced in young individuals. Older animals are much darker (stained by organic acids in the waters they inhabit) and upon initial inspection may appear uniformly black or dark brown. The belly is white, cream or yellowish often with distinct reddish-brown spots with crescent shapes (these may be irregular or absent in some individuals). Many New York specimens have thin red stripes on the face. The scales on the body, arranged in 21–25 rows, are strongly keeled, and the anal plate is divided. Males have slightly longer tails than females.

Habitat

The northern watersnake is the most aquatic snake in New York. Indeed, the genus name *Nerodia* is derived from the Greek *Nero*, meaning liquid or water. This species may be found in almost any permanent freshwater locale, whether a stream, lake, open swamp, marsh, peatland, canal, or roadside ditch. Northern watersnakes prefer cattail clumps and wet meadows. These snakes are often observed in and around human-made structures such as dikes, dams, and canals, which along with beaver lodges, muskrat houses, and streambanks, are critical basking and overwintering sites.

Natural History

In New York, northern watersnakes are active from April to October. During the spring and fall, these snakes are mainly active in the day, becoming more nocturnal during the summer months. Activity is greatest at air temperatures of 82–95°F (20.8–34.7°C).

Lizards and Snakes

Northern watersnakes are rather sedentary creatures and rarely move far from water, although young individuals may disperse overland. Radio tracking studies indicate that adults stay within a small home range, with most movements concentrated in less than 10% of the entire range (Fraker 1970, Tiebout and Carey 1987). Northern watersnakes hibernate in earth dams, floodwalls, stone causeways, levees, ant mounds, vole tunnels, and muskrat and beaver burrows.

Both sexes may reach sexual maturity at 2 years of age, with females usually larger at this time (Baumann and Metter 1977). In New York, courtship and mating occur in the spring months, soon after emergence from hibernation. Most females give birth in August and early September. The most active, rather than the largest, males secure the most matings; therefore males tend to adopt a low-energy, low-growth strategy outside of the breeding season to avoid predation and hence are smaller than females (Brown and Weatherhead 2000, Weatherhead et al. 2002). Northern watersnakes give birth to live young, and females move little during the gestation period and may not feed. Females typically give birth to 15–30 young, but litter size can range from 4–99 (larger females have larger litters). By selectively basking the parts of their bodies in which the young are developing, females are able to hasten embryonic development, permitting northern watersnakes to thrive in the colder waters of New York, where egg-laying reptiles are at a distinct disadvantage.

Northern watersnakes are excellent swimmers, both on the surface and while submerged. The snakes often forage along the water's edge, moving through water in search of prey. They prey mainly on fish and frogs (Roe et al. 2004), salamanders, and tadpoles but also take small mammals, birds, juvenile turtles, insects, and crayfish. In western New York, diets of 59 snakes were by volume 95.8% fishes, chiefly suckers and minnows, and 4.2% tadpoles (Raney and Roecker 1947). Northern watersnakes sometimes feed on carrion. Juveniles use both ambush and active searching to locate prey (Balent and Andreadis 1998). Quite remarkably, young northern watersnakes have been observed using the back half of their bodies as a barrier against which to herd schools of fish or tadpoles. Predators of northern watersnakes include most mammalian predators, hawks, herons, other snakes such as racers and larger northern watersnakes, snapping turtles, bullfrogs, and large predatory fish such as bass and northern pike. Typical escape behavior when threatened is to dive to deeper water, where northern watersnakes can stay submerged for up to 65 minutes). Longevity is 7 or more years.

Status and Distribution

Formerly thought to occur throughout New York, recent evidence suggests that northern watersnakes are absent from the St. Lawrence River valley east of the Oswegatchie River and most of the Adirondack Mountains, with the exception the lower southeastern slopes and near Lake George and Lake Champlain (map 7.11). The snakes are quite abundant across their range, but they are intolerant of certain forms of water pollution.

Other Intriguing Facts: The Truth About Northern Watersnakes

Although preferring to flee, northern watersnakes defend themselves vigorously by flattening their bodies, striking, biting, and exuding copious amounts of foul-smelling feces and anal secretions. Their saliva contains anticoagulants, thus causing profuse bleeding (their species name *sipedon*, or rottenness, refers to a serpent whose bite causes mortification). Although quite harmless if left alone, many people confuse northern watersnakes with venomous cottonmouths (also called water moccasins) and kill them for this reason. But cottonmouths do not occur in New York! Similarly, northern watersnakes are often killed because of the mistaken belief that they decimate populations of game fish. Large populations of northern watersnakes taking up residence near a bait pond or hatchery may perhaps reduce stocks, but these snakes should be captured and moved, not killed.

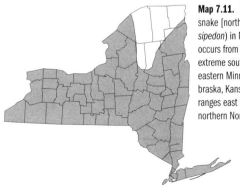

Map 7.11. Distribution of the northern watersnake [northern water snake] (*Nerodia sipedon*) in New York. Elsewhere the species occurs from southwestern Maine west through extreme southern Quebec and Ontario to eastern Minnesota and south and west to Nebraska, Kansas, and eastern Colorado. It ranges east through Oklahoma to the coast of northern North Carolina.

Lizards and Snakes

Queen Snake
Regina septemvittata [Plate 63]

Quick Identification

A relatively small snake with a dark tan back with yellow stripes on its lower sides. Extremely rare in New York, it is typically found near streams and other habitats of crayfish, its primary prey.

Description

Queen snakes are slender, relatively small snakes whose typical adult size is 15–24 in. (38–61 cm). These snakes may reach a maximum total length of 37 in. (92 cm). The background color is tan to chocolate brown to almost black with a yellow stripe on lower side of body, occupying the upper half of the first row of scales and all of the second row. Occasionally, three more narrow and dark stripes may be seen in younger individuals. The belly is yellow or reddish and marked with two distinct brown stripes along the middle of the belly and two dark stripes along the edge of the belly and lower half of the first row of scales. Dorsal scales are keeled and occur in 19 rows, and the anal plate is divided. The scientific name derives from *regina*, or queen; *septem*, or seven; and *vittata*, or striped with ribbon.

Habitat

Queen snakes require moving water and are usually found among aquatic plants, overhanging shrubs, or among or under rocks at the water's edge. Warm, shallow streams with shrubs and trees nearby are the snakes' most favored habitat, but they may be found along the edges of ponds, lakes, and marshes if crayfish—their main food—are present. Queen snakes are often seen basking on tree and shrub branches overhanging water, into which they drop when threatened. If they are in an area, it may be possible to find them by turning over flat rocks along stream edges. These snakes are vulnerable to desiccation (Stokes and Dunson 1982), so they are never far from water.

Natural History

Little is known of the biology of queen snakes in the northeastern United States. These snakes appear to be primarily diurnal, spending the evening and night under the cover of rocks and logs (Ernst 2003). Queen snakes are active from early April until October but have been observed on the surface during warm spells in late fall and winter. They hibernate in muskrat lodges, crayfish burrows, and in the structure of earth and stone dams. Female queen snakes become sexually mature in their third year of life, and mating occurs in spring (Branson and Baker 1974). Queen snakes are viviparous with extensive circulatory contact between developing young and their mother. Birth occurs from late July to September with a typical brood size of 10–14.

In New York, crayfish, particularly crayfish that are soft-shelled as a result of recently molting, are the nearly exclusive prey of queen snakes, whether newborns or older adults. Queen snakes find crayfish by probing under flat rocks and other streamside debris, primarily using their sense of smell. The snakes also occasionally consume aquatic insect nymphs, small fish, tadpoles, and frogs. In turn, queen snakes fall prey to otters, mink, raccoons, great blue herons, and other vertebrate carnivores that forage along the sides of streams.

Status and Distribution

Queen snakes in New York are known from a few river drainages south of Buffalo and from a large wetland near Rochester (map 7.12). Queen snakes are among the rarest of reptiles in New York, and few specimens have been observed in recent years. Consequently, this snake is listed as endangered; however, it may be still relatively abundant in the southern and midwestern states within its range. The species benefits from fencing to protect the riparian areas it inhabits (Homyack and Giuliano 2002).

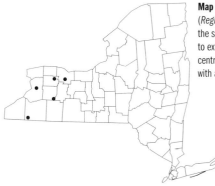

Map 7.12. Distribution of the queen snake (*Regina septemvittata*) in New York. Elsewhere the species occurs from southwestern Ontario to extreme southeastern Wisconsin south to central Mississippi and the Florida panhandle, with a disjunct population in Arkansas.

Lizards and Snakes

Other Intriguing Facts: Restricted Diets

Queen snakes are specialists in their feeding habits. In one study in western New York (Raney and Roecker 1947), 99% of the food items in the stomachs of queen snakes consisted of newly molted crayfish. Such feeding specialists are at a great disadvantage, however, when ecological conditions change and their primary food becomes scarce. Siltation and other forms of pollution (especially insecticides) often degrade streams to the extent that crayfish, so dependent on water quality, begin to disappear. Invasions by exotic crayfish are another, unexamined possibility. Queen snakes in New York may be particularly vulnerable to these threats because populations are already reduced in size and isolated at the edge of the species' range.

DeKay's Brownsnake (Brown Snake, Garden Snake, Dekay's Snake)
Storeria dekayi [Plate 64]

Quick Identification

A small, brown or grey snake with a small head and two rows of black dots running lengthwise down the back, found in many habitats, including urban areas.

Description

Rarely reaching over 20 in. (50 cm) in total length, DeKay's brownsnakes are easy to recognize by their drab brown or grey color and two rows of small black dots that run down their back. Typically adults are 9–13 in. (23–33 cm) in total length. Color variation ranges from yellowish brown or gray to dark brown. Because the skin on the back between the dots is usually lighter in color than the sides, some DeKay's brownsnakes may appear to have a wide stripe down the length of the back. The belly is cream or light pink, and a few small dark dots may be present on the edges of the ventral scales. The small head often shows dark markings beneath the eye and along the side of the neck. DeKay's brownsnakes possess keeled scales in 15–17 rows at midbody and the anal plate is divided.

This species is known to many as the DeKay's snake, named after the nineteenth century New York naturalist James DeKay. Interestingly, DeKay originally thought brownsnakes were juvenile common gartersnakes until John Holbrook, another leading herpetologist of the time, correctly determined that brownsnakes were indeed a new and separate species. These snakes are also known as "garden snakes" to many urban dwellers. DeKay's brownsnakes may be mistaken for ring-necked or eastern wormsnakes; however, both of those species have smooth scales. Adult red-bellied snakes usually have red undersides and have 15 rows of scales.

Habitat

DeKay's brownsnakes are common in most terrestrial and marshy habitats of the state where there is an abundance of objects under which they can hide, such as rocks and logs, as well as a supply of earthworms and slugs, their favorite prey. The small serpents are often found in farms, towns, and even cities under the debris left by people, and they may rival common gartersnakes in abundance. The species is even known from Central Park in New York City.

Natural History

DeKay's brownsnakes are secretive and spend most of their active season (April–October) below ground, in leaf litter, or under logs and stones. These snakes feed mostly at night. In New York they spend the winter in mammal burrows, rock crevices, rotting logs, or anthills, returning to the same spot year after year (Noble and Clausen 1936). DeKay's brownsnakes often aggregate in large numbers to hibernate and share space with other small secretive species such as smooth greensnakes and red-bellied snakes (Clausen 1936). DeKay's brownsnakes may emerge on warm winter days.

With DeKay's brownsnakes, spring mating—when males and females first emerge from winter dens—is probably the norm in New York (Clausen 1936, Noble and Clausen 1936). As with most snakes, males locate females via tracking the females' pheromone trails. Once located, the male DeKay's brownsnake moves alongside a female, twitching his tail and flicking his tongue rapidly. He brings his chin in contact with her neck and, after aligning his cloaca with hers, inserts a hemipenis. Often, several males jockey for position alongside a single female. Live birth occurs in mid-August to September in New York, and litter sizes may range from 3 to 41, with an average of 14.

DeKay's brownsnakes feed preferentially on earthworms, slugs, and snails (Judd 1954), and these snakes also eat small insects, sow bugs, and small frogs. DeKay's brownsnakes locate their prey by active searching, using olfaction as their primary cue. The snakes have little in the way of defenses aside from their secretive nature. As such, the list of potential predators is long and includes most carnivorous mammals and birds, other snakes, and large frogs.

Status and Distribuion

DeKay's brownsnake is found virtually across New York state (map 7.13), although there are few records from the northwestern Adirondack Mountains and the eastern St. Lawrence River valley. In many locations, this small snake is abundant but escapes notice due to its secretive nature.

Other Intriguing Facts: A Snake's Approach to Escargot

In addition to soft-bodied slugs, both DeKay's brownsnakes and red-bellied snakes eat snails by extracting them directly from their shells (Rossman and Myer 1990). The snakes first seize a snail by its soft parts before the snail can withdraw into its shell. If the snake grabs a snail partly by the shell, a successful extraction cannot be performed. Once grabbed, the snakes move backward until the shell becomes wedged against small stones or other objects on the ground. By twisting about and continuing to apply pressure on the muscles holding the snail to its shell, DeKay's brownsnakes can pull out the snail's body in about 10 minutes. These snakes also have longer teeth on their upper jawbone that help secure the fleshy, sticky tissue of the snails.

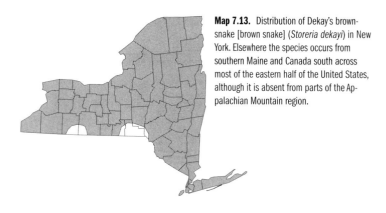

Map 7.13. Distribution of Dekay's brownsnake [brown snake] (*Storeria dekayi*) in New York. Elsewhere the species occurs from southern Maine and Canada south across most of the eastern half of the United States, although it is absent from parts of the Appalachian Mountain region.

Red-bellied Snake (Redbelly Snake)
Storeria occipitomaculata [Plate 65]

Quick Identification

A small brown or gray snake with a distinctive red belly and three light spots behind the head.

Description

The red-bellied snake is the smallest serpent found within New York's borders, averaging between 8 and 10 in. (20.3–25.4 cm) and reaching a maximum total length of 16 in (40.6 cm). Newborns may be as small as 2.75 in. (7 cm). Red-bellied snakes appear in two distinct color morphs in New York: backs that are brown or reddish brown and backs that are gray (Grudzien and Owens 1991). Four narrow black stripes and a faint light stripe in the middle of the back may be present in both morphs. Most have a distinctive red-colored belly, but it may be orange or pale yellow in some individuals. A diagnostic feature of both color morphs is the group of three spots just behind the head. In fact, its specific name, the tongue twister *occipitomaculata*, means "spot on the back of the head" in Latin. The spots are usually tan or yellow and may unite to form a collar, although this is observed in few New York individuals. In southwestern New York, individuals are occasionally found in which the dorsal and ventral surface is black, but diagnostic tan spots are still evident behind the head. Scales are keeled and occur in 15 rows at mid-body. The anal plate is divided. With this snake in hand (do not fret—this is among the most harmless of snakes!), there should be little confusion with other species in our area: ring-necked snakes and wormsnakes have smooth scales and DeKay's brownsnakes have cream or light brown bellies.

Habitat

Red-bellied snakes occur primarily in moist deciduous and mixed coniferous woods. These snakes may also be found in sphagnum bogs, swamps, upland meadows, and along river floodplains. On occasion, red-bellied snakes are found in suburbs and other residential areas but not as frequently as DeKay's brownsnakes and common garter-snakes. Rocks and other solid surface structures to hide beneath are important parts of this snake's habitat.

Lizards and Snakes

Natural History

Following a winter spent in loose soil, ant mounds, rock crevices, or under logs, red-bellied snakes emerge in mid-April across New York, perhaps earlier during particularly warm springs. In spring and fall, red-bellied snakes are active at all times of the day and evening, but they are more nocturnal in the summer months. These snakes enter hibernation in late October or November.

Red-bellied snakes give birth to live young rather than laying eggs. Mating is primarily a spring phenomenon, soon after emergence from hibernation, although some individuals have been observed copulating in late summer or fall (Trapido 1944). In summer, females swollen with developing young are most readily found under flat rocks, bark, or boards exposed to full sun. As the rock or wood warms up, the heat is conducted to the snake lying beneath, speeding development of the embryos and shortening the pregnancy. Average litter size is seven to eight (maximum of 21 reported), and both the size of the litter and mass of the offspring is positively correlated with female body size (Brodie and Ducey 1989). Birth in New York typically occurs in late July to early September, and the tiny offspring are the diameter of a toothpick. Offspring grow rapidly, feeding on ant eggs and small invertebrates, and they may become sexually mature in their second year.

Red-bellied snakes feed primarily on worms and soft-bodied insects but especially prefer slugs and snails, and the snakes occasionally consume small frogs and salamanders. In turn, other snakes, large frogs, small and large mammals, mole salamanders, lizards, and even spiders

Map 7.14. Distribution of the red-bellied snake [redbelly snake] (*Storeria occipitomaculata*) in New York. Elsewhere the species occurs from Nova Scotia to southern Manitoba south to east Texas, Georgia, and throughout the eastern United States, except most of peninsular Florida.

eat the snakes. Red-bellied snakes are harmless to people and never bite; however, some specimens appear to curl their upper lip somewhat menacingly when handled (Do Amaral 1999).

Status and Distribuion

Red-bellied snakes probably occur throughout New York State (map 7.14), but there are no recent reports from Long Island. In many locales, these snakes are abundant but are rarely observed in the open.

Other Intriguing Facts: How to Eat Food That is Wider Than Your Head

Red-bellied snakes often eat a slug or a snail that is bigger around than the diameter of their own head (a practice common to most snake species). A number of special traits facilitate accomplishing this feat (Rossman and Myer 1990). The two halves of the lower jaw of a snake do not fuse (as they do in all other reptiles). The lower jaws are also free to move independently of the skull, thereby increasing the overall potential size of the snake's "gape." In addition, some bones of the snout and upper jaw are flexibly attached to the skull to increase freedom of movement. Because snakes lack shoulders and breastbones, the ribs are not attached ventrally and are therefore free to part widely as a large object passes temporarily down the throat. When a snake's mouth is stuffed with a big prey item, it can still breathe because the opening to the trachea is at the front end rather than in the back of the throat. A snake's skin is also elastic, allowing for expansion as bulky food passes down the snake's length.

Short-headed Gartersnake (Shorthead Garter Snake)
Thamnophis brachystoma [Plate 66]

Quick Identification

A small brown gartersnake with narrow head slightly broader than neck and no alternating rows of black spots between the stripes (as in the common gartersnake).

Description

This is a small gartersnake, 10–22 in. (25–56 cm) in total length, whose narrow head is scarcely broader than the neck. The dorsal ground color ranges from dark olive to almost black, with some a distinct chocolate brown. There are three longitudinal stripes: one mid-dorsal and two lateral ones running the entire length of the body. These stripes may be prominent to obscure, ranging in color from yellowish to tan, and tending to be bordered by fine black lines. The lateral stripes are almost always located on scale rows two and three. There are no alternating rows of black spots between the stripes, as is typical for the common gartersnake. The belly color varies from yellowish-green to light tan. The dorsal scales of this snake are keeled and are arranged in 17 (rarely 19) rows. The anal plate is single (undivided), and each side of the head is adorned with six supralabial scales. The scientific name derives from *thamnos*, or shrub or bush, and *ophis*, or snake, as well as *brachys*, or short, and *stoma*, or mouth.

Habitat

This denizen of meadows and low herbaceous fields avoids deep woodlands, although it may penetrate their edges. Short-headed gartersnakes are nearly always found under some sort of cover such as boards, flat rocks, and tussocks and have been recorded at 900–2,400 ft. (275–730 m). These snakes can be most successfully sought under flat stones along the exposed edges of road cuts or in the vicinity of abandoned barns and farmhouses where the ground is covered with an abundance of boards, shingles, and other debris. These areas need not be near open water.

Natural History

Rather little is known of the biology of this species. Short-headed gartersnakes are active from April to November. Winter hibernacula in western New York have been reported as cavities in shale banks shared with eastern newts, spotted salamanders, and red-bellied snakes (Bothner 1963). In western New York, Pisani and Bothner (1970) indicated that mating occurs after emergence from hibernation in April to May. Offspring are born from July to September. Brood size can range from 5 to 14 young, averaging 7–8. Females may have a biennial reproductive cycle. Short-headed gartersnakes feed primarily on earthworms but also take small amphibians. Predators include small mammals and birds. When startled, this diminutive serpent may wriggle violently and, when in the hand, thrash about as it besmears you with its voided excrement (however, it never attempts to bite; Gray 2003).

Status and Distribution

Short-headed gartersnakes occur in south-central and southwest New York State (map 7.15) in a cluster of western counties (Allegany, Cattaraugus, Chautauqua) and a single peripheral population near Horseheads (Chemung County). Bothner (1976) suggested that the species was in decline in western New York, possibly as a result of incursions by the common gartersnake.

Other Intriguing Facts: Mysterious Declines

Up until about 1950 or so, the short-headed gartersnake was, within its range, quite abundant. Since then, it has suffered a dramatic decline in population density to the point that it was for a time listed as a species of Special Concern in New York State. Subsequent observations suggest that although still reduced, the numbers of this species have somewhat stabilized. The reasons for this dramatic decline have yet to be determined. We speculate on the following causes: (1) increases in predation (because populations of the opossum, coyote, and red fox, mammals known to feed on snakes, have escalated); (2) population expansion by milksnakes and common gartersnakes (also known to occasionally feed on or compete with, respectively, these small snakes); and (3) perhaps persistent contaminants, such as dichlorodiphenyltrichloroethane (DDT), which concentrate in earthworms and eventually in short-headed gartersnakes.

Map 7.15. Distribution of the short-headed gartersnake [shorthead garter snake] (*Thamnophis brachystoma*) in New York. The species has a rather circumscribed range, being found only in western Pennsylvania and southwestern New York.

Eastern Ribbonsnake (Eastern Ribbon Snake)
Thamnophis sauritus [Plate 67]

Quick Identification

A medium-sized snake whose slender body shows three light stripes contrasting clearly against a dark background, a distinct although small spot of yellow in front of the eye, and an exceedingly long tail.

Description

Eastern ribbonsnakes are easily mistaken for gartersnakes. Close examination of an eastern ribbonsnake reveals two bright yellow to cream stripes on the sides bordering a dark stripe and a small spot of yellow in front of the eyes. The bright lateral stripes overlie scale rows three and four, below which are light brown stripes on scale rows one and two and the edge of the belly. A third yellow stripe is found down the center of the back. All of these stripes contrast sharply with the dark body. Unlike the closely related gartersnakes, eastern ribbonsnakes have no patterns on the labial scales. The belly is yellow or green with no markings. Total length measures 45–66 in. (45.7–96.5 cm). Eastern ribbonsnakes are slender serpents with long tails that may contribute up to one-third the total length of the snake. The snakes have keeled scales in 19 rows at mid-body, and the anal plate is undivided. The species name means "lizardlike," which likely refers to the appearance of the snake's head.

Habitat

Eastern ribbonsnakes are nearly always found in wet habitats and seldom wander far from ponds, marshes, or swamps. Due to their fondness for basking, they are most commonly encountered in grassy or shrubby vegetation in wet areas without a tree canopy. Eastern ribbonsnakes readily take to water and are second only to the northern watersnakes among New York's aquatic snakes.

Natural History

Eastern ribbonsnakes are active from late March through October and are mostly diurnal, but they may be observed moving on nights when frogs are calling. These snakes do not make extensive movements but stay within a rather small area near particular ponds. Hibernation occurs in ant mounds, rodent tunnels, crayfish burrows, and among upturned tree roots at the water's edge. During especially hot and dry summers, eastern ribbonsnakes may take refuge and remain inactive for short periods.

Like all members of their genus, eastern ribbonsnakes give birth to live young (Rossman 1970). In their second or third year of life, these snakes become sexually mature and can be observed courting and mating soon after emergence from hibernation, usually by early May. There are some reports of fall breeding as well. Some 3–26 (typically 10–12) young are born in late July or August in New York.

Most studies of the prey of eastern ribbonsnakes indicate that amphibians form the bulk of their diet, with the majority being frogs in New York (Brown 1979). The snakes also consume salamanders, small fish, leeches, and arthropods. Eastern ribbonsnakes, unlike their close relatives the common gartersnakes, do not feed on earthworms. As with most snakes, olfaction is relied on to locate prey; however, vision is also important. Eastern ribbonsnakes are sometimes observed at a pond's edge with their heads held high, examining the surface for telltale movements of tadpoles and fish. Wading birds and carnivorous mammals are the major predators on adults. Young eastern ribbonsnakes are vulnerable to a wider array of potential predators, including large frogs, turtles, other snakes, and fish. Eastern ribbonsnakes take to water to escape terrestrial predators, often diving down to hide in submerged vegetation. Like common gartersnakes, eastern ribbonsnakes thrash and exude a strong-smelling musk when handled. Many

Map 7.16. Distribution of eastern ribbonsnake [eastern ribbon snake] (*Thamnophis sauritus*) in New York. Elsewhere the species occupies a broad band east of the Mississippi River from Michigan and southern Ontario to southern Maine and south through Florida and Mississippi. It is largely absent from the Appalachians and southern Ohio and Indiana.

individuals are found with tail tips missing, indicating some violent encounter in the past.

Status and Distribution

The eastern ribbonsnake's distribution across the New York State is spotty, with puzzling gaps in their distribution in the Adirondack Mountains and the southwest corner of the state (map 7.16).

Other Intriguing Facts: Hunting Strategies

All snakes are carnivores, and methods of snake foraging behavior can be loosely divided into two types: sitting and waiting for prey, and actively searching for prey. The choice is often a function of the foraging behavior of their primary prey. For example, because rattle snakes preferentially feed upon small mammals that move around considerably, the snakes can sit and wait for rodents to wander by. In contrast, eastern ribbonsnakes prefer to eat frogs that are themselves sit-and-wait predators. For this reason, eastern ribbonsnakes must be active foragers, prowling constantly along pond margins and in shallow water, looking for frogs.

Common Gartersnake (Common Garter Snake)
Thamnophis sirtalis [Plate 68]

Quick Identification

A common, small to medium-sized snake highly variable in color and pattern but usually with at least three light stripes on a darker body.

Description

Common gartersnakes are among the most variable of serpents in color and striping pattern and are often confused with other species. Most common gartersnakes have three light (usually yellow, but may be brown, green, or bluish white) stripes running from head to tail, although the central stripe may be lacking or incomplete. The lateral stripes cover scale rows two and three. The ground color is typically dark brown but may be black, green, or olive. A double row of dark spots may be present between the dorsal and lateral stripes. The coloration pattern is reminiscent of men's stocking garters—hence the common name. The underside may be yellow, green, or white, and two rows of dark spots may be visible or may be obscured by the edges of ventral scales. The labial scales are yellowish with black edges. Newborn common gartersnakes are colored much like the adults. Common gartersnakes reach adult lengths of 18–54 in. (46–137 cm). Males are smaller than similarly aged females and possess relatively longer tails (21–30% versus 17–22% of body length). The scales are keeled and are arranged in 19 rows at mid-body. The anal plate is single.

Habitat

Thamnophis is Greek for "shrub snake," but common gartersnakes may be found almost everywhere. This said, these serpents do show a preference for wetter habitats, and the most common place to find one is grassy forest edges or clearings near ponds, lakes, wetlands, or streams. Common gartersnakes may be also be quite common in urban and suburban settings (Kjoss and Litvaitis 2001), especially with abundant cover in the form of boards, rocks, or junk metal.

Natural History

Common gartersnakes usually spend the winter in groups, sometimes of just a few and sometimes of thousands. Hibernation sites include house foundations, rocky crevices, mammal burrows, and other places just below the frost line. In fact, some northern populations of common gartersnakes can tolerate brief exposure to frigid temperatures, although they cannot survive long bouts of freezing (Churchill and Storey 1992). These snakes begin to emerge on the first warm days of spring, usually early April in New York, and spend as much time as possible basking in the sun.

Sperm production occurs after the breeding season has ended, with the sperm retained over winter in the snakes' vas deferens, which permits mating soon after the snakes emerge from their winter retreats (Clesson et al. 2002). Males emerge first and wait for the females to exit the den. Females and males may then pair off to court and copulate or may form large, writhing mating balls comprised of many individuals (see Other Intriguing Facts). Young are born alive in late summer. As in nearly all snakes, there is no parental care. Newborns stay together in small groups for at least several weeks before dispersing separately.

Common gartersnakes feed heavily upon earthworms in New York
(Hamilton 1951) and also take slugs, adult and larval amphibians,
some insects, small fish, nestling birds, and small mammals (Rossman et al. 1996). Occasionally, common gartersnakes can be found
in large numbers along pond edges just at the time when frog and
toad tadpoles are transforming into air breathing, terrestrial juveniles
and are most vulnerable (Arnold 1978). Common gartersnakes have
an impressive ability to tolerate the toxic skin secretions of amphibians. Like most snakes, prey are located primarily through a well-
developed sense of smell and a forked tongue to locate and follow
scent trails. If you take a cotton ball that has been rubbed on an earth-
worm and place it in front of a hungry snake, you will observe the
rapid increase in tongue flick rate and see the snake begin its search
for this favorite prey. Gartersnakes simply grab and swallow their
prey—they do not use constriction, although there is some evidence
that gartersnake saliva may contain secretions that may incapacitate
or even kill small mammal prey (Rosenberg et al. 1985).

Status and Distribution

Common gartersnakes are indeed common and are widely encountered snake in New York State (map 7.17), occurring everywhere except at the highest elevations (over 3000 ft. [900 m]) in the Adirondack Mountains. Declines in common gartersnakes in Westchester
County in the 1960s and 1970s were attributed to widespread pesticide application (Gochfeld 1975). The species benefits from fencing
out livestock to protect riparian areas (Homyack and Giuliano 2002).

Map 7.17. Distribution of common gartersnake [common garter snake] (*Thamnophis
sirtalis*) in New York. Elsewhere the species occurs from southern British Columbia to California along the Pacific Coast and east across
the northern United States and southern
Canada to the Canadian maritime provinces.
Its range then extends south to the Gulf of
Mexico, and it is absent only from the southwestern states and western Texas.

Other Intriguing Facts: Mass Mating in Gartersnakes

At the northern edge of its range, some males of one subspecies of common gartersnake use an unusual mating tactic. All the males emerge from communal dens and congregate by the thousands, waiting for the larger females to emerge, one by one. As they do, massive mating carpets are formed, with many males courting individual females, stimulated by the pheromones females produce from their skins. Some males produce a pheromone that mimics that of the females and is attractive to other males (Mason and Crews 1985). Males that do not produce this odor waste time courting with these so-named she-males and perhaps tire themselves out, thereby reducing the competition with the "she-males" for the real females. Alternatively, the "she-males" may be trying to steal the heat of the other males—a surprisingly precious commodity for an ectothermic creature in cold northern climates in early spring. Whatever the case, studies have shown that the female mimics are more successful than the regular males at copulating with the real females (Shine et al. 2003).

Smooth Greensnake (Smooth Green Snake)
Liochlorophis [Opheodrys] vernalis [Plate 69]

Quick Identification

An unmistakable small, slender snake with bright green sides and back and a white underside.

Description

Smooth greensnakes are probably the most straightforward snake to identify in New York, although they are one of the more difficult to find. This snake is bright green in color over its entire, slender length, which may reach 26 in. (66 cm), although specimens of 12–20 in. (30–50 cm) are more common. That the green color is a mix of pigment and light reflection from the scales is observed when, soon after death, smooth greensnakes take on a distinct blue color as the yellow pigment degrades (as is the case of many road-killed specimens). The belly is white or yellowish-white. The tail is long and tapering. Newborn smooth greensnakes appear dark green or bluish gray. Scales are smooth, occur in 15 rows at the middle of the body, and the anal plate is divided. The scientific name derives from *opheos*, or snake, *drymos*, or forest, referring to arboreal habits of many members of the genus. Vernal presumably refers to the spring-like greenness of the species' coloration. The less familiar genus name *Liochlorophis* (*leio*, or smooth, and *chlor*, or green) was recently assigned to this species.

Habitat

Smooth greensnakes are primarily found on the ground in wet grassy areas that border forests, open woodlands, lakes, marshes, and peatlands, as well as within old fields and meadows. These snakes may occasionally climb into low shrubs, presumably for foraging or basking. Smooth greensnakes are most easily found by lifting cover objects such as bark, logs, boards, and flat rocks because the snakes' green coloration serves as effective camouflage as they move about in green vegetation.

Natural History

Smooth greensnakes are active from early May through late September in the northern portion of their range, including New York. The rest of the year is spent hibernating below ground. Favored locations are rodent burrows and, especially, the subsurface chambers of ant mounds (Carpenter 1953). It is not unusual to find smooth greensnakes overwintering communally with ring-necked snakes, DeKay's brownsnakes, red-bellied snakes, and common gartersnakes in these situations (Lachner 1942).

Smooth greensnakes are oviparous, depositing small clutches (most commonly four to six eggs) in rotting vegetation, beneath logs or flat stones or even in the burrows of small mammals. Often these snakes divide their eggs into two clutches in two separate locations and may nest communally with other smooth greensnakes (Gordon and Cook 1980). Eggs hatch in late August to early September in most of New York.

Most studies of the food habits of these serpents list arthropods as comprising the bulk of their diet, with soft-bodied insects predominating. Although the snakes eat spiders, millipedes, and centipedes, crickets, grasshoppers, and moth and butterfly larvae are preferred prey. Although not known to bite human handlers, these snakes make poor captives, rarely taking food and exhibiting a rather nervous disposition (Schlauch 1975).

Status and Distribution

Smooth greensnakes may be found across New York State within appropriate habitat with the exception of parts of St. Lawrence County (map 7.18). There is speculation that the species may be experiencing recent declines but smooth greensnakes are probably more common than casual observation suggests, due to their secretive nature and highly cryptic coloration.

Other Intriguing Facts: Egg Retention

Smooth greensnakes exhibit one of the shortest incubation periods of any New York egg-laying snake, anywhere from 4–23 days (Blanchard 1932). One account even suggested that young hatched within a few minutes after eggs being deposited. Apparently, female smooth greensnakes can regulate the amount of time eggs are retained within their bodies. Adult snakes adjust their body temperature to some degree by behavioral means (basking, seeking shade) and, on sunny days, they keep their body temperature above that of the air around them. Presumably, egg retention provides a means of transferring elevated body temperature to the eggs, which develop quicker at higher temperatures—a distinct advantage in cold, northern climates. But there are costs to retaining eggs, including loss of the entire clutch if the mother is killed as well as reduced mobility (which equates to less foraging opportunity and more vulnerability to predators) that may prevent egg retention from being a more widespread trait.

Map 7.18. Distribution of smooth greensnake [smooth green snake] (*Liochlorophis vernalis*) in New York. Elsewhere the species occurs from Nova Scotia across southern Canada to Saskatchewan and south to Virginia and Missouri, with disjunct populations in many western states east of the Rocky Mountains and in south Texas and Chihuahua, Mexico.

Lizards and Snakes

Copperhead
Agkistrodon contortrix [Plate 70]

Quick Identification

A large venomous snake with a coppery red, wide head and dark cross bands in an hourglass pattern down the back and no rattle at the end of the tail.

Description

Copperheads in New York are large, relatively thick-bodied snakes with weakly keeled scales, giving them an overall rough appearance. Adults typically are 24–36 in. (61–90 cm) in length, with a record length of 53 in. (134.6 cm). The body is reddish to grayish-brown, and the head is distinctly coppery red to orange. The head is unpatterned, but the body shows a succession of brown bands along its length. Bands are broader along the sides and narrow on the dorsal surface, appearing like a repeated series of hourglass shapes. Small dark spots are frequently observed between the bands. The belly is typically pink, light brown, or cream-colored. Like all pit vipers, copperheads have distinct facial pits between the eyes and nostrils, but you need to be uncomfortably close to see them. The tail is yellow or brown and lacks a rattle. The tail of the paler newborn copperhead is bright yellow. The body scales show apical pits, occur in 21–23 rows at midbody, and the anal plate is undivided. The scientific name is derived from *ankistron*, or fishhook; and *odontos*, or tooth, referring to curved fangs; and *contortrix*, possibly referring to the contorted dorsal pattern.

Habitat

The coloration of copperheads makes them remarkably difficult to see in the leaf litter of the forest floor—the preferred habitat of these snakes. Copperheads favor open areas within deciduous forests with a greater abundance of rock cover and less ground vegetation than timber rattlesnakes, with which they are often found. Exposed rocky hillsides, ledges, and talus slopes are a favorite habitat, especially just before and after hibernation. Copperheads overwinter in communal dens that extend below the frost line on rocky mountainsides, typically with a southern exposure. Dens are used for generations and are a critical resource for copperheads. Dens may be shared with timber rattlesnakes, eastern ratsnakes, and eastern racers. Copperheads are active from late April to October in New York. Especially in summer, copperheads may also occur in old fields, wet meadows, and swamp edges.

Natural History

Like all North American vipers, copperheads do not lay eggs, but instead give birth to live young. Mating has been observed both in spring (April and May) and fall (September and October), and females possess the ability to store sperm for at least one winter (Schuett 1982, Schuett and Gillingham 1986). Sexual maturity for females is reached at about 3 years of age; age at sexual maturity for males is unknown. In New York, most females do not breed every year. Gestation of young lasts about 105 days, and young are typically born in late August and September. A copperhead's brood may contain 1–20 young, with 4–8 the most common. Year-to-year variation in brood size is evidently related to environmental conditions. Like rattlesnakes, the young are born with functional fangs and venom.

As with New York's two rattlesnake species, the facial pits enable the copperhead to detect infrared radiation from warm-blooded birds and mammals against a cooler background. Small mammals such as chipmunks, young squirrels and rabbits, and rats and mice form the bulk of their diet (Fitch 1960). Copperheads, which are active mostly at night, ambush their prey along trails and fallen logs once prey odor trails have

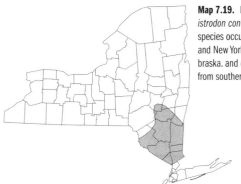

Map 7.19. Distribution of copperhead (*Agkistrodon contortrix*) in New York. Elsewhere the species occurs from southern New England and New York south and west to Kansas, Nebraska. and eastern Texas. It is largely absent from southern Georgia and Florida.

Lizards and Snakes

been located. The snakes envenomate larger prey items, release them, track them by an odor trail, and consume them once the venom has taken effect. Copperheads are not restricted to warm-blooded prey and may take insects, frogs, and other snakes and lizards. Young copperheads often wave their bright yellow tails back and forth to attract frogs and tend to be more active in search of prey than the adults. Opossums, birds of prey, and other snakes feed on copperheads.

Status and Distribution

In New York, copperheads are restricted to the southeastern corner of the state, particularly the Hudson Highlands, but do not occur on Long Island (map 7.19).

Other Intriguing Facts: The Combat Dance

Male copperheads, as well as the cottonmouth and most rattlesnakes, engage in an interesting combat dance during the breeding season (Gloyd and Conant 1990). When two males encounter each other during the breeding season, usually but not always with a female present, both males may face off and elevate the front third of their bodies off the ground. With tongues flicking furiously, the males may sway back and forth with their heads bent at an angle. At some point, one male leans forward and attempts to push the other's head to the ground. The other responds by entwining with the aggressor. Both try to pin each other. Biting has not been observed during this ritual. After anywhere from 20 minutes to 2 hours, one snake breaks contact and crawls away, leaving the other presumably as the victor.

Timber Rattlesnake
Crotalus horridus [Plate 71]

Quick Identification

A large, venomous, and stout-bodied snake that occurs in both dark and yellow color phases. It is easily identified by its wide head, facial pits, and set of rattles at the tip of the tail.

Description

Timber rattlesnakes are impressive creatures, with typical specimens measuring 36–60 in. (90–152 cm) in total length. These snakes are the largest venomous snake in New York (among all other snakes, only the eastern ratsnake is longer) and certainly the bulkiest snake of any kind in New York, weighing up to 3.9 lb. (1.76 kg) in the wild. The largest northern specimen on record, from New Jersey, was 74 in (188 cm). Males are generally larger than females.

Like all pit vipers, timber rattlesnakes possess two facial pits that are capable of detecting minute differences in the thermal field around them (see figure 7.2). In addition, timber rattlesnakes have a rattle at the end of their tails—a series of hollow structures made of a hard protein called keratin, the same material that makes up the scales . These hollow structures make a loud and distinct sound as they rub together when the snake vibrates its tail (see figure 7.2). A new rattle is added to the rattle chain each time the snake sheds. Because skin molting may occur more or even less than once per year, and older rattles wear off, one cannot tell the age of a rattlesnake by simply counting the rattles.

Although individual timber rattlesnakes are quite variable in color pattern, two pronounced color phases occur in New York. Some are nearly black or dark brown and often patterned with bands and blotches of lighter color ("black morph"). Others are yellow or tan on the back with dark brown or gray bands and blotches and a yellow head ("yellow morph"). In both morphs, the tail is uniformly black, although newborns typically have bands on the tail. Both morphs camouflage the snakes well against their typical background of leaves, grass, and dappled sunlight. The belly is white to grayish with some dark flecks. The scales are strongly keeled, and there may be as many as 26 and as few as 19 rows of scales at mid-body (typically 23). The anal plate is single. Newborn rattlers possess a small scale at the tip of the tail called a prebutton and develop their first rattle, called a button, following their first molt, which occurs a few weeks after birth. The scientific name derives from *krotalon*, or rattle, and *horridus*, or dreadful, presumably referring to the snake's venomous nature.

Warning: The timber rattlesnake, like the massasauga and copperhead, is a venomous reptile and, although the danger is often overstated, it should be treated with extreme caution. Even newborns possess fangs and venom. Fortunately, these snakes can be distinguished from others at a distance. The distinctly wide head is shared only with the copperhead, which lacks the rattles and has a coppery-red head. The timber rattlesnake's southern and eastern range in New York, large adult size, and the presence of numerous small scales on the top of the head as opposed to nine large plates distinguish it from New York's other rattler, the highly endangered massasauga.

Lizards and Snakes

Habitat

The timber rattlesnake in New York is a creature largely of deciduous forests in mountainous terrain; however, in summer, these snakes may be found in coniferous forests, mixed forests, old fields, and even near wetlands (Brown 1993). A central feature in a timber rattlesnake's life is the den where it spends the cold winter months. These dens are usually found on mountain slopes, typically with a southern exposure, where the canopy coverage is less than complete and there is access to retreats deep below ground. Large numbers may congregate there for overwintering. Following emergence, males and nonpregnant females travel widely through forested terrain in search of prey (Brown et al. 1982). Pregnant females seek rocky areas, such as outcroppings and talus slopes, with a high degree of exposure to the sun to maximize basking opportunity (Brown 1993).

Natural History

Timber rattlesnakes emerge from their winter retreats in April and early May, when air temperatures in spring begin to rise above winter levels (Brown 1992). The snakes remain in the vicinity of the dens for several weeks before moving to summer haunts. Timber rattlesnakes are mostly active during the day, although during hot spells in mid-summer they may be active at night (Brown et al. 1982). By mid-September, timber rattlesnakes begin to return to the vicinity of their dens, and by mid- to late October, most New York snakes are safely in the dens.

Female timber rattlesnakes take many years to reach sexual maturity, that is, as early as their seventh year of life to as late as their eleventh. Males mature earlier, probably in their fourth year. Mating is usually a mid- to late summer event, and sometimes several males joust to copulate with a particular female (see Copperhead, Other Intriguing Facts, for a description of this type of behavior). Females can store sperm over the winter, so fertilization usually occurs the spring following mating. Females give birth to about six to nine live snakes late in summer or in early fall. Female timber rattlesnakes likely reproduce once every 3–4 years in the northern part of their range, including New York (Brown 1991, Martin 1993).

Timber rattlesnakes may be observed moving about actively, carefully scanning the ground and air for the odors of mice, chipmunks, squirrels, and other rodents that they favor as prey. Once an odor source is located, timber rattlesnakes, like most pit vipers, become ambush predators, often lying coiled in one spot for long periods awaiting prey to approach. Because rodents are apt to use logs as travel corridors, one favorite posture for rattlesnakes is to position their head perpendicular to the long axis of a fallen log and wait to ambush passing rodents (Reinert et al. 1984). Occasionally, timber rattlesnakes have even been observed with their heads resting vertically on tree trunks (Brown and Greenberg 1992). Aside from rodents, rabbits, birds, and other warm-blooded prey, timber rattlesnakes have been known to consume lizards, other snakes, amphibians, and possibly carrion. Young rattlesnakes may take frogs and can wave their bright tails back and forth slowly as a lure. Although adult timber rattlesnakes have few enemies, young have many predators, which range from carnivorous birds and mammals to other snake species.

Status and Distribution

Timber rattlesnakes occur in New York (map 7.20) in the Hudson Highlands, the southern slopes of the Catskills and Shawangunks, a few locations in the vicinity of Lake George and Lake Champlain, one isolated population along the Mohawk River, and at several scattered locales in the west-central part of the state (Stechert 1982, Brown 1993). The timber rattlesnake is listed as a "threatened" species in New York State.

Other Intriguing Facts: Rattlesnake as Wilderness Icon

Dr. William S. Brown, a biologist at Skidmore College, who has studied the timber rattlesnake in New York for decades, eloquently stated why we should conserve this historically loathed creature and so

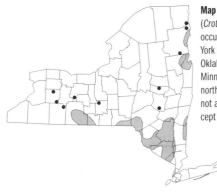

Map 7.20. Distribution of timber rattlesnake (*Crotalus horridus*) in New York. The species occurs from southern New England and New York south to northern Florida, west to Texas, Oklahoma, and Kansas and north to eastern Minnesota and western Wisconsin. In the north-central states, timber rattlesnakes do not appear north of the Ohio River valley, except for a few, isolated populations.

Lizards and Snakes

many others like it (Brown et al. 1994): "The Timber Rattlesnake is one of the last symbolic wilderness species remaining in eastern North America. Many of our mountainous deciduous forests would not have an element of pristine excitement without this species in these woodlands. Seeing one of these snakes quietly coiled on the forest floor on a warm summer day is a naturalist's or hiker's thrill of a lifetime. Saving this species for our future is a high priority of those with a sense of respect for the natural world."

Massasauga
Sistrurus catenatus [Plate 72]

Quick Identification

A highly endangered, medium-sized, gray to brown snake with nine large scales on top of the head, facial pits on the head, and a rattle on the end of the tail found at just two sites in New York.

Description

Massasaugas are medium-sized rattlesnakes (total length: 18.5–30 in. [47.0–76 cm], maximum length of 39.5 in. [100.3 cm]). Like all rattlesnakes, they have a distinct facial pit between the eyes and nostrils and a rattle at the base of the tail. The ground color of the back is gray to light brown with a mid-dorsal row of 21–50 dark brown to black blotches and three rows of smaller, similarly colored blotches on each side. The belly is black and often mottled with yellow, cream, or white marks. There are 19–27 (usually 25) rows of scales at mid-body. The dorsal scales are keeled, and the anal plate is single. Newborns are patterned much like the adult but have bright yellow tails. Massasaugas are distinguished from timber rattlesnakes by the massasaugas' smaller size and the presence of nine large plates on the top of the head as opposed to numerous small scales between the supraocular scales. Massasaugas may be confused with milksnakes, which have smooth scales, a less distinct neck, and no rattle or facial pit. The scientific name derives from *sistrum*, or rattle; *oura* or tail; and *catenatus* or chained, referring to the central row of blotches.

Habitat

Massasaugas are strongly associated with wetlands across their range, including fens, marshes, and wet prairies. Indeed the word "massasauga" has its origins in the Chippewa language and means "great

river mouth," referring to the preferred wetland habitat of these creatures. Wetlands are particularly important for overwintering. Over
much of the massasauga's range, crayfish burrows appear to be a primary hibernation situation, but in New York, where chimney-building
crayfish do not occur, massasaugas spend the winter under hummocks
of sphagnum and shrubs. Because these hummocks generally contain water, it is likely that massasaugas remain immersed in the un-
frozen part of the water table through much of the winter. Massasaugas hibernate singly, unlike other species of rattlesnake, which
gather in large numbers at den sites. During the active season, massasaugas shift from lowland and wet prairie habitat to upland habitats, likely tracking increased food availability in upland areas, especially in old fields and woodland edges (Reinert and Kodrich 1982,
Johnson 2000).

Natural History

Massasaugas emerge from their winter retreats in mid-April but do
not initiate significant movements until nearly a month later. Massasaugas are mostly diurnal and spend nights tightly coiled beneath
overhanging vegetation. Some individuals may move more than 0.5
mi. (0.8 km) from their overwintering site during the active season
but return precisely to their overwintering site in late September by as
yet unknown navigation mechanisms.

Massasaugas in New York likely reproduce every 2 years. Female
massasaugas give birth to live young, typically between mid-August
and mid-September. In New York, mating also occurs in late summer, and females probably mate one summer and give birth the next.

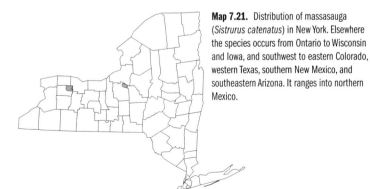

Map 7.21. Distribution of massasauga
(*Sistrurus catenatus*) in New York. Elsewhere
the species occurs from Ontario to Wisconsin
and Iowa, and southwest to eastern Colorado,
western Texas, southern New Mexico, and
southeastern Arizona. It ranges into northern
Mexico.

Females gravid with young do not appear to feed or move much over this period. Brood size varies from 3 to 19; average brood size at one New York location was 9.3 (Johnson 1995). In the wild, at least 3 years are required to reach sexual maturity.

The massasauga's diet consists primarily of small mammals such as mice, shrews, and voles. Other vertebrates, such as birds, lizards, and frogs have been reported, as well as incidental reports of insects, crayfish, and centipedes. Juveniles may eat small snakes. Newborns have been observed using a caudal luring strategy (tail twitching) to attract frogs, whereas adults adopt a sit-and-wait foraging strategy (Schuett et al. 1984). Predators include most carnivorous mammals within their range, as well as birds of prey and other snakes.

Status and Distribution

In New York this species is only known from two locations in large wetlands near Syracuse and Rochester (map 7.21). At least two other locations were recorded during the early 1900s (Whiffen 1913). Massasauga populations are susceptible to wetland drainage, habitat fragmentation, the changing of early succession vegetation to late succession plant communities, overcollecting, and human disturbance (Parent and Weatherhead 2000). The massasauga is listed as "endangered" in New York. The species is variously considered "endangered," "threatened," or of "special concern" in every state and province in which it occurs. Currently it is being evaluated for federal listing as an "endangered" or "threatened" status.

Other Intriguing Facts: Isolated Populations

All available evidence suggests that genetic exchange between massasauga populations is restricted and has been so for a long time, even long before populations were fragmented by the extensive wetland drainage across their range (Gibbs et al. 1997). Given the "threatened" status of this species everywhere, an important conservation implication of these findings is that each geographically separated population should be protected because of the unique genetic diversity found within it. By extension, moving snakes between populations for whatever reason may be a bad idea. Large regional populations are probably composed of genetically isolated subpopulations and each should be treated as a separate management unit.

8

Threats

In this chapter we first describe the history of amphibian and reptile exploitation in New York State and then follow with an examination of the major conservation issues currently facing these creatures: skewed public attitudes, introduced species, commercialization
of wild species, environmental contamination, acid rain, climate
change, and the biggest issue of all—habitat loss and fragmentation. As a result of these combined threats, there have been local extinctions of species on a massive scale, particularly in parts of the
state converted to urban areas, intensive agricultural uses, and
reservoirs. This said, just 9 of the 69 native species in the state are
listed as Endangered, and only five are listed as Threatened (see tables 2.1 and 2.2). Surprisingly, all of the species confirmed for the
state since the early 1800s can still be found. In fact, amphibians
and reptiles can be incredibly hardy creatures. For example, even
Onondaga Lake (near Syracuse), which has been subject to heavy
contamination by nitrites, ammonia, benzenes, and heavy metals
(particularly mercury) from 150 years of continual municipal and
industrial pollution, supports breeding populations of a few reptile
species (Ducey et al. 1998). Moreover, recent surveys suggest that
amphibian populations in upstate New York are doing well in wetlands that have not been destroyed (see box: Are Amphibians Declining in New York State?). In a nutshell, these creatures are surprisingly resilient, but their long-term future is very much in our
hands.

Are Amphibians Declining in New York State?

Of course they are. New York State is becoming increasingly urbanized, and there is a consistently negative association between amphibian diversity and urban development. That said, the catastrophic declines beyond direct habitat loss reported elsewhere are apparently not occurring. A recent study (Gibbs et al. 2005) contrasted counts of frogs in roadside wetlands made in 2001–2002 with a baseline of frog counts from 1973–1980 at 300 sites across upstate New York. Population disappearance was associated with elevated levels of acid deposition (American toad, spring peeper, western chorus frog, and northern leopard frog), urban development (American toad and spring peeper), increased forest cover (western chorus frog), and high-intensity agriculture (spring peeper). Population persistence was associated with increased deciduous forest cover (American toad, spring peeper, and wood frog) and low-intensity agriculture (American toad and western chorus frog). Populations of all species except western chorus frogs were evidently stable or increasing in the wetlands that had not been destroyed.

Historic Overexploitation

There are two important methods used in catching frogs. In one case men and boys tramp the borders of the lake and swamps and the upland fields, singly or in small parties, carrying clubs about three feet long. The frogs are flushed and as they alight a blow is struck with the club, killing them. In this manner from 600 to 800 frogs may be caught in a day, from July until the early winter season sets in. Mr. H. N. Coville has taken early in August 1,276 frogs between 9 A.M. and 2:30 P.M. or 5 1/2 hours of work . . . In the fall of 1915 Mr. Coville had on land in his cages about five tons of frogs, or about 150,000 frogs.

This excerpt from the "Frog Industry" section of a report entitled *Notes on Oneida Lake Fish and Fisheries* (Adams and Hankinson 1916) described the activities of frog hunters at the lake near Syracuse when the demand for frog legs peaked in the United States in the early 1900s. The wholesaler C.F. Davison in Brewerton at the outlet of Oneida Lake had 1.2 millions frogs in captivity in 1915 and grossed some $40,000/year (in 1915 dollars). Most of the frogs Davison secured from long fences made of cheesecloth that intercepted frogs retreating from fields toward the Oneida River and herded them into pits that were 2 ft. (0.6 m) deep. It was activities such as this that

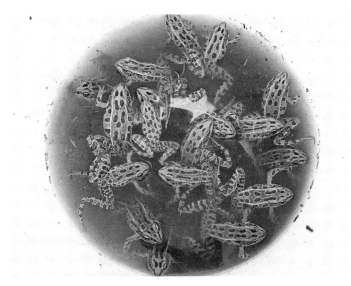

Figure 8.1. Leopard frogs (such as these confined to a translucent bucket) were a major focus of the Oneida Lake frog industry in the early 1900s. Onondaga Co., New York. (Nancy E. Karraker.)

resulted in an amendment to the state conservation law in about 1917 that prohibited the use of "a device which prevents frogs from having free access to and egress from water." Other frogs were gathered in the wake of mowing machines working wet ground. Frogs were imprisoned in metal cages half submerged in mud and snatched out as needed to fill orders. Most orders were for frog legs (a capable skinner could dress 700 frogs in 1 hour), and these were shipped on ice by trolley to Syracuse and then by train to Detroit, Buffalo, and New York City. Schools and colleges all over the country also requested live frogs for study, which were shipped on beds of wet grass in boxes. But by 1912 the market was becoming saturated. Citizens also became fed up with harvest excesses. After an individual netted 8,000 frogs one night in South Bay of Oneida Lake, local legislators began to press the state legislature for protections for the frogs (sources: archives of the *Syracuse Herald*, September 7, 1902; November 7, 1915; and Nov. 12, 1937). All the species cited as harvested commercially are still present at Oneida Lake (figure 8.1), but their current numbers pale by comparison. Much of the wetland near the lake has been drained or isolated from the lake by roads and housing development, and the fields have been converted to housing developments or have been reforested.

Exploitation by humans of New York's herpetofauna is not a new phenomenon. The state's first human inhabitants ate bullfrogs, northern leopard frogs, and wood frogs, and they used gray treefrogs for medicinal purposes (Speck and Dodge 1945). Moreover, refuse heaps of the Niantic and Sebonic people of Long Island have revealed fragments of snapping turtles, eastern box turtles, diamond-backed terrapins, painted turtles, and seaturtles (Latham 1969). Turtles were and remain cultural icons to New York's original people—the Haudenosaunee, and were a source of food, bowls, drinking ladles, burial items, and rattles as well. Some uses evidently depleted populations of some species. For example, archeologists have found a correlation between a sudden decline in the frequency of box turtle shells in middens and gravesites and a large increase in the population of Iroquoian peoples about 2700–2900 years ago (Adler 1970). Use of eastern box turtles by northeastern Native Americans ended some 350 years ago, because the turtles became scarce; now the species is extirpated from large expanses of central and western New York, where it evidently once thrived.

Although always sketchy in details, historical reports shed light on the dramatic changes that have occurred in New York's herpetofauna. In the early 1800s, Eights (1853) indicated that eastern box turtles were abundant in the sand plains between Albany and Schenectady, where today there are likely none. Eights also found tiger salamanders in Albany County and bog turtles in Rensselaer County (McKinley 2005); neither of these animals has been confirmed in those areas since his time. Ditmars (1905) stated that spotted turtles rivaled painted turtles as the most common turtle in the vicinity of New York City, but this is clearly no longer the case. And Bishop (1941) stated that the "dusky salamander is perhaps the commonest and most widely distributed species in the State," an observation that can no longer be made (that honor now clearly goes to the eastern red-backed salamander). Lastly, consider the sordid history of persecution of the timber rattlesnake in New York State (see box: Timber Rattlesnake: From Vermin to Protected Species). Manhattan Island, the Palisades of the Hudson River, and much of Long Island were once prime habitat, likely supporting large populations of timber rattlesnakes (Stechert 1982), but they are gone now. Rank overexploitation of some native reptiles still occurs on occasion in the Great Lakes region, even today (figure 8.3).

Timber Rattlesnake: From Vermin to Protected Species

According to an 1855 account, rattlesnake hunting in the region of Lake George in upstate New York was a girls' sport, the huntresses killing as many as a hundred snakes a day by taking them by their tails and snapping them. This is an exceedingly hazardous way to dispose of a heavy-bodied poisonous snake like a rattler, but perhaps girls were more rugged in those days (Minton and Minton 1969).

The timber rattlesnake is a prime example of the profound "U-turn" that public attitudes and political winds have taken in regard to amphibians and reptiles. Until 1971, the New York State government conducted an extensive (and expensive) program to rid "nuisance" animals from the state. Rattlesnakes were considered as such, with a bounty of $1.00–$5.00 per rattle paid to "rattle trappers," a colloquial name for rattlesnake hunters. One such individual operating on the east side of Lake George earned good money collecting the bounty. During a 50-year-long career, the rattle trapper collected bounties for about 18,000 rattlesnakes (*Adirondack Explorer*, August, 2001), although not all of these snakes came from the Lake George area or were necessarily collected by him. Another pathological rattlesnake hunter and commercial collector killed nearly 3,000 snakes and was eventually convicted in 1993 of federal felony charges for trafficking New York State rattlesnakes via an intermediary in Westchester County to a dealer in Florida (Brown et al. 1994). Consider that today there are only an estimated 9,000 rattlesnakes living among 180 or so dens. Aside from the bounty, the snakes were rendered into "snake oil," a lineament for all matter of ailments, particularly rheumatism, as well as for meat.

Killing of rattlesnakes with abandon occurred into the 1970s (figure 8.2). It was particularly intense during the late 1800s and early 1900s. Consider the following except from the *Walton Reporter* [Delaware County] (August 10, 1901):

> Twenty-nine rattlesnakes were killed on the mountain near East Branch Wednesday by two men and two boys. Rattlesnakes have been unusually plenty on the mountains in that vicinity this season. A rattler measuring nearly five feet was killed on the mountain opposite Francisco's last week and others were seen.
>
> Some of the more venturesome citizens concluded that there was a den of snakes on the mountain and on Wednesday two men and two boys, arming themselves with shotguns and dynamite, started out to make war on the snakes. They found a hole near where the big snake had been killed a few days before and the space around it was literally swarming with snakes. They got the dynamite where they thought it would do the most good and touched it off. There was an explosion and for a minute the air was full of snakes, squirming, hissing and rattling.
>
> A large number of snakes were killed by the explosion, but some big ones escaped and made for the hunters, hissing and rattling in a hair-raising manner. The snakes would dart toward the hunters and coil for a spring when the shot-

Figure 8.2. Rattlesnakes were heavily persecuted in New York until the 1970s. Here two patrolmen and their quarry: a 52-inch female (left) and 40-inch male (right) rid as vermin from the Hale Eddy area, Delaware County, New York. (Glenn Graves/*Walton Reporter,* August 11, 1961.)

guns were brought into play. When the slaughter was over twenty-nine snakes were gathered up, nine big ones and twenty smaller. It was the greatest snake hunt in the history of the town.

An earlier edition of the *Walton Reporter* (July 18, 1891) reported thirty snakes totaling 90 feet in length killed with shotguns and snap eel spears by two men in the same area. Based on this and other reports from the *Walton Reporter,* A.J. Lindberg (unpublished data) concluded that 58% of the dens in the western Catskills have been extirpated since the late nineteenth century.

In large part due to the success of the government-funded "rattle trappers," in 1983 New York State classified timber rattlesnakes as a Threatened species, making it illegal to possess them without a permit. Despite these new protections, timber rattlers have been slow to recover from earlier depredations. Some 8–10 years are needed for females to reach sexual maturity, and even then they reproduce only once every 3–6 years, managing to breed usually only twice per lifetime (Brown 1993). Still, if habitat loss is successfully controlled (fortunately, most remaining dens are on protected state lands), we may see a steady, slow recovery of the timber rattlesnake in New York State from an estimated halving of its historical numbers by snake collecting and bounty hunting (Stechert 1982, Brown 1993). But illegal killing and collecting continues—*notify your NYS DEC conservation officer immediately if you observe any such activity.*

Figure 8.3. Snapping turtles are subject to overexploitation in the Great Lakes region to this day, as indicated by this pile of discarded shells on the shores of Lake St. Clair, Ontario. (Ross MacColloch.)

Public Attitudes

Amphibians and reptiles are fascinating creatures for those who take the time to get to know them. For example, the Native Americans who call New York home (the Haudenosaunee) have long regarded turtles with respect and admiration (Speck 1943). Even today, the clans of the Haudenosaunee exist in the reciprocating halves of Wolves and Turtles. Turtles live a long time and thus are a symbol of life itself. Moreover, turtles appear to spend so much time in deliberate thought and are so slow to decide what to do next that some ascribe to them the virtues of wisdom and patience.

Unfortunately, the current attitude of most of the general public toward amphibians and reptiles ranges from revulsion to indifference. An opinion survey of 2,000 American households (Czech and Krausman 1997) indicated that the public valued these creatures only slightly more than invertebrates and microorganisms and significantly less than plants, birds, mammals, and fish. Moreover, a Harris Poll (#49, August 18, 1999) of 1,015 adults surveyed in the United States revealed that snakes are at the absolute top of the list of the most widespread fears. More than one-third (36%) of all adults surveyed said that they are "very afraid" of snakes (despite the fact that most people rarely, if ever, encounter a potentially dangerous snake).

Figure 8.4. A perennial sore point between New Yorkers and native reptiles relates to the perception that turtles eat game fishes yet many turtles are harmed by fishermen. (Jason Gibson.)

One particular sore point between New Yorkers and native reptiles relates to the perception that turtles eat game fishes and thereby deprive people who fish the opportunity to catch more fish (e.g., Latham 1971; figure 8.4). Worse, waterfowl hunters and wildlife managers have long viewed snapping turtles with suspicion because of their purported voracious appetite for ducklings. That turtles neither depredate upon nor compete with fish and waterfowl to any significant degree was established long ago. For example, thorough studies of food habits of painted turtles from Chautauqua Lake in western New York (table 8.1) indicate that game fishes comprise only about 3% of their diet. Turtles do not outcompete larger fishes for small fish prey. The study concluded: ". . . we doubt if [turtles] offer serious competition to desirable fish life on Chautauqua Lake, since the type of food taken is probably seldom the limiting factor affecting fish production in weedy situations where these turtles are usually found." Similar studies of snapping turtles indicate that even this maligned species mostly eats plants during much of the year (Coulter 1957), including over half of a typical individual turtle's diet in New York (Pell 1940). Although ducklings are unquestionably occasionally "snapped up," snapping turtles present no hazard to waterfowl populations (Brooks et al. 1988).

Table 8.1.

Stomach Contents of 76 Painted Turtles Collected from Chautauqua Lake, New York[a]

Food Item	Volume (%)
Plants	48.4
Snails	15.9
Game and pan fishes	3.2
Rough fishes	3.7
Fish carrion	6.9
Insects	11.6
Crayfish	8.6
Earthworms	1.2
Miscellaneous animals	0.5

[a]Raney and Lachner (1942).

The good news is that as the generations transition, we are witnessing a gradual "warming" toward and increased understanding of amphibians and reptiles. Many young adults today grew up with "Kermit the Frog" and the "Teenage Mutant Ninja Turtles" and, as a result, have positive associations (with frogs and turtles, at least).

A Sampling of Herpetologically Named Businesses in New York State

Blue Lizard Lounge Inc., Commack
Bull Frog Hotel, Jamestown
Dinosaur Bar-B-Que, Syracuse
Flying Frog Tavern & Grill, Hudson
Flying Turtles Bar & Grill Inc, Buffalo
Jumping Frog Deli, Commack
King Snake Sewer & Drain Cleaning Service, Pattersonville
Naked Turtle, Plattsburgh
Red Newt Cellars Winery and Bistro, Hector
Thirsty Turtle, White Plains
Turtle Moving & Storage, Brooklyn

Figure 8.5. Attitudes toward amphibians and reptiles are gradually changing from outright loathing and indifference in older generations to intrigue and fascination in younger ones. (David A. Steen.)

Nothing could perhaps better indicate the devotion some express toward these creatures than the recent case of a young man killed on a road near Syracuse while evidently attempting to rescue a snake (*The Post-Standard* [Syracuse], January 6, 2003). Moreover, amphibians and reptiles represent cultural icons among the people of the state, as indicated perhaps by the occasional use of "herp" names by commercial establishments (see box: A sampling of herpetologically named businesses in New York State). May this slow but steady warming in attitudes toward amphibians and reptiles continue (figure 8.5).

Introduced Species

All of New York State's significant introduced "herps" are (so far) reptiles. They have been released for a variety of reasons. One example is a translocated population from the release in 1942 of 29 eastern fence lizards to the Rossville sector of Staten Island by Carl F. Kaufeld, who hoped to establish a local source of food for lizard-eating snakes at the Staten Island Zoo (Kieran 1959). Another relates to a dealer of Florida softshell turtles who sold a "load" of the turtles to a Buddhist temple, members of which then ceremoniously released the turtles into New York Harbor as part of a religious rite (Williams 1999). Even a Texas tortoise (*Gopherus berlandieri*) has been reported from the wild on Long Island (Burnley 1968). Likely this and many other alien "herp" introductions involved released pets that grew beyond their "cute" and manageable stage. Many reptiles are sold in pet stores, at herp "expos," and over the Internet as diminutive hatchlings that grow rapidly in captivity and develop voracious appetites and much larger body sizes than expected. The potential is immense: 18.3 million live reptiles, belonging to more than 600 different species, were imported to the United States from 1989 through 1997 (Telecky 2001). Among them were 5.7 million turtles and tortoises representing 142 species. Moreover, many invasive species are an issue for amphibians and reptiles insofar as research in New York has shown. Japanese knotweed invasions reduce foraging success in green frogs most likely by reducing insect abundance (Maerz et al. 2005a), and compounds leached from purple loosestrife into wetland waters cause gill damage and thereby reduce larval survival in American toads (Maerz et al. 2005b).

Released pets are the basis for the extensive colonies of "cooters" established all over the State but particularly in the New York City area and especially on Long Island, where populations are likely sustained by continuous releases in addition to successful reproduction in the wild (see species accounts for pond sliders and northern red-bellied cooter). Fortunately, the rate of turtle releases has been slowed by bans on sales of small turtles in pet stores, but adults are still quite available. The reason for the ban has nothing to do with halting the influx of exotic turtles into New York State. Rather, most reptiles and many amphibians carry *Salmonella* bacteria. Turtles for the pet trade are often raised under extremely unsanitary conditions, and they pick up *Salmonella* from the animal and vegetable waste that they are fed. The *Salmonella* does not bother the turtles, but when humans handle amphibians and reptiles and then touch their hands to their mouths, they can infect themselves, leading to stomach cramps, fever, vomiting, and diarrhea. Small turtles and small children are a particularly bad combination. For this reason, since 1975, the US Food and Drug Administration has banned the commercial distribution of turtles measuring less than 4 inches across the shell. This action is estimated to prevent some 100,000 cases of salmonellosis among children each year. Regulations adopted under New York State Health Law also prohibit the sale of turtles less than 4 inches except for educational purposes. Some pet stores manage to declare that the turtles they are selling are strictly for educational purposes, a "loophole" of sorts that still permits sales under the ban (Grady 2005).

Species introductions to date have not been particularly noxious. If such introductions continue, however, someday New York may well end up with something truly unwanted, such as a carnivorous frog that gobbles up the native frogs. If this sounds far-fetched, consider that New York's native bullfrog has destroyed frog faunas where it has been introduced in many areas outside its native range, for example, in the western United States, Southeast Asia, and northern South America (Banks et al. 2000, Kiesecker et al. 2001). There are many candidate species in various parts of the world that could, if brought here, cause massive problems. Once established there is little anyone can do to remove them. *It is illegal in New York State to release any amphibian or reptile (native or exotic) for any reason into the wild without a permit to do so.*

Commercialization of Wild Amphibians and Reptiles

Amphibians and reptiles face a particularly serious threat that is not generally felt by wild birds and mammals: protective laws that regulate hunting, collecting and commercialization do not apply to all amphibians and reptiles. In January, 2006, New York extended protection to all "herp" species native to New York (but non-native species are for the most part unregulated). The reasons for this increased protection is that many native species are highly prized in the pet trade (Schlaepfer et al. 2005). Prices of the more intriguing or colorful of New York's turtles are typically in the hundreds of dollars and yet readily fetch buyers. A recent study by Hohn (2003) of 44 pet stores in New York found that 45 of the 68 species native to New York State could be purchased, including three species listed as either Endangered or Threatened (tiger salamander, eastern mud turtle, and eastern fence lizard). Equally alarming, many other species of Special Concern were readily available for sale: the hellbender, Jefferson salamander, long-tailed salamander, marbled salamander, spotted salamander, eastern spadefoot, southern leopard frog, diamond-backed terrapin, eastern box turtle, spiny softshell, and eastern hognosed snake. Notably, some 75% of species sold were described by sales staff as primarily collected from the wild. Such market forces are starting to deplete some wild populations to the point of local extinction.

Another legitimate debate over commercialization of wild species of amphibians and reptiles is whether it should occur at all, particularly in the case of turtles. Although few citizens are aware of it, commercial harvesting of snapping turtles, diamond-backed terrapins, and other turtles for food does occur in New York State (e.g., Coniff 1989). Commercial harvesting occurs despite the fact that contaminants have been shown to be particularly high in turtles, and eating snapping turtles in New York is likely a bad idea from a human health perspective (Stone et al. 1980, Pagano et al. 1999, de Solla et al. 2001). These activities have been regulated only reluctantly, if at all. Diamond-backed terrapins, for example, received modest protections only recently (in the 1990s) after concern, largely organized by the New York Turtle and Tortoise Society, arose over the large numbers being exploited by food markets in New York City. In New York, the commercial and illegal exploitation of diamond-backed terrapins and other native amphibians and reptiles continues to this day.

Without getting into the ethical dimensions of harvesting turtles for food, turtle harvesting is a bad idea solely on the basis of turtle biology. The problem is that although some turtles may be abundant they all reproduce slowly. Occasional sport harvesting might be tolerable, but commercial harvesting will certainly cause substantial population declines (Congdon et al. 1994). When a single commercial collector harvests 120,000 snappers over a 45-year period (Tapply 1997), it is time to reevaluate whether unregulated harvesting is sound policy.

It is remarkable just how sensitive turtle populations are to modest levels of removal (see Wood Turtle, Other Intriguing Facts). Simply put, "sustainable harvest" of turtles appears to be an oxymoron, at least in northern regions such as New York State. Many states have recently banned commercial harvesting of turtles altogether (e.g., Maine), and New York State has greatly limited the unregulated harvest of earlier years. Beginning in 2006, an individual in New York can harvest only five snapping turtles a day and a maximum of 30 per year. Similarly, many salamanders are extremely long-lived creatures and have a turtle-like demography; for example, hellbenders, are unlikely to absorb even modest levels of harvest. Lastly, there are significant legal issues associated with state government sanctioning commercial harvesting of species for which there are no effective means in place to monitor effects of such harvest on populations.

Acid Rain

Compared to other states, New York gets more than its share of acid deposition, which occurs when sulfur dioxide (SO_2) and nitrogen oxides (NO_x) generated from burning fossil fuels are warmed by the sun and react in the atmosphere with water, oxygen, and other chemicals to form a mild solution of sulfuric and nitric acids. These compounds fall as "acid rain" upon New York's landscape. New York is vulnerable to acid rain because of its geographical position; it is "downwind" of many acid rain sources (e.g., coal-burning power plants in mid-western states). The problem is compounded by poor soils, which are unable to provide a buffer against the acids that precipitate across vast swaths of the state, especially in the Adirondack and Catskill Mountain regions.

Salamanders are particularly sensitive to the acidity of their environment. In breeding ponds, water with a pH less than 4.0 can reduce egg hatching success, slow hatching time, and cause deformities to the spines and gills of larvae (Clark 1986, Freda and Dunson 1986, Portnoy 1990). Similar effects occur on land. Intensive studies of eastern red-backed salamanders conducted near Albany indicate that this species is absent from 27% of forest habitat because of low soil pH (Wyman and Hawksley-Lescault 1987). The salamanders avoid areas with pH less than 3.7. The problem is that sodium (important for making nervous systems function) leaches from the bodies of salamanders under acidic conditions (Frisbie and Wyman 1992, 1995).

The bottom line is that large-scale reductions in salamander populations associated with pond and soil acidification could result in significant changes to the forest ecosystems. This is to say nothing of the inherent tragedy of the mortality of potentially billions of these animals. How well salamander populations will fare over the vast areas of forest in New York State depends a great deal on the success of New York's congressional delegation in their fight to protect the federal Clean Air Act, which regulates the sources of acid rain, against continual attempts to weaken it.

Contaminants, Disease, and Deformities

Many environmental contaminants have direct and indirect effects on amphibians and reptiles. These include salts, metals, petroleum derivatives, pesticides and herbicides. Amphibians, for example, are susceptible to the direct effects of fertilizers as well as to the more subtle effects of hormone-mimicking contaminants, which can feminize males (Hayes et al. 2003). Similarly, some reptiles, including snapping turtles of Lake Ontario and the St. Lawrence and Hudson Rivers, accumulate heavy levels of polychlorinated biphenyls (PCBs), dieldrin, and other contaminants in tissues and eggs, to the point at which sex reversal and abnormal gonads can occur.

A case in point concerns turtles of the Akwesasne (St. Regis) Reservation on the St. Lawrence River in northern New York State (de Solla et al. 2001). Snapping turtle eggs found on the Reservation in 1999 and 2000 had total PCB concentrations of 1,900–61,000 parts per million, or 360–3,100 times higher than concentrations at uncontaminated reference sites (Ashpole et al. 2004). In 1985–1987, adult turtles in the same area had PCB concentrations of 835–11,522 parts per million in their body fat. There are no federal standards for PCB levels for turtles, but those for edible poultry are just 3 parts per million and for edible fish, 2 parts per million. Even soil with a PCB concentration of 50 parts per million on a dry-weight basis is considered a hazardous waste. Accumulated industrial pollutants from nearby heavy industry qualify many turtles on the Akwesasne Reservation as small, roving "toxic waste dumps" (Johansen and Mann 2000). This situation is unfortunate for the local people—the Iroquois—whose creation story holds that the world took shape on a giant, benevolent turtle's back and who traditionally depended on turtles for food and cultural uses.

Contaminants and disease may also interact to cause population declines, particularly in amphibians. Chronic but nonlethal chemical stressors may suppress the animals' immune systems, thereby permitting diseases to kill weakened creatures. Some biologists now consider disease to be as large a factor as habitat destruction in declines of amphibians. For an example of a poorly understood disease has been killing thousands of New York salamanders, see box: Mudpuppies: A Rash of Mysterious Deaths. Disease is also an issue for reptiles—upper respiratory tract diseases are frequent problems, particularly in terrestrial turtles, such as eastern box turtles on Long Island (Lee 2004). The risk of introducing such diseases to wild populations is one of the main reasons why release of pet turtles is generally not permitted in New York State. Although resolving these issues is important in its own right for reptile and amphibian conservation, what they indicate about the health of the environment for all species, including humans, is of concern (see box: Spots on Spotted Salamanders May Indicate Environmental Stress). One bright note is that ultraviolet-B (UV-B) radiation, often considered a threat to amphibians in the western North American, does not seem to be an issue for this species in the eastern part of the United States (Crump et al. 1999, Starnes et al. 2000).

Mudpuppy: A Rash of Mysterious Deaths

In June of 2002, thousands of mudpuppies, a large aquatic salamander, washed up along the shores of Lake Erie, most notably along the shore stretching from Erie, Pennsylvania, to Buffalo, New York. The suspected cause of death was type E botulism. The disease results from the ingestion of the toxin produced by *Clostridium botulinum*, a bacterium that naturally lives in the lake. This bacterium is better known for making types A and B botulism, which is associated with eating improperly canned food. A purified form of type A, used to smooth out wrinkles by partially paralyzing facial nerves, is more familiarly known as Botox. How might mudpuppies have become exposed to higher-than-usual levels of botulism? One theory involves zebra and quagga mussels (both species introduced decades ago) loading up on type E botulism over time as they slowly filtered lake water. The next player—the round goby, a small fish—is also an introduced species that just arrived in the lake. Gobies like to eat mussels. By unleashing stores of botulinum toxins locked into mussel tissues and releasing them to the environment, gobies might be the mechanism that increased the exposure of mudpuppies to botulism. Moreover, mudpuppies might normally withstand such an event, but during times of stress, such as the high water temperatures associated with mudpuppy die-offs, they succumbed to it. It is all speculation at this point, clearly indicating the need for more research on this topic. The story does not end with the mudpuppies. Thousands of gulls, loons, and diving ducks also died, many after ingesting botulism-laden mudpuppies.

Threats **283**

Spotting Patterns of Spotted Salamanders: A Sign of Environmental Stress

Two Cornell biologists recently examined spotting patterns in two nearby breeding populations of spotted salamanders near Ithaca, New York, one from a pond on a golf course, and the other from a pond in a nature reserve. The biologists took digital pictures of the spotting patterns of salamanders they captured as well as salamanders collected from the 1910s to the 1960s at the same two ponds that had been kept in the Cornell Museum of Vertebrates in ethanol-filled jars. Analyses revealed that spots on the golf course pond salamanders had become more asymmetrical than spots on individuals collected from that population before the golf course was constructed, but the spots on salamanders from the other pond had not. The change in spotting patterns may have been due to persistent and toxic materials applied to the golf course during the 1950s, 1960s, and 1970s. Changes in salamanders' spot patterns may seem an arcane topic, but they may be telling us something important about environmental changes that ultimately may effect us (Wright and Zamudio 2002).

Amphibian deformities, in particular, have been widely publicized in the media based on the appearance, sometimes in surprising numbers at single ponds, of frogs and toads with extra limbs and other morphological oddities. Although chemical pollution and UV radiation have been often suggested as causes of such deformities, researchers at Hartwick College in Oneonta have presented convincing evidence that the problem in many instances is caused by small parasites (trematodes) that lodge in developing limb buds and interfere with normal limb development (Sessions and Ruth 1990, Sessions et al. 1999). This is not to say that deformities are entirely a "natural" phenomenon. Elevated levels of nutrients in water caused by excessive fertilizer use may indirectly increase parasite numbers by boosting the populations of aquatic snails—the intermediate hosts for parasitic trematodes.

Climate Change

Based on projections for the next century made by the Intergovernmental Panel on Climate Change, temperatures in New York State could increase by about 5°F (2°C) by 2100 and include more episodic precipitation and increased evapotranspiration. The climatic conditions of New York in 100 years are projected to approximate those that currently exist in Indiana. In such a scenario, vernal pools would dry earlier and remain dry longer; such changes would be to the detriment of many amphibians that breed in seasonal pools (Brooks and Hayashi 2002, Brooks 2004). Global warming may also increase the likelihood of outbreaks of fungal diseases that have been implicated in worldwide declines in amphibian diversity (Pounds et al. 2006). One New York species for which climate warming could be significant is the mink frog, "the frog of the north" found only on the Tug Hill and Adirondack Plateaus. Notably, the mink frog's globular egg mass, which impedes the diffusion of oxygen to the eggs in the interior of the mass, prevents its embryos from surviving in the more poorly oxygenated and warmer waters of the southern parts of the state (Hedeen 1986). If a modest increase were to occur in surface water temperatures in the northern ponds and lakes where the frog now lives, much of its current habitat will become inhospitable. Moreover, the frog will have nowhere to go because it cannot migrate off the plateaus where it now resides. It is not likely to evolve quickly enough to keep up with climate change. Climate warming is apparently already shifting the calling patterns of frogs in the state to earlier dates (see box: Changes in the Calling Phenology of New York Frogs and Toads) and will affect all of the State's amphibians and reptiles—creatures whose biology is intimately tied to ambient moisture and temperature levels. Some species may benefit but others, such as the mink frog, likely will not.

Changes in the Calling Patterns of New York Frogs and Toads

Between 1900 and 1912 Albert Hazen Wright and his spouse Anna made daily records of calling activities of frogs in the Ithaca, New York area. These were compared to records gathered from the New York State Amphibian and Reptile Atlas Project for 1990-1999 for the same area (Gibbs and Breisch 2001). Four species—spring peeper, wood frog, bullfrog, and gray treefrog—are now calling 10-13 days earlier, two species—green frog and American toad—are unchanged, and none is calling later. The data suggest that the warming climate in central New York State during this century is associated with earlier breeding in some amphibians—a possible first indication of biological response to climate change in eastern North America. Were it not for Wright's scrupulous record keeping in the tradition of the careful naturalist, this insight would not be available to us.

Habitat Loss and Fragmentation

Habitat loss and fragmentation pose the greatest threat to New York's amphibians and reptiles. The process is one in which the environment is converted to increasing amounts of urban and in some areas agricultural land, thereby subdividing the remaining natural habitats into a mosaic of smaller pieces. This reduces populations and disrupts the movement of amphibians and reptiles within the landscape. Moreover, roads, railroads, and other barriers to movements permeate a once continuous and gradually transitioning landscape. The process is occurring all over New York State but particularly in the Hudson River Valley, Long Island, and in the peripheries of the state's larger cities (see figure 3.4; figure 8.6).

The long-term consequences of habitat loss and fragmentation for the herpetofauna are dire. For example, Schlauch (1979) provides a sobering analysis of the decline of the entire herpetofauna of Nassau County up to the 1970s, during which just 3—the bullfrog, green frog, and Fowler's toad—of 36 species remained in a nonendangered status. Ziminksi (1970) gives a similar account of the community-wide decline of native snakes as a result of habitat destruction in the vicinity of Hempstead, Long Island.

From the perspective of a salamander, frog, turtle, or snake attempting to hop, crawl, or slither across the ground's surface, these changes are significant indeed (figure 8.7). Many salamanders move each year from forests and fields, where they spend much of the year feeding, resting, and hibernating, to a wetland to breed. For example, spotted salamanders move up to 500 ft. (150 m) from breeding to over-wintering sites in small mammal burrows in the forest near Bing-hamton, New York (Madison 1997). Many aquatic turtles do the reverse. Females emerge each year from ponds, lakes, and other wetlands to dig holes in the uplands and lay their eggs (e.g., Bland-ing's turtles in Dutchess County may travel 2,625 ft. [800 m] to nesting areas; Kiviat et al. 2000, A. R. Breisch, unpublished data). Some aquatic frogs, such as green frogs, leave their summer ponds and migrate to wooded hillsides where they overwinter in the well-oxygenated waters of streams (e.g., up to 900 ft. [300 m] from breeding ponds near Binghamton; Lamoureux and Madison 1999). Even the turtles that we think of mostly as land dwellers, such as the wood turtle and eastern box turtle, move often between wet areas and uplands

Figure 8.6. Just 1 year previously, this housing development (A) was prime habitat for timber rattlesnakes. Subsequently excluded by a wire fence (B) from their traditional home range within the housing development, local rattlesnakes were noticeably perturbed. (Randy Stechert.)

throughout the warm season. Lest we fail to mention snakes, none are evidently territorial; instead, they roam widely in search of prey and mates, visiting both wetlands and uplands in their meanderings. Consider the endangered massasauga in New York, which travels about 65 ft. (20 m) per day for an average of about 1.7 mi (2,700 m) per year between wetland and upland habitats near Syracuse (Johnson 2000).

Roads are a major component of habitat fragmentation in New York and are a particularly vexing problem. The state's road network

Figure 8.7. Turtles are low-slung, slowly creeping creatures that are nevertheless extremely mobile—a trait that frequently puts them in conflict with roads. (Sean T. Giery.)

is extremely extensive (New York has the tenth highest road density in the United States). More important, traffic volumes are increasing at a much faster rate than is road expansion as New Yorkers drive more cars more frequently for longer distances. Traffic volumes on many "main" roads are commonly in the thousands to tens of thousands of vehicles per day. Such traffic volumes can translate into nearly certain death for any reptile or amphibian attempting to cross such a road (figure 8.8). Notably, "trauma" is the primary source of morbidity and mortality of reptiles brought to wildlife veterinary centers, with motor vehicle impacts the most frequent cause of trauma for eastern box turtles, painted turtles, and snapping turtles (Brown et al. 1991). Of the 59,000 records submitted to the "Herp Atlas" from 1990 to 1999, 5.4% were of "herps" found dead on the road (DOR). This included 59 of the 71 species reported. DOR reptiles outnumbered DOR amphibians, with gartersnakes, snapping turtles, painted turtles, and spotted salamanders accounting for 35% of the reported roadkills (A.R. Breisch, unpublished data).

Road mortality in amphibians and reptiles often generates jokes rather than the serious concern it warrants. Anyone who takes the time to disembark from their vehicle and observe the road surface near a wetland after a heavy rain can often witness hundreds to thousands of

Figure 8.8. Road mortality is a gruesome reality for many of New York's reptiles and amphibians, such as this American toad, that traverse the landscape attempting to complete their annual activity cycle. (Twan Leenders.)

mangled corpses along some stretches of highways, particularly adjacent to wetlands. Furthermore, some easily overlooked aspects of road engineering are particularly lethal. One example is storm water drains, which, in conjunction with vertical road edging (figure 8.9), herd hordes of "herps" to their deaths down storm grates each year.

Roads are a particular issue for turtles. The crux of the problem for turtles is the same as in the case of commercial harvest (see Commercialization of Wild Amphibians and Reptiles). The longevity and

Figure 8.9. Road edging herds hordes of "herps" to their deaths annually down storm drains. Here at the Binghamton Nature Reserve the problem is mitigated for with asphalt "salamander ramps" up to the curb's height. Broome Co., New York. (Victor S. Lamoureux.)

delayed reproduction makes turtle populations extremely sensitive to increased mortality of adults. Female turtles—the core of breeding populations—on their annual nesting migrations are those most vulnerable to road mortality (Steen and Gibbs 2004).

There has been only one systematic study of road mortality in New York. Of some 1,500 amphibians attempting to cross Route 23

Table 8.2.

Estimates of Road Mortality of Amphibians Crossing Route 23 During the Spring Breeding Season Outside Oneonta, New York in 1984-1986[a]

Species	Number Observed Crossing Road	Percent Killed
Wood Frog	551	34%
Pickerel Frog	201	34%
Spring Peeper	308	47%
American Toad	53	28%
Eastern Newt	277	56%
Spotted Salamander	169	73%
Eastern Red-backed Salamander	4	100%
Total	1563	41%

[a]From Wyman 1991.

near Oneonta in the mid-1980s (Wyman 1991), an estimated 41% were killed (table 8.2). The faster-moving frogs were killed at somewhat lower rates than the sluggish salamanders. Notably, this was a study of spring movements. But amphibians also move all summer and fall, albeit more diffusely, so the mortality was likely even higher than these figures suggest. For example, near Binghamton, New York, three of four green frogs carrying radiotransmitters (used for tracking) that approached a local roadway were killed on it (Lamoureux and Madison 1999). In nearby Ontario, one study of an approximately 2-mile (3.6-km) section of a two-lane paved causeway at Long Point over two seasons tallied more than 32,000 dead individuals. Most were amphibians, but 864 were reptiles, including painted turtles, snapping turtles, Blanding's turtles, and common gartersnakes (Ashley and Robinson 1996). Salamanders, in particular, are particularly affected by roads as barriers to movement (DeMaynadier and Hunter 2000). Roads are not just a matter of mortality but also health—in Massachusetts spotted salamanders migrating across pavement have much higher levels of stress hormones than those migrating through forest (Homan et al. 2003). Roads also are associated with

Figure 8.10. Signage on roads near wetlands where overland movement of breeding salamanders and nesting turtles is frequent can help reduce road mortality, as attempted here for Blanding's turtles at James Baird State Park, Dutchess Co., New York. (Sean T. Giery.)

increased contaminant loads in amphibians (e.g., lead) (Birdsall et al. 1986).

One approach to alleviating the problem of road mortality would be to establish a statewide network for reporting "hot spots" of amphibian and reptile mortality on roads. These could be used as the basis to identify where along the road system amphibian and reptile populations may be most seriously affected. When reengineering of particular road segments occurs, subsurface passageways under roads or even barriers to prevent "herps" from entering roadways could be constructed. Signs warning motorists can be important where endangered species are involved (figure 8.10). Much research still needs to be conducted to determine the characteristics of effective passageways. Various road-crossing structures have been piloted in different parts of the state and the preliminary results are encouraging (see Conservation Case Studies: Amphibians Cross Here: New York State's First "Herp" Tunnel). Moreover, many European countries accommodate amphibians and reptiles in a "business as usual" manner in highway planning and design. Perhaps through a similar, concerted effort, we can find ways to limit road deaths of the New York State's herpetofauna.

9

Legal Protections

Excessive harvest of turtles by European immigrants triggered in 1905 the first New York State law to protect any member of the state's herpetofauna (Breisch 1997). At this time, the state legislature amended the "Forest, Fish and Game Law" to include a section that prohibited the "taking, killing, or exposing for sale of all land turtles or tortoises, including the box and wood turtle." According to Babcock (1918), this law was passed because coal miners striking in Pennsylvania were collecting large numbers of wood turtles and eastern box turtles from the wild for food. Apparently this law was established to protect both the turtles and the people. Notably, some miners became sick from consuming the turtles, likely because of toxins the turtles had sequestered from eating mushrooms (Ernst et al. 1994). Eastern box turtles are known to heavily consume fungus toxic to humans, including on Long Island (Latham 1968b). By 1912, frogs, specifically "bullfrogs, green frogs, and spring frogs," had been added to the list of species that could be taken or possessed only during a limited open season. In contrast, an open season for wood, box, and land turtles was never allowed. In 1966, the bog turtle became the next herpetofaunal species to be protected (Breisch 1997).

Laws Regulating "Take"

Prompted by indiscriminate exploitation of the state's herpetofauna, government agencies from federal to local levels have become involved in making decisions that affect amphibian and reptile populations in New York State. The federal government enforces the

Convention on International Trade in Endangered Species of Wild
Fauna and Flora (CITES), which allows international trade in wildlife
species only when such trade is sustainable. In addition to the sea turtles, four of New York's reptiles are listed by CITES: the bog, wood,
eastern box, and common map turtles. The US Fish and Wildlife
Service (USFWS) also administers the federal Endangered Species
Act (ESA). All the sea turtles and the bog turtle are listed under the
authority of the ESA. The USFWS administers the Lacey Act, which
makes it unlawful to import, export, transport, buy or sell any species,
including amphibians and reptiles, taken or possessed in violation of
federal, state, or tribal law. Therefore, a permit is required in order for
a species to be taken from a state in which it is unprotected to a state
in which it is protected, and vice versa.

At the state level, the Environmental Conservation Law (ECL) di-
vides wildlife (all animal life existing in the wild, except fish, shellfish,
and Crustacea), into "protected wildlife" and "unprotected wildlife."
"Unprotected wildlife" can be taken from the wild at any time in un-
limited numbers by any legal means, which usually implies the possession of a hunting, fishing, or trapping license or a special permit.
Until very recently, most amphibians and reptiles, except for the few
species listed as Endangered, Threatened, or Small Game, were considered "unprotected wildlife." Legislation passed in late 2005 by
unanimous approval of the New York State Senate and Assembly and
signed by Governor George Pataki, which went into effect on January
1, 2006, designated all native amphibians and reptiles as "small game"
and gave the New York State Department of Environmental Conservation (NYS DEC) authority to regulate "take" of all the native
"herps" in the state. This new law allows limited "take" of such species
as snapping turtle, diamond-backed terrapin, and frogs while the final
regulations are being developed.

When the first list of "endangered" species in New York was
adopted in 1974, the bog turtle was the only species of herpetofauna
included. New York's endangered species law was amended in 1981 to
allow designation of Threatened species. Since then, other species
have been added to the list (see Tables 2.1 and 2.2). For Endangered
or Threatened species, no individual (or part of it) may be taken, possessed, transported, or sold without a special license from the NYS
DEC. A permit is also required to possess all non-native species that
are listed as Endangered or Threatened by the USFWS. A recent
Dutchess County court decision greatly reinforced protections of

Endangered and Threatened species and their habitats in New York State (see box: Rattlesnakes and the Law). Because New York lists species only if they are Endangered or Threatened throughout their range in the state, Westchester County has taken the initiative to develop its own list of Endangered and Threatened species mandated for protection on county lands (J. Robbins, personal communication).

Rattlesnakes and the Law

A recent, prominent state court ruling (State of New York v. Sour Mountain Realty) suggests that legal protections for timber rattlesnakes and other endangered species will remain strong (Amato and Rosenthal 2001). At issue was a 2-mile (3.2-km) long, 4-foot (1.2-m) high, snakeproof wire-mesh fence that a landowner in Dutchess County had begun to install to keep rattlesnakes off his property. The landowner was interested in expanding mining activities on the property, but doing so would have disturbed a den of rattlesnakes. The fence was to be situated some 260 feet from a rattlesnake den, and, once completed, would have reduced the snakes' habitat by 20% by blocking their access to the den. The timber rattlesnake is protected in New York State by the endangered species law, which prohibits "disturbing, harrying or worrying" of Threatened or Endangered species. The court held that building a fence so qualified and it should therefore be removed. Because this was the first court case to interpret the state's endangered species act, the decision to protect the snakes established a landmark precedent in applying the law to protect the habitat of all species threatened with extinction, not just timber rattlesnakes.

To kill or collect frogs, a small game hunting license or a fishing license is required. Only frogs of the genus *Rana* may be taken in any number from June 16 through September 30 between sunrise and sunset (special restrictions apply to southern leopard frogs on Long Island). The diamond-backed terrapin can be harvested under a "terrapin license" from the NYS DEC between August 1 and April 30. To protect both younger and older female terrapins, terrapins may be taken only with straight-line carapace lengths of 4–7 in (10–18 cm), inclusive.

Please note that you may *not* release animals into the wild without a special permit from the NYS DEC. The purpose of this law is to prevent the spread of infectious diseases from captive to wild populations and the introduction of new species that might interfere with native species, as well as to avoid polluting local gene pools. So even if you are tired of your pet turtle, have excess frogs purchased out-of-state and left over from your high school biology class, or even perhaps wish fervently to restore a population of spring peepers to Central Park by releasing individuals captured somewhere else, *you must check with the NYS DEC first!*

Laws preventing unnecessary cruelty to animals also apply to amphibians and reptiles. At present, the maximum penalty is six months in prison for subjecting any animal to cruelty. Notably, a case in 2003 in which hundreds of animals (many of them reptiles) were found dead from starvation and extreme heat in filthy conditions at a pet store in Mt. Vernon (*The Journal News* [West Nyack], August 16, 2003) recently prompted lawmakers to consider increasing the maximum penalty to two years in prison.

Some reptiles kept as family pets are inherently unsuited for that role. Witness the recent reports of, for example, a 19-year-old man who was strangled to death by his own 44-lb pet python in the Bronx (*The Buffalo News*, Oct. 10, 1996). A Newark, New Jersey, man was partially eaten and likely killed by his seven pet Nile Monitor lizards (one was 6 ft. long [1.8 m]) that had free roam of his apartment (*News Journal* (Wilmington, Delaware), Jan. 19, 2002). Or consider a Henrietta (Monroe County) man who was arrested after one of several timber rattlesnakes he had collected illegally from the wild and then transported to his home bit him and sent him to the hospital (*Rochester Democrat and Chronicle*, Jul. 17, 2002).

In an effort to prevent tragedies that result when animals attack their owners, escape from homes, or are abandoned when they become too difficult to handle, the State of New York amended the ECL (effective Jan. 1, 2005) to require a permit for private ownership of crocodilians, boas, large monitor lizards, and venomous snakes. Targeted nonvenomous species include pythons (Burmese, reticulated, African rock, Australian amethystine, Indian), anacondas (green and yellow), and monitors (Asiatic [water], Nile, and white throat, black throat and crocodile). Individuals who owned prohibited species when the new law took effect are permitted to keep their charges if they comply with stringent animal care and public safety requirements. For example, any permitted animal needs to be distinguishable from others of its species (preferably by tattoos or "PIT" tagging). None can be bred. Among other restrictions, registered owners cannot

Figure 9.1. Vernal pools are vital to reproduction in many species of amphibians (as well as a few reptiles), yet are virtually unprotected from destruction in New York State. Ulster Co., New York. (James P. Gibbs.)

openly carry permitted animals unless the animals are being taken to the veterinarian. Thus, you should not expect to see many public shows of boa constrictors wrapped around the arms of their owners on the streets of your town or city.

Laws Protecting Habitat

Some New York laws do pertain indirectly to conservation of amphibians and reptiles via protection of their habitats. The New York Freshwater Wetlands Act (ECL Article 24) provides some protection to many of the larger wetlands in the state as well as a 100-ft. (30-m) wide adjacent area surrounding the wetland. Unfortunately, such a buffer is clearly not adequate for species that move hundreds, if not thousands, of feet to and from wetlands to breed. Similarly, the Tidal Wetlands Law (ECL Article 25) protects brackish wetlands surrounding Long Island and New York City, which is vital habitat for the diamond-backed terrapin.

Unfortunately, the Freshwater Wetlands Act does not protect many of the small, temporary wetlands (less than 12.4 acres or 5 ha; figure 9.1) unless a local government has designated them as a "wetland of unique local importance." Few towns, except for those on Long Island, have done so. This represents a major gap in protection

Figure 9.2. Failure to recognize vernal pools, which are dry much of the year (such as this one in July), is a major obstacle to protecting them. St. Lawrence Co., New York. (James P. Gibbs.)

of reptile and amphibian habitats. Small, temporary pools, often known as "vernal pools," are shallow depressions that fill with icy water from snow melt and spring runoff and are usually dry by midsummer. These pools may not even be in evidence during a walk through the woods in August (figure 9.2), but they are nevertheless vital areas for larval production and feeding by adults of many species of frogs, salamanders, and turtles during the spring and early summer. Nearby states, such as Maine and Massachusetts, have taken significant steps toward generating legal protections for vernal pools, and New York should follow.

Streams are vital habitats to many amphibians and reptiles. Permanent, mapped streams are protected under the Stream Protection Law (ECL Article 15) from pollution discharges and physical alteration. The small headwater streams, seeps, and intermittent streams that are home to many of the streamside salamanders are usually not protected.

Lastly, the State Environmental Quality Review Act or SEQRA (ECL Article 8) requires review of virtually any construction or building project in the state. County and town planning and building departments are subject to its requirements but too often local officials

---

Bog Turtles and SEQRA

A two-year-long court battle recently concluded over two wetlands in Oswego County—Selkirk Fen and Deer Creek Marsh—that had been classified as "significant coastal fish and wildlife habitat" areas by the State of New York. Among the many "endangered" species lurking in the wetlands was the bog turtle (which is both a state Endangered and federal Threatened species). Adjacent to the wetlands, a golf course had been constructed with which a nonprofit, local environmental group "Friends of the Salmon River" had taken issue. Specifically, they filed a lawsuit under the State Environmental Quality Review Act (better known as SEQRA) against the owner of the golf course to stop the application of potentially dangerous pesticides to the golf course and to control sewage discharge from the golf course and an adjacent campground between the two wetlands. Ultimately the lawsuit prompted the New York State Department of Environmental Conservation (NYS DEC) to investigate the situation and subsequently determine that the owner had filled in wetlands, built septic systems without approval, and tried to compost sewage, among other violations. In the final settlement, the owner agreed to deal with the sewage issues and to stop using several potentially harmful pesticides on the golf course, as well as to dispose of the chemicals. He also agreed to permit biologists who had long studied bog turtles in the area but who had been denied access to the site to enter and conduct research on the turtles. In May of 2005 the NYS DEC also purchased 268 acres (108 ha) of the adjacent wetland. Without the collective will of a local group of concerned citizens wielding a state environmental protection law, the habitat would have progressively deteriorated, likely eliminating its value for the highly endangered bog turtle (source: archives of *The Post-Standard*, Syracuse).

---

do not seek appropriate guidance in applying its provisions (see box: Bog Turtles and SEQRA). The New York State Natural Heritage Program, a partnership of the NYS DEC and The Nature Conservancy, maintains a database of all rare plants, animals, and natural communities. Anyone can, and local government or landowners are encouraged to, file a request to see if there are any known occurrences of these sensitive species in or near a proposed development. Cooperation among informed citizens, landowners, and land managers is absolutely essential to conserving amphibian and reptile habitat in the state.

10

Habitat Conservation Guidelines

How we use the land profoundly affects amphibians and reptiles. In this chapter, we outline key considerations for conservation of habitat. These guidelines are based on our experiences working on amphibian and reptile conservation issues for several decades and also adapted in part from Mitchell et al. (2006) and Kingsbury and Gibson (2002).

Permanent Wetlands

The majority of New York's amphibians and reptiles regularly use wetlands during some part of their life cycle. Permanent wetlands hold water all year. Permanent wetlands include marshes (figure 10.1), swamps, bogs, ponds, lakes, and impoundments. It is vital to maintain native plant communities in these wetlands, as well as normal water levels and patterns of fluctuation. It is also important to maintain terrestrial habitat surrounding them. The following points are key management considerations for permanent wetlands:

- *Maintain surrounding uplands.* Scientists have estimated that the minimally effective buffer distance to accommodate the terrestrial wanderings of adults and juveniles that use the wetland (either turtles that leave the wetland to nest or salamanders and frogs that arrive at the wetland to lay eggs) is likely 300 ft. (90 m) (Semlitsch 2000, Buhlmann and Gibbons 2001). For example, local populations of gray treefrogs need a buffer of at least 200 ft. (60 m) (Johnson and Semlitsch 2003).

Figure 10.1. This marsh with a variety of aquatic vegetation as well as dead timber supports green frogs, bullfrogs, mink frogs, snapping turtles, painted turtles, common gartersnakes, and northern watersnakes. St. Lawrence Co., New York. (James P. Gibbs.)

- *Maintain critical habitats on uplands.* Radio tracking of green frogs by Lamoureux and Madison (1999) near Binghamton, New York indicated that many frogs traveled considerable distances (up to about 980 ft. [300 m] from breeding sites) to overwinter in seemingly insignificant seeps, springs, and small streams in the wooded hillsides. Such wetlands are too small or temporary to be protected under wetland laws, but their protection is nevertheless vital to the maintenance of populations of green frogs.

- *Maintain habitat connections among wetlands.* Certain open habitats (e.g., agricultural fields, roads) can be major barriers to dispersal. In contrast, native forests and grasslands can serve to "connect" and sustain populations in adjacent isolated wetlands. Therefore, consider maintaining strips of native vegetation between wetlands to permit animals to move among them and sustain their populations in the larger landscape. For example, studies from Maine indicate that wood frogs and spotted salamanders, particularly dispersing juveniles, benefit from maintenance of connectivity between upland forest habitats and aquatic breeding sites (DeMaynadier and Hunter 1999).

- *Beware of roadways.* Roads should be planned outside the buffer zone of a wetland (more than 1000 ft. [300 m] from the edge). For roads near wetlands, possible alternatives include seasonal road closures that coincide with times of overland movement, such as salamander breeding and turtle nesting, appropriate signage (see figure 8.9), or the construction of "herp" passageways under the road to reduce road mortality. People can work with their local municipal officials and highway departments to accomplish this.

- *Maintain natural patterns of water level fluctuations of all wetlands.* Stabilizing water levels usually degrades permanent wetland habitats by eliminating the seasonal flooding that generates habitat diversity. Quite often the result of water level stabilization is conversion of a complex wetland with a diverse community of amphibians and reptiles to an open water pond or a pure stand of cattail hosting a few common "herps." Permanently flooding a temporary wetland makes it attractive to fish and thereby can extirpate many amphibians. Artificially dropping water levels in winter, a common weed control method for managed ponds, may kill those amphibians and reptiles overwintering in the sediments of the pond bottom.

- *Limit chemical and sediment runoff from agricultural areas and roads.* One simple way is to leave a buffer strip of natural vegetation some 50 ft. (15 m) in width around the wetland. It is also critical to restrict or eliminate shoreline access by livestock near wetlands susceptible to shoreline erosion. Although habitat factors predominate in determining amphibian occurrence, water chemistry also contributes. In Ontario, for example, amphibian diversity declines with increasing chloride, conductivity, magnesium, total hardness, and turbidity (Hecnar and M'Closkey 1996).

- *Do not stock fish!* Fish are major predators of amphibian eggs and larvae. Introductions of fish are usually devastating to amphibian populations of isolated wetlands. For example, introductions of bluegill sunfish can devastate amphibian populations, even of such hardy species as eastern newts (Smith et al. 1999). Despite the considerable charms of having bluegills or trout in your pond, they are highly destructive of amphibians.

- *Do not introduce other non-native plants or animals.* Non-native animals might include frogs, crayfish, pet turtles, or aquarium fish.

Non-native plants can be invasive. They can eliminate native species through predation, competition, or disease.

- *Leave logs, snags, and other woody debris.* Although most folks like to neaten and "tidy things up," woody debris serves as valuable hiding places and basking sites. Add this material if it has been removed.

- *Consider creating patches of loose, well-drained soil away from edges of permanent wetlands for turtle nesting.* Turtle populations can be limited by the availability of nesting sites and will readily use a large sand and gravel pile if provided. Make sure these "created" nest sites are not shaded by tall shrubs and trees and are large enough to make the task of digging up all the nests difficult for raccoons and other predators. This may be one way to mitigate the problem caused by suburban areas that have essentially become an ecological trap for snapping turtles. The turtles "cue into" habitats with all the right features of natural areas but experience much lower nest success due to soil disturbance and predation (Kolbe and Janzen 2002).

- *Created wetlands are not yet adequate substitutes for natural wetlands.* In situations where wetlands are being destroyed and "replaced" via mitigation, permanent protection of complexes of existing wetlands off-site through acquisition or easements is usually a better strategy than attempted wetland creation on-site. How to successfully create a wetland is still largely a mystery to ecologists. This said, some progress is being made. Endangered species such as tiger salamanders, as well as common species of frogs and toads, sometimes even adopt small constructed ponds (Stevens et al. 2002, Knutson et al. 2004). Whatever the case, 5 years of postconstruction monitoring is required to assess effects on populations because many of the species of concern (e.g., spotted salamanders) are so long-lived (Petranka et al. 2003). Long-established reservoirs and larger impoundments can eventually become productive habitat if vegetation is permitted to proliferate.

- *Restore wetlands where feasible.* Some degraded wetlands can be readily restored by plugging ditches, breaking subsurface drainage tiles, and removing fill and invasive plants.

- *Embrace beavers.* The best creator and steward of amphibian and reptile habitat across much of the state is a rodent: the beaver (figure 10.2). This said, many land managers have active programs

Figure 10.2. Beavers create complex wetlands with variable water levels that are highly productive habitats for amphibians and reptiles. St. Lawrence Co., New York. (James P. Gibbs.)

to limit beaver populations to facilitate timber production and road building, even though beaver populations remain at a fraction of their former abundance (only 10% of their former numbers across the contiguous United States; Naiman et al. 1986). "Herp" conservation and beaver conservation are closely linked, and beaver recovery has permitted range expansions of several amphibian species in some parts of the United States (Russell et al. 1999). There is also strong evidence of long-term, coevolutionary relationships between beavers and some amphibians (e.g., eastern newts; Gill 1978). In a nutshell, a more enlightened view of beavers as habitat generators and stewards will directly benefit the herpetofauna of New York State.

Vernal Pools

Seasonal wetlands, which are dry part or most of the year (see figures 9.1 and 9.2), are among the most critical yet least protected habitats of New York's herpetofauna. Vernal pools, flooded with water in spring and early summer, are the best known seasonal pools. Such wetlands are small but still useful to amphibians. For, example, ponds as small as 0.1 acre (0.05 ha) are critical breeding habitats for wood frogs and spotted salamanders in the northeastern United States (Egan and Paton 2004). The ephemeral nature of these wetlands underpins their importance. Because they dry at some point during the year, fish cannot survive in them.

Despite their ephemeral nature and often diminutive size, temporary wetlands are vital. Who would guess that hundreds of spotted
salamanders depend on a single, small and unnoticed depression in
your back lot that you stroll through dry-footed most of the year? Similarly, consider that narrow swath of wet pasture that you have
thought of ditching because it occasionally bogs down the tractor. It
might well support a breeding population of several hundred western
chorus frogs.

It is important to note that although these seasonal wetlands are
vital during breeding, the rest of the lives of most species that are dependent on vernal pools is spent on the surrounding uplands. In Vermont, Faccio (2003) observed that an area extending 575 ft. (175 m)
from a pool's edge would be needed to encompass 95% of the population of Jefferson and spotted salamanders using the pool. Thus, rec-
ommendations for vernal pool protection, as developed by Calhoun
and deMaynadier (2002), take an integrated view of both the pool and
the surrounding uplands:

- *Vernal pool depression.* In the vernal pool depression itself (approximately 0.2 acre [0.08 ha]), seek good water quality and water-
  holding capacity (do not disrupt the pool substrate), and maintain
  the basin and peripheral vegetation in an undisturbed state.

- *Vernal pool protection zone.* In the vernal pool protection zone,
  maintain undisturbed an approximately 1.4-acre (0.6-ha) area encompassed by a 100-ft. (30-m) buffer around the margin of the vernal pool. Here, critical shade and organic inputs derive. This area
  also serves as critical staging habitat for juvenile amphibians. In
  forested areas, maintain at least 75% canopy cover and abundant
  coarse woody debris in this zone.

- *Amphibian life zone.* In the "amphibian life zone," maintain an approximately 13-acre (5.2-ha) area encompassed by a 400-ft. (120-m)
  buffer around the margin of the vernal pool that serves as upland
  habitat for pool breeding amphibians. In forested areas, seek to
  maintain a partially shaded forest floor with deep, moist uncompacted litter and coarse woody debris. There, maintain more than
  50% canopy closure and limit canopy openings to less than 1 acre
  (0.4 ha).

- *Keep pools seasonal.* Avoid deepening temporary pools, thereby
  converting them to permanent wetlands where fish can thrive.

Figure 10.3. The science of vernal pool creation is still in its infancy. (US Geological Survey Northeast Amphibian Research and Monitoring Initiative.)

Artificially extending the hydroperiod of wetlands by excavation occurs to the detriment of native species adapted to the naturally short hydroperiods of such wetlands (Euliss and Mushet 2004).

■ *Consider creating pools where none exist.* Artificial pools are no replacement for natural pools, but given time small created pools can eventually become useful breeding areas for many amphibians (figure 10.3).

Rivers and Streams

Along with wetlands, the flowing waters of rivers (figure 10.4) and streams (figure 10.5) are vital to many amphibians and reptiles. Maintaining rivers and streams and the integrity of adjacent terrestrial habitats is critical.

■ *Keep vegetation near the shoreline.* A buffer of native vegetation at least 100 ft. (30 m) from the edges of streams and rivers should be maintained.

■ *Maintain water quality.* Reducing sediment load and pollution runoff as well as moderate water temperatures is important and can be achieved by a healthy buffer of overhanging bank vegetation as well as limiting bank access to all-terrain vehicles and livestock. For example, abundance of the spring salamander is negatively related to logging-associated sedimentation (Lowe et al. 2004).

Figure 10.4. Small rivers with intact riparian zones, unpolluted waters, exposed sand or gravel bars, and some natural debris can support healthy populations of the hellbender, mudpuppy, wood turtle, and spiny softshell. Madison Co., New York. (James P. Gibbs.)

Figure 10.5. Unconsolidated streambeds like this one can support extremely high densities of spring salamanders, northern two-lined salamanders, and dusky salamanders despite an apparent lack of flowing water. Onondaga Co., New York. (James P. Gibbs.)

- *Provide habitat structure.* Logs, snags, and other woody debris in the watercourse and along banks help minimize erosion by slowing water flow and provide underwater refuges for many species. This debris should be kept intact as long as it does not cause flooding.

- *Protect sand and gravel bars.* Bars form where current deposits sand and gravel in slower flowing areas of the stream. These may be important nesting and basking habitat, especially for turtles, and should be protected accordingly.

- *Create holding ponds or grass filter strips.* Most water quality problems in streams and rivers arise from drainage from agricultural lands and suburban areas. Creation of holding ponds or strips of vegetation that filter inflow to watercourses helps reduce the transport of chemicals and silt into streams and rivers.

Forests

Forests cover two-thirds of the land in New York State, and how they are managed has major consequences for amphibians and reptiles (figure 10.6). At the site level, key structural microhabitat variables affecting the herpetofauna include canopy cover, litter cover, and the availability of stumps and snags. For example, salamander counts are decreased where there is high understory stem density and extensive herb cover and increased where there is greater soil organic layer depth (DeGraaf and Yamasaki 2002). Eastern red-backed salamanders benefit from addition of cover objects to a forest area (coarse woody debris) (Grover and Wilbur 2002). Buried, bulky organic matter in the soil derived from previously fallen tree trunks is a vital nursery area for young eastern red-backed salamanders (R. L. Wyman, personal communication). Uncompacted soils and healthy small mammal populations are also critical, because species such as spotted salamanders rely on tunnels made by shrews and others (Regosin et al. 2003a). At the landscape level, what is most important is to protect large patches of relatively mature forest along with key habitat components within them—pools, swamps, rock outcrops, and streamsides—in a relatively natural state and well connected to one another.

Forest management (figure 10.7) and maintenance of herpetofaunal diversity are compatible (Brooks 1999, Knapp et al. 2003). In New York State, salamanders seem to be resilient to limited disturbance of

Figure 10.6. This salamander's eye view of maturing forest highlights some key habitat components: thick leaf litter layer, closed canopy, and downed and coarse woody debris that together supports populations of eastern red-backed salamanders, efts of the eastern newt, spotted salamanders, and wood frogs. Onondaga Co., New York. (New York State Dept. Transportation.)

forests, and small-scale habitat disruption associated with harvesting firewood can even increase numbers of eastern newts and does not change numbers of eastern red-backed salamanders (Pough et al. 1987). One-year-old gaps produced by selective logging do not strongly affect the distributions of eastern red-backed salamanders in central New York (Messere and Ducey 1998). In Missouri, clear-cutting affects local populations of amphibians and reptiles through extensive "edge effects," but at the landscape scale even-aged and uneven-aged forest management had comparable effects (Renken et al. 2004). Based on research conducted to date we suggest the following as guidelines for using New York's forests while maintaining healthy populations of the amphibians and reptiles that depend on them:

- *Maintain forests of native species.* New York State has in the past promoted plantation forestry on many of its public forest lands outside the Adirondack and Catskill Mountains, and vast swaths of state lands in regions formerly dominated by northern hardwoods are planted in Norway spruce, Douglas fir, red and scotch pines, and other conifers. These areas are usually poor habitats for amphibians, especially because of the dark, cold understory and more acidic soils

Figure 10.7. Low intensity and moderate-scale forestry activities are compatible with maintaining healthy communities of forest-dependent amphibians and reptiles. St. Lawrence Co., New York. (James P. Gibbs.)

(Waldick et al. 1999). Further expansion of plantation forestry should be avoided, and existing plantations converted through forest management to native trees where possible.

- *Avoid fragmenting forests when possible.* Roads and cultivated areas should be kept out of or limited to the edges of existing forests. Connections among forests with hedgerows, forested strips, and other corridors should be retained for use by migrating amphibians and reptiles. Note that frog and salamander populations in Maine as much as 80–100 ft. (25–30 m) from forest edges are reduced (De-Maynadier and Hunter 1998).

- *Protect riparian zones and wet areas.* Areas near forest streams are important to many species that may dwell in streams but forage on the banks (such as streamside salamanders; Orser and Shure 1975). The vegetation of these areas should be maintained (minimally to 100 ft. [30 m] from the streamedge), and sources of bank erosion, particularly cattle and recreational vehicles, should be restricted. Similarly, springs and seeps are important centers of activity for many amphibians in forests and should be retained in an undisturbed state.

- *Avoid clear-cutting.* Clear-cutting can have dramatic effects on amphibians and reptiles. Research in the northeastern United States suggests that complete recovery times for eastern red-backed salamanders after clear-cutting may be 50 years or more (Pough et al. 1987, Duguay and Wood 2002, DeGraaf and Yamasaki 2002). Instead, trees should be removed selectively to retain significant canopy cover, and some of the larger diameter, older trees should not be cut to maintain cool shaded conditions in the understory as well as a source of dead wood on the ground. Also, branches, stumps, treetops, and other fallen woody debris should be left in place; such woody debris provides shelter, humid retreats, and foraging opportunities. An "untidy" approach to forest management is generally desirable for amphibians and reptiles, because coarse debris on the ground provides habitat complexity. Lastly, working during the winter months minimizes disturbance to soil and vegetation during a time when amphibians and reptiles are usually hibernating out of harm's way, far underground or in nearby wetlands and streams.

Agricultural Areas, Grasslands, and Shrublands

Agricultural areas—pastures, grasslands, fields, croplands, meadows—as well as barrens and shrublands (figures 10.8 and 10.9) host abundant insect and rodent populations, receive abundant solar energy useful to ectothermic creatures, and are particularly important foraging areas for some frogs and snakes. In New York, however, species that favor scrublands, pastures, and meadows and the wet areas within them are increasingly being "squeezed" out by habitat loss. Restoration and maintenance of parcels of early successional habitats is, for example, now a priority for maintaining snake diversity in the northeastern United States (Kjoss and Litvaitis 2001). The reason is that agricultural lands are increasingly subject to "clean farming" practices that remove natural habitats, whereas grasslands are in decline because of succession to forest or rampant conversion to housing development. For these reasons we suggest the following considerations for managing such lands while maintaining healthy populations of native amphibians and reptiles upon them:

- *Leave a few weeds.* Weed management in row-cropped fields has become so efficient that there are often virtually no areas for amphibians and reptiles to hide or forage. Even modest expansion of

Figure 10.8. Intensive agriculture can be inimical to reptiles and amphibians. Few species, if any, can make use of this dry, plowed field. although the verges can provide habitat. Chenango Co., New York. (James P. Gibbs.)

Figure 10.9. Many amphibians and reptiles thrive in the weedy edges and hedgerows of low-intensity agricultural lands, such as this pasture, particularly if some standing water, hedgerows, and moist soils are retained. Chenango Co., New York. (James P. Gibbs.)

natural cover in row-cropped areas dramatically increases habitat for amphibians and reptiles. Fencerows, surface drainage areas, and ditches are all prime areas where cover can be maintained to permit movement and foraging. No-till farming, where practicable, also can leave residual crop debris that provides some cover. A study of riparian strips in agricultural landscapes of southern Quebec indicated that amphibians and reptiles benefited from preservation of strips and hedgerows, particularly those dominated by shrubs rather than herbaceous plants (Maisonneuve and Rioux 2001). Because hedgerows and the like provide habitat for these predators of crop pests, what is likely good for amphibians and reptiles is likely also good for the farmer. In contrast, intensive grazing and off-road vehicle use eliminate much needed cover and diminish the herpetofauna; therefore, they should be avoided.

- *Mow judiciously.* Mowing in rows provides some opportunity for amphibians and reptiles to escape, whereas mowing in circles tends to concentrate animals for final slaughter. Raising a mower's deck height to 12 in. (30 cm) reduces the animals killed and leaves some residual cover for survivors. First cutting of hay in much of New York occurs in June, the peak month for turtles to be searching for nest sites. Many eastern box turtles are found with circular wounds on their carapaces; these are the few turtles that survived encounters with whirling mower blades. In orchards, infrequent mowing as needed only to prepare for harvest permits orchards to support amphibians and reptiles for much of the growing season, whereas frequent mowing to manicure the ground largely excludes them. Some agricultural operations may locally benefit wood turtles by providing a mixture of different food and cover types near wooded creeks (Kaufmann 1992a). Be aware that such areas may be a form of "ecological trap" insofar as a much larger fraction of wood turtles suffer from injuries in agricultural areas than elsewhere (Saumure and Bider 1998).

- *Use chemicals as necessary with targeted application.* Substantial amounts of fertilizers are applied to row-cropped fields, and there is much concern of disruption of amphibian reproductive cycles by commonly applied agricultural chemicals (Hayes et al. 2003). Moreover, fertilizers may reduce water quality in breeding habitats and increase levels of amphibian deformities. Spot applications of pesticides on patches of weeds or insect pests is preferable. Use of rodenticides around farm buildings and grain storage areas may have secondary effects on snakes that eat the dying mice and rats. Research on the interactions between agricultural chemicals and amphibians suggests that toxic effects of ammonium nitrate occurred in all four species of amphibians in Ontario at concentrations that are commonly exceeded in agricultural areas; thus, nitrate fertilizers may play a role in apparent global amphibian declines (Hecnar 1995). Lower frog and toad diversity and density along with reduced reproductive success of American toads and green frogs in the site dominated by agriculture was attributed to elevated ammonia, phosphorus, particulates, and nitrogen levels in the agricultural zone (Bishop et al. 1999). Fortunately, it appears that anurans may not be as sensitive to nitrogen pollution as many fishes, so water quality criteria as determined for fishes should be protective of many amphibians (Jofre and Karasov 1999). Notably, what little research has been conducted to date on orchards indicates that wetlands in apple orchards provide viable breeding habitat for both northern leopard frogs and green frogs and that contaminant loads of orchard dwelling amphibians are not abnormal (Harris et al. 1988a, b).

- *Burn carefully.* Fire is an underused tool that can create a heterogeneous grassland that benefits many amphibians and reptiles although it must be used carefully. A burn on Long Island recently killed 70 eastern box turtles. Unburned areas should be maintained adjacent to prescribed burns in grasslands to serve as refuges for snakes (Setser and Cavitt 2003). To avoid high reptile mortality, prescribed burns should be implemented during cool and overcast periods (Frese 2003).

- *Protect the wet spots.* Swales, wet meadows, shallow ditches, and other damp spots are vital components of grasslands and agricultural areas. Amphibians and reptiles require these habitats to rehydrate in an otherwise arid and exposed habitat. Even small wet meadows can provide excellent breeding habitats for diminutive species such as western chorus frogs. Where restoration of wet areas is desired, segments of the old drainage system should be broken up otherwise blocked.

Urban and Suburban Areas

The development sprawl that has consumed so much of Long Island, counties of the southern tier, and regions around all major New York metropolitan areas is largely inimical to the native herpetofauna over the long-term, although a surprising diversity of the hardier native amphibians and reptiles can survive in urban and suburban areas (see Chapter 3 box: The native herpetofauna of New York City). Unfortunately, the most species-rich regions of New York State are those experiencing among the highest development pressures, (e.g., lower Hudson River valley). Many of the habitat conservation guidelines presented earlier are germane to urban areas (figure 10.10). But residential development presents its own set of challenges that needs to be dealt with directly. Practical guidance on protecting critical habitats in areas subject to housing development in New York has been developed by Calhoun and Klemens (2002) and is summarized here:

- *Collaborate in the planning process.* It is important to establish cooperation early in any planning process among landowners, land managers, urban planners, biologists, and landscape architects so that areas with high quality habitats can be targeted for long-term conservation. Once a zoning scheme is established or a development project underway, there is little opportunity to make adjustments. The time to advocate for critical amphibian and reptile habitats is before the plan has been decided and requisite permits have been issued.

- *Minimize habitat fragmentation.* Many communities in New York attempt to protect their environment by "upzoning," that is, increasing minimum single family residential lots by 100% or more. Unfortunately, this creates a highly fragmented landscape dominated by "edge" habitats and subsidized predators. In contrast, compact developments based on traditional neighborhood design with accompanying planned "green spaces" create the opportunity for more livable communities for humans and also leave larger areas of natural habitats for native amphibians and reptiles.

- *Be frank about the habitat needs of the herpetofauna.* Many species need substantial areas to roam. For example, in a report about five New York counties near Albany, Wyman (1991) found that about 250 acres (100 ha) was required to support about half of the amphibian species present in the region but that 3,500 acres (1,400 ha) was needed to capture all 16 species in the regional pool. Others have speculated that 1,000 acres (400 ha) of natural habitat is needed in New York to adequately provide for the native herpetofaunal community of a local area. This sort of habitat set aside is

Figure 10.10. Urban and suburban natural areas can support a surprising variety of amphibians and reptiles, including DeKay's brownsnakes, painted turtles, snapping turtles, American toads, and eastern red-backed and northern dusky salamanders. However, these areas receive large numbers of unwanted pet turtles. Central Park, New York City. (James P. Gibbs.)

realistically possible only through careful long-range collaborative planning on the part of municipalities in collaboration with developers, biologists, and landowners.

- *Maintain habitat connectivity.* The effective habitat area of a set of protected natural areas in an urban zone can be enhanced by developing corridors between habitat fragments via significant buffer zones along watercourses and greenways of natural vegetation.

- *Maintain natural water regimes and native plant communities.* The tendency to stabilize water levels, convert vegetated wetlands to open water, and manicure the banks of wetlands and streams should be avoided. All of these practices are detrimental to amphibians and reptiles. Moreover, storm water ponds do not offer clean or productive ecosystems for amphibians and reptiles. Lastly, wetlands in urban areas are prone to infestation of exotic species, particularly purple loosestrife and common reed in New York State, and efforts to restore such wetlands to native plants benefit the herpetofauna.

- *Beware of "killer" engineering features and machinery.* Certain standard engineering features of modern residential developments are inimical to amphibians and reptiles. Storm drains associated with road edging structures, which may extend for miles, herding thousands of migrating amphibians and reptiles to their deaths through the grate of associated storm drains, should be reconsidered. Vertical curbing, often referred to as "Belgian block," along residential roadways can also divert all manner of amphibians and reptiles away from traditional migration routes, or trap them on a roadway where they quickly become overheated or desiccated (see figure 8.9). Straight-sided ponds and in-ground swimming pools also can be lethal. Nylon erosion netting for backing silt fences and other uses (mesh of 1 sq. in.) can be a major hazard to large-bodied snakes, which can hook their scales, get tangled in it, and die. Lawn mowers also take their toll; garden equipment–related trauma, for example, was the most frequent cause of injury for many reptiles brought into wildlife rehabilitation centers (Brown and Sleeman 2002).

- *Control "subsidized" predators.* Feral cats and dogs as well as raccoons and skunks benefit from the food and shelter we provide to them directly or indirectly. Excessive populations of these creatures limit reptile and amphibian populations in urban areas. For example, high raccoon densities usually translate to complete destruction of turtle nests in urban areas [see Chapter 11: Diamond-backed Terrapin: From Near Extinction to Near Recovery (. . . and Back Again?].

- *Retain open spaces.* Small tracts of "abandoned" lands such as old gravel mines and rights-of-way are valuable habitat and vital refuges, particularly for snakes, in urban areas. The importance of these areas should not be discounted.

11

Conservation Case Studies

Case studies help put concepts into practice. Here we provide an eclectic series of short accounts that highlight current conservation efforts in New York State. All the case studies originated from actions of concerned citizens. Collectively we hope these case studies provide a sense of the opportunities, approaches, and challenges for conserving New York's herpetofauna.

Blanding's Turtle: Conservation Through Land Acquisition, Nest-Site Creation, and "Head-Starting"

Blanding's turtle is listed as a Threatened species in New York. It is a highly mobile turtle, preferring to travel among wetlands frequently to forage, as well as to undertake long nesting migrations. It is on these overland movements that it encounters difficulties. Many conservation groups are trying to find ways to accommodate the movements of these fascinating turtles and maintain viable populations of Blanding's turtles on properties that they manage.

One example is The Nature Conservancy, which in 1987 asked Al Breisch and Jim Eckler of the New York State Department of Conservation (NYS DEC) to begin a study at one of its preserves in Dutchess County where Blanding's turtles had been discovered the year before. By attaching small, waterproof radio transmitters to turtles (figure 11.1) and following them around with handheld antennae, researchers attempted to determine if turtles nested on the preserve property. To their surprise, the turtles migrated 3,300 ft. (1,000 m)

Figure 11.1. A wood turtle having a radio signal transmitter and a wire antenna glued to its shell to permit researchers to track its movements. Saratoga Co., New York. (Kenneth Barnett.)

to nest in lawns and driveways of a nearby housing development. Because the development was only 2 years old at the time, the turtles likely had discovered it recently, which suggested that they might be convinced to nest elsewhere. Despite the willingness of the homeowners to accommodate the turtles, the turtles were at risk traversing a large open field from the wetland to the development at the time of first hay cutting. Moreover, nesting in a driveway is just not a good idea for a turtle.

In a cooperative effort among the NYS DEC, The Nature Conservancy, and Marla Emerich Briggs, a graduate student at Bard College, new openings were created in the forest nearer to the pond so that the turtles would not have to cross the hayfield or nest in driveways. After several years, turtles began using the newly created nesting sites. These initial studies showed that the preserve was home to one of the largest Blanding's turtle populations in southeastern New York—more than 80 adults captured and marked—but it had very few juveniles. It is also the home of five other turtle species, making it one of the most turtle-rich sites in the state.

Because of the lack of young turtles in the population, a parallel effort was begun in 1995 in cooperation with Dr. George Kollias at the Cornell University to collect hatchlings from the nesting areas and raise them in captivity for a year for subsequent release into the wetland complex. The idea was to bolster the population by providing more secure nesting habitat and by ushering young turtles safely through their normally hazardous first year. When the young turtles were subsequently released at about 10 months of age, they were equivalent in size to wild 4- or 5-year-old turtles. More than half of these released turtles have been recaptured after overwintering at least once.

Another ambitious and apparently successful effort to create new habitats for Blanding's turtles has also been undertaken in Dutchess County (Kiviat et al. 2000). Researchers from Hudonsonia, Ltd., led by Erik Kiviat, had been studying how Blanding's turtles use habitats for many years and were able to apply this knowledge to a situation where a Dutchess County school expansion was poised to destroy prime Blanding's turtle habitat. In a mitigation effort brokered with the NYS DEC, the proposed 1.7 acres (0.7 ha) of habitat loss associated with the school expansion was replaced with 3.5 acres (1.4 ha) of artificial wetlands and created turtle nesting areas on the uplands.

In May 1997, the artificial habitat was constructed before the school expansion destroyed the turtle's original habitat. It is no small feat to create a wetland: 40-in. (101-cm) thick pieces of sod cut from the original wetland were moved to the created habitats on something like a giant steel spatula mounted on an excavator. Also, a one-way turtle barrier to usher turtles out of the hazardous development site was constructed. The turtles are now living and breeding in the newly created habitats and, if all goes well, will continue to do so for many decades to come.

Amphibians Cross Here: New York State's First "Herp" Tunnel

When Al Breisch and Mark Fitzsimmons first started recording amphibian and reptile hotspots in Albany County in the early 1980s, Vly Swamp and Black Creek Marsh in the towns of New Scotland and Guilderland stood out as extraordinary. In addition to high species diversity, these large wetland complexes were the former stomping grounds of Sherman C. Bishop, author of the renowned volume *Salamanders of New York* (Bishop 1941). Four species of turtles, six species snakes, eight species of frogs, and twelve species of salamanders had been recorded there. Unfortunately, roads bordering both

Figure 11.2. Road crossing structure installed during the resurfacing of Meadowdale Road, which cuts through Black Creek Marsh near Guilderland. Since installation, road mortality of amphibians and reptiles, which was previously quite high, has declined to nearly zero. Albany Co., New York. (Alvin R. Breisch.)

wetlands resulted in massive slaughter of amphibians and reptiles every year. Moreover, the mortality was associated not only with breeding migrations but also with summer foraging and migrations back to overwintering sites. In 1999, during the resurfacing of Meadowdale Road, which cuts through Black Creek Marsh and nearby upland forests, an opportunity arose to place a passageway under the road to connect two sections of habitat where all 20 amphibian species had been recorded. Two 4×4 ft. (1.2×1.2 m) box culverts, backfilled with 1 ft. (0.3 m) of gravel, were placed under the road with the culverts being filled with 2 ft. (0.6 m) of native soil. Approximately 300 ft. (90 m) of permanent drift fence–barrier system, 1 ft. (0.3 m) high, keeps the amphibians and reptiles off the road surface and funnels them into the tunnels (figure 11.2). The permanent drift fence is backfilled on the side toward the road, so that if a salamander or frog somehow manages to get around the end, it is not trapped on the road. The good news is that road kills have dropped to nearly zero along this portion of Meadowdale Road.

Shedding a Little Light on the Massasauga

Cicero Swamp Wildlife Management Area is one of only two sites remaining that support massasaugas in New York. The NYS DEC manages this large and complex wetland primarily for hunting. Beginning in 1980, census efforts at this site suggested a slow and steady decline in the snake's population. Several factors were implicated, including human persecution, but most suspicion centered on habitat change due to the force of natural succession (Johnson and Breisch 1993).

In the late 1980s, a study of the massasaugas at Cicero Swamp was undertaken by Drs. Glenn Johnson and Donald Leopold of the State University of New York's College of Environmental Science and Forestry in Syracuse to determine the snakes' movements and patterns of habitat use (Johnson 1995). Their findings suggested that the snakes made seasonal movements between a 100-acre (40-ha) shrub-dominated boggy section of the swamp and the surrounding fields and forest (Johnson 2000). The bog provided the only suitable overwintering sites for massasaugas in the entire area. Each fall, the snakes would return to the bog to hibernate and then leave in the spring, presumably for better feeding opportunities in other habitats. Pregnant females would remain in the bog until they gave birth late in August.

Detailed study of movement patterns suggested that massasaugas limited their activities in the bog to two small sections with the most exposure to sunlight. A conservation initiative involving multiple approaches was begun to 1991 to simulate early stage vegetation in the bog using combinations of cutting (figure 11.3), careful burning, and limited herbicide application (Johnson and Leopold 1998). Inmates

Figure 11.3. Clearing woody vegetation to create sunny patches for the endangered massasauga. Onondaga Co., New York. (James P. Gibbs.)

from a nearby prison provided much of the labor. Although only on a small scale, these methods were successful over the short term in reducing stem density and canopy cover of woody plants and in increasing small mammal density, the principal prey of massasaugas, compared to untreated areas. Follow-up studies indicated that the snakes appeared to use treated areas at a rate of about four times their availability. Further efforts have involved placing large pieces of sheet metal for snakes to bask beneath that simultaneously suppress vegetation growth. Because it is unlikely that massasaugas can find additional suitable habitat beyond the borders of the wildlife management area, it is probable that periodic management interventions aimed at retarding natural succession will be required to provide the sunny spots needed to sustain this population of highly endangered snakes.

Diamond-Backed Terrapin: From Near Extinction to Near Recovery (. . . and Back Again?)

Populations of diamond-backed terrapins (figure 11.4) in New York State have been on a roller-coaster ride. Until the early 1900s, the species thrived at remarkable densities as the only turtle adapted to

Figure 11.4. Nesting diamond-backed terrapin (top left), terrapin nest destroyed by raccoons (top right), cages applied to terrapin nests to exclude predatory raccoons (lower left), and terrapin hatchling gathered from caged, successfully protected nest (lower right). Nassau Co., New York. (Michael Unold.)

life in coastal salt marshes. In the early 1900s, however, terrapin soup became a delicacy in great demand on the east coast of the United States. The species suffered from what Archie Carr (1952) referred to as an "innate and incontrovertible succulence." The 1918 version of Fannie Farmer's *The Boston Cooking-School Cook Book* recommended that live terrapins be ". . . plunged into boiling water" for five minutes, then lifted out, their meat removed, and copious amounts of sherry and other liquors, cream, vegetables, and cayenne be added in various combinations to create any number of variations on terrapin stew, including Terrapin à la Baltimore, Terrapin à la Maryland, and Washington Terrapin, largely accomplished by varying the amount of alcohol versus cream.

Terrapins paid dearly to feed this fad. Despite elaborate efforts on the part of the US Bureau of Fisheries to cultivate terrapins in tanks alongside estuaries to relieve some of the harvest pressure, terrapins nearly went extinct in the wild. Fortunately, the Great Depression in the 1930s put terrapins as a delicacy out of the reach of many. Moreover, Prohibition made it very difficult to locate a key ingredient of terrapin soup: sherry. Although terrapins are slow reproducers, these turtles did manage to recover to robust population levels by the 1970s.

After enjoying 20 years of "pregourmet" abundance, terrapin populations are again on the downslide, for four reasons. The first is coastal development, which has resulted in habitat destruction, particularly loss of nesting sites on barrier beach islands, and increased road mortality as terrapins attempts to cross roads to get to remaining nesting areas. Some researchers have learned how to extract eggs from road-killed females, which usually hatch successfully once buried, but these courageous efforts cannot replace the loss of adult females from the population.

The second problem is crab pots. The smelly bait used to attract crabs into crab pots attracts large numbers of terrapins, which, unable to find their way back out, drown. Redesigning crab pots to have escape hatches for terrapins offers great hope for reducing terrapin drowning but only if these modifications become required by law. Even motorboats represent a threat: some 18% of terrapins in Oyster Bay on Long Island bore scars from the propellers of outboard motors (Marganoff 1969).

The third problem concerns the escalating densities of nest predators (see figure 11.4). Dr. Russell Burke and his students from Hofstra University have conducted research on this problem at Jamaica Bay Wildlife Refuge in Queens. Terrapins are still quite abundant in the refuge and attempt to cram some 2,000 nests into the refuge's barrier beaches and islands. However, raccoons consume 92% of the nests now compared with less than 10% of the nests a few decades ago (Feinberg and Burke 2003). The raccoon issue began when freshwater ponds were dug in the 1950s for migratory birds, thereby providing a means for raccoons to survive on the islands of Jamaica Bay. It was compounded in the 1980s when workers for pest control companies started dumping raccoons trapped elsewhere in New York City into the refuge (an illegal act). Solving the raccoon problems will likely involve some combination of protecting terrapin nests with wire mesh (no small task, however, for the thousands of nests affected), an intensive management technique that has been very successful (see figure 11.4). Another possibility is stocking the beach with quail eggs injected with estrogen, which causes nausea in raccoons if eaten in sufficient quantity, in hopes of fostering an aversion in raccoons to terrapin eggs. The most logical solution, simply removing the raccoons from the islands, is mired in political battles over whether the raccoons are native to the islands and indeed belong there and, if not, over how they might best be deported.

The fourth threat—terrapin harvest for food—is once again a significant factor as immigrants to the New York City area bring with them from their homelands their taste for turtle flesh. Without addressing the issues of nesting habitat loss, crab pots, nest predation, and harvest for food, the terrapin population will decline once again despite its spectacular recovery from near extinction 80 years ago.

Herpetofaunal Restoration: "And the voice of the grey tree frog was heard again in the land . . ." (Cook 1989)

Conservation often focuses on preserving just what's left, but occasionally ambitious individuals adopt a grander vision and attempt the whole-scale restoration of habitats and species. Such is the case of Bob Cook, of the US National Park Service, who in varying capacities since 1979 has overseen restoration of the amphibian and reptile community at Jamaica Bay Wildlife Refuge in southern Brooklyn, Queens, and New York City. Originally all salt marsh, Jamaica Bay was subject to extensive dredging and landfill that created upland habitat that could be suitable for many amphibians and reptiles—if only they could reach it. Moreover, the steady urbanization and destruction of mainland areas surrounding Jamaica Bay had reduced most species to remnant populations or driven them to extinction. Cook's vision was to compensate for the loss of mainland populations by "inoculating" created habitats in Jamaica Bay with native reptiles and amphibians, thereby creating an oasis of sorts for "herps" within the bounds of New York City.

To do so, Cook and many other volunteers first manipulated the habitat on Jamaica Bay's island to ensure that food, water, cover, and other special requirements for amphibians and reptiles were met. To this end, they created small freshwater ponds by hand and brought in aquatic plants. To the uplands they added driftwood boards and piles of leaves and wood chips (refuse from urban tree management). Then they added the reptiles and amphibians, which came from local populations to ensure they were already adapted to local conditions. They also came only from populations either facing extinction or were already large enough to sustain collection. For example, breeding pairs of spring peepers, a locally common species, were gathered from beside runways at John F. Kennedy International Airport and deposited in the newly created ponds. Many eastern box turtles were rescued from almost certain oblivion on a parcel of land slated for subdivision in Suffolk County and then released on the islands. Species that were lower on the "trophic pyramid," that is, might serve as prey for others, were released first.

Some 20 species in total were released. What made Cook's efforts unusual is that he followed the "translocations" with years of careful monitoring to see which species thrived and which did not. To do so, individuals released were marked (e.g., turtles had notches placed in the margins of their shells or snakes had particular scales clipped). By ongoing capture efforts, Cook and his coworkers were able to then identify those species that were successfully breeding on their own (as indicated by the appearance of young, unmarked individuals). As of 1999, some 33 of 40 translocation efforts have been successful. These include Fowler's toad, gray treefrog, eastern red-backed salamander, DeKay's brownsnake, milksnake, black racer, snapping turtle, painted turtle, and eastern box turtle. An unanticipated downside to these efforts has been creation of permanent water sources on the islands that now sustain raccoon populations where formerly no raccoons could persist. The raccoons are now exacting a serious toll on eggs laid by diamond-backed terrapins—an increasingly contentious issue for terrapin conservation in the region. For more information on these ambitious efforts, consult Cook (1982), Cook and Pinnock (1987), Cook and Tanacredi (1990), and Cook (2002).

Spiny Softshell: A Little Help Goes a Long Way

Shortly after Jerry Czech first started watching spiny softshells at a sheltered bay along Lake Ontario in the 1980s, he became concerned about whether they could successfully nest in such a human-modified environment. The females he saw attempt to nest crawled up into a parking area of a private marina to dig in the packed gravel among the parked cars and boat trailers. In 1994, with the help of NYS DEC biologists he was able to convince the marina operator to set aside a 20×35 ft. (6×10 m) area at the edge of the marina for the turtles to nest. A mound of sand was placed in the area that was then enclosed on three sides by cyclone fencing, which allowed the turtles to enter from the bay side but kept out predators, people, and vehicles. Construction was completed by the fall of 1995, and the following June the softshells began to nest there. A hinged ramp was attached to the bulkhead along the marina so that the turtles would have access to the nest site no matter what the water level in the bay.

Figure 11.5. This nondescript, fenced off mound of sand is actually a vital nesting area for spiny softshells created by the New York State Department of Environmental Conservation in cooperation with a marina owner. Several thousand hatchling softshells have now emerged from it. Wayne Co., New York. (Jerry Czech.)

The turtles quickly learned to use the ramp. In late summer when hatching began, plastic netting was suspended over the nesting site to protect the hatchlings from gulls and herons until they had a chance to reach the water. Since that first successful nesting, more than 2,800 hatchling softshells have emerged from this area (figure 11.5).

12

Finding and Studying Amphibians and Reptiles

For most of us, our first encounters in nature with amphibians and reptiles were unplanned. We might have happened upon a bright orange eft wandering through a forest or a snapping turtle nesting on a roadside. These serendipitous encounters often were the seeds of the beginning of a lasting intrigue with amphibians and reptiles (figure 12.1).

Young or old, amateur or professional, you will find that the best way to cultivate your interest is simple: go out in the field, get your feet wet, and explore and observe. Take notes and photographs of the amphibians and reptiles you encounter. As experience accumulates, you will reach the point that where knowing the time of year, habitat, and your location within the state will allow you to predict accurately what species you will encounter at a given site on a particular day. Moreover, you can make significant contributions to New York State herpetology, as the recent discovery of significant range extensions for eastern spadefoots (e.g., Tierny and Stewart 2001) and Blanding's turtles (e.g., Johnson and Wills 1997) within New York indicate. Who knows . . . your interests may eventually lead to a career in herpetology (figure 12.2).

By all means carry a field notebook with you when you go outdoors. Get in the habit of recording the circumstances surrounding an observation or capture. Jot down the date, time, weather, precise location, and exactly where an animal was found (e.g., under a fallen white pine log, in a limestone seep, on the edge of a pond). What was the animal doing at the time? A few photographs will add considerably

Figure 12.1. "Herps" are easy to find, study and enjoy with very little equipment, as is the case of these boys and their box turtle. The best way to cultivate an interest in amphibians and reptiles is simple: go out in the field, explore, and observe. (US Geological Survey Northeast Amphibian Research and Monitoring Initiative.)

to the value of these notes. Nothing is more valuable and rewarding than field observations written down at the site of discovery. Although not necessary, an inexpensive digital camera and hand-held global positioning system unit for securing location information greatly enhances the value of field records.

Once you discover where to look for the animals, you must learn how to search for them. Most frogs and salamanders prefer aquatic or

Figure 12.2. We can all make contributions to the study of amphibians and reptiles either through volunteering for such efforts as the New York State Amphibian and Reptile Atlas Project or perhaps even by pursing a career in herpetology. Here a researcher is pleased to have completed setting up her field experiment. Each bucket contains water with a different concentration of road salt as well as a single wood frog egg mass. In 2 weeks she will compare the hatching success of the eggs under the different road salt treatments. Essex Co., New York. (James P. Gibbs.)

moist situations and should be sought where these conditions prevail. Frogs can also be located by the male's mating call during the breeding season. Many compact discs, tapes, records, and Internet-distributed sound files are available that identify each species of frog by its call (bird watchers have used these for decades [see Resources]). Knowing the seasonality of the calls is also important. The seasonality of calling by frogs and toads in New York State is described in table 5.1.

For most species, there is a difference of one month in timing of first calling between the southern and northern parts of the state. You may hear these species outside these dates, but it will be a rare occurrence. Often you will also find evidence of frogs and toads in the form of their eggs, so becoming familiar with these is important.

During the day, salamanders are almost always found under rocks and other debris, as are surprisingly large numbers of frogs. The mostly-to-fully aquatic salamanders conceal themselves beneath stones under the water or on the immediate banks. *Remember to return all the boards, rocks, and other cover objects under which you looked back to their original positions!* In fact, frequent overturning of the same object makes it unsuitable by destroying the delicate microclimate beneath; be sure to roll over and replace logs and rocks judiciously. Even when rocks are returned, repeatedly surveying the same area can lead to declines in amphibian populations (R. L. Wyman, personal communication).

During hard rains in spring, especially after dark, large numbers of amphibians migrate to the water for breeding activities. These can be found on roads (although many may be squashed beyond recognition). For the sake of safety, be sure to pick a secondary, lightly traveled road. If you drive slowly, you will be rewarded. Start your road hunting when you first hear spring peepers calling. If you are walking along the roadway, wear reflective clothing; roads are very hazardous places at night. For night observation away from car headlight beams, light supplied by a flashlight or headlamp is vital. The former is easier to aim, but the latter leaves both hands free.

Turtles may be found in both terrestrial and aquatic habitats, yet all the females must lay their eggs on land. Roadsides, gravel pits near wetlands, and railroad berms are good places for finding nesting turtles, particularly snapping and painted turtles in June. They are also often encountered crossing roads; do assist them in their perilous passage, but be careful to stay out of biting range and be very wary of traffic. Do not overlook the value of binoculars for finding turtles. Basking turtles are skittish, so a good set of binoculars can be invaluable for securing an identification from cover. Moreover, binoculars are a good way to spot softshells from promontories as they wend their way over sandy lake bottoms.

Snakes and lizards in contrast are primarily terrestrial, especially the lizards, which are usually found basking or under some sort of cover. Most snakes have similar patterns of behavior, although some, such as the northern watersnake and eastern ribbonsnake, prefer the vicinity of aquatic areas. Also, snakes are not infrequently found on roads, especially in spring and autumn when they are leaving or returning to their hibernating sites. Although we have emphasized spring, summer, and fall as the peak times to find reptiles and amphibians in New York State, "herping" in winter is not out of the question (see box: "Herping" in Winter). Mudpuppies are a reliable mid-winter quarry in exposed, running waters within their range.

"Herping" in Winter

Most people associate looking for "herps" with balmy summer nights or hard spring rains, but winter presents some interesting opportunities. Dust off the icy surface of a vernal pool in the southern part of New York State and you might see brownish tadpoles with golden-flecks swimming beneath. These are larval marbled salamanders, which hatched in the fall, biding their time until the pools thaw in spring when their primary prey—other amphibian larvae—appear. Peer into the outlets of lakes and reservoirs; tadpoles of green frogs and bullfrogs are active all winter and can often be seen in the flowing, well-oxygenated water. Even turtles, especially northern map turtles, can be seen paddling around beneath the ice, usually seeking pockets of air trapped under the ice to breathe so that they might recover a bit from the severe oxygen debt and lactic acid buildup they are experiencing trapped under the ice.

By far the most efficient and sensitive implement of securing a specimen for closer observation is your hand (obviously, this statement does not apply in the case of venomous snakes). Quickly (and gently) press the flat of the hand over the animal; do not try to curl your fingers around it, for it is apt to scurry away before it can be grasped. Having immobilized it, you can grasp it with the other hand with much less chance of losing or crushing it.

Good ecological manners for handling amphibians:
- Be inquisitive; turn over rocks and logs, but always turn the rock or log back, leaving the "home" as you found it.
- Never tromp through a pond or other small body of water as a large group; instead, send out a single scout, so as to leave the habitat as undisturbed as possible.

- If you catch an adult amphibian, wet your hands before holding it, and hold it only for a very short period. Do not pass it around. Its skin is fragile and dries out very quickly.
- Never over collect—observe and put back.

From Tyler (1994, used by permission, *Northeastern Naturalist*)

Be respectful of the sensitivity of amphibians' skins; a salty palm or insect repellent–saturated fingers will cause them great distress. Holding plethondontid salamanders in warm hands dries out their skin and can rapidly result in suffocation, especially in juvenile salamanders. Young eastern red-backed salamanders can go into shock in less than one minute in a warm hand on a dry day! Dip your hands in water frequently if you are handling frogs and salamanders (see box: Good ecological manners for handling amphibians). Many lizards and some salamanders are able to voluntarily break off their tails when grasped by the the tail, so when collecting these animals be sure to grasp them by the body, not the tail. If it is a female, you may deny her a chance to reproduce, because tail fat is converted to add yolk in the eggs. Lizards can be surprisingly swift, so it is easier to collect them by seeking them under cover early in the morning when they are still cool and lethargic.

In some circumstances, the hand is not sufficient for securing reptiles and amphibians. A long-handled net is useful for collecting frogs from a boat or when wading along the edge of a pond. A smaller dip net can be equally useful for catching small aquatic salamanders or tadpoles, and many authorities suggest using a tea strainer or aquarium net for this purpose. Turtles are quite elusive when in the water but are sometimes encountered on their overland nesting migrations. Note that turtles can bite, and some, such as the snapping turtle and the spiny softshell, can inflict serious damage. Handling them is best done by grasping them by the rear part of the shell and lifting firmly and well away from your body. Although it is commonly recommended, *do not lift turtles by the tail!* The force of their own mass can easily cause severe and lasting damage to their tail vertebrae and spinal cord (figure 12.3).

For observing serpents, some sort of a snake stick is of great help. This is simply a staff or shaft some 2 or 3 feet in length with an L-shaped end (a Y-shaped stick is virtually worthless and a noose, used by early snake hunters, almost always causes serious injury to

Figure 12.3. How to not hold (left) and how to hold (right) a snapping turtle. (left: Neg./Trans. no. 260474, American Museum of Natural History Library; right: James P. Gibbs.)

the snake even if not immediately evident). The snake stick is handy for lifting boards, flat rocks, and other cover objects to see what lies beneath. It also can be used to lift or herd snakes from locations where they are difficult to grab to more open areas. A No. 2 iron from a set of golf clubs makes an excellent snake stick, because its durability and strength allow one to lift large rocks and even old railroad ties without having to expose your fingers to whatever is beneath. Simply have the head of the golf club ground down to form an "L" configuration with the shaft. Alternatively, one can fashion a stick by attaching an angle iron to the end of a broomstick (this will not be nearly as strong as the golf club).

As with turtles, snakes should not be held by their tails. A thrashing snake held by its tail causes serious injury to itself. Support the body at several points without using a "death grip" around its neck. Let it relax and crawl on your arm.

If you keep exotic amphibians or reptiles as pets, do not use the same equipment to handle them as you use when studying native species in the field without first sterilizing the equipment. The same applies to moving among habitats. Novel forms of aquatic fungi and other threats to amphibians are readily transported on your equipment. Quickly dunking your equipment (and boots) in bleach between site visits is a good way to disinfect. And never house a wild caught animal that will be released back to the wild with a captive animal, even if it is the same species. Serious diseases, including slow-acting and difficult-to-detect viruses, have been transferred to wild populations by just such practices.

Collecting animals is rarely ethical and yet some still practice it, so a few words on collecting are warranted: know and abide by the laws regarding the taking of these creatures (see chapter 9, Legal Protections). *Collecting protected species without requisite permits is illegal. Similarly, releasing animals (native or exotic) for any reason into the wild without a permit is also illegal.*

13

Folklore

The lives of amphibians, reptiles, and humans have been long intertwined in New York State. The "unnatural history" of reptiles and amphibians, as recorded in the tales and myths we tell about them, is as interesting as their biology. It also reveals as much about us as it does about them.

Aboriginal Lore

The first residents of the State, the Haudenosaunee or members of the Six Nations, had a strong cultural identification with reptiles. Indeed, the creation story of the Haudenosaunee features turtles prominently (see Frontispiece) and is just one of many renditions of the story. On the basis of this myth, even today many Native Americans and environmentalists call North America "Turtle Island" (figure 13.1).

A particularly beautiful story rendered by Merrill (1957) that explains the geology of the Canandaigua Lake area comes from the lore of the Senecas, members of the Haudenosaunee:

> Long ago the Creator caused the earth to open and out of the side of a massive hill the ancestors of the Senecas came into being. For a time they lived in peace there. A boy of the tribe found a little snake in the woods. It was an unusual serpent for it had two heads. The boy took it home, made a pet of it and fed it the choicest deer meat. The thing grew to incredible size and its hunger knew no bounds. Its master could not obtain enough

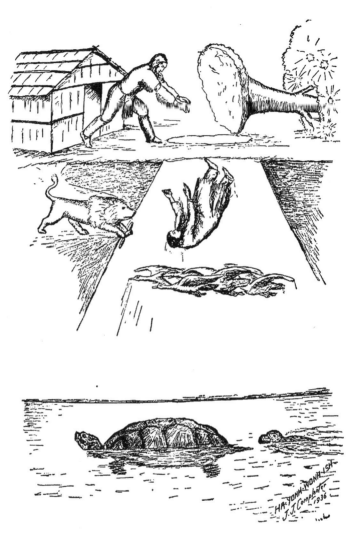

Figure 13.1. "The beginning of the present world and all the living things as they are now." This drawing by Jesse Cornplanter (Hayonhwonhish), 1889–1957 (Seneca) depicts Sky-woman carrying corn earthwards after she was pushed through the hole caused by the uprooting of the Tree of Light. Beneath is a flock of birds with locked wings prepared to softly arrest her fall. Further below is the muskrat bringing up a mouthful of wet earth from the bottom to place on the back of the Great Snapping Turtle. The turtle volunteered to hold up the living earth and all living creatures that have since materialized upon it (Cornplanter 1938). The book's frontispiece presents another version of this tale.

game for its voracious appetite. The people of the tribe came to fear it as a monster.

Finally, the great serpent encircled the hill and barred the gate with its opened, double jaws so that none could escape. Driven by hunger, the people tried to get away and, one by one, they were eaten by the monster. At last only a young warrior and his sister remained of all the People of the Hill.

One night the young brave had a vision. If he would fletch his arrows with his sister's hair, they would possess a fatal charm over the enemy. He followed his dream and shot his magic arrows straight into the serpent's heart. The reptile was mortally hurt and in agony writhed his way down Bare Hill, tearing out trees and flailing the earth until he finally slid into the lake.

As the snake rolled down the hill, he disgorged the skulls of the Seneca he had devoured. In the area have been found large rounded stones weirdly like human heads. And to this day nothing has ever grown in the path of the serpent down old Bare Hill. Its somber peak stands out above the rich and fruitful Vine Valley.

An old European folk tale of devotion recorded by Witthoft (1947) followed settlers to northern New York State near the Canadian border. The Ojibwa of Ontario borrowed the story, and their version is very moving:

> One time there was an Indian and his wife living. They had a young daughter about twelve years old. This girl would never eat with them, she would take her plate and tea-milk out some place behind a big tree. They began to take notice of her. The Indian said to his wife, "Today at noon I will follow her and see where she will go." This girl did the same again, and her father followed her. She went and sat down under this big elm tree. Her father was watching her. After a while he saw a hole right at the foot of the tree. A big serpent came out of there. The serpent and the girl ate together. The man felt awful bad. He went home and got his rifle, came back, and shot the serpent. This girl felt awful bad. She would not eat. She said to her father, "Why did you kill the best friend that I had?" They told her everything they could, thinking that she might forget the serpent, but she died a couple of days afterwards, she was that sorry for the serpent.

Serpent of Silver Lake

Scotland has its Loch Ness Monster, and Lake Champlain has its ple-
siosaur "Champ," but for ingenuity and drama they are more than
matched by the appearance of the Serpent of Silver Lake in
Wyoming County, New York, in July, 1855:

> [A party of five] were just leaving the landing on an evening's fish-
> ing excursion. The story of their voyage and its incident is theirs as
> related to us in all sincerity, and we give it with the remark that
> the party had no liquor in their boat, nor was there any in or about
> the party.
>
> About 9 o'clock . . . McKnight called attention to what had the
> semblance of a long tree trimmed off [which] appeared to be 80 or
> 100 feet long. After watching it a few minutes, [he] exclaimed:
> "Boys, that thing is moving!" . . . [On its fourth appearance] all in
> the boat had a fair view of the creature and concur in representing
> it as a most horrid and repulsive monster . . . [As to the size of
> the portion above the water] as large in circumference as a flour
> barrel . . . [or] the size of a butter firkin in circumference.
>
> The party reached shore in safety, but frightened most out of
> their senses . . . These men are persons of character; they would be
> believed in this community in any ordinary matter between man
> and man. (Hawley 1946)

It seems that there was a legend of a serpent in Silver Lake among
the native peoples of the region, and that indeed the people would
not fish in Silver Lake despite its reputation as having "catfish or bull-
heads . . . as thick as grasshoppers in a wheat field" (Hawley 1946).
Whatever the case, after its initial appearance in July, 1855, there were
numerous sightings of the serpent, bringing many visitors to A. B.
Walker's hotel on the lake in hopes of seeing the monster. Some lo-
cals assembled harpoons and similar equipment to capture it:

> During August and September thousands of curious persons
> crowded the hotels and private homes. Even scientists were alerted
> as the news went abroad that in Wyoming County there was a liv-
> ing specimen of the Age of Reptiles. The consensus was that the
> serpent was of a beautiful dark green color and had vivid yellow
> spots shimmering on a smooth skin. A head, variously estimated as
> one foot or several feet in length, supported red eyes and a savage-
> looking mouth equipped with sharp fangs and a long, pointed

tongue. The lining of the mouth was an intense scarlet. Surely, it was a denizen from out of the depths of the earth and had an ancestry countless ages old. (Douglass 1956)

Alas for the Serpent of Silver Lake, its last sighting was in the late summer of 1855, although hopeful spectators and would-be captors watched the lake in vain for the next 2 years. "On December 19, 1857, flames swept the upper portion of the Walker House. The firemen stumbled upon a strange conglomeration of coiled wire and canvas. It was recognized as the *corpus delicti* of the late inhabitant of the lake" (Douglass 1956).

It emerged that A. B. Walker, finding business slow at his hotel, had conspired with some close friends to purchase materials from Boston to construct the serpent, which was operated by means of a large pair of bellows concealed in the basement of a shanty adjacent to the lake, from which a trench extended to the lake concealing the body of the serpent.

> After a period of several weeks of genuine excitement, pleasure, and a greatly increased business at the hotel, it began to dawn upon the men that things would be mighty hot for them in this section of the country if their mischief were found out. On two or three occasions only a miracle seemed to have prevented discovery, and finally after one of these narrow escapes it was decided that the giant serpent had done its full duty, had accomplished the purpose for which it was constructed and now must disappear forever. Accordingly, it was taken from the lake and stored in the attic of the hotel. (Hawley 1946)

One wonders, upon reading this narrative of a classic hoax, what treasures might reside in attics near Loch Ness.

The Empeyville Frog

A tall tale to rival the tallest comes from Empeyville, north of Oneida Lake in central New York, where the legend of Joshua the giant frog has been told since his birth in the early 1850s (Littler 1958): "Joshua is more than one hundred years old. When ready to jump he stands four feet tall. His hind legs are six feet long and his front legs are three feet long. Each time he jumps into Empeyville pond, the water sprays about thirty feet into the air and the pond becomes six feet wider." Joshua reportedly dined on chipmunks, squirrels, rabbits, and large insects. He was a useful and valued community member (Littler 1958): "Joshua was employed as an assistant sawman at Empeyville. He hauled logs and pulled the things that were too heavy for a horse to draw. He is noted for having straightened out roads. A chain was hooked to the road and in just one of Joshua's mighty leaps the road became straight."

Rattlesnake Stories

All that is necessary to frighten some people is to mention snakes. The mention of rattlesnakes generally scares them cold (figure 13.2). And yet rattlesnakes can make interesting neighbors. When folklorist Alf Evers moved to Lewis Hollow in the Town of Woodstock, he inquired about these intriguing inhabitants of the area. His neighbor confirmed that the reptiles were present: "Sure, but I wouldn't let that bother my time none. A rattlesnake is like a jug of whiskey. You leave it alone, and it'll leave you alone." Despite this commonsense advice, the neighbor went on to explain that there were two kinds of rattlesnakes. "There's the kind you and me might see. And then there's the kind a fella down the road kilt a couple of years ago. The

Figure 13.2. The timber rattlesnake, now highly endangered, is the disproportionate focus of "herp"-related folklore in New York State. Columbia Co., New York. (© 2005, David N. Edwards, All rights reserved.)

snake this fella kilt was as long as most snakes are—about forty-two inches. Six months after, this fella was telling me about the snake he kilt. Said it was fifty inches long. Well, a year after that it was sixty inches long. Yessir, this fella sure found a new kind of rattlesnake—it keeps right on growing after its kilt and buried." (Evers 1951).

Exaggeration is common in rattlesnake stories. Evers (1951) remarked: "If a forty-inch rattler is seen in the Hollow on a Monday, by Saturday this snake has multiplied into a dozen, the smallest of which is five feet long and 'as big around as your arm, and I ain't kidding.' Over the weekend he may even develop into forty or fifty in the local bars, where conditions are favorable to the growth and multiplication of snakes."

Catching rattlesnakes was a nasty business. A rattlesnake hunter working the Lake George area described the equipment he used to secure snakes:

Well, it's really a broomstick with a wire run through eyelets along the side. They's a handle at your end and at the business end it's got a pair of steel jaws like pincers an' they work the same way. When I see a rattler I get up on him and get his neck between them jaws. Then I pull on the handle an' the jaws close on his neck, an' I've got him. I usually carry a basket to put him in because he might be a her and have five or six little ones down her gullet. I git jest as much bounty for little rattlers as I do for big ones. But if I'm in a hurry I jest put my foot on his neck and jerk off his head with my tongs. Then I bury his head under a stone and go ahead. (Carmer 1995)

Rattlesnakes had many uses, including medicinal. "The rattlesnake was a walking—or rather, crawling—drugstore" (Evers 1951). The galls were mixed with chalk to make a remedy for common children's diseases for export. Rattlesnake soup was said to be "efficacious against consumptions" (Evers 1951). Rattlesnake oil was sold at drugstores and at fairs and medicine shows. Because Native Americans were revered during the nineteenth century as a fountain of medical knowledge, the discovery of the value of snake oil was attributed to them. But "Indian Oil" was not always the real thing. "Proprietors of medicine shows were not above fleecing the gullible by selling them oils of nonsnake origin in bottles decorated—with the intent to deceive—by pictures of Indians and serpents" (Evers 1951).

In 1851, the *Niagara Democrat* carried a story of the man who may have been one of the only proprietors and vendors of authentic rattlesnake oil. This man was perhaps a significant contributor and certainly a witness to the diminution of rattlesnake populations in New York State. Rattlesnake hunting was indeed an art:

> The first warm spring day he would stealthily approach a den, and having commenced the slaughter, leave only a few to perpetuate the race, thus insuring him a source for his 'Ile.'
>
> Our young men saw him, armed with a small stick of blue beech and a forked one which he first secured the snake astride the neck to prevent it from biting itself and thus rendering its oil poisonous.
>
> When first observed he was standing motionless, his body half inclined with the wooden fork lifted for a space of two or three minutes. Then there was a thrust of the fork and a blow from the beech, and another writhing victim was tossed on a heap of those already slain . . .
>
> In a short time the snake hunter, dragging a string of snakes on a stick as boys string eels they have caught, came down the hill. 'Poor luck, this morn,' he complained, 'but some are pretty fat and larger than the general run.' He counted, 'Only seventy-one. Poor luck. Less and less every year. By this time another year comes around they'll hardly be worth hunting. The Canawl is going to spile the business with new settlers, they'll bring hogs, and they are wonderful critters for these snakes, sure death on 'em . . .'
>
> His predictions proved true. In another year his trade in oil was ruined. (Winner 1958)

Other rattlesnake hunters no doubt contributed to the species' decline:

> They used to have a lot of rattlesnakes up on south Mountain, up on Rattlesnake Den, they call it, where you look down into South Holler, two or three hundred feet. Rowell and his brother they used to go up there and Rowell would take his fiddle and get up there and entertain the rattlesnakes. They'd come out to hear him play and sing and while Rowell played his brother would pick them off . . . between the two of them they killed twenty-six rattlesnakes in one day. And if the rattlesnakes hadn't bit themselves when they were shot Uncle Rowell would skin them and put their skins up against the cabin, and the fat he'd fry out. (Studer (1959)

Then there are those individuals hardy enough to play with rattlers. One father of "twelve to fifteen children" in Lewis Hollow reportedly collected rattlesnakes to amuse his horde, because "it would have taken more money to keep these kids in toys for one year than the father ever saw in ten. So he'd go up to the Overlook and catch a dozen rattlesnakes. He'd put the snakes in a barrel and head the barrel up. When the kids took a stick and whacked the side of the barrel, all them snakes would rattle to once. Could hear it all over the Hollow. Made a nice rattle for the kids, at that" (Evers 1951).

Seaman (1963) relates the story of the Storm family's experience with the rattlesnakes near Lake George:

> Long ago, Diamond Island, near the south end of Lake George, was so overrun with rattlesnakes that few men dared land on its shores. It happened that seven hogs bound for market escaped from Storm family onto Diamond Island. Unfortunate events prevented their retrieval during the next three years, until finally Jim Storm and a friend secretly went to over to the island.
>
> They were dressed in the thick leather jackets, pants, boots and mittens of the time, and they carried stout hickory sticks.
>
> As they approached Diamond Island they saw no snakes, much to their amazement. Cautiously they searched the island but found only one pindling creature which they quickly slew. At last they came upon not seven, but sixteen of the fattest hogs a farmer could hope to raise on the best corn.
>
> It took three trips to transport the hogs to the Storm pens. During the fall some of the hogs were butchered. They were full of rattlesnakes, the old folks say, and some of them were still alive! The Storms made and sold a lot of sausage that season. It is reported that one of his neighbors complained to Storm, "What do you mean by selling me sausage that crawls out of the frying pan?"
>
> The following spring, some of the unbutchered hogs had pigs. Most of these piglets had rattles on their tales!

As charming as this story is, it highlights the frequently used and highly destructive practice used by settlers to "clean up" an area of rattlesnakes, that is, releasing thick-skinned, fat-protected hogs that relished eating any rattlesnakes present.

A common cure for rattlesnake bite was to plunge the bite, or the victim, into mud. Chewing tobacco placed on the bite is also recommended. A rattlesnake bite meant good fortune to this man in the days when a stiff drink was thought to be a cure:

> There used to be a man who liked his liquor. Liked it a little too much. One day this man—he didn't have a cent. His friends wouldn't help him. But he was thirsty as all get out, My God, he was thirsty! So this man took a pail and went up the mountain to pick huckleberries. Thought he might sell the berries for enough money to buy a drink, you see. While he was picking away, a rattler up and bit him. This man he threw down his pail and ran down the mountain. He busted right into the first house he came to, without wasting time knocking on the door. "Glory be to God," he shouted, "this is my lucky day. I'm bit by a rattler. Get out your jug and fill me up." (Evers 1951)

Hoop Snakes

From Fair Haven, New York, comes this story that even Paul Bunyan would relish:

> Now, I remember the time when I was hoeing corn out on the hill-side beyond the farmhouse. Along about noontime, my mother called me in to dinner. I stuck the hoe in the ground where I had left off and started for the house. Just before I went in, something caught my attention. I turned around just in time to see a "hoop snake" a-coming right down the row where I'd been working. Of course, you know what a hoop snake is. It's a snake that puts his tail in his mouth and then just rolls like a hoop.
>
> Well, I paid it no mind and went on in to dinner, but when I went back to finish the hoeing, I found the snake must have bitten that hoe. When Pa arrived home, we hitched up the team and wagon, loaded on that swollen hoe, and headed for the saw mill.
>
> "Well, I hope to tell you, we got ten 2 by 4s; twelve 2 by 6s; five 2 by 8s; and ten 1 by 6s from that hoe handle." (Larson 1962)

Epilogue

Having read thus far, you may have gathered that much is known about the status, distribution, natural history, and conservation of New York's amphibians and reptiles. You may also have realized that a surprising amount remains to be learned. You are therefore encouraged to contribute to the ongoing expansion of our knowledge about New York's herpetofauna by reporting your observations in standardized fashion using the facsimile of the "Herp Atlas" Report Card provided. Doing so will help biologists, land use planners, regulators, and policy makers develop better strategies to conserve these magnificent creatures. In fact, with some intelligent planning, a dose of compassion, and a smidgeon of sacrifice, we can find ways to live compatibly with our herpetofaunal neighbors over the long term. Our children's children will be grateful to us for trying. Let's hope that as a result of our collective efforts, perhaps this among the first of impressions of New York State ever recorded in written form will apply long into its future:

> . . . yet the South-side is not without Brooks and Riverets, which empty themselves into the Sea; yea, you shall scarce travel a mile, but you shall meet with one of them whose Christal streams run so swift . . . and in every pond and brook green silken Frogs, who warbling forth their untun'd tunes strive to bear a part in this musick.

—From "A Brief Description of New York"
by Daniel Denton (1670)

"Herp Atlas" Survey Card

The New York State Amphibian and Reptile Atlas project is an on-going effort to accumulate information on the distribution of "herps" in the state. You can help, as many hundreds of volunteers already have. Any information you provide will further our knowledge and conservation of these organisms. To do so, photocopy and fill out the "Herp Atlas" Survey Card below and mail it to New York Amphibian and Reptile Atlas Project, 108 Game Farm Road, Wildlife Resources Center, Delmar, NY 12054. Further guidance follows after the card.

Instructions for Filling Out "Herp Atlas" Survey Cards

A separate "herp" survey card should be used for each site and each date. If you visit the same site on two separate dates or if you visit two separate sites on one date, the information must be recorded on two separate cards. Please ask for more survey cards as you need them. The information *cannot* be entered into the computer unless it includes your name, the date, county, town, topographic quad, species and verification codes. Please print clearly using the following guidelines:

- County/Town. Double check your location before you record it. There are 62 counties and approximately 1,000 towns and cities in New York State. Towns (sometimes called townships) and cities are incorporated subunits of the county and should not be confused with villages, hamlets or all those other place names that have no real geographic boundaries. Town and city boundaries are depicted on most county maps or state atlases. The New York State Atlas and Gazetteer published by DeLorme has the most useful format we've found.

- Topographic Quadrangle. The 7½-minute topographic quadrangle is the basic unit for reporting observations.

82-15-61 (9/94)—10g NEW YORK STATE DEPARTMENT OF ENVIRONMENTAL CONSERVATION

HERP SURVEY CARD

COUNTY	TOWN		TOPOGRAPHIC QUAD NAME	DATE OBSERVED (one per card)
				Year / Month / Day

DETAILED LOCATION: (one site per card)

PRINCIPAL OBSERVER: (list additional observers on back)

Name _____

Address _____

City/State/Zip _____

Telephone: ( ) _____

SPECIES	VERIFICATION CODES	SPECIES		VERIFICATION CODES
1.		5.		
2.		6.		
3.		7.		
4.		8.		

PLEASE USE A NEW CARD IF MORE THAN 8 SPECIES OBSERVED

This project is supported by: NYS DEC, Division of Fish and Wildlife

Please return completed card to:

**NEW YORK AMPHIBIAN AND REPTILE ATLAS PROJECT
108 GAME FARM ROAD, WILDLIFE RESOURCES CENTER
DELMAR, NY 12054**

NEW YORK AMPHIBIAN AND REPTILE ATLAS PROJECT

SPECIES VERIFICATION CODES

(use at least one code from each category):

1. **Method of Documentation** (you may use more than one code if appropriate)

   VS—voucher specimen. This code is to be used only by individuals with a permit to collect. List accession number and museum where specimen is deposited under "notes".

   PH—photograph. Must show distinctive field marks.

   CAP—hand-captured, trapped or dip netted and released after identifying.

   OBS—observed without capturing, collecting or photographing.

   VOC—vocalization, frogs only.

2. **Type of Evidence** (you may use more than one code if appropriate)

   DOR—dead on road.

   KLL—found carcass dead (except roadkills).

   BON—bones, empty shell.

   SHD—shed skin, snakes only.

   EGG—eggs, eggmass.

   LRV—salamander larva, tadpoles.

   ADL—adult or immature.

   TRK—tracks.

   OTH—other distinctive parts or signs (specify).

OTHER OBSERVERS (include address):

NOTES:

- Date Observed. Record year, three-letter abbreviation for month, and day.

- Detailed Location. This block should include information that identifies the geographic area (e.g., "south end of Vly Swamp" or "1.2 mi. north of intersection of Rts. 32 and 201"). This is especially important if you are unsure of the name of the topographic quad or town.

- Principal Observer. Fill out your complete name and the address where you would like to receive additional mailings. Please notify the "Herp Atlas" project of a change in your name or address.

- Species. Use the names as indicated in tables 2.1 and 2.2. If you encounter a species that is not on the list, use the name given in the field guide you used to identify it. There are a number of species or subspecies that are difficult or impossible to identify in the field. For any observation, unless you are 100% sure of your identification, do not record it!!! You may be asked for supporting information for any observation that appears questionable or which is clearly beyond the known range. Use only distinctive field marks to identify the species in question.

- Verification Codes. The codes listed on the survey card should be used to describe your encounter. List a species only once for each location with all the codes that are applicable. Each species report should be followed by *at least one code* for the method of documentation and *at least one code* for the type of evidence. For instance, "CAP-LRV" indicates that you dip-netted some tadpoles, or "OBS-VOC-ADL" would mean you heard frogs calling and saw at least one individual. The "voucher specimen" (VS) code is to be used only by individuals who have been issued a permit to make collections.

- Notes. This block is to be used for recording species information that cannot simply be explained with the verification codes. Use this block to record number of individuals, sex, biological information (e.g., eggs were hatching), or environmental date (e.g., heavy rains, air temp. 49°F).

Recording Negative Data

Many people have favorite sites that they return to repeatedly each year watching or listening for the first or last occurrence of some event. In such a case, it is appropriate to record negative observations. For instance, if spring peepers are calling at a site on a particular day, but you visited that site just a few days earlier and did not hear them, it would be beneficial to submit a record card for the day that you did not hear the calling, and a separate card for the first day you did hear calling. In such a case, record the species with the verification code "OTH" and explain "OTH" in the "Notes" section of the card.

Please return the report cards promptly.

Resources

New York-based Organizations

Coastal Research and Education Society of Long Island (CRESLI). A group concerned with welfare of sea turtles around Long Island: http://cresli.org/

Cortland Herpetology Connection. A general source of information for high school students and others about New York's amphibians and reptiles: http://www.cortland.edu/herp/

Long Island Herpetological Society. Local events, care sheets, and adoptions: http://www.lihs.org/

New York Herpetological Society. Founded in 1954, one of the oldest herp societies in the United States: http://www.nyhs.org/

New York State Department of Environmental Conservation. The governmental authority responsible for protective regulations and granting of permits of use for amphibians and reptiles in New York State: http://www.dec.state.ny.us/

New York Turtle and Tortoise Society (NYTTS). A group committed to the welfare of turtles and tortoises in New York State and beyond: http://www.nytts.org/

Riverhead Foundation. Sea Turtle and Marine Mammal Stranding Network: http://www.riverheadfoundation.org/

Upstate Herpetological Association. Devoted to promoting responsible reptile handling, education, and conservation, with chapters in Albany, Binghamton, and Syracuse: http://www.upstateherp.org/

National and International Organizations

American Society of Ichthyologists and Herpetologists (ASIH). Producers of the journal *Copeia:* http://www.utexas.edu/depts/asih

Amphibian Research Monitoring Initiative (ARMI). A US Geological Survey–hosted group seeking to coordinate amphibian research and monitoring in the United States: http://armi.usgs.gov/

Center for North American Herpetology (CNAH). A general repository on information about North American amphibians and reptiles: http://www.cnah.org/

Chelonian Research Foundation (CRF). A group focused on the biology and conservation of turtles and tortoises: http://www.chelonian.org/

Declining Amphibian Populations Task Force (DAPTF). A United Kingdom–based group that serves as a clearinghouse on issues related to declining amphibians: http://www.open.ac.uk/daptf/index.htm

Herpetologists League (HL). Producers of the journals *Herpetologica*, and *Herpetological Monographs*: http://www.inhs.uiuc.edu/cbd/HL/HL.html

North American Amphibian Monitoring Program (NAAMP). A US Geological Survey–based program promoting standardized amphibian monitoring (excellent opportunities for contributions from volunteers): http://www.pwrc.usgs.gov/naamp/

Partners in Amphibian and Reptile Conservation (PARC). A professional organization with a northeastern chapter focused on the complexities of reptile and amphibian conservation, and producers of *Habitat Management Guidelines for Amphibians and Reptiles* and *Model State Herpetofauna Regulatory Guidelines*: http://www.parcplace.org

Society for the Study of Amphibians and Reptiles (SSAR). Producers of the *Journal of Herpetology, Herpetological Review*, and *Catalog of American Amphibians and Reptiles*: http://www.ukans.edu/~ssar/

Identification of Larvae

Tadpoles of the United States and Canada. A tutorial and key: http://www.pwrc.usgs.gov/tadpole/

Sources of Frog Calls

Savannah River Ecology Laboratory. A source of calls of some of New York's frogs and toads: http://www.uga.edu/srelherp/

Sounds of North America Frogs, Charles M. Bogert, 1998, Smithsonian Folkways Recordings, SFCD 45060.

The Calls of Frogs and Toads, Lang Elliott, 1994, Naturesound Studios, NorthWord Press, P.O. Box 1360, Minocqua, WI 54548.

Related Field Guides

Behler, J.L. and F.W. King. 1997. National Audubon Society Field Guide to North American Amphibians and Reptiles. Alfred A. Knopf, New York, New York.

Bider, J.R. and S. Matte. 1996. The Atlas of Amphibians and Reptiles of Quebec. St. Lawrence Valley Natural History Society and Ministere de l'Environnement et de la Faune du Quebec, Direction de la faune et des habitats, Quebec 106 pp.

Conant, R. and J.T. Collins. 1998. A Field Guide to the Amphibians and Reptiles: Eastern and Central North America. Houghton Mifflin Company, New York, New York.

Harding, J.H. 1997. Amphibians and Reptiles of the Great Lakes Region. The University of Michigan Press. Ann Arbor, Michigan.

Hulse, A.C., C.J. McCoy, and E. Censky. 2001. Amphibians and Reptiles of Pennsylvania and the Northeast. Comstock Publishing Associates, Ithaca.

MacCulloch, R.D. 2002. The ROM Field Guide to Amphibians and Reptiles of Ontario. McClelland and Stewart.

Smith, H.M. 1978. Amphibians of North America: A Guide to Field Identification. Golden Press, New York.

Smith, H.M. and E.D. Brodie. 1982. Reptiles of North America: A Guide to Field Identification. Golden Press, New York.

Schwartz, V. and D.M. Golden. 2002. Field Guide to Reptiles and Amphibians of New Jersey. New Jersey Division of Fish and Wildlife.

Reference Books

Amphibians

Bishop, S.C. 1941. The Salamanders of New York. New York State Museum Bulletin No. 324. The University of the State of New York, Albany, New York.

Bishop, S.C. 1994. Handbook of Salamanders: The Salamanders of the United States, of Canada, and of Lower California. Comstock Publishing Associates, A Division of Cornell University Press, Ithaca, New York.

Dickerson, M.C. 1969. The Frog Book: North American Toads and Frogs, with a Study of the Habits and Life Histories of Those of the Northeastern States. Dover Publications, Inc., New York.

Petranka, J.W. 1998. Salamanders of the United States and Canada. Smithsonian Institution Press, Washington, DC.

Pfingsten, R.A. and F.L. Downs. 1989. Salamanders of Ohio. Bulletin of the Ohio Biological Survey Vol. 7, No. 2. College of Biological Sciences, The Ohio State University, Columbus, Ohio.

Wright, A.H. and A.A. Wright. 1995. Handbook of Frogs and Toads of the United States and Canada. Comstock Publishing Associates, A Division of Cornell University Press, Ithaca, New York.

Reptiles

Carr, A. 1995. Handbook of Turtles: The Turtles of the United States, Canada, and Baja California. Comstock Publishing Associates, A Division of Cornell University Press, Ithaca, New York.

Ernst, C.H. and R.W. Barbour. 1989. Snakes of Eastern North America. George Mason University Press, Fairfax, Virginia.

Ernst, C.H. and E.M. Ernst. 2003. Snakes of the United States and Canada. Smithsonian Books, Washington, D.C.

Ernst, C.H., J.E. Lovich, and R.W. Barbour. 1994. Turtles of the United States and Canada. Smithsonian Institution Press, Washington, D.C.

Klauber, L.M. 1982. Rattlesnakes: Their Habits, Life Histories, and Influence on Mankind, Abridged Edition. University of California Press, Berkeley and Los Angeles, California.

Klemens, M. 2000. Turtle Conservation. Smithsonian Institution Press. Washington, D.C.

Levell, J.P. 1995. A Field Guide to Reptiles and the Law. Serpent's Tale Natural History Books, Excelsior, Minnesota.

Mitchell, J.C. 1994. The Reptiles of Virginia. Smithsonian Institution Press, Washington, D.C.

Smith, H.M. 1995. Handbook of Lizards: Lizards of the United States and Canada. Comstock Publishing Associates, A Division of Cornell University Press, Ithaca, New York.

Wright, A.H. and A.A. Wright. 1957. Handbook of Snakes of the United States and Canada, Volumes 1 and 2. Comstock Publishing Associates, Ithaca, New York.

Related Texts

Duellman, W.E. and L. Trueb. 1994. Biology of Amphibians. The Johns Hopkins University Press, Baltimore, Maryland.

Heyer, W.R., M.A. Donnelly, R.W. McDiarmid, L-A.C. Hayek, and M.S. Foster. 1994. Measuring and Monitoring Biological Diversity: Standard Methods for Amphibians. Smithsonian Institution Press, Washington, D.C.

Pough, F.H., R.M.Andrews, J.E.Cadle, M.L. Crump, A.H. Savitzky and K.D. Wells. 2004. Herpetology, 3rd Ed. Pearson Prentice Hall, Upper Saddle River, New Jersey.

Powell, R., J.T. Collins, and E.D. Hooper, Jr. 1998. A Key to the Amphibians and Reptiles of the Continental United States and Canada. University Press of Kansas, Lawrence, Kansas.

Stebbins, R.C. and N.W. Cohen. 1995. A Natural History of Amphibians. Princeton University Press, Princeton, New Jersey.

Tyning, T.F. 1990. A Guide to Amphibians and Reptiles. Stokes Nature Guides. Little Brown and Company, Boston.

West, L. and W.P. Leonard. 1997. How to Photograph Reptiles and Amphibians. Stackpole Books, Mechanicsburg, Pennsylvania.

Zug, G.R. 1993. Herpetology: An Introductory Biology of Amphibians and Reptiles. Academic Press, San Diego, California.

Glossary

Amplexus – Position used by male and female frogs during egg laying and external fertilization, usually involving male clasping female's back.

Anal plate – The scales, usually numbering one or two, that cover the cloacal opening of lizards and snakes.

Annelid – Member of the invertebrate phylum Annelida; the segmented worms, including the earthworms.

Anuran – Lacking tail; referring to frogs and toads (Order Anura).

Arthropod – Member of the invertebrate phylum Arthropoda; animals with jointed legs, such as insects, crustaceans, millipedes, centipedes, and spiders.

Barbel – A fleshy protrusion from the body.

Bog – A kind of peatland in which there is little or no inflow or outflow of water that typically supports acid-loving mosses such as *Sphagnum*.

Carapace –The top part of a turtle's shell (see also plastron).

Clade – Any group of two or more species that includes the common ancestor and all of its descendents.

Cloaca – The single common chamber for the end products of the digestive, reproductive, and excretory systems of amphibians and reptiles. It opens to the outside of the animal through the vent.

Conspecific – Referring to a member of the same species.

Costal grooves – Folds in the skin of salamanders that correspond with the location of the ribs.

Cranial crests – Raised edges on the top of the heads of toads.

Cryptic – Serving to conceal, as in cryptic coloration.

Dewlap – Loose, pendulous skin beneath the throat.

Dimorphic – Occurring in two forms; sexually dimorphic refers to the morphological differences between males and females.

Disjunct – Referring to a population that is separated from the main distribution of a species so that reproduction between the two is unlikely.

Dorsal – Referring to the back.

Dorsolateral fold – A glandular longitudinal ridge on the upper side of some frogs.

Eft stage – A terrestrial juvenile stage of newts.

Endangered –Used to describe any native species in imminent danger of extirpation or extinction in New York State.

Estivation – A state of inactivity during long periods of drought or high temperatures.

Fen – A kind of peatland where some surface or underground water from the surrounding area flows through and is typically dominated by grass-like plants.

Fossorial – Living below ground.

Friable – Easily broken apart or burrowed through; dry, sandy soils are often friable and are home to a number of burrowing organisms.

Granular gland – Skin glands of amphibians that produce noxious or toxic secretions.

Gravid – Containing eggs or young, referring to females.

Keeled scales – Scales of reptiles, particularly some snakes, with a raised longitudinal ridge.

Hemipenes – Paired copulatory structures of male snakes and lizards (singular: hemipenis).

Hibernaculum – A communal overwintering site for amphibians and reptiles.

Intergrade – A population or individual that exhibits a combination of characteristics of two or more subspecies or species.

Labial – Referring to the lips, as in labial scales.

Larvae/Larval – Refers to the immature stage of some amphibians.

Lateral – Refers to the side.

Mental gland – A gland beneath the chin in some male salamanders, which secretes a substance sexually stimulating to females.

Metamorph – A young amphibian that is newly transformed to the adult stage.

Metamorphosis – Transformation from one stage of an amphibian's life to another.

Mollusk – Member of the invertebrate phylum Mollusca; the snails, slugs, bivalves, squid, and octopus.

Morph – One of at least two distinct morphological variations of a species; may include color varieties.

Nasolabial groove – A small groove connecting the upper lip to the nostril of salamanders in the family Plethodontidae that aids in sensing chemicals from conspecifics and prey.

Niche – The functional role of a species in a biological community, defined by such parameters as where it lives, when it is active, and what food it eats.

Northern hardwoods – A term to collectively describe the tree species composition of forests in the northeastern and north-central United States and southeastern Canada where the dominant species are American beech, yellow and paper birch, red and sugar maple and white ash.

Oviparous – Egg laying soon after fertilization.

Ovoviviparous – Egg retention for variable lengths of time, even up to parturition, with very little or no maternal nutritional contribution other than yolk production.

Papillae – A rounded nipple-like projection.

Parotoid gland – The toxin-producing shoulder glands of toads.

Parturition – Birth.

Peatland – A type of wetland where production of organic material far outweighs its decomposition, resulting in a buildup of peat; includes bogs and fens.

Pheromone – A class of hormone, or chemical messenger, often used for communication between conspecifics.

Plastron – Underside of a turtle's shell, connected to the carapace (top part) by the bridge.

Posterior – Toward the rear; back end.

Riparian – Of or pertaining to the bank of a river.

Scute – Individual keratin plates that comprise the outer layer of a turtle's shell.

Sexual dimorphism – Referring to readily observable differences in shape or color between males and females of a species.

Special Concern – Used to describe any native species for which a welfare concern or risk of endangerment has been documented in New York State.

Spermatophore – Small packet of sperm perched on a tiny pedestal produced by male salamanders and inserted by females into their bodies.

Squamate – Referring to lizards and snakes (Order Squamata).

SVL – Snout-to-vent length; the measurement from the tip of the snout to the anterior angle of the vent (cloaca).

Sympatric – Occurring in the same area.

Tadpole – A name for the aquatic larvae of frogs.

Talus – Rock debris that accumulates on a mountain slope or at the base of a cliff.

Terrestrial – Living on land.

Threatened – Used to describe any native species likely to become an endangered species within the foreseeable future in New York State.

Tympanum – The eardrum; can be used to distinguish sex in some species where the males have larger tympanums than the females.

Unisexual – Refers to populations that consist of only one sex, as in those groups of mole salamanders that are all females and reproduce by a form of parthenogenesis.

Vent – See cloaca.

Venter – Belly or bottomside

Vernal – Of or relating to the spring season.

Viviparous – Bearing of live young with some maternal nutritional contribution, generally via a placental connection, beyond addition of yolk to eggs.

Wetland – An area seasonally or permanently inundated with water and underlain by hydric soils.

Literature Cited

Adams, C.C., and T.L. Hankinson. 1928. The ecology and economics of Oneida Lake fishes. Roosevelt Wildlife Annals 3/4:235–548.

Adams, M.J. 2000. Pond permanence and the effects of exotic vertebrates on anurans. Ecological Applications 10:559–568.

Adler, K. 1970. The influence of prehistoric man on the distribution of the box turtle. Annals of the Carnegie Museum 41:263–280.

Alerich, C., and D.A. Drake. 1995. Forest statistics for New York: 1980 and 1993. Resource Bulletin NE-132. USDA Forest Service, Northeastern Forest Experiment Station, Radnor, Pennsylvania.

Alford, R.A., and H.M. Wilbur. 1985. Priority effects in experimental pond communities: Competition between *Bufo* and *Rana*. Ecology 66:1097–1105.

Amato, C.A., and R. Rosenthal. 2001. Endangered species protection in New York after State v. Sour Mountain Realty, Inc. New York University Environmental Law Journal 10:117–145.

Anderson, J.D. 1967. *Ambystoma opacum*. Catalogue of American Amphibians and Reptiles 46:1–2.

Anderson, J.D., and P.J. Martino. 1967. Food habits of *Eurycea longicauda longicauda*. Herpetologica 23:105–108.

Arndt, R.G. 1994. Predation on hatchling diamondback terrapin, *Malaclemys terrapin* (Schoepff), by the ghost crab, *Ocypode quadrata* (Fabricius). Florida Scientist 57:1–5.

Arnold, S.J. 1976. Sexual behavior, sexual interference, and sexual defense in the salamanders *Ambystoma maculatum*, *Ambystoma tigrinum*, and *Plethodon jordani*. Zeitschrift fur Tierpsychologie 42:247–300.

———. 1978. Differential predation on metamorphic anurans by garter snakes (*Thamnophis*): Social behavior as a possible defense. Ecology 59:1014–1022.

———. 1982. A quantitative approach to antipredator performance: Salamander defense against snake attack. Copeia 1982:247–253.

Arvisais, M., J-C. Bourgeois, E. Levesque, C. Daigle, D. Masse, and J. Jutras. 2002. Home range and movements of a wood turtle (*Clemmys insculpta*) population at the northern limit of its range. Canadian Journal of Zoology 80: 402–408.

———. 2004. Habitat selection by the wood turtle (*Clemmys insculpta*) at the northern limit of its range. Canadian Journal of Zoology 82:391–398.

Ashley, E.P., and J.T. Robinson. 1996. Road mortality of amphibians, reptiles and other wildlife on the Long Point Causeway, Lake Erie, Ontario. Canadian Field-Naturalist 110:403–412.

Ashpole, S.L., C.A. Bishop, and R.J. Brooks. 2004. Contaminant residues in common snapping turtle (*Chelydra s. serpentina*) eggs from the Great Lakes-St. Lawrence River basin (1999 to 2000). Archives of Environmental Contamination and Toxicology 47:240–252.

Ashton, R.E., Jr. 1975. A study of movement, home range, and winter behavior of *Desmognathus fuscus* (Rafinesque). Journal of Herpetology 9:85–91.

Ashton, R.E., Jr., and P.S. Ashton. 1978. Movements and winter behavior of *Eurycea bislineata* (Amphibia, Urodela, Plethodontidae). Journal of Herpetology. 12:295–298.

Babbitt, K.J., M.J. Baber, and T.L. Tarr. 2003. Patterns of larval amphibian distribution along a wetland hydroperiod gradient. Canadian Journal of Zoology 81:1539–1552.

Babcock, H.L. 1918. The turtles of New England. Memoirs of the Boston Society of Natural History 8:323–431.

———. 1971. Turtles of the northeastern United States. Dover Publications, New York.

Bachman, M.D., R.G. Carlton, J.M. Burkholder, and R.G. Wetzel. 1986. Symbiosis between salamander eggs and green algae: Microelectrode measurements inside eggs demonstrate effect of photosynthesis on oxygen concentration. Canadian Journal of Zoology 64:1586–1588.

Bahret, R. 1996. Ecology of lake dwelling *Eurycea bislineata* in the Shawangunk Mountains, New York. Journal of Herpetology 30:399–401.

Bailey, L.L., T.R. Simons, and K.H. Pollock. 2004. Spatial and temporal variation in detection probability of *Plethodon* salamanders using the robust capture-recapture design. Journal of Wildlife Management 68:14–24.

Baldauf, R.J. 1952. Climatic factors influencing the breeding migration of the spotted salamander, *Ambystoma maculatum* (Shaw). Copeia 1952:178–181.

Baldwin, E.A., M.N. Marchand, and J.A. Litvaitis. 2004. Terrestrial habitat use by nesting painted turtles in landscapes with different levels of fragmentation. Northeastern Naturalist 11:41–48.

Balent, K.L., and P.T. Andreadis. 1998. The mixed foraging strategy of juvenile northern water snakes. Journal of Herpetology 32:575–579.

Banks, B., J. Foster, T. Langton, and K. Morgan. 2000. British bullfrogs? British Wildlife 11:327–330.

Barbour, R.W. 1960. A study of the worm snake, *Carphophis amoenus*, Say in Kentucky. Transactions of the Kentucky Academy of Science 21:10–16.

Barbour, R.W., J.W. Hardin, J.P. Schafer, and M.J. Harvey. 1969a. Home range, movements, and activity of the dusky salamander, *Desmognathus fuscus*. Copeia 1969:293–279.

Barbour, R.W., M.J. Harvey and J.W. Hardin. 1969b. Home range, movements, and activity of the eastern worm snake, *Carphophis amoenus amoenus*. Ecology 50:470–476.

Barr, G.I., and K.I. Babbitt. 2002. Effects of biotic and abiotic factors on the distribution and abundance of larval two-lined salamanders (*Eurycea bislineata*) across spatial scales. Oecologia 133:176–185.

Barton, A.J., and J.W. Price. 1955. Our knowledge of the bog turtle, *Clemmys muhlenbergi*, surveyed and augmented. Copeia 1955:159–165.

Barzilay, S. 1980. Aggressive behavior in the wood turtle, *Clemmys insculpta*. Journal of Herpetology 14:89–91.

Baumann, M.A., and D.E. Metter. 1977. Reproductive cycle of the northern watersnake, *Natrix s. sipedon*. Journal of Herpetology 11:51–59.

Bayless, L.E., 1975. Population parameters for *Chrysemys picta* in a New York pond. American Midland Naturalist 93:168–176.

Bell, E.L. 1955. An aggregation of salamanders. Proceedings of the Pennsylvania Academy of Sciences 29:265–266.

Bennett, R.M., R.M. Ross, W.A. Lellis, and L.A. Redell. 2003. Terrestrial salamander preference for artificial cover objects made from four species of wood. Journal of the Pennsylvania Academy of Science 76:77–79.

Berrill, M., S. Bertram, L. McGillivray, M. Kolohon, and B. Pauli. 1994. Effects of low concentrations of forest-use pesticides on frog embryos and tadpoles. Environmental Toxicology and Chemistry 13:657–664.

Berrill, M., S. Bertram, P. Tosswill, and V. Campbell. 1992. Is there a bullfrog decline in Ontario? Declines in Canadian amphibian populations: Designing a national monitoring strategy. Occasional paper, Canadian Wildlife Service 76:32–36.

Berven, K.A. 1990. Factors affecting population fluctuations in larval and adult stages of the wood frog (*Rana sylvatica*). Ecology 71:1599–1608.

Birdsall, C.W., C.E. Grue, and A. Anderson. 1986. Lead concentrations in bullfrog *Rana catesbeiana* and green frog *R. clamitans* tadpoles inhabiting highway drainages. Environmental Pollution 40:233–247.

Bishop, C.A., N.A. Mahony, J. Struger, P. Ng, and K.E. Pettit. 1999. Anuran development, density and diversity in relation to agricultural activity in the Holland River watershed, Ontario, Canada (1990–1992). Environmental Monitoring and Assessment 57:21–43.

Bishop, S.C. 1926. Notes on the habits and development of the mudpuppy *Necturus maculosus* (Rafinesque). New York State Museum Bulletin 268:1–38.

———. 1941. The salamanders of New York. New York State Museum Bulletin No. 324.

Blanchard, F.C. 1932. Eggs and young of the smooth green snake *Liopeltis vernalis* (Harlan). Papers of the Michigan Academy of Science, Arts, and Letters 17:493–508.

Blanchard, F.N., M.R. Gilreath, and F.C. Blanchard. 1979. The eastern ringneck snake (*Diadophis punctatus edwardsii*) in northern Michigan (Reptilia, Serpentes, Colubridae). Journal of Herpetology 13:377–402.

Blem, C.R., J.W. Steiner, and M.A. Miller. 1978. Comparison of jumping abilities of the cricket frogs *Acris gryllus* and *Acris crepitans*. Herpetologica 34:288–291.

Blouin-Demers, G., K.A. Prior, and P.J. Weatherhead. 2002. Comparative demography of black rat snakes (*Elaphe obsoleta*) in Ontario and Maryland. Journal of Zoology 256:1–10.

Blouin-Demers, G., and P.J. Weatherhead. 2001. Habitat use by black rat snakes (*Elaphe obsoleta obsoleta*) in fragmented forests. Ecology 82:2882–2896.

Blouin-Demers, G., P.J. Weatherhead, and J.R. Row. 2004. Phenotypic consequences of nest-site selection in black rat snakes (*Elaphe obsoleta*). Canadian Journal of Zoology 82:449–456.

Boatright-Horowitz, S.S., C.A. Cheney, and A.M. Simmons. 1999. Atmospheric and underwater propagation of bullfrog vocalizations. Bioacoustics 9:257–280.

Bogart, J.P. 1982. Ploidy and genetic diversity in Ontario salamanders of the *Ambystoma jeffersonianum* complex revealed through an electrophoretic examination of larvae. Canadian Journal of Zoology 60:848–855.

Bogart, J.P., R.P. Elinson, and L.E. Licht. 1989. Temperature and sperm incorporation in polyploid salamanders. Science 246:1032–1034.

Bogart, J.P. and M. W. Klemens. 1997. Hybrids and genetic interactions of mole salamanders (*Ambystoma jeffersonianum* and *A. laterale*) (Amphibia: Caudata) in New York and New England. American Museum Novitates 3218: 1–78.

Bogart, J.P., L.A. Lowcock, C.W. Zeyl, and B.K. Mable. 1987. Genome constitution and reproductive biology of the *Ambystoma* hybrid salamanders on Kelly's Island in Lake Erie. Canadian Journal of Zoology 65:2188–2201.

Bolek, M.G. and J.R. Coggins. 2002. Observations on myiasis by the calliphorid, *Bufolucilia silvarum*, in the American toad (*Bufo americanus americanus*) from southeastern Wisconsin. Journal of Wildlife Diseases 38: 598–603.

Bonin, J., J-L. DesGranges, C.A. Bishop, J. Rodrigue, A. Gendron, and J.E. Elliott. 1995. Comparative study of contaminants in the mudpuppy (Amphibia) and the common snapping turtle (Reptilia), St. Lawrence River, Canada. Archives of Environmental Contamination and Toxicology 28:184–194.

Boogaard, M.A., T.D. Bills, and D.A. Johnson. 2003. Acute toxicity of TFM and a TFM/Niclosamide mixture to selected species of fish, including lake sturgeon (*Acipenser fulvescens*) and mudpuppies (*Necturus maculosus*), in laboratory and field exposures. Journal of Great Lakes Research 29:529–541.

Boone, M.D., and S.M. James. 2003. Interactions of an insecticide, herbicide, and natural stressors in amphibian community mesocosms. Ecological Applications 13:829–841.

Bossert, M., M. Draud, and T. Draud. 2003. *Bufo fowleri* (Fowler's toad) and *Malaclemys terrapin terrapin* (northern diamondback terrapin) refugia and nesting. Herpetological Review 34:135.

Bothner, R.C. 1963. A hibernaculum of the short-headed garter snake, *Thamnophis brachystoma* Cope. Copeia 1963:572–573.

———. 1976. *Thamnophis brachystoma*. Catalog of American Amphibians and Repiles 190.1–190.2.

Bothner, R.C and A.R. Breisch. 2001. Snakes of New York — a sampler of our most common species. Conservationist 56(1):15–18.

Brainerd, E.L., J.S. Ditelberg, and D.M. Bramble. 1993. Lung ventilation in salamanders and the evolution of vertebrate air-breathing mechanisms. Biological Journal of the Linnean Society 49:163–183.

Branch, L.C., and R. Altig. 1981. Nocturnal stratification of three species of *Ambystoma* larva. Copeia 1981:870–873.

Brandon, R.A., and J.E. Huheey. 1981. Toxicity of the plethodontid salamanders *Pseudotriton ruber* and *Pseudotriton montanus* (Amphibia, Caudata). Toxicon 19:25–31.

Branson, B.A. and E.C. Baker. 1974. An ecological study of the queen snake, *Regina septemvittata*, in Kentucky. Tulane Studies in Zoology and Botany 18: 153–171.

Braun, J., and G.R. Brooks, Jr. 1987. Box turtles (*Terrapene carolina*) as potential agents for seed dispersal. American Midland Naturalist 117:312–318.

Breder, R.B. 1927. The courtship of the spotted salamander. Zoological Society Bulletin 30:50–56.

Breisch, A. 1997. The status and management of turtles in New York. Pages 11–14 In: Status and Conservation of Turtles of the Northeastern United States. A Symposium. (T.F. Tyning, editor). Serpent's Tale, Lanesboro, Minnesota.

Breisch, A.R., and J.L. Behler. 2002. Turtles of New York State. Conservationist 57(1):15–18.

Breisch, A.R., and P.K. Ducey. 2003a. Woodland and vernal pool salamanders of New York State. Conservationist 57(6):15–18.

Breisch, A.R., and P.K. Ducey. 2003b. Lake, pond and stream salamanders of New York State. Conservationist 57(5):15–18.

Breisch, A.R., and J.P. Gibbs. 2002. Frogs and toads of New York State. Conservationist 56(5):15–18.

Breisch, A.R. and R.C Bothner. 2006. Snakes of New York Part 2. Conservationist 60(6):15–18.

Breisch, A.R. and J.W. Jaycox. 2006. Lizards of New York State. Conservationist 61(1):15–18.

Breitenbach, G.L. 1982. The frequency of communal nesting and solitary brooding in the salamander, *Hemidactylium scutatum*. Journal of Herpetology 16:341–346.

Brodie, E.D., Jr. 1968. Investigations on the skin toxin of the red-spotted newt, *Notophthalmus viridescens*. American Midland Naturalist 80:276–280.

———. 1977. Salamander antipredator postures. Copeia 1977:523–535.

———. 1981. Phenological relationships of model and mimic salamanders. Evolution 35:988–994.

———. 1982. Toxic salamanders. Journal of the American Medical Association 247:1408.

Brodie, E.D., Jr., and E.D. Brodie, III. 1980. Differential avoidance of mimetic salamanders by free-ranging birds. Science 208:181–183.

Brodie, E.D., Jr., T. G. Dowdy, and C. D. Anthony. 1989. Salamander antipredator strategies against snake attack: Biting by *Desmognathus*. Herpetologica 45: 167–171.

Brodie, E.D., Jr., and D.R. Formanowicz, Jr. 1981. Palatability and antipredator behavior of the treefrog *Hyla versicolor* to the shrew *Blarina brevicauda*. Journal of Herpetology 15:235–236.

Brodie, E.D., Jr., D. Robert, T. Nowak, and W.R. Harvey. 1979. The effectiveness of antipredator secretions and behavior of selected salamanders against shrews. Copeia 1979:270–274.

Brodie, E.D., III and P.K. Ducey. 1989. Allocation of reproductive investment in the redbelly snake, *Storeria occipitomaculata*. American Midland Naturalist 122:51–58.

Brodman, R.,M. Kolaczyk, R.A. Pulver, A.J. Long, and T. Bogard. 2003. Mosquito control by pond-breeding salamander larvae. Herpetological Review 34:116–119.

Brooks R.J., D.A. Galbraith, E.G. Nancekivell, and C.A. Bishop. 1988. Developing management guidelines for common snapping turtles. Pages 174–179 In: Management of amphibians, reptiles, and small mammals in North America (Szaro R.C., K.E. Severson, and D.R. Patton, editors). USDA Forest Service General Technical Report RM-166.

Brooks, R.J., G.P. Brown, and D.A. Galbraith. 1991. Effects of a sudden increase in natural mortality of adults on a population of the common snapping turtle (*Chelydra serpentina*). Canadian Journal of Zoology 69:1314–1320.

Brooks, R.J., C.M. Shilton, G.P. Brown, and N.W.S. Quinn. 1992. Body size, age distribution, and reproduction in a northern population of wood turtles (*Clemmys insculpta*). Canadian Journal of Zoology 70:462–469.

Brooks, R.T. 2004. Weather-related effects on woodland vernal pool hydrology and hydroperiod. Wetlands 24:104–114.

Brooks, R.T. 1999. Residual effects of thinning and high white-tailed deer densities on northern redback salamanders in southern New England oak forests. Journal of Wildlife Management 63:1172–1180.

Brooks, R.T., and M. Hayashi. 2002. Depth-area-volume and hydroperiod relationships of ephemeral ("vernal") forest pools in southern New England. Wetlands 22:247–255.

Brooks, S.P., B.A. Dawson, D.B. Black, and K.B. Storey. 1999. Temperature regulation of glucose metabolism in red blood cells of the freeze-tolerant wood frog. Cryobiology 39:150–157.

Brown, E.E. 1979. Stray food records from New York and Michigan snakes. American Midland Naturalist 102:200–203.

Brown, G.P. and P.J. Weatherhead. 2000. Thermal ecology and sexual size dimorphism in northern water snakes, *Nerodia sipedon*. Ecological Monographs 70:311–330.

Brown, J.D. and J.M. Sleeman. 2002. Morbidity and mortality of reptiles admitted to the Wildlife Center of Virginia, 1991 to 2000. Journal of Wildlife Diseases 38:699–705.

Brown, W.S. 1991. Female reproductive ecology in a northern population of the timber rattlesnake, *Crotalus horridus*. Herpetologica 47:101–115.

———. 1992. Emergence, ingress, and seasonal captures at dens of northern timber rattlesnakes, *Crotalus horridus*. Pages 251–258 In: Biology of the pitvipers (J.A. Campbell and E.D. Brodie, Jr., editors). Selva, Tyler, Texas.

———. 1993. Biology, status, and management of the timber rattlesnake (*Crotalus horridus*): A guide for conservation. SSAR Herpetological Circular 22: 1–78.

Brown, W.S. and D.B. Greenberg. 1992. Vertical-tree ambush posture in *Crotalus horridus*. Herpetological Review 15:75–76.

Brown, W. S., L. Jones, and R. Stechert. 1994. A case in herpetological conservation: Notorious poacher convicted of illegal trafficking in timber rattlesnakes. Bulletin of the Chicago Herpetological Society 29:74–79.

Brown, W.S. and W.S. Parker. 1976. Movement ecology of *Coluber constrictor* near communal hibernacula. Copeia 1976:225–242.

Brown, W.S., D.W. Pyle, K.R. Greene, and J.B. Friedlaender. 1982. Movements and temperature relationships of timber rattlesnakes (*Crotalus horridus*) in northeastern New York. Journal of Herpetology 16:15–16.

Buhlmann, K.A. and J.W. Gibbons. 2001. Terrestrial habitat use by aquatic turtles from a seasonally fluctuating wetland: Implications for wetland conservation boundaries. Chelonian Conservation and Biology 4:115–127.

Burger, J. 2002. Metals in tissues of diamondback terrapin. New Jersey Environmental Monitoring and Assessment 77:255–263.

Burger, J. and W.A. Montevecchi. 1975. Nest site selection in the terrapin *Malaclemys terrapin*. Copeia 1975:113–119.

Burghardt, G.M. 1973. Chemical release of prey attack: Extension to naive newly hatched lizards, *Eumeces fasciatus*. Copeia 1973:178–181.

Burke, R.L., A. A. Hussain, J. M. Storey, and K. B. Storey. 2002. Freeze tolerance and supercooling ability in the Italian wall lizard, *Podarcis sicula*, introduced to Long Island, New York. Copeia 2002:836–842.

Burke, R.L. and R. Mercurio. 2002. Food habits of a New York population of Italian wall lizards, *Podarcis sicula* (Reptilia, Lacertidae). American Midland Naturalist 147:368–375.

Burke, R.L. and S. Ner. 2005. Seasonal and daily activity patterns of the Italian wall lizard, *Podarcis sicula*, in New York, USA. Northeastern Naturalist 12: 349–360.

Burke, V.J., J.W. Gibbons, and J.L. Greene. 1994. Prolonged nesting forays by common mud turtles (*Kinosternon subrubrum*). American Midland Naturalist 131:190–195.

Burke, V.J., S.J. Morreale, and A.G. Rhodin. 1993. Testudines, *Lepidochelys kempii* Kemp's ridley sea turtle and *Caretta caretta* loggerhead sea turtle diet. Herpetological Review 24:31–32.

Burke, V.J., S.J. Morreale, and E.A. Standora. 1994. Diet of the Kemp's ridley sea turtle, *Lepidochelys kempii*, in New York waters. Fishery Bulletin 92:26–32.

Burke, V.J., R.D. Nagle, M. Osentoski, and J.D. Congdon. 1993. Common snapping turtles associated with ant mounds. Journal of Herpetology 27:114–115.

Burke, V.J., S.L. Rathbun, J.R. Bodie, and J.W. Gibbons. 1998. Effect of density on predation rate for turtle nests in a complex landscape. Oikos 83:3–11.

Burke, V.J., and E.A. Standora. 1993. Diet of juvenile Kemp's ridley and loggerhead sea turtles from Long Island, New York. Copeia 1993:1176–1180.

Burke, V.J., E.A. Standora, and S.J. Morreale. 1991. Factors affecting strandings of cold-stunned juvenile Kemp's ridley and loggerhead sea turtles in Long Island, New York. Copeia 1991:1136–1138.

Burmeister, S.S., A.G. Ophir, M.J. Ryan, and W. Wilczynski. 2002. Information transfer during cricket frog contests. Animal Behaviour 64:715–725.

Burnley, J. M. 1968. Some nonindigenous turtles recorded on Long Island. Engelhardtia 1:11–12.

———. 1973. Eastern spadefoots, *Scaphiopus holbrooki*, found on the south fork of Long Island during 1973. Engelhardtia 6:10.

Burton, T.M. and G.E. Likens. 1975a. Energy flow and nutrient cycling in salamander populations in the Hubbard Brook Experimental Forest, New Hampshire. Ecology 56:1068–1080.

Burton, T.M., and G.E. Likens. 1975b. Salamander populations and biomass in the Hubbard Brook Experimental Forest, New Hampshire. Copeia 1975: 541–5456.

Bury, R.B. 1979. Review of the ecology and conservation of the bog turtle, *Clemmys muhlenbergii*. US Fish and Wildlife Services Special Science Report–Wildlife 219.

Bush, F.M. and E.F. Menhinick. 1962. The food of *Bufo woodhousei fowleri* Hinckley. Herpetologica 18:110–114.

Cadi, A., and P. Joly. 2003. Competition for basking places between the endangered European pond turtle (*Emys orbicularis galloitalica*) and the introduced red-eared slider (*Trachemys scripta elegans*). Canadian Journal of Zoology 81:1392–1398.

Caldwell, J.P. 1986. Selection of egg deposition sites: A seasonal shift in the southern leopard frog, *Rana sphenocephala*. Copeia 1986:249–253.

Calhoun, A.J.K., and P. deMaynadier. 2002. Forestry habitat management guidelines for vernal pool wildlife in Maine. Maine Department of Inland Fisheries and Wildlife, Augusta, Maine.

Calhoun, A.J.K. and M. W. Klemens. 2002. Best development practices for vernal pools: Conserving pool-breeding amphibians in commercial and residential developments in the northeastern US. Wildlife Conservation Society Technical Paper #5. Rye, New York.

Cameron, K.D., S.B. Broyles, P.K. Ducey. 1998. Non-lethal technique for obtaining tissue for molecular studies of *Ambystoma* salamanders. Herpetological Review 29:20–23.

Carmer, C. 1995. My Kind of Country: Favorite Writings about New York. Syracuse University Press, Syracuse, New York.

Carpenter, C.C. 1953. A study of hibernacula and hibernating associations of snakes in Michigan. Ecology 34:74–80.

Carr, A. 1952. Handbook of Turtles. Cornell University Press, Ithaca, New York.

Carr, L.W., and L. Fahrig. 2001. Effect of road traffic on two amphibian species of differing vagility. Conservation Biology 15:1071–1078.

Carter, S.L., C.A. Haas, and J.C. Mitchell. 1999. Home range and habitat selection of bog turtles in southwestern Virginia. Journal of Wildlife Management 63:853–860.

———. 2000. Movements and activity of bog turtles (*Clemmys muhlenbergii*) in southwestern Virginia. Journal of Herpetology 34:75–80.

Churchill, T.A., and K.B. Storey. 1992. Freezing survival of the garter snake *Thamnophis sirtalis parietalis*. Canadian Journal of Zoology 70:99–105.

Clark, D.R. Jr. 1967. Experiments into selection of soil type, soil moisture level, and temperature by five species of small snakes. Transactions of the Kansas Academy of Sciences 70:490–496.

———. 1970. Ecological study of the worm snake *Carphophis vermis* (Kennicott). University of Kansas Publication of the Museum of Natural History 19:85–194.

Clark, J.P., A.M. Ewert, and E.C. Nelson. 2001. Physical apertures as constraints on egg size and shape in the common musk turtle, *Sternotherus odoratus*. Functional Ecology 15:70–77.

Clark, K.L. 1986. Responses of spotted salamanders, *Ambystoma maculatum*, populations in central Ontario to habitat acidity. Canadian Field-Naturalist 100:463–469.

Clausen, H.J. 1936. Observations on the brown snake *Storeria dekayi* (Holbrook), with especial reference to the habit and birth of young. Copeia 1936: 98–102.

Clausen, R.T. 1938. Notes on *Eumeces anthracinus* in central New York. Copeia 1938:3–7.

Clesson, D., A. Bautista, D.D. Baleckaitis, and R.W. Krohmer. 2002. Reproductive biology of male eastern garter snakes (*Thamnophis sirtalis sirtalis*) from a denning population in central Wisconsin. American Midland Naturalist 147: 376–386.

Clevenger, A.P., M. McIvor, D. McIvor, B. Chruszcz, and K. Gunson. 2001. Tiger salamander, *Ambystoma tigrinum*, movements and mortality on the Trans-Canada highway in southwestern Alberta. Canadian Field-Naturalist 115:199–204.

Cole, R.V., and T.E. Helser. 2001. Effect of three bycatch reduction devices on diamondback terrapin *Malaclemys terrapin* capture and blue crab *Callinectes sapidus* harvest in Delaware Bay. North American Journal of Fisheries Management 21:825–833.

Collins, J.T., and J.L. Knight. 1980. *Crotalus horridus*. Catalogue of American Amphibians and Reptiles 253:1–2.

Collins, J.T., and T.W. Taggart. 2005. Standard Common and Current Scientific Names for North American Amphibians, Turtles, Reptiles, and Crocodilians. 5th ed. http://www.cnah.org

Compton, B.W., J.M. Rhymer, and M. McCollough. 2002. Habitat selection by wood turtles (*Clemmys insculpta*): An application of paired logistic regression. Ecology 83:833–843.

Congdon, J.D., A.E. Dunham, and R.C. van Loben Sels. 1993. Delayed sexual maturity and demographics of Blanding's turtles (*Emydoidea blandingii*): Implications for conservation and management of long-lived organisms. Conservation Biology. 7:826–833.

———. 1994. Demographics of common snapping turtles (*Chelydra serpentina*): Implications for conservation and management of long-lived organisms. American Zoologist 34:397–408.

Congdon, J.D., R.D. Nagle, O.M. Kinney, M. Osentoski, H.W. Avery, R.C. Van Loben Sels, and D.W. Tinkle. 2000. Nesting ecology and embryo mortality: Implications for hatchling success and demography of Blanding's turtles (*Emydoidea blandingii*). Chelonian Conservation and Biology 3:569–579.

Coniff, R. 1989. King of the snappers. Yankee, June: 64–69, 110–114.

Cook, R.P. 1982. Representative animal community being created at Jamaica Bay. Park Science 2:3–4.

———. 1983. Effects of acid precipitation in embryonic mortality of *Ambystoma* salamanders in the Connecticut Valley of Massachusetts. Biological Conservation 27:77–88.

———. 1989. And the voice of the grey treefrog was heard again in the land. Park Science 9:6–7.

———. 2002. Herpetofaunal community restoration in a post-urban landscape (New York and New Jersey). Ecological Restoration 20:290–291.

Cook, R.P., and C.A. Pinnock. 1987. Recreating a herpetofaunal community at Gateway National Recreation Area. Pages 151–154 In: Integrating man and nature in the urban environment (L.W. Adams and D.L. Leedy, editors). National Institute for Urban Wildlife, Columbia, Maryland.

Cook, R.P. and Tanacredi, J.T. 1990. Management strategies for increasing habitat and species diversity in an urban national park. Pages 248–250 In:

Environmental Restoration: Science and Strategies for Restoring the Earth (J.J. Berger, editor). Island Press, Washington, DC.

Cooper, W.E., Jr. and N. Burns. 1987. Social significance of ventrolateral coloration in the fence lizard, *Sceloporous undulatus*. Animal Behavior 35: 526–532.

Cooper, W.E., Jr., and L.J. Vitt. 1985. Blue tails and autotomy: Enhancement of predation avoidance in juvenile skinks. Zeitschrift fur Tierpsychologie 70:265–276.

Cornplanter, J. J. 1938. Legends of the Longhouse. J.B. Lippincott Co., Philadelphia.

Cortwright, S.A., and C.E. Nelson. 1990. An examination of multiple factors affecting community structure in an aquatic amphibian community. Oecologia 83:123–131.

Coulter, M.W. 1957. Predation by common snapping turtles upon aquatic birds in Maine marshes. Journal of Wildlife Management 21:17–21.

Courtois, D., R. Leclair, Jr., S. Lacasse, and P. Magnan. 1995. Habitat preferences of Ranidae in oligotrophic lakes in the Laurentian Shield, Quebec. Canadian Journal of Zoology 73:1744–1753.

Craig, R.J., M.W. Klemens, and S.S. Craig. 1980. The northeastern range limit of the eastern mud turtle *Kinosternon s. subrubrum* (Lacepede). Journal of Herpetology 14:295–297.

Crocker, C.E., T.E. Graham, G.R. Ultsch, and D.C. Jackson. 2000. Physiology of common map turtles (*Graptemys geographica*) hibernating in the Lamoille River, Vermont. Journal of Experimental Zoology 286:143–148.

Crother, B.I. 2000. Scientific and standard English names of amphibians and reptiles of North America north of Mexico, with comments regarding confidence in our understanding. SSAR Herpetological Circular 29.

Crother, B.I., J. Boundy, J.A. Campbell, K. DeQueiroz, D. Frost, D.M. Green, R. Highton, J.B. Iverson, R.W. McDiarmid, P.A Meylan, T.W. Reeder, M.E. Seidel, J.W. Sites, Jr., S.G. Tilley, and D.B. Wake. 2003. Scientific and standard English names of amphibians and reptiles of North America north of Mexico. Update. Herpetological Review 34:196–203.

Crump, D., M. Berrill, D. Coulson, D. Lean, L. McGillivray, and A. Smith. 1999. Sensitivity of amphibian embryos, tadpoles, and larvae to enhanced UV-B radiation in natural pond conditions. Canadian Journal of Zoology 77:1956–1966.

Cundall, D., J. Lorenz-Elwood, and J.D. Groves. 1987. Asymmetric suction feeding in primitive salamanders. Experientia 43:1229–1231.

Czech, B., and P. R. Krausman. 1997. Public opinion on species and endangered species conservation. Endangered Species Update 14:7–10.

Dahl, T.E. 1990. Wetland Losses in the United States 1780s to 1980s. US Fish and Wildlife Service, Washington, D.C.

Daigle, C., P. Galois, and Y. Chagnon. 2002. Nesting activities of an eastern spiny softshell turtle, *Apalone spinifera*. Canadian Field-Naturalist 116:104–107.

Dale, J.M., B. Freedman, and J. Kerekes. 1985. Acidity and associated water chemistry of amphibian habitats in Nova Scotia. Canadian Journal of Zoology 63:97–105.

Davenport, J. 1997. Temperature and the life-history strategies of sea turtles. Journal of Thermal Biology 22:479–488.

Davenport, J., M. Spikes, S.M. Thornton, and B.O. Kelly. 1992. Crab-eating in the diamondback terrapin *Malaclemys terrapin*: Dealing with dangerous prey. Journal of the Marine Biological Association of the United Kingdom, Plymouth 72:835–848.

Davic, R.D., and H.H. Welsh, Jr., 2004. On the ecological role of salamanders. Annual Review of Ecology and Systematics 35:405–434.

Davidson, J.A. 1956. Notes on the food habits of the slimy salamander *Plethodon glutinosus glutinosus*. Herpetologica 12:129–131.

Davis, D.D. 1946. Observations on the burrowing behavior of the hog-nosed snake. Copeia 1946:75–78.

Davis, D.S., and J. Gilhen. 1982. An observation of the transportation of pea clams, *Pisidium adamsi*, by blue-spotted salamanders, *Ambystoma laterale*. Canadian Field-Naturalist 96:213–214.

de Solla, S.R., C.A. Bishop, H. Lickers, and K. Jock. 2001. Organochlorine pesticides, PCBs, dibenzodioxin, and furan concentrations in common snapping turtle eggs (*Chelydra serpentina serpentina*) in Akwesasne, Mohawk Territory, Ontario. Archives of Environmental Contamination and Toxicology 40:410–417.

de Solla, S.R., and K.J. Fernie. 2004. Characterization of contaminants in snapping turtles (*Chelydra serpentina*) from Canadian Lake Erie Areas of Concern: St. Clair River, Detroit River, and Wheatley Harbour. Environmental Pollution 132:101–112.

DeGraaf, R. M., and M. Yamasaki. 2002. Effects of edge contrast on redback salamander distribution in even-aged northern hardwoods. Forest Science 48: 351–363.

DeMaynadier, P.G., and M.L. Hunter, Jr. 1999. Forest canopy closure and juvenile emigration by pool-breeding amphibians in Maine. Journal of Wildlife Management 63:441–450.

———. 2000. Road effects on amphibian movements in a forested landscape. Natural Areas Journal 20:56–65.

Dickerson, M.C. 1969. The Frog Book: North American Toads and Frogs, with a Study of the Habits and Life Histories of Those of the Northeastern States. Dover Publications, Inc., New York.

Dickinson, N.R. 1979. A division of southern and western New York State into ecological zones. Special Report, Bureau of Wildlife, New York State Department of Conservation, Albany. 56 pp.

DiGiovanni, M., and E.D. Brodie, Jr. 1981. Efficacy of snake glands in protecting the salamander *Ambystoma opacum* from repeated attacks by the shrew *Blarina brevicauda*. Herpetologica 37:234–237.

Ditmars, R.L. 1905. The reptiles of the vicinity of New York City. Journal of the American Museum of Natural History. 5:93–140.

Do Amaral, J.P.S. 1999. Lip-curling in redbelly snakes (*Storeria occipitomaculata*): Functional morphology and ecological significance. Journal of Zoology 248:289–293.

DonnerWright, D.M., M.A. Bozek, J.R. Probst, and E.M. Anderson. 1999. Responses of turtle assemblage to environmental gradients in the St. Croix River in Minnesota and Wisconsin, U.S.A. Canadian Journal of Zoology 77:989–1000.

Douglas, M.E. 1979. Migration and sexual selection in *Ambystoma jeffersonianum*. Canadian Journal of Zoology 57:2303–2310.

Douglass, H.S. 1956. The legend of the serpent. New York Folklore Quarterly 12: 37–42.

Dowdey, T.G., and E.D. Brodie, Jr. 1989. Antipredator strategies of salamanders: Individual and geographic variation in responses of *Eurycea bislineata* to snakes. Animal Behaviour 37:707–711.

Draud, M., M. Bossert, and S. Zimnavoda. 2004. Predation on hatchling and juvenile diamondback terrapins (*Malaclemys terrapin*) by the Norway rat (*Rattus norvegicus*). Journal of Herpetology 38:467–470.

Ducey, P.K. 1988. Variation in the antipredator behavior of *Ambystoma* salamanders. Ph.D. dissertation. University of Michigan, Ann Arbor.

———. 1989. Agonistic behavior and biting during intraspecific encounters in *Ambystoma* salamanders. Herpetologica 45:155–160.

Ducey, P.K., and E.D. Brodie, Jr. 1983. Salamanders respond selectively to contacts with snakes: Survival advantage of alternative antipredator strategies. Copeia 1983:1036–1041.

Ducey, P.K. and J. Dulkiewicz. 1994. Ontogenetic variation in antipredator behavior of the newt *Notophthalmus viridescens*: Comparisons of terrestrial adults and efts in field and laboratory tests. Journal of Herpetology 28:530–533.

Ducey, P.K., and J. Heuer. 1991. Effects of food availability on intraspecific aggression in salamanders of the genus Ambystoma. Canadian Journal of Zoology 69:288–290.

Ducey, P.K., W. Newman, K.D. Cameron, and M. Messere. 1998. Herpetofauna of the highly-polluted Onondaga Lake Ecosystem, Onondaga County, New York. Herpetological Review 29:118–119.

Ducey, P.K., and P. Ritsema. 1988. Intraspecific aggression and responses to marked substrates in *Ambystoma maculatum* (Caudata: Ambystomatidae). Copeia 1988:1008–1013.

Ducey, P.K., K. Schramm, and N. Cambry. 1994. Interspecific aggression between the sympatric salamanders, *Ambystoma maculatum* and *Plethodon cinereus*. American Midland Naturalist 131:320–329.

Duguay, J.P, and P.B. Wood. 2002. Salamander abundance in regenerating forest stands on the Monongahela National Forest, West Virginia. Forest Science 48:331–335.

Durner, G.M., and J.E. Gates. 1993. Spatial ecology of black rat snakes on Remington Farms, Maryland. Journal of Wildlife Management 57:812–826.

Dundee, H.A., and D.A. Rossman. 1989. Amphibians and Reptiles of Louisiana. State University Press, Baton Rouge.

Eckert, S.A., and C. Luginbuhl. 1988. Death of a giant. Marine Turtle Newsletter 43:2–3.

Edmonds, J.H., and R.J. Brooks. 1995. Demography, sex ratio, and sexual size dimorphism in a northern population of common musk turtles (*Sternotherus odoratus*). Canadian Journal of Zoology 74:918–928.

Egan, R.S., and P.W.C. Paton. 2004. Within-pond parameters affecting oviposition by wood frogs and spotted salamanders. Wetlands 24:1–13.

Eights, J. 1853. Scraps from a naturalist's notebook. The Country Gentleman (Albany) 2:140–141.

Ernst, C.H. 1971. *Chrysemys picta*. Catalogue of American Amphibians and Reptiles 106:1–4.

———. 1982. *Malaclemys, M. terrapin*. Catalogue of American Amphibians and Reptiles 299:1–4.

———. 1986. Ecology of the turtle, *Sternotherus odoratus*, in southeastern Pennsylvania. Journal of Herpetology 20:341–352.

———. 2001. Some ecological parameters of the wood turtle, *Clemmys insculpta*, in southeastern Pennsylvania. Chelonian Conservation and Biology 4:94–99.

———. 2003. Natural history of the queen snake, *Regina septemvittata*, in southeastern Pennsylvania, U.S.A. Herpetological Bulletin 85:2–11.

Ernst, C.H. and R.W. Barbour. 1989. Snakes of Eastern North America. George Mason University Press, Fairfax, Virginia.

Ernst, C.H., and E. M. Ernst. 2003. Snakes of the United States and Canada. Smithsonian Books, Washington, D.C.

Ernst, C.H., J.E. Lovich, and R.W. Barbour. 1994. Turtles of the United States and Canada. Smithsonian Institution Press. Washington, D.C.

Euliss, N.H., Jr., and D.M. Mushet. 2004. Impacts of water development on aquatic macroinvertebrates, amphibians, and plants in wetlands of a semi-arid landscape. Aquatic Ecosystem Health and Management 7:73–84.

Evers, A. 1951. Rattlesnake lore. New York Folklore Quarterly 7:109–115.

———. 1960. The time old Bella lost her cud. New York Folklore Quarterly 16:269–279.

Ewert, M.A., and C.E. Nelson. 1991. Sex determination in turtles: Diverse patterns and some possible adaptive values. Copeia 1991:50–69.

Faccio, S.D. 2003. Postbreeding emigration and habitat use by Jefferson and spotted salamanders in Vermont. Journal of Herpetology 37:479–489.

Feinberg, J.A., and R.L. Burke. 2003. Nesting ecology and predation of diamondback terrapins, *Malaclemys terrapin*, at Gateway National Recreation Area, New York. Journal of Herpetology 37:517–526.

Ferriero, C., S. Miller, M. Chapman, and P.K. Ducey. 1998. *Gyrinophilus porphyriticus* (spring salamander) coloration. Herpetological Review 29:229.

Finkler, M.S. and A.E. Schultz. 2003. *Sternotherus odoratus* (common musk turtle) and *Chelydra serpentina* (common snapping turtle) reproduction. Herpetological Review 34:58.

Fisher, D. W. 1981. The world of Coelophysis—a New York dinosaur of 200 million years ago. New York State Museum and Science Service, Geological Survey, Circular 49.

Fitch, H.S. 1954. Life history and ecology of the five-lined skink, *Eumeces fasciatus*. University of Kansas Publications of the Museum of Natural History 8:1–156.

———. 1960. Autecology of the copperhead. University of Kansas Publications of the Museum of Natural History 13:85–288.

———. 1975. A demographic study of the ringneck snake (*Diadophis punctatus*) in Kansas. University of Kansas Museum of Natural History Miscellaneous Publications 62:1–53, Lawrence, Kansas.

———. 2003. A comparative study of loss and regeneration of lizard tails. Journal of Herpetology 37:395–399.

Flores-Nava, A. 2000. Bullfrog *Rana catesbeiana* farming in Latin America: An overview. World Aquaculture 31:22–29.

Forester, D.C. 1977. Comments on the female reproductive cycle and philopatry by *Desmognathus ochrophaeus* (Amphibia, Urodela, Plethodonitidae). Journal of Herpetology 11:311–316.

———. 1979. The adaptivenes of parental care in *Desmognathus ochrophaeus* (Urodela: Plethodontidae). Copeia 1979:332–341.

———. 1981. Parental care in the salamander *Desmognathus ochrophaeus*: Female activity pattern and trophic behavior. Journal of Herpetology 15:29–34.

———. 1984. Brooding behavior by the mountain dusky salamander: Can the females presence reduce clutch desiccation? Herpetologica 40:105–109.

Forester, D.C. and K.J. Thompson. 1998. Gauntlet behaviour as a male sexual tactic in the American toad (Amphibia: *Bufonidae*) Behaviour 135:99–119.

Formanowicz, D.R., Jr. and E.D. Brodie, Jr. 1982. Relative palatabilies of members of a larval amphibian community. Copeia 1982:91–97.

———. 1993. Size-mediated predation pressure in a salamander community. Herpetologica 49:265–270.

Frair, W.R., R.G. Ackman, and N. Mrosovsky. 1972. Body temperature of *Dermochelys coriacea*: Warm turtle from cold water. Science 177:791–793.

Fraker, M.A. 1970. Home range and homing in the watersnake, *Natrix sipedon sipedon*. Copeia 1970:665–673.

Frazer, N.B. 1991. Life history and demography of the common mud turtle *Kinosternon subrubrum* in South Carolina, USA. Ecology 72:2218–2231.

Freda, J., and W.A. Dunson. 1986. Effects of low pH and other chemical variables on the local distribution of amphibians. Copeia 1986:454–466.

Frese, P.W. 2003. Tallgrass prairie amphibian and reptile assemblage. Fire mortality. Herpetological Review 34:159–160.

Frisbie, M.P., and R.L. Wyman. 1992. The effect of soil chemistry on sodium balance in the red-backed salamander: A comparison of two forest types. Journal of Herpetology 26:434–442.

———. 1995. A field simulation of the effect of acidic rain on ion balance in a woodland salamander. Archives of Environmental Contamination and Toxicology 28:327–333.

Galbraith, D.A., B.N. White, R.J. Brooks, and P.T. Boag. 1993. Multiple paternity in clutches of snapping turtles (*Chelydra serpentina*) detected using DNA fingerprints. Canadian Journal of Zoology 71:318–324.

Gall, S.B., C.D. Anthony, and J.A. Wicknick. 2003. Do behavioral interactions between salamanders and beetles indicate a guild relationship? American Midland Naturalist 149:363–374.

Galois, P., M. Leveille, L. Bouthillier, C. Daigle, and S. Parren. 2002. Movement patterns, activity, and home range of the eastern spiny softshell turtle (*Apalone spinifera*) in northern Lake Champlain, Quebec,Vermont. Journal of Herpetology 36:402–411.

Garber, S.D., and J. Burger. 1995. A 20-yr study documenting the relationship between turtle decline and human recreation. Ecological Applications 5:1151–1162.

George, C. J., C.W. Bayles, and R.B. Sheldon. 1977. The presence of the red-spotted newt, *Notophthalmus viridescens rafinesque* (Amphibia, Urodela, Salamandridae) in water exceeding 12 meters in Lake George, New York. Journal of Herpetology 11:87–90.

Gibbons, J.W., S.S. Novak, and C.H. Ernst. 1988. *Chelydra serpentina*. Catalogue of American Amphibians and Reptiles 420:1–4.

Gibbs, H.L., K.A. Prior, P.J. Weatherhead ,and G. Johnson. 1997. Genetic structure of populations of the threatened eastern massasauga rattlesnake, *Sistrurus c. catenatus*: Evidence from microsatellite DNA markers. Molecular Ecology 6:1123–1132.

Gibbs, J.P. 1998a. Amphibian movements in response to forest edges, roads, and streambeds in southern New England. Journal of Wildlife Management 62:584–589.

———. 1998b. Distribution of woodland amphibians along a forest fragmentation gradient. Landscape Ecology 13:263–268.

Gibbs, J.P., and A.R. Breisch. 2001. Climate warming and calling phenology of frogs near Ithaca, New York, 1900–1999. Conservation Biology 15:1175–1178.

Gibbs, J.P., K.K. Whiteleather, and F.W. Schueler. 2005. Changes in frog and toad populations over 30 years in New York State. Ecological Applications 15:1148–1157.

Gilbert, B. 1993. The reptile that stakes its survival on snap decisions. Smithsonian 24:93–99.

Gilbert, P.W. 1941. Eggs and nests of *Hemidactylum scutatum* in the Ithaca region. Copeia 1941:47.

Gilhen, J. 1984. Amphibians and reptiles of Nova Scotia. Nova Scotia State Museum, Halifax.

Gill, D.E. 1978. The metapopulation ecology of the red-spotted newt, *Notophthalmus viridescens* (Rafinesque). Ecological Monographs. 48:145–166.

Given, M.A. 2005. Vocalizations and reproductive behavior of male pickerel frogs, *Rana palustris*. Journal of Herpetology 39:223–233.

Gist, D.H., and J.D. Congdon. 1998. Oviductal sperm storage as a reproductive tactic of turtles. Journal of Experimental Zoology 282:526–534.

Gloyd, H.K., and R. Conant. 1990. Snakes of the *Agkistrodon* complex: A monographic review. Society for the Study of Amphibians and Reptiles, Cont. Herpetol. 6:1–614.

Gochfeld, M. 1975. The decline of the eastern garter snake, *Thamnophis sirtalis sirtalis*, in a rural residential section of Westchester County, New York. Engelhardtia 6:23–34.

Gordon, D.M., and F.R. Cook. 1980. An aggregation of gravid snakes in the Quebec Laurentians. Canadian Field-Naturalist 94:456–457.

Gordon, D.M., and R.D. MacCulloch. 1980. An investigation of the ecology of the map turtle, *Graptemys geographica* (Le Sueur), in the northern part of its range. Canadian Journal of Zoology 58:2210–2219.

Gossweiler, W.A. 1975. European lizards established on Long Island. Copeia 1975:584–585.

Grady, D. 2005. Tiny pet turtles return; *Salmonella* does, too. The New York Times, 3/15/05.

Graham, T.E., and A.A. Graham. 1997. Ecology of the eastern spiny softshell, *Apalone spinifera spinifera*, in the Lamoille River, Vermont. Chelonian Conservation Biology, 2:767 769.

Graham, T.E., C.B. Graham, C.E. Crocker, and G.R. Ultsch. 2000. Dispersal from and fidelity to a hibernaculum in a northern Vermont population of common map turtles, *Graptemys geographica*. Canadian Field-Naturalist 114: 405–408.

Graham, T.E., and R.W. Guimond. 1995. Aquatic oxygen consumption by wintering red-bellied turtles. Journal of Herpetology 29:471–474.

Grant, G.S., H. Malpass, and J. Beasley. 1996. Correlation of leatherback turtle and jellyfish occurrence. Herpetological Review 27:123–125.

Grant, J.B. 2001. *Rana palustris* (pickerel frog) production of odor. Herpetological Review 32:183.

Grant, K.P., and L.E. Licht. 1993. Acid tolerance of anuran embryos and larvae from central Ontario. Journal of Herpetology 27:1–6.

Gray, B.S. 2003. *Thamnophis brachystoma* (short-headed gartersnake) defensive behavior. Herpetological Review 34:158.

Green, D.M., and C. Parent. 2003. Variable and asymmetric introgression in a hybrid zone in the toads, *Bufo americanus* and *Bufo fowleri*. Copeia 2003:34–43.

Greene, H.W. 1988. Antipredator mechanisms in reptiles. Pp 1–152 in C. Gans and R.B. Huey (eds.) Biology of the Reptilia, Volume 16, Alan R.Liss, New York.

Grogan, W.L., Jr. 1974. Effects of accidental envenomation from the saliva of the eastern hognose snake, *Heterodon platyrhinos*. Herpetologica 30:248–249.

Grover, M.C., and H.M. Wilbur. 2002. Ecology of ecotones: Interactions between salamanders on a complex environmental gradient. Ecology 83:2112–2123.

Grudzien, T.A. and P.J. Owens. 1991. Genic similarity in the gray and brown color morphs of the snake *Storeria occipitomaculata*. Journal of Herpetology 25:90–92.

Guerry, A.D., and M.L. Hunter. 2002. Amphibian distributions in a landscape of forests and agriculture: An examination of landscape composition and configuration. Conservation Biology 16:745–754.

Guimond, R.W., and V.H. Hutchison. 1973. Aquatic respiration: An unusual strategy in the hellbender *Cryptobranchus alleganiensis* (Daudin). Science 182:1263–1265.

Haenel, G.J., L.C. Smith, and H.B. John-Alder. 2003a. Home-range analysis in *Sceloporus undulatus* (Eastern Fence Lizard). I. Spacing patterns and the context of territorial behavior. Copeia 2003:99–112.

———. 2003b. Home-range analysis in *Sceloporus undulatus*. II. A test of spatial relationships and reproductive success. Copeia 2003:113–123.

Hairston, N.G. 1983. Growth, survival, and reproduction of *Plethodon jordani*: Trade-offs between selective pressures. Copeia 1983:1024–1035.

Hall, R.J. 1976. Summer foods of the salamander, *Plethodon wehrlei* (Amphibia, Urodela, Plethodontidae). Journal of Herpetology 10:129–131.

Hall, R.J., P.F.P. Henry, and C.M. Bunck. 1999. Fifty-year trends in a box turtle population in Maryland. Biological Conservation 88:165–172.

Hall, R.J., and D.P. Stafford. 1972. Studies in the life history of Wehrle's salamander, *Plethodon wehrlei*. Herpetologica 28:300–309.

Halverson, M.A., D.K. Skelly, J.M. Kiesecker, and L.K. Freidenburg. 2003. Forest mediated light regime linked to amphibian distribution and performance. Oecologia 134:360–364.

Hamilton, W.J., Jr. 1930. Notes on the food of the American toad. Copeia 1930:45.

———. 1940. The feeding habits of larval newts with reference to availability and predilection of food items. Ecology 21:351–356.

———. 1943. Winter habits of the dusky salamander in central New York. Copeia 1943:192.

———. 1948. The food and feeding behavior of the green frog, *Rana clamitans* Latreille, in New York state. Copeia 1948:203–207.

———. 1951. The food and feeding behavior of the garter snake in New York. American Midland Naturalist, 46:385–390.

Harlan, R.A., and R.F. Wilkinson. 1981. The effects of progressive hypoxia and rocking activity on blood oxygen tension for hellbenders, *Cryptobranchus alleganiensis*. Journal of Herpetology 15:383–384.

Harris, J.P., Jr. 1959. The natural history of *Necturus*: III. Food and feeding. Field and Lab 28:105–111.

Harris, M.L., C.A. Bishop, J. Struger, M.R. van den Heuvel, G.J. Van der Kraak, D.G. Dixon, B. Ripley, and J.P. Bogart. 1988a. The functional integrity of northern leopard frog (*Rana pipiens*) and green frog (*Rana clamitans*) populations in orchard wetlands. I. Genetics, physiology, and biochemistry of breeding adults and young-of-the-year. Environmental Toxicology and Chemistry 17:1338–1350.

Harris, M.L., C.A. Bishop, J. Struger, B. Ripley, and J.P. Bogart. 1988b. The functional integrity of northern leopard frog (*Rana pipiens*) and green frog (*Rana clamitans*) populations in orchard wetlands. II. Effects of pesticides and eutrophic conditions on early life stage development. Environmental Toxicology and Chemistry 17:1351–1363.

Harris, R.N., and P.M. Ludwig. 2004. Resource level and reproductive frequency in female four-toed salamanders, *Hemidactylium scutatum*. Ecology 85:1585–1590.

Haskell, A., T.E. Graham, C.R. Griffin, and J.B. Hestbeck. 1996. Size related survival of headstarted redbelly turtles (*Pseudemys rubriventris*) in Massachusetts. Journal of Herpetology 30:524–527.

Hawley, H. J. 1946. The sea serpent of Silver Lake. New York Folklore Quarterly 2:191–196.

Haxton, T. 2000. Road mortality of snapping turtles, *Chelydra serpentina*, in central Ontario during their nesting period. Canadian Field-Naturalist 114:106–110.

Haxton, T., and M. Berrill. 1999. Habitat selectivity of *Clemmys guttata* in central Ontario. Canadian Journal of Zoology 77:593–599.

Hayes, T., K. Haston, M. Tsui, A. Hoang, C. Haeffele, and A. Vonk. 2003. Atrazine-induced hermaphroditism at 0.1 ppb in American leopard frogs (*Rana pipiens*): Laboratory and field evidence. Environmental Health Perspectives 111:568–575.

Healy, W.R. 1974. Population consequences of alternative life histories in *Notophthalmus v. viridescens*. Copeia 1974:221–229.

Heatwole, H. 1962. Environmental factors influencing local distribution and activity of the salamander, *Plethodon cinereus*. Ecology 43:460–472.

Hecnar, S.J. 1994. Nest distribution, site selection, and brooding in the five-lined skink (*Eumeces fasciatus*). Canadian Journal of Zoology 72:1510–1516.

———. 1995. Acute and chronic toxicity of ammonium nitrate fertilizer to amphibians from southern Ontario. Environmental Toxicology and Chemistry 14:2131–2137.

Hecnar, S.J., and R.T. M'Closkey. 1996. Amphibian species richness and distribution in relation to pond water chemistry in south-western Ontario. Canada Freshwater Biology 36:7–15.

———. 1997. Changes in the composition of a ranid frog community following bullfrog extinction. American Midland Naturalist 137:145–150.

———. 1998. Effects of human disturbance on five-lined skink, *Eumeces fasciatus*, abundance and distribution. Biological Conservation 85:213–222.

Hedeen, S.E. 1977. *Rana septentrionalis*. Catalogue of American Amphibians and Reptiles 202:1–2.

———. 1986. The southern geographic limit of the mink frog, *Rana septentrionalis*. Copeia 1986:239 244.

Hedges, S.B. 1986. An electrophoretic analysis of holarctic hylid frog evolution. Systematic Zoology 35:1–21.

Heinen, J.T. 1994. The significance of color change in newly metamorphosed American toads (*Bufo a. americanus*) Journal of Herpetology 28:87–93.

Hess, Z.J., and R.N. Harris. 2000. Eggs of *Hemidactylium scutatum* (Caudata: Plethodontidae) are unpalatable to insect predators. Copeia 2000:597–600.

Highton, R., G.C. Maha, and L.R. Maxson. 1989. Biochemical evolution in the slimy salamanders of the *Plethodon glutinosus* complex in the eastern United States. University of Illinois Biological Monographs 57:1–153.

Highton, R., and T. Savage. 1961. Functions of the brooding behavior in the female red-backed salamander, *Plethodon cinereus*. Copeia 1961:95–98.

Hileman, K.S., and E.D. Brodie, Jr. 1994. Survival strategies of the salamander *Desmognathus ochrophaeus*: Interaction of predator-avoidance and anti-predator mechanisms. Animal Behaviour 47:1–6.

Hillis, R.E., and E.D. Bellis. 1971. Some aspects of the ecology of the hellbender, *Cryptobranchus alleganiensis alleganiensis* in a Pennsylvania stream. Journal of Herpetology 5:121–126.

Hohn, S.M. 2003. A survey of New York state pet stores to investigate trade in native herpetofauna. Herpetological Review 34:23–27.

Holomuzki, J.R. 1982. Homing behavior of *Desmognathus ochrophaeus* along a stream. Journal of Herpetology 16:307–309.

———. 1995. Oviposition sites and fish-deterrent mechanisms of two stream anurans. Copeia 1995:607–613.

Hom, C.L. 1987. Reproductive ecology of female dusky salamanders, *Desmognathus fuscus* (Plethodontidae), in the southern Appalachians. Copeia 1987: 768–777.

Homan, R.N., J.V. Regosin, D.M. Rodrigues, J.M. Reed, B.S. Windmiller, and L.M. Romero. 2003. Impacts of varying habitat quality on the physiological stress of spotted salamanders (*Ambystoma maculatum*). Animal Conservation 6:11–18.

Homyack, J.D., and W.M. Giuliano. 2002. Effect of streambank fencing on herpetofauna in pasture stream zones. Wildlife Society Bulletin 30:361–369.

Horne, M.T., and W.A. Dunson. 1994. Exclusion of the Jefferson salamander, *Ambystoma jeffersonianum*, from potential breeding ponds in Pennsylvania: Effects of pH, temperature, and metals on embryonic development. Archives of Environmental Contamination and Toxicology 27:323–330.

Hotchkin, P.E., C.D. Camp, and J.L. Marshall. 2001. Aspects of the life history and ecology of the coal skink, *Eumeces anthracinus* in Georgia. Journal of Herpetology 35:145–148.

Howard, R.D. 1978. The influence of male-defended oviposition sites on early embryo mortality in bullfrogs. Ecology 59:789–798.

Howard, R.D., R.S. Moorman, and H.H. Whiteman. 1997. Differential effects of mate competition and mate choice on eastern tiger salamanders. Animal Behaviour 53:1345–1356.

Howard, R.R., and E.D. Brodie, Jr. 1971. Experimental study of mimicry in salamanders involving *Notophthalmus viridescens viridescens* and *Pseudotriton ruber schencki*. Nature 233:277.

Howes, B.J., and S.C. Lougheed. 2004. The importance of cover rock in northern populations of the five-lined skink (*Eumeces fasciatus*). Herpetologica 60:287–294.

Hudson, D.M., and P.L. Lutz. 1986. Salt gland function in the leatherback sea turtle, *Dermochelys coriacea*. Copeia 1986:247–249.

Hudson, R.G. 1955. Observations on the larvae of the salamander *Eurycea bislineata bislineata*. Herpetologica 11:202–204.

Huheey, J.E. 1958. Some feeding habits of the eastern hog-nosed snake. Herpetologica 14:68.

Hulse, A.C., C.J. McCoy, and E. Censky. 2001. Amphibians and Reptiles of Pennsylvania and the Northeast. Comstock Publishing Associates, Ithaca.

Hurd, L.E., G.W. Smedes, and T.A. Dean. 1979. An ecological study of a natural population of diamondback terrapins (*Malaclemys t. terrapin*) in a Delaware salt marsh. Estuaries 2:28–33.

Ireland, P.H. 1989. Larval survivorship in two populations of *Ambystoma maculatum*. Journal of Herpetology 23:209–215.

Irwin, J.T., J.P. Costanzo, and R.E. Lee, Jr. 1999. Terrestrial hibernation in the northern cricket frog, *Acris crepitans*. Canadian Journal of Zoology 77:1240–1246.

Jackson, M.E., D.E. Scott, and R.E. Estes. 1989. Determinants of nest success in the marbled salamander (*Ambystoma opacum*). Canadian Journal of Zoology 67:2277–2281.

Jacger, R.G. 1978. Plant climbing by salamanders: Periodic availability of plant dwelling prey. Copeia 1978:686–691.

382 Literature Cited

———. 1984. Agonistic behavior of the red-backed salamander. Copeia 1984: 309–314.

Jaeger, R.G. and W.F. Gergits. 1979. Intra- and interspecific communication in salamanders through chemical signals on the substrate. Animal Behaviour 27: 150–156.

Jaeger R.G., J.K. Schwartz, and S.E. Wise. 1995a. Territorial male salamanders have foraging tactics attractive to gravid females. Animal Behaviour 49:633–639.

Jaeger, R.G., J.A. Wicknick, M.R. Griffs, and C.D. Anthony. 1995b. Socioecology of a terrestrial salamander: Juveniles enter adult territories during stressful foraging periods. Ecology 76:533–543.

Jansen, K.P., A.P. Summers, and P.R. Delis. 2001. Spadefoot toads (*Scaphiopus holbrookii holbrookii*) in an urban landscape: Effects of nonnatural substrates on burrowing in adults and juveniles. Journal of Herpetology 35:141–145.

Janzen, F.J. 1994. Vegetational cover predicts the sex ratio of hatching turtles in natural nests. Ecology 75:1593–1599.

Jensen, H.N. 2004. Herpetofaunal interactions with wetland vegetation as mediated by regulation of St. Lawrence River water levels. M.S. Thesis, S.U.N.Y. Coll. Environ. Sci. and Forestry, Syracuse, New York.

Jofre, M.B., and W.H. Karasov. 1999. Direct effect of ammonia on three species of North American anuran amphibians. Environmental Toxicology and Chemistry 18:1806–1812.

Johansen, B.E., and B.A. Mann. 2000. Encyclopedia of the Haudenosaunee (Iroquois Confederacy). Greenwood Press, Westport, Connecticut.

Johnson, G. 1995. Spatial ecology, habitat preferences, and habitat management of the eastern massasauga, *Sistrurus c. catenatus*, in a New York transition peatland. Ph.D. Thesis, S.U.N.Y. Coll. Environ. Sci. and Forestry, Syracuse, New York.

———. 2000. Spatial ecology of the eastern massasauga (*Sistrurus c. catenatus*) in a New York peatland. Journal of Herpetology, 34:186–192.

Johnson, G., and A.R. Breisch. 1993. The eastern massasauga rattlesnake in New York: Occurrence and habitat management. Pages 48–54 In: Proceedings of the International Symposium and Workshop on the Conservation of the Eastern Massasauga Rattlesnake, *Sistrurus catenatus catenatus* (B. Johnson and V. Menzies, editors). Metro Toronto Zoo, West Hill, Ontario. 136 pp.

Johnson, G., and D.J. Leopold. 1998. Habitat management for the eastern massasauga in a central New York peatland. Journal of Wildlife Management. 62:84–97.

Johnson, G., and T.C. Wills. 1997. *Emydoidea blandingii* (Blanding's turtle). Herpetological Review 28:209.

Johnson, J.R., and R.D. Semlitsch. 2003. Defining core habitat of local populations of the gray treefrog (*Hyla versicolor*) based on choice of oviposition site. Oecologia 137:205–210.

Johnson, W.S., and E.F. Yearicks. 1981. Hibernation of the northern diamondback terrapin, *Malaclemys terrapin terrapin*. Estuaries 4:78–80.

Joyal, L.A., M. McCollough, and M.L. Hunter, Jr. 2000. Population structure and reproductive ecology of Blanding's turtle (*Emydoidea blandingii*) in

Maine near the northeastern edge of its range. Chelonian Conservation and Biology 3:580–588.

———. 2001. Landscape ecology approaches to wetland species conservation: A case study of two species in southern Maine. Conservation Biology 15:1755–1762.

Judd, W.W. 1954. Observations on the food of the little brown snake, *Storeria dekayi*, at London, Ontario. Copeia 1954:62–64.

———. 1957. The food of Jefferson's salamander, *Ambystoma jeffersonianum*, in Rondeau Park, Ontario. Ecology 38:77–81.

Juterbock, J.E. 1987. The nesting behavior of the dusky salamander, *Desmognathus fuscus*. II. Nest site tenacity and disturbance. Herpetologica 43:361–368.

Kaminsky, S.K. 1997. *Bufo americanus* (American toad) reproduction. Herpetological Review 28:84.

Kaplan, R.H., and M.L. Crump. 1978. The non-cost of brooding in *Ambystoma opacum*. Copeia 1978:99–103.

Karlin, A.A., and S.I. Guttman. 1981. Hybridization between *Desmognathus fuscus* and *Desmognathus ochrophaeus* (Amphibia: Urodela: Plethodontidae) in northeastern Ohio and northwestern Pennsylvania. Copeia 1981:371–377.

Kaufmann, J.H. 1992a. Habitat use by wood turtles in central Pennsylvania. Journal of Herpetology 26:315–321.

———. 1992b. Home ranges and movements of wood turtles, *Clemmys insculpta*, in central Pennsylvania. Copeia 1995:22–27.

Keen, W.H. 1979. Feeding and activity patterns in the salamander *Desmognathus ochrophaeus* (Amphibia, Urodela, Plethodontidae). Journal of Herpetology 14:461–467.

Keen, W.H., and L.P. Orr. 1980. Reproductive cycle, growth, and maturation of northern female *Desmognathus ochrophaeus*. Journal of Herpetology 14:7–10.

Khan, R.N., and M.G. Frick. 1997. *Erpobdella punctata* (Hirudinea: Erpobdellidae) as phoronts on *Ambystoma maculatum* (Amphibia: Ambystomatidae). Journal of Natural History 31:157–161.

Kieran, J. 1959. Natural history of New York City. Houghton Mifflin, New York City.

Kiesecker, J.M., A. R. Blaustein, and C.L. Miller. 2001. Potential mechanisms underlying the displacement of native red-legged frogs by introduced bullfrogs. Ecology 82:1964–1970.

Kingsbury, B., and J. Gibson. 2002. Habitat management guidelines for amphibians and reptiles of the Midwest. Partners in Reptile and Amphibian Conservation.

Kinneary, J.J. 1993. Salinity relations of *Chelydra serpentina* in a Long Island estuary. Journal of Herpetology 27:441–446.

Kiviat, E.A. 1997. Blanding's turtle habitat requirements and implications for conservation in Dutchess County, New York. Pages 377–382 In: Proceedings of the 1993 International Conference 11–16 July 1993, State University of New York at Purchase.

———. 1980. Hudson River tidemarsh snapping turtle population. Transactions of the Northeast Sections of the Wildlife Society 37:158–168.

Kiviat, E., and J.G. Barbour. 1996. Wood turtles, *Clemmys insculpta*, in the freshtidal Hudson River. Canadian Field-Naturalist Ottawa 110:341–343.

Kiviat, E., and J. Stapleton. 1983. *Bufo americanus* (American toad) estuarine habitat. Herpetological Review 14:46.

Kiviat, E., and G. Stevens. 2003. Environmental deterioration of the outwash plains: Necropsy of a landscape. News from Hudsonia, 18:3–5.

Kiviat, E., G. Stevens, R. Brauman, S. Hoeger, P.J. Petokas, and G.G. Hollands. 2000. Restoration of wetland and upland habitat for Blanding's turtle, *Emydoidea blandingii*. Chelonian Conservation Biology, 3:650–657.

Kjoss, V.A., and J.A. Litvaitis. 2001. Community structure of snakes in a human-dominated landscape. Biological Conservation 98:285–292.

Klemens, M.K. 1993. Amphibians and reptiles of Connecticut and adjacent regions. State Geological and Natural History Survey of Connecticut, Bulletin No. 112.

———. 2001. Bog turtle (*Clemmys muhlenbergii*) northern population recovery plan. US Fish and Wildlife Service. 110 pp.

Klemens, M.W., E. Kiviat, and R.E. Schmidt. 1987. Distribution of the northern leopard frog, *Rana pipiens*, in the lower Hudson and Housatonic River valleys. Northeastern Environmental Science 6:99–101.

Klimstra, W.D. 1959. Foods of the racer, *Coluber constrictor*, in southern Illinois. Copeia 1959:210–214.

Knapp, S.M., C.A. Haas, D.N. Harpole, and R.L. Kirkpatrick. 2003. Initial effects of clearcutting and alternative silvicultural practices on terrestrial salamander abundance. Conservation Biology 17:752–762.

Knutson, M.G., W.B. Richardson, D.M. Reineke, B.R. Gray, J.R. Parmelee, and S.E. Weick. 2004. Agricultural ponds support amphibian populations. Ecological Applications 14:669–684.

Knutson, M.G., J.R. Sauer, D.A. Olsen, M.J. Mossman, L.M. Hemesath, and M.J. Lannoo. 2000. Landscape associations of frog and toad species in Iowa and Wisconsin, USA. Journal of the Iowa Academy of Science 107:134–145.

Koffler, B.R., R.A. Seigel, M.T. Mendonca, and B.R. Koffler. 1978. The seasonal occurrence of leeches on the wood turtle, *Clemmys insculpta* (Reptilia, Testudines, Emydidae). Journal of Herpetology 12:571–572.

Kolbe, J.J., and F.J. Janzen. 2002. Impact of nest-site selection on nest success and nest temperature in natural and disturbed habitats. Ecology 83:269–281.

Kolozsvary, M.B., and R.K. Swihart. 1999. Habitat fragmentation and the distribution of amphibians: Patch and landscape correlates in farmland. Canadian Journal of Zoology 77:1288–1299.

Kramek, W.C. 1976. Feeding behavior of *Rana septentrionalis* (Amphibia, Anura, Ranidae). Journal of Herpetology 10:251–252.

Kraus, F., P.K. Ducey, P. Moler, and M. M. Miyamoto. 1991. Two new triparental unisexual *Ambystoma* from Ohio and Michigan. Herpetologica 47:429–439.

Krawchuk, M.A., N. Koper, and R.J. Brooks. 1997. Observations of a possible cleaning symbiosis between painted turtles, *Chrysemys picta* and snapping turtles, *Chelydra serpentina*, in central Ontario. Canadian Field-Naturalist 111:315–317.

Kroll, J.C. 1976. Feeding adaptations of hognose snakes. Southwestern Naturalist 20:537–557.

Krzysik, A.J. 1979. Resource allocation, coexistance, and the niche structure of a streambank salamander community. Ecological Monographs 49:173–194.

Kumpf, K.F.., and S.C. Yeaton, Jr. 1932. Observations on the courtship behavior of *Ambystoma jeffersonianum*. American Museum Novitates 546:1–7.

Labanick, G.M. 1976. Prey availability, consumption and selection in the cricket frog, *Acris crepitans* (Amphibia, Anura, Hylidae). Journal of Herpetology 10: 293–298.

Lachner, E.A. 1942. An aggregation of snakes and salamanders during hibernation. Copeia 1942:262–263.

Lamoureux, V.S., and D.M. Madison. 1999. Overwintering habitats of radio-implanted green frogs, *Rana clamitans*. Journal of Herpetology 33:430–435.

Lamoureux, V.S., J.C. Maerz, and D.M. Madison. 2002. Premigratory autumn foraging forays in the green frog, *Rana clamitans*. Journal of Herpetology, 36:245–254.

Lancaster, D.L. and S.E. Wise. 1996. Differential response by the ringneck snake, *Diadophis punctatus*, to odors of tail-autotomizing prey. Herpetologica 52: 98–108.

Larson, M.R. 1962. The taller the better. New York Folklore Quarterly 18:217–234.

Latham, R. 1968a. Common snapping turtles in combat. Engelhardtia 1:28.

———. 1968b. Fungus-eating habits of the eastern box turtle on Long Island. Engelhardtia 1:12.

———. 1968c. Notes on some hibernating Fowler's toads. Engelhardtia 1:17.

———. 1969. Sea turtles recorded in the Southold Township region of Long Island. Engelhardtia 2:7.

———. 1971. Fishermen pay bounty on turtles. Engelhardtia 4:53.

Laurin, M., and R.R. Reisz. 1995. A reevaluation of early amniote phylogeny. Zoological Journal of the Linnean Society 113:165–223.

Layne, J.R., Jr., and A.L. Jones. 2001. Freeze tolerance in the gray treefrog: Cryoprotectant mobilization and organ dehydration. Journal of Experimental 290:1–5.

Layne, J.R., Jr., and J. Kefauver. 1997. Freeze tolerance and postfreeze recovery in the frog *Pseudacris crucifer*. Copeia 1997:260–264.

Lazell, J.D. 1980. New England waters: Critical habitat for marine turtles. Copeia 1980:290–295.

Lee, S.M. 2004. Repatriation and health assessment of eastern box turtles (*Terrapene c. carolina*) at Caumsett State Park, New York. M.S. Thesis, Hofstra University.

Lehtinen, R.M., and S.M. Galatowitsch. 2001. Colonization of restored wetlands by amphibians in Minnesota. American Midland Naturalist 145:388–396.

Levell, J.P. 2000. Commercial exploitation of Blanding's turtle, *Emydoidea blandingii*, and the wood turtle, *Clemmys insculpta*, for the live animal trade. Chelonian Conservation and Biology 3:665–674.

Lewis, T.L., J.M. Ullmer, and J.L. Mazza. 2004. Threats to spotted turtle (*Clemmys guttata*) habitat in Ohio. The Ohio Journal of Science 104:65–71.

Linzey, D.W. 1967. Food of the leopard frog, *Rana p. pipiens* in central New York. Herpetologica 23:11–17.

Littler, J. 1958. The Empeyville frog. New York Folklore Quarterly 14:146–474.

Litzgus, J.D., and R.J. Brooks. 1998. Growth in a cold environment: Body size and sexual maturity in a northern population of spotted turtles, *Clemmys guttata*. Canadian Journal of Zoology 76:773–782.

———. 2000. Habitat and temperature selection of *Clemmys guttata* in a northern population. Journal of Herpetology 34:178–185.

Litzgus, J.D., J.P. Costanzo, R.J. Brooks, and R.E. Lee, Jr. 1999. Phenology and ecology of hibernation in spotted turtles (*Clemmys guttata*) near the northern limit of their range. Canadian Journal of Zoology 77:1348–1357.

Lotter, F., and N.J. Scott, Jr. 1977. Correlation between climate and distribution of the color morphs of the salamander *Plethodon cinereus*. Copeia 1977:681–690.

Lovich, J.E., and J.W. Gibbons. 1990. Age at maturity influences adult sex ratio in the turtle *Malaclemys terrapin*. Oikos 59:126–134.

Lowe, W.H., and D.T. Bolger. 2002. Local and landscape-scale predictors of salamander abundance in New Hampshire streams. Conservation Biology 16: 183–193.

Lowe, W.H., K.H. Nislow, and D.T. Bolger. 2004. Stage-specific and interactive effects of sedimentation and trout on a headwater stream salamander. Ecological Applications 14:164–172.

Lykens, D.V., and D.C. Forester. 1987. Age structure in the spring peeper: Do males advertise longevity? Herpetologica 43:216–223.

Macauley, J. 1829. The natural, statistical and civil history of the State of New York in three volumes. Volume 1:430–520.

MacNamara, M.C. 1977. Food habits of terrestrial adult migrants and immature red efts of the red-spotted newt *Notophthalmus viridescens*. Herpetologica 33:127–132.

MacNamara, M.C., and W.N. Harman. 1975. Further studies of the Mollusca of the Otsego Lake area. Nautilus 89:87–90.

Madison, D.M. 1997. The emigration of radio-implanted spotted salamanders, *Ambystoma maculatum*. Journal of Herpetology 31:542–552.

———. 1998. Habitat-contingent reproductive behaviour in radio-implanted salamanders: A model and test. Animal Behaviour 55:1203–1210.

Madison, D.M., and L. Farrand, III. 1998. Habitat use during breeding and emigration in radio-implanted tiger salamanders, *Ambystoma tigrinum*. Copeia 1998:402–410.

Maerz, J.C., B. Blossey, and V. Nuzzo. 2005a. Green frogs show reduced foraging success in habitats invaded by Japanese knotweed. Biodiversity and Conservation 14:2901–2911.

Maerz, J.C., C.J. Brown, C.T. Chapin, and B. Blossey. 2005b. Can secondary compounds of an invasive plant affect larval amphibians? Functional Ecology 19:970–975.

Maerz, J.C., and D.M. Madison. 2000. Environmental variation and territorial behavior in a terrestrial salamander. Pages 395–406 In: The biology of plethodontid salamanders (R.C. Bruce, R.G. Jaeger, and L.D. Houck, editors). Kluwer Academic/Plenum Publishers, New York.

Maisonneuve, C., and S. Rioux. 2001. Importance of riparian habitats for small mammal and herpetofaunal communities in agricultural landscapes of southern Quebec. Agriculture, Ecosystems and Environment 83:165–175.

Marchand, M.N., and J.A. Litvaitis. 2004. Effects of habitat features and landscape composition on the population structure of a common aquatic turtle in a region undergoing rapid development. Conservation Biology 18:758–767.

Marganoff, B.I. 1969. Northern diamondback terrapins scarred by motor craft. Engelhardtia 2:34.

Martin, W.H. 1993. Reproduction of the timber rattlesnake (*Crotalus horridus*) in the Appalachian Mountains. Journal of Herpetology 27:133–143.

Martof, B.S. 1970. *Rana sylvatica*. Catalogue of American Amphibians and Reptiles 86:1–4.

Mason, R.T, and D. Crews. 1985. Female mimicry in garter snakes. Nature 316:59–60.

Mathis, A. 1991. Large male advantage for access to females: Evidence of male-male competition and female discrimination in a territorial salamander. Behavioral Ecology and Sociobiology 29:133–138.

Mathis, A., R.G. Jaeger, W.H. Keen, P.K. Ducey, S.C. Walls, and B.W. Buchanan. 1995. Aggression and territoriality by salamanders and a comparison with the territorial behavior of frogs. Pages 633–676 In: Amphibian Biology, Vol. 2, Social Behaviour (H. Heatwole and B. K. Sullivan, editors). Surrey Beatty and Sons. Chipping Norton, NSW, Australia.

Mays, C.E., and M.A. Nickerson. 1973. A population study of the Ozark hellbender salamander, *Cryptobranchus alleganiensis bishopi*. Proceedings of the Indian Academy of Sciences (Math. Sci.) 81:339–340.

McAlister, W.H. 1963. Evidence of mild toxicity in the saliva of the hognose snake (*Heterodon*). Herpetologica 19:132–137.

McAllister, A.J. 1995. Wetland habitat use by the black rat snake, *Elaphe obsoleta*, in eastern Ontario. Canadian Field-Naturalist 109:449–451.

McCoy, C.J. 1982. Amphibians and reptiles in Pennsylvania: Checklist, bibliography and atlas distribution. Carnegie Museum of Natural History Special Publication Number 6.

McGregor, J.H., and W.R. Teska. 1989. Olfaction as an orientation mechanism in migrating *Ambystoma maculatum*. Copeia 1989:779–781.

McKinley, D.L. 2005. James Eights; 1798–1882. Antarctic Explorer, Albany Naturalist, His Life, His Times, His Works. New York State Museum Bulletin 505. University of the State of New York, Albany, NY 455pp.

McLeod, R.F., and J.E. Gates. 1998. Response of herpetofaunal communities to forest cutting and burning at Chesapeake Farms, Maryland. American Midland Naturalist 139:164–177.

Mecham, J.S. 1967. *Notophthalmus viridescens*. Catalogue of American Amphibians and Reptiles 53:1–4.

Meeks, R.L. 1990. Overwintering behavior of snapping turtles. Copeia 1990:880–884.

Merovich, C.E., and J.H. Howard. 2000. Amphibian use of constructed ponds on Maryland's eastern shore. Journal of the Iowa Academy of Science 107:151–159.

Merrell, D.J. 1977. Life History of the Leopard Frog, *Rana pipiens*, in Minnesota. Bell Museum of Natural History, University of Minnesota, Minneapolis, Minnesota.

Merrill, A. 1957. Old legends never die. New York Folklore Quarterly 13:54–62.

Messere, M., and P.K. Ducey. 1998. Forest floor distribution of northern redback salamanders, *Plethodon cinereus*, in relation to canopy gaps: First year following selective logging. Forest Ecology and Management 107:319–323.

Michener, M.C., and J.D. Lazell, Jr. 1989. Distribution and relative abundance of the hognose snake *Heterodon platyrhinos*, in eastern New England. Journal of Herpetology 23:35–40.

Milam, J.C., and S.M. Melvin. 2001. Density, habitat use, movements, and conservation of spotted turtles (*Clemmys guttata*) in Massachusetts. Journal of Herpetology 35:418–427.

Miller, K., and V.H. Hutchison. 1979. Activity metabolism in the mudpuppy, *Necturus maculosus*. Physiological Zoology 52:22–37.

Mills, M.S., and S.R. Yeomans. 1993. *Heterodon platirhinos* (eastern hognose snake) diet. Herpetological Review 24:62.

Minton, S.A., Jr., and M. R. Minton 1969. Venomous reptiles. Charles Scribner's Sons, New York.

Mitchell, J.C. 1974. Statistics of *Chrysemys rubriventris* hatchlings from Middlesex County, Virginia. Herpetological Review 5:71.

Mitchell, J.C., A.R. Breisch, and K.A. Buhlmann. 2006. Habitat management guidelines for amphibians and reptiles of the northeastern United States. Partners in Amphibian and Reptile Conservation, Technical Publication HMG-3.

Mitro, M.G. 2003. Demography and viability analyses of a diamondback terrapin population. Canadian Journal of Zoology 81:716–726.

Moreno, G. 1989. Behavioral and physiological differentiation between the color morphs of the salamander, *Plethodon cinereus*. Journal of Herpetology 23: 335–341.

Moriarty, E.C., and D.C. Cannatella. 2004. Phylogenetic relationships of the North American chorus frogs (Pseudacris: Hylidae). Molecular Phylogenetics and Evolution 30:409–420.

Moriarty, J.J. and A.M. Bauer. 2000. State and provincial amphibian and reptile publications for the United States and Canada. SSAR Herpetological Circular 28.

Morreale, S.J., A.B. Meylan, S.S. Sadove, and E.A. Standora. 1992. Annual occurrence and winter mortality of marine turtles in New York waters. Journal of Herpetology 26:301–308.

Morrow, J.L., J.H. Howard, D.K. Poppel, D.K. Poppel, and S.A. Smith. 2001. Home range and movements of the bog turtle (*Clemmys muhlenbergii*) in Maryland. Journal of Herpetology 35:68–73.

Mullin, S.J. 1999. Caudal distraction by rat snakes (*Colubridae, Elaphe*): A novel behavior used when capturing mammalian prey. Great Basin Naturalist 59: 361–367.

Mushinsky, H.R., and E.D. Brodie, Jr. 1975. Selection of substrate pH by salamanders. American Midland Naturalist 93:440–443.

Myers, C.W. 2000. A history of herpetology at the American Museum of Natural History. Bulletin of the American Museum of Natural History 252:1–232.

Myers, E.M., and K.R. Zamudio. 2004. Multiple paternity in an aggregate breeding amphibian: The effect of reproductive skew on estimates of male reproductive success. Molecular Ecology 13:1951–1963.

Naiman R.J., J.M. Melillo, and J.E. Hobbie. 1986. Ecosystem alteration of boreal forest streams by beaver (*Castor canadensis*). Ecology 67:1254–1269.

Nichols, J.T. 1939. Range and homing of individual box turtles. Copeia 1939: 125–7.

———. 1947. Notes on the mud turtle. Herpetologica 3:147–148.

Nickerson, M.A. 2000. *Sternotherus odoratus* (common musk turtle) aerial basking. Herpetological Review 31:238–239.

Nickerson, M.A., K.L. Krysko, and R.D. Owen. 2003. Habitat differences affecting age class distributions of the hellbender salamander, *Cryptobranchus alleganiensis*. Southeastern Naturalist 2:619–629.

Niewiarowski, P.H. 1995. Effects of supplemental feeding and thermal environment on growth rates of eastern fence lizards, *Sceloporus undulatus*. Herpetologica 51:487–496.

Noble, G.K. 1926. The Long Island newt: A contribution to the life history of *Triturus viridescens*. American Museum Novitates 228:1–11.

Noble, G.K., and M.K. Brady. 1933. Observations on the life history of the marbled salamander, *Ambystoma opacum* Gravenhorst. Zoologica 11:89–132.

Noble, G.K., and H.J. Clausen. 1936. The aggregation behavior of *Storeria dekayi* and other snakes, with special reference to the sense organs involved. Ecological Monographs 6:269–316.

Oliverio, M., R.L. Burke, M.A. Bologna, A. Wirz, and P. Mariottini. 2001. Molecular identification of native (Italy) and introduced (USA) *Podarcis sicula* populations (Reptilia, Lacertidae). Italian Journal of Zoology 68:121–124.

Organ, J.A., and D.J. Organ. 1968. Courtship behavior of the red salamander, *Pseudotriton ruber*. Copeia 1968:217–223.

Orser, P.M., and D.J. Shure. 1975. Population cycles and activity patterns of the dusky salamander, *Desmognathus fuscus fuscus*. American Midland Naturalist 93:403–410.

Oseen, K.I., and R.I. Wassersug. 2002. Environmental factors influencing calling in sympatric anurans. Oecologia 133:616–625.

Pace, A.E. 1974. Systematic and biological studies of the leopard frogs (*Rana pipiens* complex) of the United States. Miscellaneous Publications of the Museum of Zoology, University of Michigan 148:1–140.

Packard, G.C., and M.J. Packard. 2002. Cold-tolerance of hatchling painted turtles (*Chrysemys picta bellii*) from the southern limit of distribution. Journal of Herpetology 36:300–304.

Packard, G.C., M.J. Packard, J.W. Lang, and J.K. Tucker. 1999. Tolerance for freezing in hatchling turtles. Journal of Herpetology 33:536–543.

Packard, G.C., J.K. Tucker, D. Nicholson, and M.J. Packard. 1997. Cold tolerance in hatching slider turtles (*Trachemys scripta*). Copeia 1997:339–345.

Pagano, J.J, P.A. Rosenbaum, R.N. Roberts, G.M. Sumner, and L.V. Williamson. 1999. Qualitative and quantitative assessment of maternal contaminant burden by analysis of snapping turtle eggs. Journal of Great Lakes Research 25:950–961.

Palis, J.G. 2000. *Scaphiopus holbrookii* (eastern spadefoot) predation. Herpetological Review 31:42–43.

Parent, C., and P.J. Weatherhead. 2000. Behavioral and life history responses of eastern massasauga rattlesnakes (*Sistrurus catenatus catenatus*) to human disturbance. Oecologia 125:170–178.

Parham, J.F., and C.R. Feldman. 2000. Generic revisions of Emydine turtles. Turtle and Tortoise Newsletter 6:28–30

Park, D., S.C. Hempleman, and C.R. Propper. 2001. Endosulfan exposure disrupts pheromonal systems in the red-spotted newt: A mechanism for subtle effects of environmental chemicals. Environmental Health Perspectives 109:669–673.

Parren, S.G., and M.A. Rice. 2004. Terrestrial overwintering of hatchling turtles in Vermont nests. Northeastern Naturalist 11:229–233.

Parris, M.J. 1998. Terrestrial burrowing ecology of newly metamorphosed frogs (*Rana pipiens* complex). Canadian Journal of Zoology 76:2124–2129.

Paton, P.W., and W.B. Crouch. 2002. Using the phenology of pond-breeding amphibians to develop conservation strategies. Conservation Biology 16:194–204.

Peacor, S.D., and E.E. Werner. 2000. Predator effects on an assemblage of consumers through induced changes in consumer foraging behavior. Ecology 81:1998–2010.

Pearse, D.I., F.I. Janzen, and J.I. Avise. 2002. Multiple paternity, sperm storage, and reproductive success of female and male painted turtles (*Chrysemys picta*) in nature. Behavioral Ecology and Sociobiology 51:164–171.

Pell, S.M. 1940. Notes on the food habits of the common snapping turtle. Copeia 1940:131.

Peterson, C.L. 1987. Movement and catchability of the hellbender, *Cryptobranchus alleganiensis*. Journal of Herpetology 21:197–204

Petokas, P.J. 1981. Snapping turtle predation on Ring-billed gulls. Maryland Herpetological Society Bulletin 17:111–115.

Petokas, P.J., and M.M. Alexander. 1980. The nesting of *Chelydra serpentina* in northen New York. Journal of Herpetology 14:239–244.

Petokas, P.J,. and M.M. Alexander. 1981. Occurrence of the Blanding's turtle in northern New York. New York Fish and Game Journal 28:119–120.

Petranka, J.W. 1990. Observations on nest site selection, nest desertion, and embryonic survival in marbled salamanders. Journal of Herpetology 24:229–234.

———. 1998. Salamanders of the United States and Canada. Smithsonian Institution Press, Washington.

Petranka, J.W., J.J. Just, and E.C. Crawford. 1982. Hatching of amphibian embryos: The physiological trigger. Science 217:257–259.

Petranka, J.W., C.A. Kennedy, and S.M. Murray. 2003. Response of amphibians to restoration of a southern Appalachian wetland: A long-term analysis of community dynamics. Wetlands 23:1030–1042.

Petranka, J.W. and S.M. Murray. 2001. Effectiveness of removal sampling for determining salamander density and biomass: A case study in an Appalachian streamside community. Journal of Herpetology 35:36–44.

Petranka, J.W., and J.G. Petranka. 1980. Selected aspects of the larval ecology of the marbled salamander *Ambystoma opacum* in the southern portion of its range. American Midland Naturalist 104:352–363.

————. 1981. On the evolution of nest selection in the marbled salamander, *Ambystoma opacum*. Copeia 1981:387–391.

Petranka, J.W., and D.A.G. Thomas. 1995. Explosive breeding reduces egg and tadpole cannibalism in the wood frog, *Rana sylvatica*. Animal Behaviour 50:731–739.

Pfingsten, R.A., and F.L. Downs. 1989. Salamanders of Ohio. Bulletin of the Ohio Biological Survey Vol. 7, No. 2. College of Biological Sciences, The Ohio State University, Columbus, Ohio.

Pinder, A.W., and S.C. Friet. 1994. Oxygen transport in egg masses of the amphibians *Rana sylvatica* and *Ambystoma maculatum*: Convection, diffusion and oxygen production by algae. Journal of Experimental Biology 197: 17–30.

Pisani, G.R., and R.C. Bothner. 1970. The annual reproductive cycle of *Thamnophis brachystoma*. Science Studies 26:15–34.

Platt, D.R. 1969. Natural history of the hognose snakes *Heterodon platyrhinos* and *Heterodon nasicus*. University of Kansa Publications of the Museum of Natrual History 18:253–420.

Plummer, M.V., and J.W. Goy. 1997. *Sternotherus odoratus* (common musk turtle) mortality. Herpetological Review 28:88.

Plummer, M.V., and N.E. Mills. 1996. Observations on trailing and mating behaviors of hognose snakes (*Heterodon platirhinos*). Journal of Herpetology 30: 80–82.

————. 2000. Spatial ecology and survivorship of resident and translocated hognose snakes (*Heterodon platirhinos*). Journal of Herpetology 34:565–575.

Porej, D., M. Micacchion, and T.E. Hetherington. 2004. Core terrestrial habitat for conservation of local populations of salamanders and wood frogs in agricultural landscapes. Biological Conservation 120:399–409.

Portnoy, J.W. 1990. Breeding biology of the spotted salamander *Ambystoma maculatum* (Shaw) in acidic temporary ponds at Cape Cod, USA. Biological Conservation 53:61–75.

Pough, F.H. 1971. Leech-repellent property of eastern red-spotted newts, *Notophthalmus viridescens*. Science 174:1144–1146.

Pough, F.H., E.M. Smith, D.H. Rhodes, and A. Collazo. 1987. The abundance of salamanders in forest stands with different histories of disturbance. Forest Ecology and Management 20:1–9.

Pough, F.H., R.M. Andrews, J.E.Cadle, M.L. Crump, A.H. Savitzky, and K.D. Wells. 2004. Herpetology, 3rd Ed. Pearson Prentice Hall, Upper Saddle River, New Jersey.

Pough, F.H., and R.E. Wilson. 1977. Acid precipitation and reproductive success of *Ambystoma* salamanders. Water Air and Soil Pollution 7:307–316.

Pounds, J.A., R. Martín, L.A. Bustamante, L.A. Coloma, J.A. Consuegra, M.P.L. Fogden, P.N. Foster, E. La Marca, K.L. Masters, A. Merino-Viteri, R. Puschendorf, T. Santiago R., G.A. Sánchez-Azofeifa, C.J. Still, and B. E. Young. 2006. Widespread amphibian extinctions from epidemic disease driven by global warming. Nature 439:161–167.

Prior, K.A., and P.J. Weatherhead. 1996. Habitat features of black rat snake hibernacula in Ontario. Journal of Herpetology 30:211–218.

Pryor, G.S. 1996. Observations of shorebird predation by snapping turtles in eastern Lake Ontario. Wilson Bulletin 108:190–192.

Purgue, A.P. 1997. Tympanic sound radiation in the bullfrog *Rana catesbeiana*. Journal of Comparative Physiology, A 181:438–445.

Ralin, D.B. 1968. Ecological and reproductive differentiation in the cryptic species of *Hyla versicolor* complex (Hylidae). Southwestern Naturalist 13:283–300.

Raney, E.C., and E.A. Lachner. 1942. Summer food of *Chrysemys picta marginata*, in Chautauqua Lake, New York. Copeia 1942:83–85.

Raney, E.C., and R.M. Roecker. 1947. Food and growth of two species of watersnakes from western New York. Copeia 1947:171–174.

Reese, S.A., C.E. Crocker, M.E. Carwile, D.C. Jackson, and G.R. Ultsch. 2001. The physiology of hibernation in common map turtles. Comparative Biochemistry and Physiology, A 130:331–340.

Reese, S.A., D.C. Jackson, and G.R. Ultsch. 2003. Hibernation in freshwater turtles: Softshell turtles (*Apalone spinifera*) are the most intolerant of anoxia among North American species. Journal of Comparative Physiology, B 173: 263–268.

Regosin, J.V., B.S. Windmiller, and J.M. Reed. 2003a. Influence of abundance of small-mammal burrows and conspecifics on the density and distribution of spotted salamanders (*Ambystoma maculatum*) in terrestrial habitats. Canadian Journal of Zoology 81:596–605.

———. 2003b. Terrestrial habitat use and winter densities of the wood frog (*Rana sylvatica*). Journal of Herpetology 37:390–394.

Reilly, E.M., Jr. 1955. Snakes of New York. Conservationist 9(6):22–26.

Reilly, E.M., Jr. 1957. Salamanders and lizards of New York. Conservationist 11(6):23–28, 35.

Reilly, E.M., Jr. 1958. Turtles of New York. Conservationist 12(6):22–27.

Reinert, H.E., D. Cundall, and L.M. Bushar. 1984. Foraging behavior of the timber rattlesnake, *Crotalus horridus*. Copeia 1984:1057–1059.

Reinert, H.E., and W.R. Kodrich. 1982. Movements and habitat utilization by the massasauga, *Sistrurus catenatus catenatus*. Journal of Herpetology 16:162–171.

Relyea, R.A., and J.T. Hoverman. 2003. The impact of larval predators and competitors on the morphology and fitness of juvenile treefrogs. Oecologia 134: 596–604.

Renken, R.B., W.K. Gram, D.K. Fantz, S.C. Richter, T.J. Miller, K.B. Ricke, B. Russell, and X. Wang. 2004. Effects of forest management on amphibians and reptiles in Missouri Ozark forests. Conservation Biology 18:174–188.

Reschke, C. 1990. Ecological communities of New York State. New York Natural Heritage Program, Department of Environmental Conservation, Latham, New York.

Resetarits, W.J., Jr. 1995. Competitive asymmetry and coexistence in size-structured populations of brook trout and spring salamanders. Oikos 73: 188–198.

Richmond, N.D. 1947. Life history of *Scaphiopus holbrookii holbrookii* (Harlan). Part I: Larval development and behavior. Ecology 28:53–67.

Richter, S.C. 2000. Larval caddisfly predation on the eggs and embryos of *Rana capito* and *Rana sphenocephala*. Journal of Herpetology 34:590–593.

Rittmann, S.E., E. Muths, and D.E. Green. 2003. *Pseudacris triseriata* (western chorus frog) and *Rana sylvatica* (wood frog) Chytridiomycosis. Herpetological Review 34:53.

Roe, J.H., B.A. Kingsbury, and N.R. Herbert. 2004. Comparative water snake ecology: Conservation of mobile animals that use temporally dynamic resources. Biological Conservation 118:79–89.

Roggenbuck, M.E., and T.A. Jenssen. 1986. The ontogeny of display behavior in *Sceloporus undulatus* (Sauri: Iguanidae). Ethology 71:153–165.

Rohr, J.R., and D.M. Madison. 2003. Dryness increases predation risk in efts: Support for an amphibian decline hypothesis. Oecologia 135:657–664.

Roman, J. and B.W. Bowen. 2000. The mock turtle syndrome: Genetic identification of turtle meat purchased in the south-eastern United States of America. Animal Conservation 3:61–65.

Roosenburg, W.M., W. Cresko, M. Modesitte, and M.B. Robbins. 1997. Diamondback terrapin (*Malaclemys terrapin*) mortality in crab pots. Conservation Biology 11:1166–1172.

Roosenburg, W.M., and J.P. Green. 2000. Impact of a bycatch reduction device on diamondback terrapin and blue crab capture in crab pots. Ecological Applications 10:882–889.

Rosen, P.C. 1991. Comparative ecology and life history of the racer (*Coluber constrictor*) in Michigan. Copeia 1991:897–909.

Rosen, M., and R.E. Lemon. 1974. The vocal behavior of spring peepers, *Hyla crucifer*. Copeia 1974:940–950.

Rosenberg, H.I., A. Bdolah, and E. Kochva. 1985. Lethal factors and enzymes in the secretion from Duvernoy's gland of three colubrid snakes. Journal of Experimental Zoology 233:5–14.

Rossman, D.A. 1970. *Thamnophis sauritus*. Catalogue of American Amphibians and Reptiles 99:1–2.

Rossman, D.A., N.B. Ford, and R.A. Seigel. 1996. The Garter Snakes: Evolution and Ecology. University of Oklahoma Press, Norman, Oklahoma.

Rossman, D.A., and P.A. Myer. 1990. Behavioral and morphological adaptations for snail extraction in North American brown snakes (Genus *Storeria*). Journal of Herpetology 24:434–438.

Rowe, C.L., W.J. Sadinski, and W.A. Dunson. 1992. Effects of acute and chronic acidification on three larval amphibians that breed in temporary ponds. Archives of Environmental Contamination and Toxicology 23:339–350.

Rowe, J.W. 2003. Activity and movements of midland painted turtles (*Chrysemys picta marginata*) living in a small marsh system on Beaver Island, Michigan. Journal of Herpetology 37:342–353.

Rubbo, M.J., V.T. Townsend, Jr., S.D. Smyers, and R.G. Jaeger. 2003. An experimental assessment of invertebrate/vertebrate predation: The interaction between wolf spiders (*Gladicosa pulchra*) and terrestrial salamanders (*Ambystoma maculatum*). Journal of Zoology 261:1–5.

Rumph, W.T. 1979. The rediscovery of a Plethodontid salamander on Staten Island. Staten Island Institute of Arts and Sciences 30:2 3.

Russell K.R., C.E. Moorman, J.K. Edwards, B.S. Metts, and D.C. Guynn. 1999. Amphibian and reptile communities associated with beaver (*Castor canadensis*) ponds and unimpounded streams in the piedmont of South Carolina. Journal of Freshwater Ecology 14:149–158.

Russell, R.W., S.J. Hecnar, and G.D. Haffner. 1995. Organochlorine pesticide residues in southern Ontario spring peepers. Environmental Toxicology and Chemistry 14:815–817.

Ryan, M.J. 1980. The reproductive behavior of the bullfrog (*Rana catesbeiana*). Copeia 1980:108–114.

Saba, V.S., and J.R. Spotila. 2003. Survival and behavior of freshwater turtles after rehabilitation from an oil spill. Environmental Pollution 126:213–223.

Saenz, D., J.B. Johnson, C.K. Adams, and G.H. Dayton. 2003. Accelerated hatching of southern leopard frog (*Rana sphenocephala*) eggs in response to the presence of a crayfish (*Procambarus nigrocinctus*) predator. Copeia 2003: 646–649.

Saumure, R.A., and J.R. Bider. 1998. Impact of agricultural development on a populaton of wood turtles (*Clemmys insculpta*) in southern Quebec, Canada. Chelonian Conservation Biology 3:37–45.

Saumure, R.A., and D. Rodrigue. 1998. An albino snapping turtle, *Chelydra serpentina*, from Quebec. Canadian Field-Naturalist 112:344.

Schlaepfer, M.A., C. Hoover, and C.K. Dodd. 2005. Challenges in evaluating the impact of the trade in amphibians and reptiles on wild populations. BioScience 55:256–264.

Schlauch, F.C. 1975. Agonistic behavior in a suburban Long Island population of the smooth green snake, *Opheodrys vernalis*. Engelhardtia 6:25–26.

———. 1979. New methodologies for measuring species status and their application to the herpetofauna of a suburban region. Engelhardtia, 6:30–41.

Schmidt, K.P. 1953. A check list of North American amphibians and reptiles. 6th ed. American Society of Ichthyologists and Herpetologists, Chicago, IL. 280 pp.

Schmidt, R.E., T.W. Hunsinger, T. Coote, E. Griffin-Noyes, and E. Kiviat. 2004. The mudpuppy (*Necturus maculosus*) in the tidal Hudson River with comments on its status as native. Northeastern Naturalist 11:179–188.

Schueler, F.W. 1975. Geographic variation in the size of *Rana septentrionalis* in Quebec, Ontario, and Manitoba. Journal of Herpetology 9:177–186.

Schueler, F.W., and P.W. Schueler. 1977. An unstriped morph of *Desmognathus ochrophaeus* (Amphibia, Urodela, Plethodontidae) from western New York. Journal of Herpetology 11:103–105.

Schuett, G.W. 1982. A copperhead (*Agkistrodon contortrix*) brood produced from autumn copulations. Copeia 1982:700–702.

Schuett, G.W., D.L. Clark, and F. Kraus. 1984. Feeding mimicry in the rattlesnake *Sistrurus catenatus*, with comments on the evolution of the rattle. Animal Behavior 32:625–626.

Schuett, G.W., and J.C. Gillingham. 1986. Sperm storage and multiple paternity in the copperhead, *Agkistrodon contortrix*. Copeia 1986:807–811.

Scott, D.E. 1994. The effect of larval density on adult demographic traits in *Ambystoma opacum*. Ecology 75:1383–1396.

Seale, D.B. 1982. Physical factors influencing oviposition by the wood frog, *Rana sylvatica*, in Pennsylvania. Copeia 1982:627–635.

Seaman, R. 1963. Tales our fathers told us. New York Folklore Quarterly 19: 275–280.

Seburn, C.N.L. 1993. Spatial distribution and microhabitat use in the five-lined skink (*Eumeces fasciatus*). Canadian Journal of Zoology 71:445–450.

Seburn, D.C. 2003. Population structure, growth, and age estimation of spotted turtles, *Clemmys guttata*, near their northern limit: An 18-year follow-up. Canadian Field-Naturalist 117:436–439.

Semlitsch, R.D. 1980. Geographic and local variation in population parameters of the slimy salamander *Plethodon glutinosus*. Herpetologica 36:6–16.

———. 1983. Burrowing ability and behavior of salamanders of the genus Ambystoma. Canadian Journal of Zoology 61:616–620.

———. 2000. Principles for management of aquatic breeding amphibians. Journal of Wildlife Management 64:615–631.

Sessions, S. K. 1982. Cytogenetics of diploid and triploid salamanders of the *Ambystoma jeffersonianum* complex. Chromosoma 84:599–621.

Sessions, S.K., R.A. Franssen, and V.L. Horner. 1999. Morphological clues from multilegged frogs: Are retinoids to blame? Science 284:800–802.

Sessions, S.K., and S.B. Ruth. 1990. Explanation for naturally occurring supernumerary limbs in amphibians. Journal of Experimental Zoology 254: 38–47.

Setser, K., and J.F. Cavitt. 2003. Effects of burning on snakes in Kansas, USA, tallgrass prairie. Natural Areas Journal 23:315–319.

Sever, D.M., J.D. Krenz, K.M. Johnson, and L.C. Rania. 1995. Morphology and evolutionary implications of the annual cycle of secretion and sperm storage in spermathecae of the salamander *Ambystoma opacum* (Amphibia: Ambystomatidae). Journal of Morphology 223:35–46.

Sexton, O.J. 1979. Remarks on defensive behavior of hognose snakes, *Heterodon*. Herpetological Review 10:86–87.

Sexton, O.J., J. Bizer, D.C. Gayou, P. Freiling, and M. Moutseous. 1986. Field studies of breeding spotted salamanders, *Ambystoma maculatum* in eastern Missouri, USA. Milwaukee Public Museum Contributions in Biology and Geology 67:1–19.

Shepard, D.B., and A.R. Kuhns. 2000. *Pseudacris triseriata* (western chorus frog). Calling sites after drought. Herpetological Review 31:235–236.

Shine, R., T. Langkilde, and R.T. Mason. 2003. Confusion within mating balls of garter snakes: Does misdirected courtship impose selection on male tactics? Animal Behaviour 66:1011–1017.

Shirose, L.J., R.J. Brooks, J.R. Barta, and S.S. Desser. 1993. Intersexual differences in growth, mortality, and size at maturity in bullfrogs in central Ontario. Canadian Journal of Zoology 71:2363–2369.

Silliman, B.R., and M.D. Bertness. 2002. A trophic cascade regulates salt marsh primary production. Proceedings of the National Academy of Sciences, USA 99:10500–10505.

Simoes, J.C., and R.M. Chambers. 1999. The diamondback terrapins of Piermont Marsh, Hudson River, New York. Northeastern Naturalist 6:241–248.

Skelly, D.K. 1996. Pond drying, predators, and the distribution of *Pseudacris* tadpoles. Copeia 1996:599–605.

Skelly, D.K., E.E. Werner, and S.A. Cortwright. 1999. Long-term distributional dynamics of a Michigan amphibian assemblage. Ecology 80:2326–2337.

Smith, C.K., and J.W. Petranka. 1987. Prey size distribution and size specific foraging success of *Ambystoma* larvae. Oecologica 71:239–244.

Smith, D.C. 1987. Adult recruitment in chorus frogs: Effects of size and date at metamorphosis. Ecology 68:344–350.

Smith, D.C., and J. Van Buskirk. 1995. Phenotypic design, plasticity, and ecological performance in two tadpole species. American Naturalist 145:211–233.

Smith, E.M., and F.H. Pough. 1994. Intergeneric aggression among salamanders. Journal of Herpetology 28:41–45.

Smith, G.R., and J.B. Iverson. 2002. Sex ratio of common musk turtles (*Sternotherus odoratus*) in a north-central Indiana lake: A long-term study. American Midland Naturalist 148:185–189.

Smith, G.R., J.E. Rettig, G.G. Mittelbach, J.L. Valiulis, and S.R. Schaack. 1999. The effects of fish on assemblages of amphibians in ponds: A field experiment. Freshwater Biology 41:829–837.

Smith, G.R., A. Todd, J.E. Rettig, and F. Nelson. 2003. Microhabitat selection by northern cricket frogs (*Acris crepitans*) along a west-central Missouri creek: Field and experimental observations. Journal of Herpetology 37:383–385.

Smith, H.H., R.T. Zappalorti, A.R. Breisch, and D.L. McKinley. 1995. The type locality of the frog *Acris crepitans*. Herpetological Review 26:14.

Smith, H.M., and F.N. White. 1955. Adrenal enlargement and its significance in the hognose snakes (*Heterodon*). Herpetologica 11:137–144.

Smith, H.M. 1995. Handbook of Lizards: Lizards of the United States and Canada. Comstock Publishing Associates, Cornell University Press, Ithaca, New York.

Smith, P.W. 1963. *Plethodon cinereus*. Catalogue of American Amphibians and Reptiles 5:1–3.

Speck, F. G. 1923. Reptile lore of the northern Indians. Journal of American Folklore 36:273–280.

———. 1943. Turtle music. Fauna 5:82–84.

Speck, F.G., and E.S. Dodge. 1945. Amphibian and reptile lore of the Six Nations Cayuga. Journal of American Folklore 58:306–309.

Standing, K.L., T.B. Herman, and I.P. Morrison. 2000. Predation of neonate Blanding's turtles (*Emydoidea blandingii*) by short-tailed shrews (*Blarina brevicauda*). Chelonian Conservation and Biology 3:658–660.

Starnes, M.S., A.C. Kennedy, and W.J. Petranka. 2000. Sensitivity of embryos of southern Appalachian amphibians to ambient solar UV-B radiation. Conservation Biology 14:277–282.

Stechert, R. 1982. Historical depletion of timber rattlesnake colonies in New York State. Bulletin of the New York Herpetological Society 17:23–24.

Steen, D.A., and J.P. Gibbs. 2004. Effects of roads on the structure of freshwater turtle populations. Conservation Biology 18:1143–1148.

Stegeman, E. and A.R. Breisch. 2005. Sea turtles of New York. Conservationist 59(4):15–18.

Stenhouse, S.L. 1987. Embryo mortality and recruitment of juveniles of *Ambystoma maculatum* and *Ambystoma opacum* in North Carolina. Herpetologica 43:496–501.

Stenhouse, S.L., N.G. Hairston, and A.E. Cobey. 1983. Predation and competition in *Amybstoma* larvae: Field and laboratory experiments. Journal of Herpetology 17:210–220.

Stevens, C.E., A.W. Diamond, and T.S. Gabor. 2002. Anuran call surveys on small wetlands in Prince Edward Island, Canada restored by dredging of sediments. Wetlands 22:90–99.

Stewart, M.M. 1983. *Rana clamitans*. Catalogue of American Amphibians and Reptiles 337:1–4.

Stewart, M.M., and J. Rossi. 1981. The Albany Pine Bush: A northern outpost for southern species of amphibians and reptiles in New York. American Midland Naturalist 106:282–292.

Stewart, M.M., and P. Sandison. 1972. Comparative food habits of sympatric mink frogs, bullfrogs, and green frogs. Journal of Herpetology 6:241–244.

Stickel, L.F. 1950. Populations and home range relationships of the box turtle, *Terrapene c. carolina* (Linnaeus). Ecological Monographs 20:351–378.

———. 1978. Changes in the box turtle population during three decades. Copeia 1978:221–225.

Stinner, J., N. Zarlinga, and S. Orcutt. 1994. Overwintering behavior of adult bullfrogs, *Rana catesbeiana*, in northeastern Ohio. Ohio Journal of Science 94:8–13.

Stokes, G.D., and W.A. Dunson. 1982. Permeability and channel structure of reptilian skin. American Journal of Physiology 242:681–689.

Stone, P.A., J.L. Dobie, R.P. Henry. 1992. Cutaneous surface area and bimodal respiration in soft-shelled (*Trionyx spiniferus*), stinkpot (*Sternotherus odoratus*), and mud turtles (*Kinosternon subrubrum*). Physiological Zoology 65:311–330.

Stone, W.B., E. Kiviat, and S.A. Butkas. 1980. Toxicants in common snapping turtles. New York Fish and Game Journal 27:39–50.

Storey, K.B., J.R. Layne, Jr., M.M. Cutwa, T.A. Churchill, and J.M. Storey. 1993. Freezing survival and metabolism of box turtles, *Terrapene carolina*. Copeia 3:628–634.

Studer, N. 1959. Turning back the waters of the Ashokan. New York Folklore Quarterly 15:168.

Sugalski, M.T., and D.L. Claussen. 1997. Preference for soil moisture, soil pH, and light intensity by the salamander, *Plethodon cinereus*. Journal of Herpetology 31:245–250.

Sullivan, B.K. 1983. Sexual selection in Woodhouse's toad (*Bufo woodhousei*). II. Female choice. Animal Behaviour 31:1011–1017.

Sutton, K.K., and J.L. Christiansen. 1999. The habitat and distribution of the stinkpot, *Sternotherus odoratus*, in Iowa. Journal of the Iowa Academy of Science 106:63–65.

Swain, T.A., and H.M. Smith. 1978. Communal nesting in *Coluber constrictor* in Colorado (Reptilia: Serpentes). Herpetologica 34:175–177.

Swanson, D.L., B.M.Graves, and K.L. Koster. 1996. Freezing tolerance/intolerance and cryoprotectant synthesis in terrestrially overwintering anurans in the Great Plains, USA. Journal of Comparative Physiology B: Biochemical, Systemic, and Environmental Physiology 166:110–119.

Swanson, P.L. 1948. Notes on the amphibians of Venango County, Pennsylvania. American Midland Naturalist 40:362–371.

Taber, C.A., R.F. Wilkenson, Jr., and M.S. Topping. 1975. Age and growth of hellbenders in the Niangua River, Missouri. Copeia 1975:633–639.

Tangredi, B.P., and R.H. Evans. 1997. Organochlorine pesticides associated with ocular, nasal, or otic infection in the eastern box turtle (*Terrapene carolina carolina*). Journal of Zoo and Wildlife Medicine 28:97–100.

Tapply, W.G. 1997. King of the snappers. Field and Stream (April) 26.

Telecky, T.M. 2001. United States import and export of live turtles and tortoises. Turtle and Tortoise Newsletter 4:8–13.

Tennessen, J.A., and K.R. Zamudio. 2003. Early male reproductive advantage, multiple paternity and sperm storage in an amphibian aggregate breeder. Molecular Ecology 12:1567–1576.

Test, F.H., and H. Heatwole. 1962. Nesting sites of the red-backed salamander, *Plethodon cinereus*, in Michigan. Copeia 1962:206–207.

Thompson, E.L., J.E. Gates, and G.J. Taylor. 1980. Distribution and breeding habitat selection of the Jefferson salamander, *Ambystoma jeffersonianum*, in Maryland. Journal of Herpetology 14:113–120.

Tiebout, H.M., and J.R. Carey. 1987. Dynamic spatial ecology of the water snake, *Nerodia sipedon*. Copeia 1987:1–18.

Tierney, D., and M.M. Stewart. 2001. *Scaphiopus holbrookii holbrookii* (eastern spadefoot) Herpetological Review 32:56.

Tinkle, D.W., and R.E. Ballinger. 1972. *Sceloporus undulatus*: A study of the intraspecific comparative demography of a lizard. Ecology 53:570–584.

Townsend, C.H. 1926. An old tortoise. Bulletin of the Zoological Society of New York 29:217–218.

Trapido, H. 1944. The snakes of the genus *Storeria*. American Midland Naturalist 31:1–84.

Trauth, S.E. 1982. *Ambystoma maculatum* (Ambystomatidae) in the diet of *Heterodon platirhinos* (Colubridae) from northern Arkansas. Southwest Naturalist. 27:230.

Tucker, A.D., J.W. Gibbons, and J.L. Greene. 2001. Estimates of adult survival and migration for diamondback terrapins: Conservation insight from local extirpation within a metapopulation. Canadian Journal of Zoology 79:2199–2209.

Tucker, J.K., and J. Janzen. 1998. Order of oviposition and egg size in the redeared slider turtle (*Trachemys scripta elegans*). Canadian Journal of Zoology 76:377–380.

Turtle, S.L. 2000. Embryonic survivorship of the spotted salamander (*Ambystoma maculatum*) in roadside and woodland vernal pools in southeastern New Hampshire. Journal of Herpetology 34:60–67.

Tyler, M.S. 1994. Stalking amphibians. Maine Naturalist 2:33–44.

Ultsch, G.R., and J.T. Duke. 1990. Gas exchange and habitat selection in the aquatic salamanders *Necturus maculosus* and *Cryptobranchus alleganiensis*. Oecologia 83:250–258.

Ultsch, G.R., T.E. Graham, and C.E. Crocker. 2000. An aggregation of overwintering leopard frogs, *Rana pipiens*, and common map turtles, *Graptemys geographica*, in northern Vermont. Canadian Field-Naturalist 114:314–315.

Ultsch, G.R., G.M. Ward, C.M. LeBerte, B.R. Kuhajda, and E.R. Stewart. 2001. Intergradation and origins of subspecies of the turtle *Chrysemys picta*: Morphological comparisons. Canadian Journal of Zoology 79:485–498.

Uzzell, T. M., Jr. 1964. Relations of the diploid and triploid species of the *Ambystoma jeffersonianum* complex (Amphibia, Caudata). Copeia 1964:257–300.

———. 1967. *Ambystoma laterale*. Catalog of American Amphibians and Reptiles 48.1–48.2.

Van Snik Gray, E., W.A. Lellis, J.C. Cole, and C.S. Johnson. 2002. Host identification for *Strophitus undulatus* (Bivalvia: Unionidae), the creeper, in the Upper Susquehanna River Basin, Pennsylvania. American Midland Naturalist 147:153–161.

Vandewalle, T.J., and J.L. Christiansen. 1996. A relationship between river modification and species richness of freshwater turtles in Iowa. Journal of the Iowa Academy of Science 103:1–8.

Vitt, L.J., and W.E. Cooper. 1986. Tail loss, tail color, and predator escape in *Eumeces* (Lacertilia: Scincidae): Age specific differences in costs and benefits. Canadian Journal of Zoology 64:583–592.

———. 1989. Maternal care in skinks (*Eumeces*). Journal of Herpetology 23:29–34.

Walde, A.D., and J.R. Bider, C. Daigle, D. Masse, J.-C. Bourgeois, J. Jutras, and R.D. Titman. 2003. Ecological aspects of a wood turtle, *Glyptemys insculpta*, population at the northern limit of its range in Quebec. Canadian Field-Naturalist 117:377–388.

Waldick, R.C., B. Freedman, and R.J. Wassersug. 1999. The consequences for amphibians of the conversion of natural, mixed-species forests to conifer plantations in southern New Brunswick. Canadian Field-Naturalist 113:408–418.

Waldman, B. 1982. Adaptive significance of communal oviposition in wood frogs (*Rana sylvatica*). Behavioral Ecology and Sociobiology 10:169–174.

Waldman, B. 1985. Olfactory basis of kin recognition in toad tadpoles. Journal of Comparative Physiology 156:565–577.

Walls, S.C. 1991. Ontogenetic shifts in the recognition of siblings and neighbors by juvenile salamanders. Animal Behaviour 42:423–434.

Walls, S.C., and A.R. Blaustein. 1995. Larval marbled salamanders, *Ambystoma opacum*, eat their kin. Animal Behaviour 50:537–545.

Walls, S.C., A. Mathis, G. Jaeger, and W.F. Gergits. 1989. Male salamanders with high quality diets have faeces attractive to females. Animal Behavior 38:546–548.

Walls, S.C., and R.E. Roudebush. 1991. Reduced aggression toward siblings as evidence of kin recognition in cannibalistic salamanders. American Naturalist 138:1027–1038.

Weatherhead, P.J., G. Blouin-Demers, and K.A. Prior. 2002. Synchronous variation and long-term trends in two populations of black rat snakes. Conservation Biology 16:1602–1608.

Weatherhead, P.J., G. Blouin-Demers, and K.M. Cavey. 2003. Seasonal and prey-size dietary patterns of black ratsnakes (*Elaphe obsoleta obsoleta*). American Midland Naturalist 150:275–281.

Weatherhead, P.J., M.R. Prosser, H.L. Gibbs, and G.P. Brown. 2002. Male reproductive success and sexual selection in northern water snakes determined by
microsatellite DNA analysis. Behavioral Ecology 13:808–815.

Weeber, R.C., and M. Vallianatos. 2000. The Marsh Monitoring Program 1995–
1999: Monitoring Great Lakes wetlands and their amphibian and bird inhabitants. Bird Studies Canada, Port Rowan, Ontario, Canada.

Weinstein, S.A., C.F. DeWitt, and L.A. Smith. 1992. Variability of venom
neutralizing properties of serum from snakes of the colubrid genus *Lampropeltis*. Journal of Herpetology 26:452–461.

Wells, K.D. 1976. Multiple egg clutches in the green frog (*Rana clamitans*). Herpetologica 32:85–87.

———. 1977. Territoriality and male mating success in the green frog (*Rana
clamitans*). Ecology 58:750–762.

Werner, E.E., and K.S. Glennemeier. 1999. Influence of forest canopy cover on
the breeding pond distributions of several amphibian species. Copeia 1999:
1–12.

Wheeler, B.A., E. Prosen, A. Mathis, and R.F. Wilkinson. 2003. Population declines of a long-lived salamander: A 20+-year study of hellbenders, *Cryptobranchus alleganiensis*. Biological Conservation 109:151–156.

Whiffen, E.T. 1913. The massasauga in New York State. Bulletin of the Zoological Society of New York 16:949–950.

Whitaker, J.O., Jr. 1971. A study of the western chorus frog, *Pseudacris triseriata*,
in Vigo County, Indiana. Journal of Herpetology 5:127–150.

Whitaker, J.O., Jr., D. Rubine, and J.R. Munsee. 1977. Observations on food
habits or four species of spadefoot toads, genus *Scaphiopus*. Herpetologica
33:468–475.

Whitford, W.G., and A. Vinegar. 1966. Homing, survivorship, and overwintering
of larvae in spotted salamnders, *Ambystoma maculatum*. Copeia 1966:
515–519.

Will, G.D., R.D. Stumvoll, R.F. Gootie, and E.S. Smith. 1982. The ecological
zones of northern New York. New York Fish and Game Journal 29:1–25.

Williams, E.E., R. Highton, and D.M. Cooper. 1968. Breakdown of polymor-
phism of the red-backed salamander on Long Island. Evolution 22:76–86.

Williams, K.L. 1994. *Lampropeltis triangulum*. Catalogue of American Amphibians and Reptiles 594:1–10.

Williams, T. 1999. The terrible turtle trade. Audubon 101:44, 46–48, 50–51.

Winner, J.H. 1958. The rattlesnake hunter. New York Folklore Quarterly 14:
273–5.

Witters, L.R., and L. Sievert. 2001. Feeding causes thermophily in the Woodhouse's toad (*Bufo woodhousii*). Journal of Thermal Biology 26:205–208.

Witthoft, J. 1947. A snake tale from northern New York. New York Folklore Quarterly, 3:134–137.

Woodford, J.E., and M.W. Meyer. 2003. Impact of lakeshore development on
green frog abundance. Biological Conservation 110:277–284.

Wright, A.H. 1955. Frogs and toads of New York. Conservationist 10:23–26.

Wright, A.H., and A.A. Wright. 1949. Handbook of frogs and toads. Comstock
Publishing Associates, Ithaca, New York.

————. 1957. Handbook of snakes of the United States and Canada. Vol. 1. Comstock Publishing Associates, Ithaca, New York.

Wright, A.N., and K.R. Zamudio. 2002. Color pattern asymmetry as a correlate of habitat disturbance in spotted salamanders (*Ambystoma maculatum*). Journal of Herpetology 36:129–133.

Wyman, R.L. 1988. Soil acidity and moisture and the distribution of amphibians in five forests of southcentral New York. Copeia 1988:394–399.

————. 1991. Global climate change and life on Earth. Routledge, Chapman and Hall, New York.

————. 1998. Experimental assessment of salamanders as predators of detrital food webs: Effects on invertebrates, decomposition and the carbon cycle. Biodiversity and Conservation 7:641–650.

Wyman, R.L., and D.S. Hawksley-Lescault. 1987. Soil acidity affects distribution, behavior, and physiology of the salamander *Plethodon cinereus*. Ecology 68: 1819–1827.

Young, R. A. 1992. Effects of Duvernoy's gland secretions from the eastern hognose snake, *Heterodon platirhinos*, on smooth muscle and neuromuscular junction. Toxicon 30(7):775–779.

Zampella, R.A., and J.F. Bunnell. 2000. The distribution of anurans in two river systems of a coastal plain watershed. Journal of Herpetology 34:210–221.

Ziminski, S.W. 1970. Notes on the decline of snakes at the Long Island village of Hempstead and its vicinities. Engelhardtia 3:2.

Zweifel, R.G. 1989. Long-term ecological studies on a population of painted turtles, *Chrysemys picta*, on Long Island, New York. American Museum Novitates 2952:1–55.

Index